DEPARTMENT OF ECONOMIC AND SOCIAL AFFAIRS

E/1999/50/Rev.1
ST/ESA/268

WORLD ECONOMIC AND SOCIAL SURVEY 1999

TRENDS AND POLICIES IN THE WORLD ECONOMY

UNITED NATIONS • NEW YORK 1999

Note

Symbols of the United Nations documents are composed of capital letters combined with figures

E/1999/50/Rev.1

ST/ESA/268

ISBN 92-1-109135-7

PREFACE

Each year for over half a century, the United Nations Secretariat takes stock of the world economy. The idea is to look at where we have recently been in order to see where we are going. This year, in addition to its traditional review of the macroeconomic situation, the **World Economic and Social Survey** *tries to put in perspective how the financial sector has been changing around the world and where it is going.*

The reason for this focus is not hard to see. The world economy has just gone through yet another financial crisis in the emerging economies, a conflagration that started in mid-1997 in East Asia, engulfed the Russian Federation in mid-1998 and then spread to Latin America. It set back development for millions of people, caused political upheavals, and added large numbers of people to the world's poor. Recovery will be a long struggle.

In autumn 1998 we even witnessed a serious scare at the centre of world finance, which momentarily shook the self-assurance of the world's money mandarins.

Other concerns, too, drew our attention to finance. Most finance is local, and local financial systems have been changing in developed, developing and transition economies. Around the world, government has been withdrawing from the provision of credit, and markets have absorbed some of the traditional business of institutions. New financial institutions have taken root, such as venture capital for one type of entrepreneur and microcredit for another.

It seemed essential that the economic and social policy community try to grasp what has been happening in the esoteric but internationally integrated world of finance. A well functioning financial system is as essential for a global economy as it is for a national one. When other aspects of the economy are also functioning well, the efficiency of the financial system helps to raise production. But if other things go wrong, it can actually multiply the factors of instability. In itself it also reproduces the inequalities within societies, rather than correcting them. Public oversight is needed to make sure financial systems are fair as well as effective.

With that in mind, the international community has decided to put "financing for development" on the agenda for discussion in the United Nations. The General Assembly has agreed to organize a major event in 2001 for the consideration of a wide range of financial policy matters, including ones pertaining to financial sector development, as discussed in the present **Survey***. We expect that Governments will be drawing on the expertise in their foreign, finance and other ministries in preparing for this event, just as we in the Secretariat will be cooperating with our colleagues in the International Monetary Fund and the World Bank. We offer this* **Survey** *as a contribution to this process.*

KOFI A. ANNAN

Secretary-General

FOREWORD

Many parts of the world economy were sent reeling in the past two years by the fragility of financial systems and their international connectedness. On the whole, we seem to have hit bottom and most of the affected countries are moving towards recovery. Yet we see none of the buoyancy in international trade and finance on the horizon that earlier in this decade held out such promise to economies that had successfully positioned themselves to take advantage of it. We are impatient for more rapid economic growth in the developing world, particularly in Africa and especially in the least developed countries. As we review the progress being achieved towards our goals in the social, environmental and development fields, we have to have very mixed emotions. We thought we would be much further along than we are. A more dynamic world economy is one factor that could help, but we frankly do not foresee it in the short run. This is the outlook in part one of *World Economic and Social Survey, 1999.*

As the Secretary-General noted in his preface, part two of the *Survey* is a contribution to the international consideration of "financing for development". It seeks to give a perspective on the major changes that have been taking place in recent decades in the banking and financial systems of developed, developing and transition economies. In preparing the present analysis, our staff drew on a number of outside experts and practitioners who deepened our perceptions of the revolution that has been under way in financial systems. Several of them assembled in April of this year in New York for a meeting that helped sharpen our analysis. I would like to express the gratitude of the Department of Economic and Social Affairs of the United Nations Secretariat for their willingness to devote the time then and in the numerous follow-up consultations. We know full well the cost of time of the individuals involved and we appreciate their support. They included John Buehler (Global Training and Development Group), Sakiko Fukuda-Parr (United Nations Development Programme), Jan Kregel (United Nations Conference on Trade and Development), Raymond Loveridge (Said Business School, Oxford University), Martin Mayer (Brookings Institution), J.D. von Pischke (Frontier

Finance International), William Rapp (Center for International and Area Studies, Yale University), Kenneth Rind (Israel Infinity Venture Capital Fund), Christopher Rude (New School for Social Research), Adrian Tschoegl (Wharton School, University of Pennsylvania), Paul Wachtel (Stern School of Business, New York University) and Christian Weller (Centre for European Integration Studies, University of Bonn).

The *1999 World Economic and Social Survey* was prepared in the Development Policy Analysis Division of the Department of Economic and Social Affairs, drawing upon ongoing cooperation with the regional commissions of the United Nations, the International Monetary Fund, the World Bank and the United Nations Conference on Trade and Development.

Nitin Desai
Under-Secretary-General
for Economic and Social Affairs

CONTENTS

PART ONE. STATE OF THE WORLD ECONOMY

TABLES

FIGURES

EXPLANATORY NOTES

The following symbols have been used in the tables throughout the report

.. **Two dots** indicate that data are not available or are not separately reported.

– **A dash** indicates that the amount is nil or negligible.

- **A hyphen (-)** indicates that the item is not applicable.

- **A minus sign (-)** indicates deficit or decrease, except as indicated.

. **A full stop (.)** is used to indicate decimals.

/ **A slash (/)** between years indicates a crop year or financial year, for example, 1990/91.

- **Use of a hyphen (-)** between years, for example, 1990-1991, signifies the full period involved, including the beginning and end years.

Reference to "tons" indicates metric tons and to "dollars" ($) United States dollars, unless otherwise stated.

Annual rates of growth or change, unless otherwise stated, refer to annual compound rates.

In most cases, the growth rate forecasts for 1998 are rounded to the nearest quarter of a percentage point.

Details and percentages in tables do not necessarily add to totals, because of rounding.

The following abbreviations have been used:

ADR	American Depositary Receipt
ASEAN	Association of Southeast Asian Nations
BIS	Bank for International Settlements (Basel)
CCL	Contingent Credit Lines (IMF)
CIS	Commonwealth of Independent States
COMESA	Common Market for Eastern and Southern Africa
COMTRADE	United Nations External Trade Statistics Database
DAC	Development Assistance Committee (of OECD)
EAP	Enhanced Access Policy (IMF)
EASDAQ	European Association of Securities Dealers Automated Quotation
EBRD	European Bank for Reconstruction and Development
ECA	Economic Commission for Africa
ECB	European Central Bank
ECE	Economic Commission for Europe
ECLAC	Economic Commission for Latin America and the Caribbean
ESAF	Enhanced Structural Adjustment Facility (IMF)
EU	European Union

FDI	foreign direct investment
f.o.b.	free on board
GAAP	generally accepted accounting principles
GAB	General Arrangements to Borrow (IMF)
GCC	Gulf Cooperation Council
GDP	gross domestic product
GDR	Global Depositary Receipt
GNP	gross national product
HICP	Harmonized Index of Consumer Prices
HIPC	heavily indebted poor countries
IADB	Inter-American Development Bank
ICP	International Comparison Programme
IDA	International Development Association
IFC	International Finance Corporation (World Bank)
ILO	International Labour Organization
IMF	International Monetary Fund
INTRASTAT	system of data collection for intra-EU trade
IPF	investment privatization fund
IPO	initial public offering
MERCOSUR	Southern Cone Common Market
MIGA	Multilateral Investment Guarantee Agency (World Bank)
MNB	multinational bank
NAB	New Arrangements to Borrow (IMF)
Nasdaq	National Association of Securities Dealers Automated Quotations System
ODA	official development assistance
OECD	Organisation for Economic Cooperation and Development
OPEC	Organization of the Petroleum Exporting Countries
ppp	purchasing power parity
Project LINK	international collaborative research group for econometric modelling, coordinated jointly by the Development Policy Analysis Division of the United Nations Secretariat, and the University of Toronto
SADC	Southern African Development Community
SAF	Structural Adjustment Facility (IMF)
SDRs	special drawing rights (IMF)
SFF	Supplementary Financing Facility (IMF)
SITC	Standard International Trade Classification
SOE	State-owned enterprise
SRF	Supplemental Reserve Facility (IMF)
STF	Systemic Transformation Facility (IMF)
UNCTAD	United Nations Conference on Trade and Development
UN/DESA	Department of Economic and Social Affairs of the United Nations Secretariat
UNDP	United Nations Development Programme
UNIDO	United Nations Industrial Development Organization
VAT	value-added tax

The designations employed and the presentation of the material in this publication do not imply the expression of any opinion whatsoever on the part of the United Nations Secretariat concerning the legal status of any country, territory, city or area or of its authorities, or concerning the delimitation of its frontiers or boundaries.

The term "country" as used in the text of this report also refers, as appropriate, to territories or areas.

For analytical purposes, the following country groupings and sub-groupings have been used:

Developed economies (developed market economies):
   Europe, excluding the European transition economies
   Canada and the United States of America
   Japan, Australia and New Zealand.

Major developed economies (the Group of Seven):
   Canada, France, Germany, Italy, Japan, United Kingdom of Great Britain and Northern Ireland, United States of America.

European Union:
   Austria, Belgium, Denmark, Finland, France, Germany, Greece, Ireland, Italy, Luxembourg, Netherlands, Portugal, Spain, Sweden, United Kingdom of Great Britain and Northern Ireland.

Economies in transition:
   Central and Eastern European transition economies (CEETEs, sometimes contracted to "Eastern Europe"):
      Albania, Bulgaria, Czech Republic, Hungary, Poland, Romania, Slovakia and successor States of the Socialist Federal Republic of Yugoslavia, namely, Bosnia and Herzegovina, Croatia, Slovenia, the former Yugoslav Republic of Macedonia, Yugoslavia.
   Baltic States
      Estonia, Latvia and Lithuania.
   Commonwealth of Independent States (CIS)
      Armenia, Azerbaijan, Belarus, Georgia, Kazakhstan, Kyrgyzstan, Republic of Moldova, Russian Federation, Tajikistan, Turkmenistan, Ukraine, Uzbekistan.

Developing economies:
   Africa
   Asia and the Pacific (excluding Japan, Australia, New Zealand and the member States of CIS in Asia)
   Latin America and the Caribbean.

Sub-groupings of Asia and the Pacific:
   Western Asia plus Islamic Republic of Iran (commonly contracted to "Western Asia"):
      Bahrain, Cyprus, Iran (Islamic Republic of), Iraq, Israel, Jordan, Kuwait, Lebanon, Oman, Qatar, Saudi Arabia, Syrian Arab Republic, Turkey, United Arab Emirates, Yemen.

Eastern and Southern Asia:
   All other developing economies in Asia and the Pacific (including China, unless listed separately). This group has in some cases been subdivided into:
      China
      South Asia: Bangladesh, India, Nepal, Pakistan, Sri Lanka
      East Asia: All other developing economies in Asia and the Pacific.

Sub-grouping of Africa:
   Sub-Saharan Africa, excluding Nigeria and South Africa (commonly contracted to "sub-Saharan Africa"):
      All of Africa except Algeria, Egypt, Libyan Arab Jamahiriya, Morocco, Nigeria, South Africa, Tunisia.

For particular analyses, developing countries have been subdivided into the following groups:

Net-creditor countries:
   Brunei Darussalam, Kuwait, Libyan Arab Jamahariya, Oman, Qatar, Saudi Arabia, Singapore, Taiwan Province of China, United Arab Emirates.

Net-debtor countries:
   All other developing countries.

Fuel-exporting countries:
   Algeria, Angola, Bahrain, Bolivia, Brunei Darussalam, Cameroon, Colombia, Congo, Ecuador, Egypt, Gabon, Indonesia, Iran (Islamic Republic of), Iraq, Kuwait, Libyan Arab Jamahiriya, Mexico, Nigeria, Oman, Qatar, Saudi Arabia, Syrian Arab Republic, Trinidad and Tobago, United Arab Emirates, Venezuela, Viet Nam.

Fuel-importing countries:
   All other developing countries.

Least developed countries:
   Afghanistan, Angola, Bangladesh, Benin, Bhutan, Burkina Faso, Burundi, Cambodia, Cape Verde, Central African Republic, Chad, Comoros, Democratic Republic of the Congo (formerly Zaire), Djibouti, Equatorial Guinea, Eritrea, Ethiopia, Gambia, Guinea, Guinea-Bissau, Haiti, Kiribati, Lao People's Democratic Republic, Lesotho, Liberia, Madagascar, Malawi, Maldives, Mali, Mauritania, Mozambique, Myanmar, Nepal, Niger, Rwanda, Samoa, Sao Tome and Principe, Sierra Leone, Solomon Islands, Somalia, Sudan, Togo, Tuvalu, Uganda, United Republic of Tanzania, Vanuatu, Yemen, Zambia.

The designation of country groups in the text and the tables is intended solely for statistical or analytical convenience and does not necessarily express a judgement about the stage reached by a particular country or area in the development process.

---

a   Names and composition of geographical areas follow those of "Standard country or area codes for statistical use" (ST/ESA/STAT/SER.M/49/Rev.3), with one exception, namely, Western Asia, which in the *Survey* includes the Islamic Republic of Iran (owing to the large role of the petroleum sector in its economy) and excludes the transition economies of the region. Also, "Eastern Europe", as used in this *Survey,* is a contraction of "Central and Eastern Europe"; thus the composition of the region designated by the term differs from that of the strictly geographical grouping.

PART ONE | STATE
OF THE
WORLD
ECONOMY

I | THE WORLD ECONOMY IN 1999

After two years of financial turbulence and a marked slowdown in global economic growth, the world economy is no longer weakening. Led by the easing of monetary policy in major developed economies since the autumn of 1998, economic prospects have improved and global financial markets have shown signs of stabilization. Most noticeably, financial contagion from the Brazilian currency crisis at the beginning of 1999 was contained and there has been some restoration of capital flows to a number of emerging markets. There has also been a rebound in the price of oil since early 1999. The international prices of other commodities, which experienced a sharp decline in 1997-1998 and were an economic setback to many developing countries, have also stabilized.

In spite of these short-term developments, economic growth in 1999 remains inadequate and markedly lower than at mid-decade, particularly for the majority of developing and transition economies (see table I.1). The outlook for the rest of 1999 and beyond suggests only a minor overall improvement; in a number of cases, the economic situation will continue to deteriorate. In the majority of countries, growth for the foreseeable future will fall far short of what is necessary to effect a substantial improvement in living standards and a reduction in the number of people living in poverty.

In 1998, output per head rose, despite the slowdown, in all developed countries except Japan and New Zealand. However, of the 95 developing countries for which reliable data are available, the number experiencing a decline in output per capita more than doubled from 18 in 1997 to 40 in 1998. About one person in four in the developing world, roughly 1.2 billion people, lived in countries that suffered a decline in per capita output in 1998. This compares with less than 4 per cent of the population of developing regions, 160 million people, in 1996. Moreover, for developing countries, even rising output per person is a minimal growth criterion. A growth rate of output per capita of 3 per cent, if sustained, is of the order of magnitude that would allow some progress to be made in raising employment opportunities and reducing poverty. Whereas 39 developing countries met that criterion in 1996, only 23 did so in 1998. Forecasts are that only 13, including China, will meet it in 1999: 1 in Latin America, as opposed to 9 in 1996; 6 in South and East Asia, as opposed to 13 in 1996; and 6 in Africa, as opposed to 14 in 1996 (see table I.2).

These data demonstrate that adjustments in real economic sectors will take a much longer period of time to be implemented and to bear fruit than changes in financial and monetary indicators. Recovery in employment and in real wages, and reversing the social setbacks brought about by the economic crisis will trail well behind the resumption of output growth. Above all, changes in the economic structures of many countries and reforms of the international financial system will be a protracted process. While there appears to be a consensus on the need for reforming the architecture of the international financial and monetary systems, progress to date has been limited. Without successful systemic reforms, the global economy remains highly vulnerable to future international crises.

THE INTERNATIONAL ECONOMIC ENVIRONMENT

The difficulty of recovery in individual countries is aggravated by the unfavourable international economic environment that has evolved as a result of the disruptions of the past two years. World trade grew by about 3.5 per

Table I.1.
GROWTH OF WORLD OUTPUT AND TRADE, 1981-1999

Annual percentage change										
	1981-1990	1991	1992	1993	1994	1995	1996	1997	1998[a]	1999[b]
World output[c]	2.7	0.9	1.9	1.5	3.1	2.7	3.5	3.4	1.9	2
of which:										
Developed economies	2.9	0.8	1.6	0.8	2.6	2.2	3.0	2.8	2.0	1¾
Economies in transition	1.5	-8.6	-10.5	-6.1	-5.1	0.6	0.7	2.4	0.2	-½
Developing economies	2.4	3.2	5.0	5.2	5.7	4.8	5.7	5.5	1.7	2½
World trade[d]	4.5	4.3	5.7	4.6	10.5	8.6	5.5	9.2	3.3	3½
Memorandum items:										
World										
Number of countries with rising per capita output	..	71	75	67	99	109	122	121	97	98
Number of countries in sample	..	129	143	144	144	144	144	144	144	144
Developing economies										
Number of countries with rising per capita output	..	56	59	51	64	72	81	77	55	63
Number of countries in sample	..	93	94	95	95	95	95	95	95	95
World output growth with PPP-based weights[e]	3.1	1.4	2.1	2.5	3.6	3.6	4.1	4.1	2.4	2¾

Source: UN/DESA.

[a] Partly estimated.
[b] Forecast, based in part on Project LINK.
[c] Calculated as a weighted average of individual country growth rates of gross domestic product (GDP), where weights are based on GDP in 1993 prices and exchange rates.
[d] Average of the growth rates of the volume of exports and imports.
[e] Employing an alternative scheme for weighting national growth rates of GDP, based on purchasing power parity (PPP) conversions of national currency GDP into international dollars (see introduction to annex: statistical tables).

cent in 1998. This is the smallest increase of the decade and markedly less than half the rate of 1997. It resulted from the almost 5 per cent decline in imports of developing countries, mainly owing to the collapse of imports of the crisis countries of East Asia, and the 10 per cent import drop in Japan. The 1999 outlook is for import levels to begin to recover, albeit slowly, with import volumes rising 2½ per cent in the developing countries, and ¼ per cent in Japan (see table A.13).

The value of world trade in dollars fell in 1998. The fact that commodity prices, particularly of oil, plunged during the year negatively affected the export earnings, and therefore the import demand, of many economies. Africa's exports, for instance, declined by 15 per cent in nominal terms in 1998, while in Western Asia, the value of merchandise exports shrank by about 25 per cent.

Table I.2.
GROWTH OF PER CAPITA OUTPUT IN DEVELOPING COUNTRIES, BY REGION, 1996-1999

	Number of countries monitored	Decline in GDP per capita				Growth of GDP per capita exceeding 3 per cent			
		1996	1997	1998[a]	1999[b]	1996	1997	1998[a]	1999[b]
Frequency of high and low growth of per capita output (number of countries)									
Developing countries	95	14	18	40	32	39	34	23	13
of which:									
Latin America	24	5	3	8	9	9	8	4	1
Africa	38	6	8	13	8	14	11	12	6
East and South Asia	18	0	3	10	5	13	12	6	6
Western Asia	15	3	4	9	10	3	3	1	0
Memo items:									
Least developed countries	40	12	9	17	14	11	9	7	3
Sub-Saharan Africa	31	5	4	10	5	12	9	9	6
Percentage of population									
Developing countries	95	3.7	9.8	26.7	19.2	73.8	72.1	60.5	53.3
of which:									
Latin America	24	8.2	3.1	55.1	54.4	34.9	37.6	22.1	1.7
Africa	38	12.3	24.3	42.3	24.4	27.5	27.6	24.0	9.7
East and South Asia	18	0.0	6.8	15.9	8.5	93.9	90.9	79.3	76.2
Western Asia	15	16.5	18.5	59.1	59.5	34.9	36.9	9.3	0.0
Memo items:									
Least developed countries	40	19.7	13.0	33.6	26.1	52.4	39.9	28.7	6.7
Sub-Saharan Africa	31	19.5	16.5	32.6	27.2	38.0	29.6	17.2	16.4

Source: UN/DESA, including population estimates and projections from *World Population Prospects: The 1998 Revision* (United Nations publication, Sales No. E.99.XIII.9).
[a] Preliminary estimates
[b] Forecast, based in part on Project LINK.

In response to the agreement among world oil producers in March 1999 to reduce their output, by May 1999 international prices of oil had rebounded by over 50 per cent from their lows at the end of 1998. However, oil prices are expected to retreat in the second half of 1999, resulting in smaller improvement on average over the year. Prices of other commodities have not followed the surge in oil prices, but signs of stabilization and even recovery appeared in several markets during the first quarter of 1999. Overall commodity prices are expected to increase slightly in 1999-2000, but to remain below prices earlier in the decade.

Developments in international financial markets had an unfavourable impact on developing countries in 1998. These countries had received a net transfer of financial resources between 1991 and 1996, which enabled them to finance an excess of imports over exports. The crisis reversed this flow. In particular, the South and East Asian region, whose past growth had inspired confidence in its future and attracted foreign capital, was faced with a massive withdrawal of funds. Financial transfers to the region declined from a net inflow of $31 billion in 1996 to a net outflow of over $110 billion in 1998 (see table II.1).

Until the third quarter of 1998, monetary policies worldwide had been restrictive, and thus did not provide a stimulus to the global economy, the significant exception among major economies being Japan. Policy makers in the United States of America were focusing on the inflationary potential from stronger-than-expected growth and most European Governments and central banks were concentrating on achieving the convergence criteria, notably for inflation, interest rates and fiscal deficits, for entry of their economies into the monetary union due to be inaugurated in early 1999. During the same period, interest rates in many emerging economies surged in a fruitless attempt to retain—and possibly to attract more—foreign capital and thus to stabilize their currencies. Facing the growing threat of a global deflationary spiral, central banks in the major developed economies, led by the monetary authorities—the Federal Reserve System or Fed—of the United States, started to ease monetary policy in the last quarter of 1998. The Fed made three interest-rate cuts in October-November 1998, and most developed economies reduced interest rates substantially. As recently as April 1999, the European Central Bank (ECB) cut interest rates by 50 basis points. Interest rates in some of the crisis countries, which had been declining since mid-1998, approached pre-crisis levels.

The exchange rates of many Asian developing economies stabilized in 1998. In the crisis countries, currency depreciations in 1997-1998 ranged from 20 to 80 per cent. Countries hit by renewed turbulence in early 1999 succeeded in stabilizing their currency faster than anticipated. However, exchange rates for a majority of countries have remained at values far below their pre-crisis levels although a few recovered some of their value against the United States dollar. Similarly, after a temporary weakening caused by the Brazilian crisis, equity prices have rebounded in most cases, with some emerging equity markets having returned to price levels close to their all-time highs.

The limited magnitude and duration of the contagion effects of the crisis in Brazil in January 1999 suggest that stability was returning to world financial

markets and that confidence in emerging markets was being rebuilt. One indicator of the improved financial situation was the spread between the yields of
sovereign debts of the emerging economies and yields of Treasury bonds of the
United States. As the spread between these two kinds of financial instruments
moved downward in 1998, it indicated both renewed confidence by investors
and lower external financing costs of emerging countries. Despite the reduction
in interest rates for the majority of potential borrowing countries, these spreads
remain higher than before the Asian crisis and act as a disincentive to borrow.
More importantly, there continues to be some reluctance to lend to most developing and transition economies, almost regardless of the interest rate. One
reflection of this reluctance is the large flow of funds to the United States,
which corresponds to its high and rising current-account deficit.

Given a continuing reluctance of investors to lend outside of a few preferred
countries, net capital flows to emerging markets seem unlikely to improve over
their 1998 level of $70 billion, a substantially lower level than the peak at over
$200 billion recorded in 1996. However, if global financial stability is main-
tained, net capital flows could increase in 2000, possibly making up about half
the decline that occurred between 1996 and 1998. Meanwhile, competition
among developing economies for capital inflows is expected to rise as the
Asian economies recover.

This stabilization of financial markets in mid-1999, while welcome, does
not signal that the requisite changes in the global financial architecture have
been effected. However, easing of the sense of financial crisis in 1999 has
allowed time for more systemic changes to be made, while the continuing
effects of the devastation caused by the 1997-1998 crises have made the need
for such reforms ever more apparent.

THE SETBACK IN 1998

At less than 2 per cent, the growth of world output in 1998 was about half of
that in 1997 (see table I.1). Growth in all groups of countries slowed down but
the setback to the developing countries was greatest. Their average growth of
only 1.7 per cent in 1998 was below that of the developed countries for the first
time since the 1980s and contrasted markedly with the average growth of 5 per
cent or more that they had achieved earlier in the decade. However, China and
India were able to sustain rapid growth in 1998 and are expected to continue to
do so in 1999. Their continued economic success augurs well for the large proportion of the world's poorest who are citizens of these two countries.

Earlier prospects of improved aggregate growth in the economies in transition evaporated in 1998, largely as a result of the crisis in the Russian
Federation. Total output in these countries as a group was almost unchanged in
1998 but economic performances varied widely across countries: for example,
Azerbaijan grew by 10 per cent but Romania, for the second year in a row,
declined by some 7 per cent. As in 1997, 5 of these 26 economies recorded a
fall in per capita output.

In contrast with the developing and transition economies, all the developed
countries, with the exception of Japan and New Zealand, maintained or slightly increased their output in 1998. Growth in the United States exceeded expec-

tations and Japan fell into a severe recession. Both developments had important implications for the world economy at large. The United States functioned as the main—and almost the only—engine of growth in the world economy, while Japan's difficulties dampened prospects elsewhere but particularly in the East Asia region where economic stimulus was most needed. Japan's recession and its banking crisis have been mutually reinforcing, showing that the banking crisis would have to be addressed in order to resurrect the economy.

The pattern of output growth across nations is widening the disparity between levels of living and personal incomes in the developed countries and those in the rest of the world. In order to narrow the gap between rich and poor countries, output per capita in the latter group has to increase faster than in the former.[1] Since the Asian currency crisis, the opposite has occurred. Moreover, the prices of exports produced by developing and transition countries have fallen relative to those for the goods produced by the developed world. This shift in relative prices over the past two years has amplified the deterioration in the position of the average person in the developing and transition countries: not only has average output fallen, but average incomes have fallen even more.

In contrast, and with the currently *sui generis* exception of Japan, the average consumer in the developed world has not been adversely affected by the international financial crises of the last two years. Overall economic growth has slowed, but output per capita has continued to increase and, because of the changes in relative prices mentioned above, real incomes have increased even faster than real output. Individual consumers in most developed countries have benefited directly from lower prices for primary commodities and for imports of a number of manufactured goods.

In addition to the increased income gap, developing countries and the economies in transition have to confront the social consequences of the financial crises they experienced. In social terms, what the crises have done is to delay or push back the movement of people from poverty into the more modern commercial sectors. An increase in the numbers entering formal employment, paying taxes to the government, obtaining loans from the financial system to expand their businesses and thereby providing employment opportunities to those currently in the informal sector should have been the result of continuing liberalization and globalization. Yet the financial crises in Asia and in the Russian Federation have put at risk the continued expansion of the more modern sector in these countries. Thus, whereas in recent years many of the developed countries were able to take advantage of globalization, the effects on many developing and transition countries have been perverse. The vulnerability of their economies meant that an external shock set back and even reversed their efforts to foster the expansion of the modern sectors at the very point when they seemed set to take fuller advantage of their integration in the global economy. The personal tragedy of those thrown out of work and reduced to poverty by the present crises represents a severe setback for development efforts at a broader level, impacting on a much larger number of people.

[1] Because population growth is faster in poor countries than in rich ones, there has to be an even larger difference between the rates of increase in total output in the two groups of countries.

THE NEAR-TERM OUTLOOK: SLOWER GROWTH IN MANY DEVELOPING AND TRANSITION ECONOMIES

Despite the return of a degree of stability to world financial markets, the short-term outlook for the real economy remains poor, particularly by the standards of three years ago. Gross world output is forecast to rise only 2 per cent in 1999, growth being almost the same as in 1998, and is expected to increase by only 2½ per cent in 2000.[2] Not only is this pace of expansion far from satisfactory for many countries, but in addition some serious downside risks remain.

Growth in the developing economies is expected to recover only gradually from the sharp deceleration in 1998 and reach rates of 2½ and 4½ per cent in 1999 and 2000, respectively. Although a number of afflicted developing countries and transition economies show signs of a slow recovery, others are expected to remain in, or to enter, economic recession. The recession that swept over several countries in South-East Asia in late 1997 and 1998 hit a number of Latin American countries in late 1998; and it is expected to persist in 1999 but to moderate in the course of the year, with growth returning in 2000 .

The South-East Asian developing countries have begun to recover from their financial crises but none is likely to return in the near future to the high growth rates achieved before the crisis. China's growth is expected to decelerate, but to remain in the 7-8 per cent range. India's strong growth should continue. African developing countries are expected to grow by about 3 per cent on average but, because of the relatively fast growth of population, substantial gains in per capita output are unlikely. In the Caribbean and Central America, several countries will have to overcome the damage inflicted by El Niño and severe hurricanes in 1998. Latin America as a whole is experiencing a recession in 1999 owing to adjustment measures in Brazil and other countries.

The outlook for growth in the economies in transition remains discouraging (see table A.3). Even with a recovery in oil markets, Kazakhstan, the Republic of Moldova, the Russian Federation and Ukraine are expected to see their gross domestic product (GDP) decline in 1999. Elsewhere in the Commonwealth of Independent States (CIS), the outlook is very mixed. In the Baltic countries, the pace of growth is likely to slow to under 2 per cent from about 4 per cent in 1998. The economies of Central and Eastern Europe, including those that were performing well, in particular Poland, are also likely to see a slowdown. Output in the Czech Republic and Romania is expected to continue to fall and Croatia and Slovakia could also go into recession. The confrontation over Kosovo and its aftermath will have a marked negative impact on neighbouring countries.

Inflation is likely to remain subdued in most developing and transition economies. However, some of the countries that experienced large currency devaluations are likely to experience higher inflation, in a process of adjustment to the overshooting in the depreciation of their real exchange rates.

Unemployment in most developing countries and economies in transition has worsened as a result of the recession or slowdown in these economies. This holds even for the economies in transition where the unemployment rate, which had soared rapidly during the first years of their transformation process, began to fall when the recovery finally started gaining momentum (see table A.7). Given the magnitude of the problem and since recovery in labour demand as a

[2] The outlook reported in the present *Survey* is partly based on Project LINK, an international consortium of global economic forecasts and policy analysis supported by the Department of Economic and Social Affairs of the United Nations Secretariat. Documentation of detailed forecasts and the policy assumptions can be found in the various reports prepared for the spring LINK meeting, which was held in New York, 3-6 May 1999. These documents are available on the Internet (http://www.un.org/esa/analysis/link).

rule lags the recovery of output growth, the unemployment problem in these countries will remain for at least several years.

The outlook for the developed economies as a group is that, on average, they will grow at about 2 per cent in 1999 and 2000, almost the same rate as in 1998. They will continue to enjoy low inflation.

The United States is expected to register growth of 3½ per cent in 1999, after growth of nearly 4 per cent between 1996 and 1998 (see table A.2). The long stretch of expansion has brought unemployment close to 4 per cent, yet at the same time inflation has fallen to about 2 per cent. The key policy concern of the United States is how to avoid a "hard landing" for the economy in the face of stretched labour markets, a marked appreciation of stock prices, and record external deficits.

In spite of several substantial government stimuli, Japan's GDP declined by 2.9 per cent in 1998. The baseline forecast, drawn up in May 1999, was that the Japanese economy would contract by 1.4 per cent in 1999. However, the very strong preliminary estimates of growth in the first quarter of 1999 (released in June 1999) mean that, even if output were to remain flat for the rest of the year, Japan's economic growth in 1999 would be 0.9 per cent. The difference in over 2 percentage points in Japan's forecast growth would have major implications for the world economy, and especially for Japan's neighbours (as examined in box I.1).

Box I.1

GLOBAL CONSEQUENCES OF A REBOUND IN JAPAN

In the baseline outlook, which was based on information available as of the end of April 1999, a mild recovery in Japan's economy in the second half of 1999 was forecast, although gross domestic product (GDP) for the year as a whole was expected to contract owing to the decline expected in the first half. However, information in June 1999 suggested a stronger-than-expected rebound of the Japanese economy in the first quarter of 1999, after five consecutive quarters of decline. GDP growth of 1.9 per cent in the first quarter (or 7.9 per cent at an annual rate) was supported by a recovery in domestic demand, including a 1.2 per cent growth in private consumption, 1.2 per cent growth in residential investment and 2.5 per cent growth in business investment. Although there are concerns about the data-consistency of this preliminary estimate and even more concerns about the sustainability of this recovery—as indicated by a further decline in some industrial activities in April—there is a greater probability than before that Japan may register mild growth for 1999, rather than a further contraction.

Recovery in Japan would be not only important for Japan, but also crucial for supporting global growth, especially for boosting the recovery of the crisis-affected developing economies in Asia. A quantitative indication of this can be derived from the models of Project LINK. In a simulation using the LINK models, it was assumed, partly for simplicity, that Japan's GDP will register an average quarterly growth of zero for the remaining three quarters in 1999, implying annual GDP growth of 0.9 per cent for the year. This represents a 2.3 percentage point improvement from the forecast rate of growth.

Based on this more optimistic outlook for Japan, world output growth for 1999 would increase by 0.4 percentage points from the baseline, with world export volume increasing by 0.5 percentage points (see table). While GDP of the developed

In the last quarter of 1998, largely because of a reduction in output in Germany and Italy, Europe experienced a deceleration of growth which is expected to persist into 1999. The slowdown, however, will be short-lived, in part because of the cut in interest rates in April 1999, together with buoyant consumer spending. Growth should be stronger in the second half of 1999 and so overall growth of 2 per cent in 1999 is likely to accelerate to 2½ per cent in 2000.

The unemployment picture in the developed countries reflected their growth performance (see table A.7). The unemployment rate in the United States has fallen to a level not observed since the late 1960s and is now lower than Japan's, which has been rising. High unemployment persists in many countries of the European Union, but depends only to a limited degree on the business cycle. While there was some improvement in recent years, especially in countries with the highest rates, such as Spain, rates are still above 10 per cent in many European countries. The reduction of unemployment continues to be a major policy issue for the European Union.

Major uncertainties

Even though stability appears to have returned to global financial markets and the world economy, the past two years have demonstrated that globalization has increased the uncertainties and downside risks faced by individual

---

Box I.1 (continued)

economies would rise by 0.6 percentage points (reflecting Japan's own contribution to the total, as well as the benefit of trade impulses on other countries), GDP for developing countries would increase by 0.2 percentage points. GDP in South-East and East Asia will be lifted noticeably because of the strong trade and financial links: for example, 20 per cent of Japan's imports come from the region. The Republic of Korea, in particular, would have an additional 1 percentage point of GDP growth in 1999, while the GDP of Indonesia would shrink by 0.6 per cent less than forecast.

EFFECTS ON OUTPUT OF A STRONG RECOVERY IN JAPAN

	Growth rate for 1999 under scenario (annual percentage change)	Change from the baseline forecast (percentage points)
World	2.4	0.4
Developed economies	2.4	0.6
Japan	0.9	2.5
Developing economies	2.8	0.2
China	7.7	0.2
Indonesia	-1.9	0.6
Republic of Korea	4.5	1.1
World export volume	4.0	0.5

Source: UN/DESA, based on Project LINK.

countries and the world economy. These risks themselves are not necessarily associated with a group of countries; they can stem from a national problem that, because of today's integrated world economy, has global consequences. The above forecast should thus be understood as subject to errors that could produce slower or faster growth than the forecasts show, albeit with a preponderance of downside risks.

One downside risk, possibly the worst, is that of a hard landing for the United States, either because of a stock-market crash, which would reduce the wealth of economic actors, or because the authorities reacted to a sign of inflationary pressures by tightening monetary policy so sharply as to produce a decline rather than a moderate deceleration of output growth. What has hitherto been the main stimulus to world output could therefore go into reverse.

Among developing and transition countries, there are several downside risks: Brazil still faces a formidable task in addressing its large fiscal-sector imbalances; growth in China's export sector is declining faster than expected and consumer demand is also weak; there is a risk of a further decline in output in the Russian Federation, especially given the uncertainty surrounding the Government's economic policy and whether it will be able to achieve the required cutbacks in fiscal expenditures, increases in fiscal revenues, and structural reforms in the real and financial sectors. Setbacks in Brazil, China or the Russian Federation would have adverse consequences primarily for their neighbours and trading partners.

In order to examine one specific set of these downside risks, a study was undertaken, utilizing the models of Project LINK, of the possible impact on the world economy of another major financial crisis, on this occasion entailing a sizeable stock-market correction and credit rationing, with currency realignments and shrinkage in international capital flows. The results (see box I.2) suggest that such a sequence of events would set off a severe contraction not

---

Box I.2

THE IMPLICATIONS OF ANOTHER FINANCIAL CRISIS

The present simulation examines the outcome of another financial shock, this time originating in the developed countries. The assumed shock takes the form of a decline in equity markets in the United States of America and Europe of 40 per cent from their peaks. Although this would be double the relative decline experienced at the height of the financial crunch in the fall of 1998, such a drop would bring the price-earnings ratio down to about its historical average. It is assumed that the collapse in equity prices would cause institutions such as hedge funds to fail, leading to a surge in corporate interest rates. An increase of 200 basis points in the yield spreads between corporate bonds and United States Treasury notes is posited. It is also assumed that the public rescue fund for banking reform in Japan will not have been fully successful in restoring the banks' lending capacities and that the fiscal stimuli are therefore less effective.

The impact on the emerging economies of such a severe contraction in the developed economies would occur through changes in international trade and capital flows. The meltdown of equity markets in developed economies would trigger a decrease of net capital flows to developing countries and economies in transition. Reflecting this, China is assumed to face a drop of $30 billion in foreign direct investment, which is about two thirds of the foreign investment it received in 1998.

Box I.2 (continued)

   The simulations indicate that a financial crisis of this nature would cause a loss of world output of 1.7 per cent over two years, relative to the baseline, and world trade would slow by 4.8 per cent in the same period (see table). The loss for the developed economies as a whole would be 1.6 per cent of their total gross domestic product (GDP) over two years. This would emerge through several channels. First, the equity-market meltdown would cause a drop in business confidence and in consumer sentiment which, through a self-fulfilling expectation process, would reduce both business investment and private consumption (particularly of durable goods). Next, a credit crunch would result in a higher cost for capital and this would impose another adverse shock on business investment.

   Furthermore, as the credit crunch spread from corporate credit markets to consumer loans, private consumption would also be lowered. Finally, the large drop in asset prices would cause a fall in consumption owing to a wealth effect. Along with a decline in domestic economic activity, it is estimated that import demand in the developed economies would shrink by about 6 per cent over two years.

   For the developing economies as a group, there would be a loss of 2 per cent of GDP over two years. Another financial shock would make it more difficult, if not impossible, for Asia and Latin America to recover. With the specific assumptions of a decline in foreign capital inflows into China and a devaluation of the yuan by 15 per cent to the rate that prevailed in unofficial markets in the summer of 1998, China's growth would drop to just above 3 per cent.

GROSS DOMESTIC PRODUCT AND WORLD TRADE

Percentage difference from the baseline[a]	Year 1	Year 2
World	-1.2	-1.7
Developed market economies	-1.1	-1.6
Canada	-1.3	-1.8
France	-1.0	-1.2
Germany	-1.5	-2.2
Italy	-1.3	-1.4
Japan	-1.4	-2.2
United Kingdom	-0.5	-1.8
United States	-1.5	-1.8
Developing countries	-1.4	-2.0
Latin America	-1.1	-1.5
South and East Asia	-1.1	-1.6
China	-4.2	-5.8
World exports, volume	-3.1	-4.8

   a   See table I.1.

only in developed countries but also, through their trading and financial links, in developing and transition economies. While the orders of magnitude in such a scenario depend on the assumptions made, the results indicate that world growth would slow down markedly and be accompanied by a further contraction in global trade. The impact on developing countries would be particularly pronounced. Because of the intensive trading and financial links between many of the economies in transition and the European Union, the former would experience a sharp drop in their growth rates as well.

TAKING STOCK OF POLICY AFTER TWO CRISIS YEARS

At the onset of the Asian crisis, the scale and form of the contagion that subsequently took place were not envisaged and the policy responses were correspondingly disappointing. The actions taken initially followed traditional approaches, with adjustments being made as shortcomings were exposed. However, even these adjustments were often a venture into the unknown.

The period since the crisis erupted has provided new experiences and a new perspective to economic policy-making at the national level. Because of the increased interdependence in the world economy, there has been a change in the balance between domestic and international considerations in many national policy choices. However, the differences among countries and in their degree of integration into the world economy suggest that, although there are some common elements, the optimal policy choices will depend on country circumstances.

In this era of heightened financial volatility, the importance of sound macroeconomic fundamentals has become paramount: a sustainable fiscal position and current-account balance, a low or moderate rate of inflation, and consistency between the rate of inflation and the exchange rate are indispensable for any economy, as all economies are open (albeit to different degrees). Equally important, however, is the need for a number of structural and institutional conditions to be met in order to reduce the likelihood that growth will be interrupted by international or domestic financial crises.

The past two years have prompted much discussion about the desirable policies and targets for key macroeconomic variables, the actions necessary to avoid future crises and the trade-offs that have to be addressed in striking the correct balance in policy. In many of these cases, experience to date provides no definitive answer to the debate, other than that the response is likely to vary from case to case.

Macroeconomic policy and financial crises

A first question concerns the desirability of raising interest rates to the heights that were reached in crisis countries. Some increase in interest rates is inescapable, owing to the exit of funds from domestic financial markets. In general, policy makers in the crisis economies faced a dilemma. When exchange rates began to depreciate, monetary tightening was viewed as a means of preventing a depreciation-inflation spiral and of discouraging further capital outflows. However, it was recognized that monetary tightening would also seriously weaken economic activity and have other negative effects. In the recent cases, nominal interest rates were raised to very high levels and often kept there for a long period, giving rise to unusually high real interest rates. Nevertheless, exchange rates plunged.

Advocates of the high interest-rate policy argue that it was necessary to restore international market confidence in order to stabilize exchange rates. Opponents argue that this policy was not based on sound theory or evidence. They have shown that circumstances exist, and these may have characterized the situation in the Asian economies in crisis, when raising interest rates weakens the economy and leads to further currency depreciation. As such, this policy may have caused an unnecessarily deep recession, besides failing to stabilize the exchange rate.

Moreover, neither monetary nor fiscal policy excesses were the source of the crises that erupted in the Asian economies in 1997. These crises were caused largely by financial problems in the private, rather than in the public, sector; fiscal balances in most of these economies were sound, having been in surplus for many years prior to the crisis. Nevertheless, the initial policy involved adopting tight fiscal as well as monetary policies. This policy was eventually relaxed when the economic recession turned out to be deeper and more widespread than had initially been anticipated. There now seems to be some agreement that the extent of the fiscal austerity initially pursued by these economies was inappropriate.

Much of the deterioration in fiscal positions in 1998 was beyond the control of Governments. For commodity-dependent countries, the decline of commodity prices in international markets in 1998 led to significant reductions in public revenues. While the losses were particularly acute in oil-exporting countries, lower prices for non-oil commodities adversely affected many countries, mainly in Africa, that rely on international trade in commodities as a source of fiscal revenues. More generally, the necessary compression of imports, combined with longer-term programmes of reductions in tariffs as a part of trade liberalization measures, reduced tariff revenue, an important source of fiscal revenue in many developing countries. In addition, the overall slowdown in economic activity that took place in most economies tended to lower other government revenues.

In the Asian cases, increasing the fiscal deficit was an appropriate response to the crisis. In 1998, however, the widening of fiscal deficits was one of the causes of the crisis in the Russian Federation and Brazil. In considering this difference, a distinction needs to be made between the cyclical and structural portions of a country's fiscal position.[3] In the Russian Federation and Brazil, the deficits have been structural and were likely to persist unless there were major policy changes. In the Asian case, the deficits are cyclical and appropriate in order to stimulate economic activity, as well as to enable Governments to address some of the social consequences of the slowdown, and are expected to disappear as recovery proceeds.

For countries that are integrated into the world financial markets, views regarding the likely behaviour of market participants now play an increasing role in the determination of a Government's fiscal options. This limits the room for manoeuvre that Governments have in using fiscal policy to address purely domestic policy objectives. Governments have to balance the perceptions of these markets with their own policy objectives and domestic political con-

[3] For a discussion of alternative measures of the fiscal deficit, see *World Economic and Social Survey 1997* (United Nations publication, Sales No. E.97.II.C.1 and corrigenda).

straints. Because of the sensitivity of these markets, the costs of a loss of confidence and the time it takes to regain confidence, there is an inbuilt pressure on Governments to adopt restrictive fiscal policies. In 1998, Governments in most instances were under pressure to reduce fiscal deficits, despite the need to allow automatic stabilizers to take effect and possibly to complement them with an anti-cyclical relaxation of policy. In the Asian crisis countries, for example, it was only when the severity of the recession and its social consequences became apparent that fiscal packages involving tax cuts to prop up domestic demand and increased social expenditures were adopted. Elsewhere, in cases where the consequences of the crisis have been less severe, fiscal policy remains generally restrictive. However, as illustrated in the Asian cases, this may not be desirable domestically from either an economic or a social perspective. In the present era of slow global growth, it may also not be optimal from the perspective of the world at large.

Coordinated international measures to accelerate recovery

The international response to the crises in South-East and East Asia was essentially restricted to the provision of large-scale financial assistance intended to meet the crisis countries' short-term needs for international liquidity. As indicated above, this financial assistance was initially accompanied by restrictive polices in the countries concerned but no changes in policies elsewhere were deemed necessary to address the consequences of the crisis. The result of this approach was not only a dramatic contraction in the countries concerned but also a slowdown in growth in the rest of the world. Particularly in the light of the present poor short-term prospects for the world economy, it is of interest to explore whether the use of international measures, rather than reliance purely on domestic action, might have achieved a more positive outcome for the countries concerned and, at the same time, might have boosted global economic growth.

One possibility could have been an internationally coordinated plan to cut interest rates in the major developed economies and increase official transfers to the Asian crisis economies. There are four reasons for such a set of policy actions.

First, the past two years have demonstrated that it is counter-productive for the global economy as a whole to have the initial burden of adjustment borne chiefly by the crisis economies through a tightening of aggregate demand. It would have been preferable if all countries with room for stimulating domestic consumption (such as the European economies) had contributed to the adjustment effort. The major European countries adopted measures of this nature when they started cutting interest rates beginning in the last quarter of 1998 in response to fears of a slowdown in their domestic economies. To the extent that this slowdown was a consequence of the initial crisis, these measures were a belated and indirect response to that crisis; if they had been taken earlier, the slowdown in their economies would probably not have occurred. In addition, the cuts were not coordinated at the global level (although they were coordinated within the euro zone, even before it officially came into operation).

This presents a second reason for such measures, namely, that a coordinated interest-rate reduction would stabilize the differentials in interest rates among countries and would therefore be more efficient; it would also have fewer adverse side effects for the world economy than country-driven interest rate changes which largely ignore the impact on rates elsewhere.

Third, an external demand stimulus would have been more effective in promoting recovery of the Asian economies because an important part of the idle capacity that was created in these countries was oriented towards exports.

Fourth, an additional official transfer of resources from the developed economies to the crisis countries would have not only stimulated these economies, but also fed back positive demand impulses to the developed economies through trade and other links. Foreign demand could have provided a stimulus to domestic activity in cases where weak domestic demand has since proved resistant to stimuli.

Addressing the social and human dimensions

The policy measures adopted in response to the crises in the Asian countries, in particular, brought into sharp relief the need to ensure consistency between short-term economic objectives, such as financial stability, and longer-term social and developmental goals, such as the eradication of poverty and the development of human capital. In some instances, there may be no incompatibility between economic and social objectives but this is not necessarily the case. In the Asian crisis countries, the policies initially adopted to address the crises abruptly reversed much of the long-term progress that had been achieved in reducing poverty and improving social conditions. This experience underlined the need to ensure that the social dimension is integrated into the formulation of economic policies, so as to avoid treating any negative social effects as by-products to be addressed later.

Negative social consequences of economic policies can arise through a variety of channels. The prime example of this occurs when budgetary cutbacks introduced to restore macroeconomic stability undermine the ability to deliver health care and education and to provide safety nets (such as food subsidies for the poorest). However, monetary policy can also have social consequences; for example, tight monetary policy restricts the availability of credit, and this is likely to impinge more on small and higher-risk borrowers than on major enterprises. Higher interest rates may discourage new investment in productive capacity, thus negatively affecting prospects for increased demand for labour. On the other hand, one of the key objectives of restrictive policies is often to control inflation, and success in this area has direct benefits for the poor. In Indonesia, for example, inflation since the crisis has been a major source of the increase in poverty.

These social consequences of the crisis not only entail short-term human costs but also cut into the ability of the countries concerned to build up their human capital and lift their standards of living over the longer term. For example, both declining school enrolment and worsening nutrition among children reduce the potential of those individuals to contribute to the economic and social development of their societies over the longer term.

The international community has long accepted the principle that the social and economic dimensions of policy should not be treated in isolation. Implementing that principle, however, has proved elusive. It is now increasingly recognized that the response to crises has to address the domestic social consequences of any economic measures that are adopted and should not be restricted to restoring macroeconomic stability and international financial confidence. Various social safety nets have been introduced in the crisis countries as a result. However, it has also become apparent that social protection mechanisms are more effective if they are in place before a crisis strikes than if they are hastily put together after a country faces a severe recession. The social dimension therefore needs to be incorporated in economic policy as a matter of course.

Strengthening the financial architecture

The crises of the past two years are attributable less to traditional macroeconomic imbalances than to vulnerabilities that arose from the way financial liberalization had been pursued and the phenomenal growth of private sector exposures to large amounts of risk which were underappreciated and not very well understood. The result has been widespread recognition of the need to devise new financial regimes which would be less susceptible to these types of crisis. This policy initiative has domestic and international dimensions and has come to be called "renewing the international financial architecture"[4].

As a first principle, it is universally accepted that the governance of financial markets and institutions must be strengthened in developed, developing and transition economies, albeit without assuming that one set of practices fits all situations. Private financial institutions need to be able to cope with volatility in the markets in which they operate. This means having capital adequate to their risk exposure and the capacity to monitor and manage their risk. The role of government is to establish incentives and sanctions that force financial firms in this direction. This entails strengthened regulation and supervision, bankruptcy and foreclosure laws, corporate transparency and governance.

These improvements require the development of human and institutional capital in most developing and transition economies, which takes time. For this reason, financial sector liberalization needs to be paced with the build-up of regulatory capacity and appropriate professional and managerial capacity in financial institutions. This implies that the appropriate pace of liberalization will be determined by the country's stage of development and capacity to make effective use of international expertise in both private and public sectors.

Governments need flexibility in considering the use of controls on movements of capital into and out of their economies, in particular as regards short-term flows. Views differ on the usefulness and effectiveness of different types of capital controls and no single model will be appropriate for all countries. Thus, the international community should not discourage countries from adopting policies to inhibit potentially volatile inflows and outflows. The experience of the past few years is an argument for experimentation and against dogmatism.

The damage that can arise when the uncertainty of private financial actors turns to fear and flight is much better appreciated than before. To lessen uncertainty, Governments and the International Monetary Fund (IMF) have worked recently to increase the amount of information in the public domain and the speed with which it is provided. International organizations have also enhanced cooperation so as to provide more reliable information, such as on financial

[4]   As a contribution to this project, the most senior officials of the United Nations Organization in the economic and social arena, through the Executive Committee on Economic and Social Affairs, prepared a set of proposals in a report entitled "Towards a new international financial architecture" (available on the Internet at www.un.org/esa/coordination/ecesa/eces99-1.htm).

flows and debt, and to do so more quickly. These are important initiatives that need the support and participation of creditor and debtor countries, of Governments and the private sector.

The policy community has become sensitive to the expectations of international private creditors that they would be bailed out by the international public sector when currencies and banking systems of emerging market economies went into crisis. Those expectations caused excessively risky lending practices —the "moral hazard" problem—and huge bailouts (financed at market interest rates and substantial cost for most countries). The international community is seeking to develop mechanisms to involve creditors in the working out of a future crisis and to reduce moral hazard by asking creditors (banks and bondholders) to shoulder more risk. Beyond general principles, however, there is little agreement on mechanisms or instruments to effect this change. This is an important area for further work.

At the same time, the international community favours providing adequate liquidity to countries in crisis, especially when these countries have followed sound policies and are hit by contagion from a crisis that is spreading internationally. A step was taken in this direction in April 1999 when IMF agreed to establish the Contingent Credit Line. Countries that meet certain policy criteria will be able to arrange a line of credit at IMF from which they can draw on short notice in the event of a financial emergency stemming from international developments beyond their control. This is to supplement their primary line of defence, holdings of their own reserve assets.

Beyond these policy developments, there has been a new intellectual ferment in respect of trying to better understand how financial sectors operate. It is clear that the financial sector in developed countries has been evolving rapidly in recent decades, especially the banking systems. The liberalization drive in developing countries has plunged these countries into a new, highly competitive world of finance, as has the adoption of market-based financial systems in the economies in transition. Technology has so evolved that the uncertainties, asymmetries and market failures inherent in finance can wreak extensive damage with unprecedented speed, as we have been witnessing over the past two years. In order to help take stock of our understanding in this area, part two of the present *Survey* is devoted to an examination of financial development in the globalizing world.

II | THE INTERNATIONAL ECONOMY

The international economic environment confronting developing and transition economies was not conducive to growth in 1998. The prices of many non-oil commodities dropped to record lows and the price of oil itself reached its lowest average nominal level in more than two decades. The net transfer of financial resources to developing countries as a group became markedly negative during the year, reflecting the changes in private investors' sentiments towards these economies. On the positive side, official flows from both multilateral financial organizations and bilateral creditors to developing and transition economies increased, but this was mostly in the form of rescue packages orchestrated by these organizations and was not sufficient to offset the outflows of private finance.

The decline in net transfers required countries to curb their imports, with the result that there was a significant slowdown in international trade. Weak import demand by Japan compounded the problem. The balance-of-payments adjustments by developing countries and economies in transition were paralleled by a widening of the current-account deficit of the United States of America owing to the strong import demand by the United States economy and increased inflows of private capital. The latter reflected investors' search for "quality" investment opportunities.

Private capital flows to developing countries have shown some signs of recovery during the first half of 1999 but they are unlikely to reach the levels recorded before the emergence of the Asian crisis in 1997. Moreover, although interest rates on bond issues by developing countries and economies in transition have declined, they remain high for some countries, reducing these countries' access to fresh financial resources.

Prospects for commodity prices in 1999 are not encouraging, despite the remarkable recovery in oil prices after March. International trade will grow slowly in 1999, not providing much of a stimulus for economic expansion in most countries. As of mid-1999, the international economic environment, although improved, will not provide developing and transition economies with a basis for a strong recovery from the events of the previous two years.

TURBULENCE IN INTERNATIONAL TRADE

The financial crises of 1997-1998 depressed international trade substantially. The slowdown in the growth of world output, especially the contraction in South-East and East Asia, and tightened external financing constraints in many developing and transition economies reduced the demand for imports to such an extent that the growth of world merchandise trade (in terms of export volume) was only 3.6 per cent in 1998 (see table A.13). This was less than half the rate for 1997 and the lowest of the decade. The setback was most pronounced for the developing countries whose volume of trade decreased in 1998, having grown at an annual rate in the region of 10 per cent for much of the decade (see figure II.1). At the same time, a large drop in commodity prices (see below) led to a decline in export revenues for many countries, mostly developing and transition economies. Measured in current United States dollars, the value of total world exports of goods declined by 2.3 per cent in 1998. In addition, the value of exports of services (transport, travel and other commercial services) is estimated to have dropped by about 2 per cent, the first decline since 1983.

Crisis-driven shifts in the volume and pattern of trade

The international financial crisis caused not only a general slowdown in world trade but also, because of its differentiated impact, a change in the pattern of international trade flows. One of the most noticeable changes was that imports of developing countries dropped by 10 per cent in value terms and about 5 per cent in volume terms in 1998. This decline was brought about by the fall in real incomes, adverse changes in the terms of trade and external financing constraints in many developing economies. The most severe case was that of the South-East and East Asian economies, where declines in national income, large currency devaluations and sharp reversals in foreign capital flows necessitated large cuts in imports. Total imports of the subregion fell by

Figure II.1.
GROWTH OF WORLD IMPORTS, 1992-1998

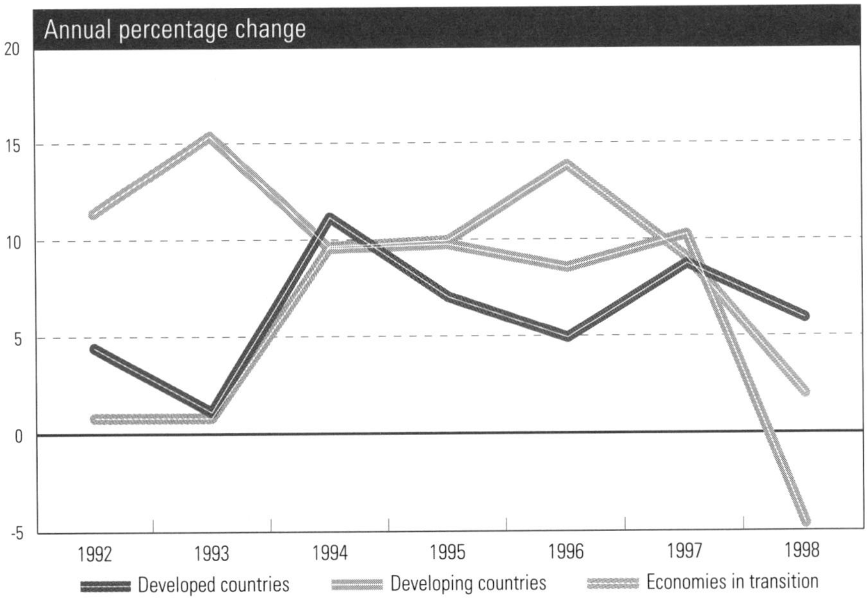

more than 20 per cent in value terms and 13 per cent in volume terms in 1998. At the same time, many economies in West Asia registered a decline in imports as the drop in the price of oil reduced their export revenues and thus their capacity to import. Conversely, imports by the Latin America and Caribbean region increased, but by substantially less than during the past few years. Imports into Mexico and Central American economies continued to grow strongly owing to their links with North America. Imports into Africa also grew in 1998, but at a slower rate than in recent years.

In contrast, most developed economies, except for Japan, maintained a relatively strong growth of imports in 1998. To some extent, the factors that contributed to the decline in import demand in developing economies worked in the opposite direction for developed economies. For example, while the drop in commodity prices caused a deterioration in the terms of trade and reduced import demand in many developing economies, it created terms-of-trade gains for many developed economies and boosted their demand for imports. Meanwhile, the large capital flows that retreated from developing and transition economies returned to the developed economies and provided them with additional financing for imports. Cheaper exports from Asia, brought about by devaluations in several countries, and strong demand growth in North America were also important factors. These factors caused imports into North America to grow by 10 per cent in volume in 1998 and those into Western Europe by 6 per cent. Japan was a special case: its decline of 2.8 per cent in output was associated with a fall in the volume of imports of 10 per cent in 1998.

Economies in transition as a group maintained their 1997 import levels but the situation varied widely within the group. The imports of Central and Eastern European economies grew by 10 per cent in volume, reflecting these economies' strengthened trade links with Western Europe. In contrast, the volume of imports into the Russian Federation and other Commonwealth of Independent States (CIS) economies declined 15 per cent. The Russian default in August 1998 and its subsequent financial and economic fallout led to a drop in the level of domestic economic activity and hence to reduced absorption of imports. The plunge in commodity prices, particularly oil, compounded the problem as it negatively affected the purchasing power of these countries' exports.

Export performance also differed across countries, but to a lesser extent. Many developing economies increased their volume of exports in 1998. Leading the group was the Latin America and Caribbean region, where export volume grew by almost 8 per cent, largely owing to a strong export performance by Mexico. However, the export growth of the Asian developing economies was almost zero, despite their large currency devaluations and the corresponding potential gains in international competitiveness. This contrasted with the double-digit rates of growth recorded earlier in the decade. Credit constraints in these economies and the large drop in demand from Japan, the region's largest importer, as well as from other economies of the region, were the major causes for this weak export performance. The collapse of regional markets and the recession in Japan also resulted in a deceleration in the growth of Chinese exports to about 4 per cent in 1998 from 26 per cent in the previous year.

A marked feature for developing economies in 1998 was the overall decline in export revenues, largely because of the sharp drop in commodity prices. The value of merchandise exports measured in United States dollars declined by 7 per cent for developing economies as a whole. All major developing regions experienced a contraction in their export earnings. The worst-hit region was Western Asia where the value of merchandise exports dropped by almost a quarter in 1998. Africa also experienced a significant decline in export earnings owing to lower commodity prices and the dominance of commodities in the region's exports.

Most developed economies managed to register moderate export growth. Exports of Western European countries grew by over 5 per cent in 1998 thanks to dynamic intra-trade among European Union (EU) member countries. North American exports, however, decelerated in 1998 but could yet register a positive growth. Conversely, Japan's export volume shrank by 4 per cent in 1998.

The export performance of economies in transition differed across two sub-groups. Central and Eastern European economies achieved double-digit growth in both the volume and value of exports. On the other hand, the value of exports of the CIS economies fell by about one sixth, even though their volume was almost unchanged.

The uneven development of international trade across nations in 1998 was associated with major changes in external balances. There was some improvement in the current-account balance for the developing economies. This, however, mainly reflected the substantial import compression by Asian countries in response to the sharp decline in net capital inflows. Other developing regions experienced a deterioration in their current-account balances. At the same time, there was a substantial widening of the external deficit of the United States. This was brought about by both a large increase in imports (because of strong domestic demand), and a weakening of United States exports (due to the economic slowdown in the rest of the world) as well as the strengthening of the dollar.

It is a testimony to the strength of the global trading system that the turbulence in the world economy, particularly the slowdown in world trade, has not given rise to significant trade conflicts. However, if there is a continuation of slow growth of world output and world trade, together with widening imbalances in the latter, tensions in international trade are likely to rise. In particular, the record external imbalances of the United States, if they continue, may give rise to protectionist pressures and may even destabilize the exchange rates for major currencies. At the same time, paradoxically, continued strong import demand from the United States and other developed economies remains an important factor for stimulating economic recovery in many developing economies. It is often recalled that following the peso crisis, Mexico was able to come out of recession relatively quickly owing to strong import demand by the United States. In contrast, Japan has not served as a source of demand growth for crisis-hit countries in Asia, as the country itself is immersed in economic recession. Some innovative forms of international cooperation are called for in order to ensure that the current period of slow growth, in addition to being a problem in itself, does not also imperil progress made in recent years towards such longer-term global objectives as freer trade.

Non-oil commodity prices plummet

During 1998, the prices of most non-oil commodities exported by developing countries collapsed, after having shown mounting signs of weakness following the emergence of the Asian crisis in mid-1997. Overall, the drop in prices of non-fuel commodities in 1998 was more than 12 per cent in dollar terms (see table A.17).[1] An annual decrease of this magnitude had not occurred since 1985. This dramatic plunge—to record lows for the majority of commodities—stemmed from a number of developments that coincided in most markets.

Weak demand in Japan and in the South-East and East Asian economies in crisis, which were large importers of primary commodities, was a critical factor. It was exacerbated by the direct and indirect effects of the general slowdown in the world economy emanating from the financial crisis. The speed of the decline in prices was accelerated by oversupply in many markets. In general, producers were reluctant to cut back production, preferring to build up stocks.

These short-term developments were superimposed on structural factors that have produced a longer-term downward trend in prices. One has been the continued shift in the composition of world output from manufacturing towards services and higher value added products, which has contributed to reducing global demand for raw materials. Second, technological progress has increased the possibilities for using other inputs to replace primary commodities. It has also bolstered the supply of some commodities by raising productivity and lowering production costs.

The prices of manufactured goods exported by industrialized countries, which constitute the bulk of imports by developing economies, also fell, but by less than 3 per cent. As a result, the purchasing power of the commodity export revenues of developing countries in terms of their imports of manufactures from industrialized countries, the "real" price of non-fuel commodities, fell by almost 10 per cent. This large annual decrease in purchasing power came on top of the long-term decline in commodity prices relative to those of manufactures.

This negative price shock led to a severe deterioration in the external and fiscal balances of the many developing countries that are heavily dependent on commodity-export revenues. For example, non-oil commodity shipments account for over 45 per cent of the export earnings of sub-Saharan African countries. In the case of Latin American countries, about 30 per cent of export revenues is accounted for by non-oil commodities. Depressed non-oil commodity prices also adversely affected a wide range of economies in transition, especially the CIS members, and developed countries like Australia, Canada and New Zealand, which are important commodity exporters.

The collapse in prices during 1998 applied to all groups of commodities except vegetable oilseeds and oils, which gained 7 per cent (see figure II.2). Notably, the price of palm oil increased more than 22 per cent owing to declines in production in Indonesia and Malaysia, the world's dominant producers, as a result of the damage caused by El Niño. There were also increases in the prices for soybean, sunflower and linseed oils.

Among other commodity groups, tropical beverage prices fell 17 per cent in 1998, after substantial gains in 1997. The decline was due mainly to the sharp fall in the price of arabica coffee at the end of the year as a result of Brazil's bumper crop. Nevertheless, some African and Asian countries were relatively unaffected because they produce robusta coffee, whose price rose slightly in 1998. Other producers of beverage crops also fared comparatively well, with prices for cocoa and tea increasing slightly.

[1]   The combined index of prices of non-fuel commodities expressed in terms of special drawing rights (SDRs) dropped by almost the same amount because the value in dollars of the SDRs' component currencies remained about the same in 1998.

Figure II.2.
NON-FUEL COMMODITY PRICES, 1993-1998

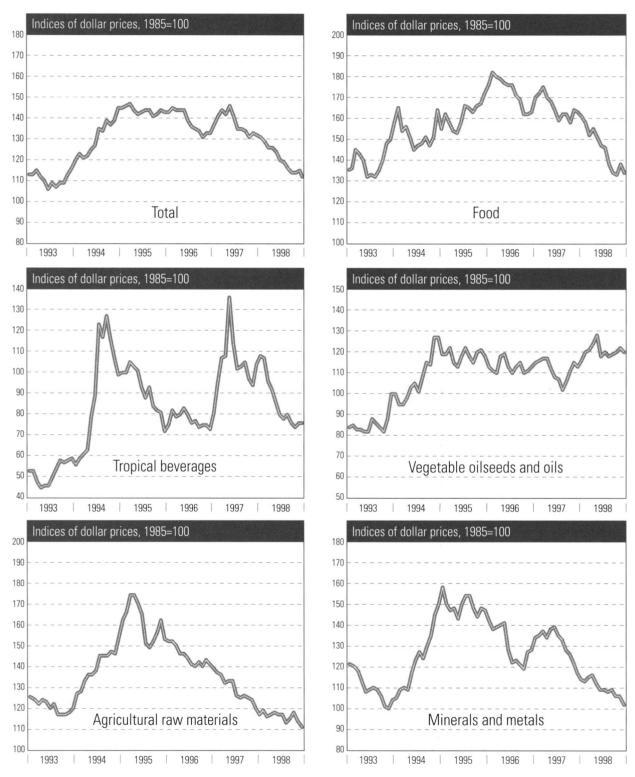

Source: UNCTAD, *Monthly Commodity Price Bulletin.*

Supply gluts and weak demand pushed down prices of food products by an average of 13 per cent, but prices for beef and sugar fell more sharply. In 1998, prices for the grain sub-group also dropped to very low levels. This applied mainly to wheat and maize, while rice maintained its average 1997 price. However, global cereal demand exceeded supply by more than expected owing to weather-related problems. Food aid by major donors in the form of grain also rose. This held especially for aid to Asia and to some of the countries of the former Soviet Union, notably the Russian Federation, where the 1998 crop was very low and the country's financial ability to import fell after the devaluation of the ruble.

Prices of some agricultural raw materials were particularly hard hit by supply shocks, mainly owing to unfavourable weather conditions, and declined on average by 11 per cent in 1998. Prices for cotton, rubber, timber and wool dropped by even more.

The falling price for natural rubber led to the virtual collapse of the International Natural Rubber Agreement (INRA), the last remaining international commodity agreement with a price-stabilization clause. At the beginning of 1999, Thailand, the world's biggest producer of this commodity, decided to leave the organization and withhold its contribution to the group's buffer stocks. This decision followed the announcement some months earlier of the abandonment of the Agreement by Malaysia which is trying to create its own buffer-stock system and to encourage Indonesia and Thailand to do likewise. These three countries together produce around 80 per cent of the world's natural rubber.

Cotton prices fell by 10 per cent in 1998, partly owing to the shrinkage of world demand, but also because of China's emergence as a major cotton exporter. Traditional cotton-producing countries (such as India, Pakistan and Turkey) were affected, but the fall in prices was especially discouraging for several francophone West African countries that had boosted production in recent years. Burkina Faso, for example, almost tripled its cotton output between 1993 and 1997, but its earnings in 1998 declined. Some economies in transition, including Turkmenistan and Uzbekistan, were similarly affected.

With some exceptions, including iron ore, phosphates, silver and tin, metals and minerals suffered large declines in prices in 1998. This was due, on the one hand, to rising stocks and the completion of new plants and, on the other hand, to shrinking demand in developing countries. On average, prices fell by 16 per cent in 1998. There were, however, much larger decreases for some metals: nickel dropped by almost 34 per cent, copper by 28 per cent, zinc by 21 per cent and aluminium by 15 per cent.

The loss of revenue from copper exports in 1998 had consequences for the budget and current account of Chile, the world's largest producer, and Zambia. For the latter, price erosion came at a crucial juncture in its long-standing effort to sell off its large copper mines, which generate about 90 per cent of the country's foreign exchange earnings and are the most important employer in the economy. Apart from these two countries, copper is a key export earner for smaller producers, like Mongolia, which were also severely affected.

Gold experienced a fall in price of some 11 per cent in 1998, continuing the decline observed during the past two decades. This erosion has been due partly to the gradual decrease in the role of gold as a store of wealth. Nowadays gold behaves more like a traditional primary commodity, that is to say , one with a price driven by current supply and demand. The fall in prices in 1998 affected not only the biggest producers (Australia, Canada, China, the Russian Federation, South Africa and the United States), but also some economies in transition. In the Caucasus and Central Asia, the production of gold has increased in recent years and exports are especially important for Kyrgyzstan and Uzbekistan.

Two events of early 1999 may have direct implications for the overall evolution of non-oil commodity prices. One was the devaluation of the real in mid-January by Brazil (discussed in chap. III). Because Brazil is a leading exporter of many commodities, this has the potential to affect the evolution of international commodity prices. The recession in the country may reinforce the effect of the real's devaluation in encouraging Brazil to increase current and prospective production and to export more, hereby further driving down the prices of such commodities as aluminium, coffee, soybeans, steel, sugar and wheat.

The other event was the strong and quick recovery of oil prices after the agreement in March among oil producers to restrict output. Some observers considered this movement a harbinger of an upturn in the prices of non-fuel commodities as well and, for a short period in early 1999, the prices of some commodities increased. However, oil prices are not a leading indicator of turning points for non-fuel commodities. All producer cartels for non-oil products have collapsed, many commodity markets are plagued by oversupply and most of the proposals by producers to reduce output lack credibility.

Consequently, even if some prices were showing evidence of bottoming out in the spring of 1999, the upturn in prices in early 1999 is likely to be difficult to maintain. The outlook for the year as a whole is for price weakness. As far as tropical beverages are concerned, the surge in global production is expected to push markets into surplus, given, at best, weak growth in demand. Prices, therefore, are not expected to improve much. On the other hand, despite sluggish demand and the large stocks held by major exporting countries, a modest recovery in grain prices could occur in 1999, as crop forecasts for the 1999/2000 season are lower than those for the previous year. Meanwhile, the outlook for 1999 for minerals and metals is for continued low prices. Nevertheless, production will tend to be maintained in the short to medium run, because closing plants is expensive and producers are reluctant to make big capacity cuts. To the contrary, several new mines came on line recently and there are ongoing expansion projects. The large stocks in many markets will therefore need to be drawn down before a price reversal can be anticipated.

In the particular case of gold, prospects for 1999 are not encouraging because of the decline in the status of gold as an official reserve and the fact that many central banks have started to pare their gold holdings in order to raise the returns on their portfolios. Australia announced the adoption of such a policy in 1998. In the spring of 1999, the United Kingdom of Great Britain and Northern Ireland, following Switzerland, announced that it will join this trend. Both decisions had an impact on the international gold markets, because British and Swiss gold holdings represent about 30 per cent and 50 per cent of the world's current annual output respectively. Also, the prospect that the International Monetary Fund (IMF) might sell gold reserves to help fund debt relief for poor countries, a proposal supported by several industrialized countries, has had a depressing impact on the market.

In all, global demand for non-oil commodities is expected to remain sluggish as a consequence of the slowdown in Latin America, continuing woes in Japan, and the weakening of the major Western European economies. The continued strength of the United States economy, and, especially, the turnaround of the Asian crisis economies, which would raise their consumption of commodities, could prompt a recovery of commodity prices by the second half of 1999. However, this recovery is likely to slow and could falter.

Historic declines in oil prices

After the increase in 1996, the average price of a barrel of crude-oil[2] dropped from $18.70 in 1997 to $12.30 in 1998—the lowest average nominal price since 1977. This represented the largest relative collapse of prices (some 34 per cent) since 1986 (see table A.17). As a result, all oil-producing and oil-exporting countries faced a very difficult economic environment in 1998. For the 11 members of the Organization of the Petroleum Exporting Countries (OPEC),[3] the plunge of oil prices in 1998 relative to 1997 led to a loss in export revenues of around $50 billion.

The rapid drop in prices was due to excess supply as rising production coincided with a sharp downturn in global demand. Total output rose by almost 1 million barrels a day, equivalent to 1.3 per cent in 1998 (see table A.18) but global oil demand grew by only 0.4 million barrels a day (0.5 per cent)—less than one fourth of the rise in 1997. This increased the existing aggregate imbalance between demand and supply to some 1.5 million barrels a day on average.

Production surged because output in several non-OPEC countries rose and most producers did not join OPEC's attempt to avert the price erosion. Moreover, the oversupply was exacerbated by Iraq's exports of crude oil under the "oil-for-food" programme of the United Nations, whose limits were increased in February 1998.[4] Although a member of OPEC, Iraq did not subscribe to the OPEC agreements, and it pushed exports to capacity in order to maximize its foreign exchange revenues.

The fall in demand initially stemmed from the weakness of Japan's economy and the reduction in oil demand by the countries most affected by the financial crisis in Asia. It was subsequently exacerbated by the mild winter in the northern hemisphere and then by the more generalized slowdown in the world economy.

Oil prices were on a downward trend from the beginning of 1997 (see figure II.3), but dropped rapidly from late 1997 onwards. OPEC's decision to raise output ceilings by 10 per cent in November 1997 contributed to the price erosion. From its peak of $19.50 in October 1997, the price per barrel tumbled to $12.40 in March 1998; it recovered slightly in April and May in response to the pledge by oil producers to cut production. While there was some easing of the oil glut, by June oil prices resumed their downward trend and fell below $12 a barrel. A second agreement in June to cut supplies led to a brief rally, with prices recovering to nearly $13 in September. Since the agreements to reduce supplies were not adhered to by several producers, with some even raising output, prices resumed their fall. Efforts to agree on further cuts failed and prices dropped further, albeit with some fluctuations, reaching a monthly average of $9.70 per barrel in December.

[2] The price indicator for oil used here is the average spot price of the basket of seven crudes produced by the members of the Organization of the Petroleum Exporting Countries (OPEC).

[3] Algeria, Indonesia, the Islamic Republic of Iran, Iraq, Kuwait, the Libyan Arab Jamahiriya, Nigeria, Qatar, Saudi Arabia, the United Arab Emirates and Venezuela.

[4] In its resolution 1153 (1998), the Security Council raised the limit to $5.256 billion from the earlier $2 billion per semester.

Figure II.3.
AVERAGE SPOT PRICES OF OPEC BASKET OF CRUDE OILS,
JANUARY 1997-APRIL 1999

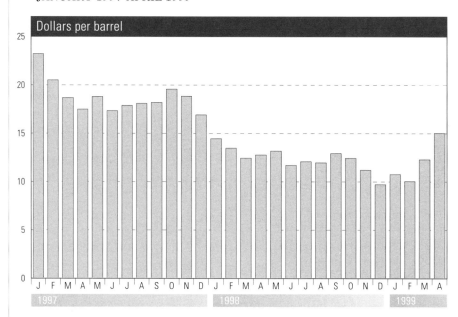

Source: *Middle East Survey* (http://www.mees.com/
dotcom/opec_basket). Accessed on 19 May 1999.

5   The members are Bahrain, Kuwait, Oman, Qatar,
Saudi Arabia and the United Arab Emirates.

The large export-revenue loss of oil-exporting countries was partially offset in some cases by the lower prices for their imports of commodities and, to a lesser extent, of manufactures. Nevertheless, for the majority, especially in Africa and the Middle East, the net loss was substantial. African oil-exporting countries, such as Angola, the Congo, Gabon, the Libyan Arab Jamahiriya and Nigeria, depend on oil for more than half of their export revenues and import relatively few commodities. Oil is also a major export earner for Algeria, Cameroon, Egypt and Equatorial Guinea. For the countries of the Gulf Cooperation Council (GCC),[5] oil revenues account for over 90 per cent of exports and over 80 per cent of budget revenues, in spite of diversification efforts. Several net oil-exporting countries were compelled to reduce government expenditures and to undertake other fiscal adjustments to reduce already high budget deficits (see chap. III).

The impact of the depression in oil markets in 1998 was also felt in some of the members of the CIS, including Azerbaijan, Kazakhstan, the Russian Federation and Uzbekistan. Rapidly declining export revenues was, because of the plunge in oil prices, one of the key triggers of the August 1998 events in the Russian Federation. In Latin America, notably in Ecuador and Venezuela (where oil accounts for 80 per cent of export revenues), and to a lesser extent in Colombia and Mexico, the collapse in oil prices had a pronounced impact on overall economic activity. In many of these countries, as in some other producers, oil-exploration and -exploitation plans based on the expectation of substantial inflows of foreign direct investment (FDI) were temporarily interrupted; some may be left unimplemented for quite some time.

Oil-producing industrialized countries and the large oil companies were adversely affected by lower oil prices. Norway was the hardest-hit developed economy. Its oil production dropped substantially owing to its support of the OPEC agreements and its budget revenues from oil declined correspondingly. Mergers and acquisitions in oil-sector companies increased sharply as companies sought to reduce costs and lift profit margins to more normal levels.

Oil prices improved substantially in March 1999, after the major oil-producing countries reached an agreement that was subsequently ratified by OPEC members. Anxious about the erosion of oil prices to below $10, oil producers agreed on coordinated action to cut crude oil production by 2.1 million barrels per day for one year. OPEC agreed to reduce oil output by 1.7 million barrels a day and some non-OPEC producers by about 400,000 barrels a day. If implemented and adhered to, the agreement would not only cut the total supply of oil by about 3 per cent but also reduce inventories. These were estimated to be between 300 million and 400 million barrels (equivalent to 4-5 per cent of estimated total demand for 1998) on the eve of the agreement.

As was not the case for the agreements reached in 1998, the political commitment and unity shown by oil-producing countries in March 1999 lent credibility to the agreement, and markets reacted accordingly. Oil prices rose by $2 at the end of March to more than $12 per barrel (see figure II.3). They have since risen to over $15 per barrel, suggesting that market actors continue to believe in the oil producers' commitment. However, it remains uncertain whether the price rise can be sustained. The failure of past efforts to enact agreed cutbacks suggests that ensuring compliance is difficult. Some producers, especially those experiencing domestic and external-payment constraints, even though they are persuaded of the need for collective action to sustain prices, may find it hard to resist the temptation to raise production with a view to realizing the higher prices that such action has brought about. On the other hand, low oil prices from late 1997 until early spring 1999 led to sharp reductions in expenditures on maintenance, exploration and development in many actual or potential oil-producing and oil-exporting countries. This may reduce the ability of these countries to raise output in the short run if they wish to do so.

Although oil prices rose sharply in March and April 1999, the outlook is for only small year-on-year gains, even if the output limits agreed in March are honoured. Current inventories are so high that, without further output cutbacks and much stronger than expected growth in the global economy, it will take months to reduce inventories to normal levels. They will therefore continue to exert downward pressure on prices for the rest of the year. In addition, some of the countries that did not participate in the last agreement are expected to raise production, offsetting the shutdown of many marginal wells in high-cost production areas undertaken at the end of 1998 and the beginning of 1999. Moreover, if prices were to rise further, some exploration projects completed in recent years could be put into production and new, previously uneconomic fields could be exploited using more modern technologies.[6]

World demand for oil in 1999 is expected to remain weak, owing to the slowdown in Western Europe and the easing of the pace of growth in the United States. Oil demand from developing countries continues to be uncertain. Latin America, which was the main sources of the growth in oil demand in 1998, is expected to experience a mild recession in 1999 because of the crisis in Brazil;

[6] Horizontal drilling, computer seismology and better offshore loading, among other recent innovations, have increased productivity and reduced operating costs.

oil prices would languish accordingly. On the other hand, if the signs of recovery in several of the Asian crisis countries are extended and strengthened throughout the year, the prospects for oil prices could improve.

INTERNATIONAL TRANSFER OF FINANCIAL RESOURCES

The net effect of the foregoing changes in trade of developing countries was a shift from a deficit in trade in goods and services to a large surplus. These countries had financed their excess of imports over exports in 1996 with a net inward transfer of financial resources, but they made a net transfer of $11 billion abroad in 1997 and this soared to about $60 billion in 1998 (see table II.1). A counterpart to this adjustment by developing countries was the sharp increase in net financial transfer to the United States, as its imports swelled along with capital inflows. There was also an increase in the net outward transfer by Japan (reflected in a net build-up of Japanese dollar claims), as its trade surplus rose because of weak imports.

These dynamics were mirrored on the financial side by the abrupt changes in investor sentiment that began in Asia in mid-1997 and then spread to other emerg-

Table II.1.
NET TRANSFER OF FINANCIAL RESOURCES OF GROUPS OF DEVELOPING COUNTRIES, 1988-1998[a]

Billions of dollars											
	1988	1989	1990	1991	1992	1993	1994	1995	1996	1997	1998[b]
All developing countries	-14.8	-21.3	-42.2	28.6	40.4	63.0	29.0	31.3	8.6	-10.8	-59.5
Africa *of which:*	3.9	0.6	-10.3	-5.8	0.9	2.9	7.6	10.5	-1.1	6.3	19.0
Sub-Saharan Africa[c]	7.8	5.9	8.5	9.2	11.4	9.9	8.1	7.6	8.0	10.2	14.0
Latin America and the Caribbean	-22.0	-27.7	-27.6	-9.1	7.8	14.3	16.9	-1.0	-1.5	23.1	45.5
West Asia	23.8	16.7	3.9	50.8	39.4	38.9	9.7	10.4	-0.7	4.6	35.5
Other Asia *of which:*	-20.5	-12.5	-10.4	-9.4	-5.7	6.9	-5.2	11.5	12.0	-44.7	-159.5
China	3.9	4.9	-10.8	-11.8	-5.2	11.4	-8.0	-12.3	-19.2	-44.9	-47.5
Other South and East Asia	-24.4	-17.2	1.0	2.7	-0.6	-4.4	3.6	24.4	31.2	0.2	-112.0
Memorandum item:											
Least developed countries[d]	8.8	8.4	8.7	9.8	11.6	11.6	9.2	11.0	11.2	12.2	16.0

Source: UN/DESA, based on data of IMF, and official national and other sources.

[a] Expenditure basis (negative of balance of payments on goods, services and private transfers, excluding investment income).
[b] Preliminary estimate.
[c] Excluding Nigeria and South Africa.
[d] Covering 42 out of 48 least developed countries.

ing markets, leading to the August 1998 Russian debt moratorium and the financial pressure on Brazil in late 1998, which culminated in the Brazilian devaluation in January 1999. The "flight to quality" among international investors intensified in 1998, particularly in the aftermath of the Russian crisis, resulting in large flows of portfolio investment to the United States, particularly purchases of government securities. Earlier in the year, there were large foreign purchases of United States equity shares as well. At the same time, purchases of international securities by United States residents fell sharply during the year.

The surge in financial flows out of developing countries in 1998 marked the second consecutive year of negative net transfer, following several years of strong inflows. The shift in financial flows was concentrated in East and South-East Asia, excluding China, owing to the massive withdrawal of private lending in the aftermath of the Asian crisis. Net portfolio equity investment rebounded somewhat from very low levels in 1997.

The net financial transfer to Latin America rose in 1998, reflecting the widening trade deficit brought about, in part, by low commodity prices. The much larger trade deficit was financed substantially by drawing down reserves. This was a departure from the steady reserve accumulation in the present decade. Foreign financial inflows declined in 1998, although they remained substantial, as the region benefited from a shift in portfolio investment from Asia to Latin America early in 1998 and from continued strong FDI flows (see below).

In Africa as well, the deterioration of the trade balance, due primarily to the sharp decline in commodity prices, was financed largely by a drawdown of reserves, a reversal of the large increase in reserves in 1997. Net financial flows to Africa declined in 1998, mainly owing to a drop in private financial inflows, as FDI flows weakened and portfolio investment and foreign banking also decreased. In contrast, official financial flows improved somewhat.

Private lending flows

Net flows of medium- and long-term private lending to developing countries as a group in 1998 were only about half their 1997 levels, with a large net outflow of commercial bank credit. This reflects the progressive decline of bond issues and loan commitments during 1998: the average monthly amount dropped from $25 billion in 1997 to $18 billion in the first half of 1998 and to $12 billion by the second half of the year.[7] Declines were concentrated in Asia where they were most severe in the first half of 1998.[8] Portfolio investors shifted funds to Latin America and Eastern Europe in early 1998, following the spread of financial contagion in Asia. Later in the year, flows to these other regions dwindled with the worsening financial situation in Brazil and the Russian debt moratorium in August. Oil-exporting countries with large assets and China, which has substantial foreign reserves, were those best able to maintain access to international credit.

Private lending to the economies in transition dropped sharply after the Russian debt crisis in August. Net flows of bank credit to those economies declined but bond flows for the year as a whole increased because of major issues in the early part of the year. The spillover from the Russian crisis onto private credit flows to other economies in transition was smallest for those countries, such as Hungary and Poland, that are less economically integrated with the Russian Federation than others in the region.

[7] World Bank, *Global Development Finance, 1999* (Washington, D.C., April 1999), pp. 24 and 28.

[8] Bank for International Settlements, "BIS consolidated international banking statistics for end-1998" (21/1994E), p. 1.

Short-term lending to developing countries in 1998 also plunged from 1997 levels. The decline was particularly severe in East and South Asia, where there was a large net reduction in the high level of short-term debt in a number of countries because creditors stopped rolling over their loans after the crisis erupted. In addition, part of the resolution of the crisis involves restructuring short-term debt into instruments with longer maturities, as in the Republic of Korea.

Paralleling the decline in bond issues and new loan commitments in 1998 was the rise in the cost of funds, which deterred even creditworthy borrowers. The interest rate on emerging market credit can be interpreted as comprising two components—a base interest rate for risk-free capital and an additional element ("spread") for the higher risk of lending to these countries. Although interest rates on riskless securities fell during the year (for example, the interest rate on the 10-year United States Treasury bond fell from about 5.6 per cent in the first quarter of 1998 to a low of 4.5 per cent in October), spreads on emerging market sovereign bonds rose substantially (see figure II.4). After rising sharply in October 1997, they rose further in April 1998 and soared in August of the same year, reflecting investors' reassessment of the risk of lending to emerging markets. While investors differentiated among countries in their risk assessment following the Asian crisis, their perception of sharply increased risk of investment in emerging markets following the Russian crisis was widespread. With the stabilization of the international financial situation in early 1999, these interest rate spreads began to come down.

Figure II.4.
YIELD SPREADS ON EMERGING MARKET BONDS,
JULY 1997-MAY 1999

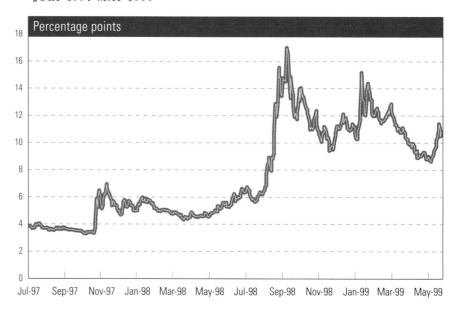

Source: J P Morgan, Emerging Markets Bond Index (EMBI) data.

Foreign direct investment

FDI flows to developing and transition economies in 1998 declined by about 5 per cent from the peak in 1997, a modest reduction in relation to the effects on other capital flows of the spread of the Asian financial crisis to global proportions. FDI flows are generally much less volatile than portfolio flows. The decline was modest in all regions, even in the Asian economies most affected by the financial crisis. Weakening economic growth worldwide as well as economic deterioration in individual countries had a depressing effect on FDI flows but this was mitigated in some countries by economic developments and policies that created a favourable environment for direct investment.

FDI in East and South Asia was notably resilient in 1998 considering the financial instability and economic recession in a number of economies. Flows to South Asia in 1998 were unchanged after several years of growth. FDI flows to China, the largest recipient in the region, also maintained their 1997 level.

Economic recession in a number of East Asian economies created poor conditions for direct investment. In Indonesia, poor economic conditions were compounded by political and social instability and FDI flows collapsed. The sharp economic slowdown throughout the region, as well as continued recession in Japan, severely depressed usually large intra-Asian FDI flows.

However, other developments offset some of these negative factors and FDI rose significantly in the Republic of Korea and Thailand. For foreign investors, the substantial currency depreciations since the latter part of 1997 reduced production costs and reinforced the collapse of domestic asset prices, making them much more attractive. At the same time, there were efforts throughout the region to promote FDI. In the crisis countries, liberalization of FDI, including cross-border mergers and acquisitions, was an integral part of adjustment programmes which involved extensive restructuring of the banking and corporate sectors. In these countries, such mergers and acquisitions increased by almost 60 per cent in value in 1998 and constituted 57 per cent of total FDI flows.[9] Furthermore, the long-term factors that had created a favourable environment for FDI—natural and human resources, infrastructure and access to major markets—were still in place.

FDI in Latin America was also quite stable in 1998, with significant increase in flows to Brazil offsetting declines in Argentina, Colombia and Mexico. Privatization of the large telecommunications company and financial companies in Brazil provided the main impetus to FDI as financial conditions and prospects for growth deteriorated during the year.

FDI flows to Africa as a whole declined slightly but there were notable increases to Egypt and Morocco where there has been progress in economic reform, particularly privatization. FDI in sub-Saharan Africa (excluding South Africa and Nigeria) increased slightly but remained concentrated in the mining and oil sectors. The largest flows, as in years past, went to South Africa, although there was a decline in 1998, owing to a variety of factors, including dwindling investment from Asian countries which had become an increasingly important source of investment.

FDI in the economies in transition as a group also remained stable in 1998, although flows to the Russian Federation dropped by half owing to the financial turmoil and economic problem in the country. The main impetus to foreign investment in some of the European economies in transition was their contin-

[9] UNCTAD, "Foreign direct investment into developing Asia has weathered the storm", TAD/INF/2803, 27 April 1999, p. 2.

ued progress in economic reform and privatization and expectations of their accession to the EU. In the Central Asian economies in transition, FDI was directed at the oil sector.

International response to the financial crisis

Balance-of-payments difficulties in a number of countries that were caught in the wake of the Asian financial crisis prompted increases in various components of official flows to developing countries. IMF took the lead role in arranging rescue packages.

During 1998, IMF approved total lending of $29.5 billion to the developing countries (down from the $38.4 billion committed in 1997), with almost the entire amount ($28.2 billion) going to the crisis-affected Asian countries and to those countries deemed vulnerable to contagion.[10] During the same period, total IMF lending to the transition economies reached $3.4 billion, up from $2.1 billion in 1997. Ukraine received the lion's share of the total (a $2.2 billion loan), as the Russian programme agreed in July became moot after August.

Because lending commitments are disbursed over time, the flow of financial resources from IMF to the developing economies increased from $12 billion in 1997 to $14 billion in 1998, with the gain coming mainly from the rise in net Fund lending through the extended (non-concessional) facility (see table A.19). In the concessional loans category, during the same period the Fund shifted from being a small net receiver of repayments to a small net provider of credit. IMF net lending to the transition economies was the highest in the decade, owing both to an increase in disbursements from regular facilities (in particular under extended programmes) and to flows from the Compensatory and Contingency Financing Facility in response to the drop in commodity prices (see table A.20).

IMF financing initiatives in 1998 and early 1999

When IMF arranged to provide $11.2 billion in financial assistance to the Russian Federation in July 1998 in support of its economic and financial reforms, it had to supplement its regular resources with a drawing from the General Arrangements to Borrow (GAB).[11] The rescue packages arranged for Asia in 1997 and 1998 and the delay in approval of the IMF quota increase by member countries had left the Fund strained for lendable resources. Its liquidity ratio (the share of available resources to liquid liabilities) had plunged to 44 per cent by mid-1998 from over 120 per cent in early 1997. After the financial commitment to the Russian Federation, the Fund had less than $25 billion available (from both GAB and its own resources) to cope with future crises.

By early 1999, the Fund's resource situation had improved considerably. First, the New Arrangements to Borrow (NAB) became effective in November 1998 with the adherence of Germany and the United States.[12] NAB was activated for the first time in December to help finance Brazil's drawing under a standby facility in support of the Government's economic adjustment programme.

In October, the United States legislature ended a year of debate over IMF funding and approved the United States share of the IMF quota increase (more than $18 billion). The action pushed membership votes for the quota increase over the 85 per cent required to approve it. As a result, quota resources

[10] For example, large standby facilities were approved for Brazil ($17.7 billion committed), Indonesia ($6.3 billion), Argentina ($2.8 billion) and the Philippines ($1.4 billion).

[11] The General Arrangements to Borrow (GAB), established in 1962 to deal with external payments deficits in the major developed economies, is a credit line extended by member countries of the Group of Ten (G-10). It has been activated nine times, previously in 1978, for use by the United States.

[12] The New Arrangements to Borrow (NAB) is a set of credit arrangements between IMF and 25 members and institutions to provide additional resources to IMF to forestall or cope with an impairment of the international monetary system or to deal with an exceptional situation that poses a threat to the stability of that system. The NAB does not replace the existing GAB, which remains operational. With combined total resource of $48 billion, it doubles the amount available under the GAB alone.

increased from $204 billion to $297 billion, and the Fund's "usable resources" were estimated to rise by about $63 billion.

In addition to adding to the Fund's lending capacity, IMF adopted a new policy to make credit available on short notice to qualifying countries. This is intended to help avert a financial crisis in member countries that follow sound policies. The initiative, adopted in April 1999, established a new mechanism, the Contingent Credit Lines (CCL), to quickly provide to member countries IMF financing to overcome balance-of-payments crises that might result from international financial contagion.[13] The CCL, established for a two-year trial period and to be reviewed after a year in operation, will be another tool, in addition to the Supplemental Reserve Facility (SRF), established in 1997. While the SRF is for use by members already in the grip of a financial crisis, the role of the CCL is preventive, being intended for countries that have been pursuing strong policies but are concerned about vulnerability to contagion from crises abroad. The Fund's approval of financing will signify its confidence in the member's economic policies and its determination to assist them should contagion occur (although disbursement of funds to countries having active Contingent Credit Lines would still require an Executive Board decision).

Increasing the private financial role in crises

The amount of official financial resources that need to be deployed in a crisis depends in part on the behaviour of private sector financial agents. One objective of policy makers in the recent crisis has been to encourage private creditors to roll over or reschedule their obligations as part of the response to a crisis. The banking community has not wished to embrace such policy as a general principle. For its part, the international community has been reluctant to have foreign banks presume that they would be bailed out of a crisis.

In October 1998, the Interim Committee (IMF) called for greater "involvement of the private sector" in preventing and resolving financial crises. IMF endorsed and considered extending under carefully designed conditions and on a case-by-case basis the policy of "lending into arrears" that had been promulgated in 1989, whereby member countries in arrears to their private creditors could receive IMF loans provided they continued to implement economic policy reforms and to work towards normalizing their external obligations. The Fund also stated that much experience had been gained in involving the private sector in several country cases and in better identifying the sources of risk in country exposure, as well as the main preventive measures to be followed up. IMF surveillance is also being strengthened in these areas, both globally and in respect of the activities of the domestic economy.

Official financial flows for development

In 1998, total official development assistance (ODA) from member countries of the Development Assistance Committee (DAC) of the Organisation for Economic Cooperation and Development (OECD) to the developing countries and multilateral development agencies rose by $3.2 billion to $51.5 billion, according to preliminary estimates.[14] The rise in ODA—almost 9 per cent measured in constant prices and exchange rates—breaks a five-year decline. The increase was mainly in contributions to multilateral agencies and in response to

[13] Contigent Credit Lines (CCL) commitments, to be made for up to one year, will not be subject to general access limits, but would be expected to be in the range of 300 to 500 per cent of the member's IMF quota, unless otherwise warranted by exceptional circumstances and with due regard to IMF's liquidity position. Members drawing under the CCL are expected to repay within one to one and a half years of the date of each disbursement (extendable by the Board by up to one additional year).

[14] See "Financial flows to developing countries in 1998", OECD press release, Paris, 10 June 1999 (for background on official development assistance (ODA) flows by source, destination and type through 1997, see tables A.21 and A.22).

the Asian crisis; however, it also reflected commitments by several DAC members to boost aid. The increase in ODA flows included additional assistance from Japan (mainly to the crisis-affected Asian countries) and from the United States (through increased contributions to multilateral development banks and food aid, notably to Africa).

Total commitments of concessional and non-concessional resources by the multilateral development institutions (MDIs) rose nearly 30 per cent in 1998 measured in constant prices. They continued their response to the financial crisis through the arrangement of significant additional lending programmes (see table A.23). For instance, commitments by the International Bank for Reconstruction and Development (IBRD), the non-concessional lending arm of the World Bank, jumped by 64 per cent, mainly owing to the sharp increases in loans to the financial sector in Asia and loans to the social sector in Latin America.[15] At the same time, International Development Association (IDA) credits, the World Bank's concessional loans, surged by 37 per cent, overcoming the decline in 1997, as commitments to Africa rose by about 75 per cent and those to South Asia almost doubled. After falling by 25 per cent in 1997, International Finance Corporation (IFC) commitments stabilized during the year.

At the Inter-American Development Bank (IADB), lending commitments rose 67 per cent in 1998, a response not only to the economic problems brought about by the financial crisis but also to the natural catastrophe that had befallen the region. IADB's concessional commitments jumped 71 per cent. In addition, IADB authorized a new one-year emergency lending programme of up to $9 billion to sustain economic reforms and to provide support to the most vulnerable segments of society suffering from the effects of the financial crisis.[16]

The Asian Development Bank approved in March 1999, as part of its Special Fund Operations, the establishment of a $3 billion Asian Currency Crisis Support Facility (ACCSF). Funding for the ACCSF will come through contributions to the Bank from the Government of Japan. The ACCSF seeks to augment regular Bank lending to the crisis-affected countries and to help mobilize co-financing and private finance for projects and programmes approved during the period 1999-2002.[17]

Concessional commitments at the African Development Bank fell 25 per cent in 1998 after a major expansion in 1997. A return to the higher magnitude is expected, following the completion of negotiations for the replenishment of the Bank's concessional lending facility, the African Development Fund (ADF), in January 1999. A total of $3.38 billion was agreed for the period 1999-2001. ADF resources are expected to receive an additional boost from the agreement in December 1998 between the Government of Switzerland and the Bank whereby Switzerland would contribute to the Supplementary Financing Mechanism. This facility was set up in 1997 to provide ADF loans to help low-income member countries meet interest payments on outstanding non-concessional loans.

At the European Bank for Reconstruction and Development (EBRD), funding issues were resolved during 1998 and led to a healthy increase in loan commitments. However, the Russian Federation's default on its financial obligations in August caused the Bank to increase its loan loss provisions and resulted in a loss in operations for 1998.

[15] The World Bank also announced a new scheme to assist developing and transition economies to raise money on private capital markets by offering to guarantee part of loans raised from those markets, provided such countries were implementing World Bank-approved structural adjustment policies and reforms.

[16] This facility allows the Inter-American Development Bank (IADB) to exceed the traditional limits for sector loans and to provide finance to the higher-income economies in the region. The loans, to be funded from the Bank's ordinary capital, will be disbursed in shorter time-frames (less than 18 months) than ordinary loans. In 1998, the Bank approved two financial emergency loans: a $2.5 billion sector adjustment and banking safeguards loan to Argentina, and a $350 million loan to the power sector in Colombia.

[17] The Asian Currency Crisis Support Facility (ACCSF) will provide grants to help in the payment of interest charges on Bank-assisted projects and programmes, technical assistance, and guarantees to support generating financial resources in conjunction with bank loans.

A \$1 billion funding package, which will double the capital base of the Multilateral Investment Guarantee Agency (MIGA), an arm of the World Bank that insures foreign direct investors against political and related risks in developing and transition economies, has been endorsed by the agency's Board of Governors and sent to the Council of Governors for approval.

Official debt relief for heavily indebted poor countries

Aside from the recent debt restructuring for countries caught in the Asian financial crisis, debt problems requiring extraordinary measures have been increasingly the preserve of low-income countries (see table A.27). The initiative for the heavily indebted poor countries (HIPCs) has been the focus of the international effort to address the debt problems of these countries. Since its inception in September 1996, a commitment to provide future debt relief has been given to seven countries (Bolivia, Burkina Faso, Guyana, Côte d'Ivoire, Mali, Mozambique and Uganda); by May 1999, debt relief had been given to only three countries (Bolivia, Guyana and Uganda),[18] with Mozambique scheduled to receive that relief in July 1999.

There has been growing support among debtors, creditors and civil society for speeding up the process, broadening the number of countries that would benefit from relief and deepening the amount of relief. The need to address the special conditions of post-conflict HIPCs has also been emphasized in international discussions.

In response to the wide-ranging proposals for change in the initiative, IMF and the World Bank undertook a review of the options as well as an analysis of the costs entailed.[19] A general approach to modifying the initiative was suggested, including: (a) lowering key target ratios to give deeper debt relief; (b) earlier provision of relief; (c) a tighter link between debt relief and poverty reduction and social policy in the debtor countries; (d) increased bilateral debt relief and official bilateral assistance; and (e) commitment by member countries to seeking prompt solutions to fund the relief.

The IMF Interim Committee at its April 1999 meeting endorsed the review and agreed to work on furthering debt reduction under the HIPC initiative. It asked the Executive Board of IMF together with the Executive Board of the World Bank to develop specific proposals to enhance the HIPC framework which it will consider at its next meeting. It also stressed the need to intensify efforts to secure full funding of these changes and urged the Executive Boards to adopt the necessary decisions to this end.

At their Economic Summit Cologne 99, the Group of Seven (G-7) countries launched the Cologne Debt Initiative[20] which endorsed enhancement of the HIPC framework that was generally in line with the review. The Cologne Initiative did not put forward detailed funding arrangements but called for concrete proposals by the time of the Annual Meetings of IMF and World Bank in autumn 1999.

The new Initiative proposed to speed up the process by shortening the six-year track record requirement for countries that meet policy conditions ahead of schedule. To lighten debt-servicing burdens, it also called for interim debt relief to be extended before the completion point and for a front-loading of debt reduction. To achieve deeper relief and broaden the number of countries

[18]   For a consideration of the heavily indebted poor countries (HIPC) process, see report of the Secretary-General entitled "Debt situation of the developing countries as of mid-1998" (A/53/373), paras. 27-37; and World Bank, *Global Development Finance, 1999* (Washington, D.C., April 1999), pp. 76-78.

[19]   See "Heavily-Indebted Poor Countries (HIPC) Initiative Progress Report by the Managing Director of IMF and the President of the World Bank", 22 April 1999.

[20]   See the report of G-7 Finance Ministers on the Cologne Debt Initiative to the Cologne Economic Summit, Cologne, Germany, 18-20 June 1999 (www.library.utoronto.ca/g7/finance/fm061899.htm).

that would qualify for relief, it proposed that the target ratios for debt sustainability and debtor countries' fiscal positions be reduced. It is estimated that these changes would increase the number of countries under the HIPC initiative to 36 from 29.

To achieve coordinated debt relief of HIPCs, the Cologne Debt Initiative appealed for deeper forgiveness of commercial debt of qualified HIPCs by bilateral official creditors. It also called on all creditor countries to forgive bilateral ODA debt of qualifying HIPCs and to provide new ODA in the form of grants.

To help meet the additional cost of their proposals, the G-7 countries supported "a limited and cautiously-phased" sale of up to 10 million ounces of IMF's gold reserves. The proceeds would be invested and the earnings on the investment would be used for debt relief. With regard to bilateral contributions to the HIPC Trust Fund, the parties to the Cologne Initiative pledged to "consider in good faith" further contributions and called for appropriate burden-sharing among donors. However, the Cologne Initiative did not contain any specific proposals for amounts and allocation of contributions.

The original HIPC proposal had been a crucial advance in the international treatment of debt, in particular on two counts: it set a goal of exit from perpetual debt renegotiation for poor countries, as they were to be brought to a sustainable debt situation at the end of the process; and it acknowledged that all creditors, including multilateral institutions, had to share in the relief to be accorded. The implementation of these core ideas disappointed expectations and resulted in the new Cologne Initiative. With this history, some proponents of relief remain skeptical of the new Initiative and some have called for a bolder approach.[21] The advances that were recently agreed were the result of intense public scrutiny of the HIPC process. That scrutiny will continue to be needed to ensure that the debt crises of low-income countries are finally and expeditiously resolved.

[21] For a review of some of these and a set of United Nations Secretariat recommendations, see report of the Executive Committee on Economic and Social Affairs entitled "Finding solutions to the debt problems of developing countries", 20 May 1999 (www.un.org/esa/coordination/ecesa/eces99-2.htm).

III   THE CURRENT SITUATION IN THE WORLD'S ECONOMIES

The economic performance of individual countries in 1998 reflected the deterioration of the international economic environment during the year. Forecasts of global economic growth were repeatedly revised downwards in 1998 as the reverberations from the Asian and, later during the year, the Russian crises became a generalized slowdown affecting most developing and transition economies.

Among the developed economies, Japan descended into a severe recession. Nonetheless, the majority of developed countries maintained, or even improved, the rate of growth they had achieved in 1997, the most notable case being the United States of America which was able to extend an unusually lengthy and strong expansion. However, there was a slowdown in many of these countries in the second half of 1998 and this is expected to continue into the first part of 1999. On the other hand, Japan is expected to begin to emerge from its recession.

The economies in transition did poorly in 1998, with their combined gross domestic product (GDP) barely growing during the year. This group of countries was the worst hit by the Russian crisis and the difficulties in the Russian Federation will continue to have a negative impact in 1999. However, the outcome within this group of countries is far from homogeneous. The economies of Central and Eastern Europe and the Baltic region will continue to grow—albeit not as rapidly as in the recent years—while output in the Commonwealth of Independent States (CIS) will show a sizeable decline in 1999, repeating its performance of 1998.

Developing countries also experienced a deceleration in their growth rates in 1998. During the period 1992-1997, this group of countries grew, on average, by 5.3 per cent. In 1998, their rate of growth plunged to below 2 per cent. Latin America and Western Asia suffered a marked slowdown and East Asia, excluding China, recorded negative growth. However, China and India, the most populous developing economies, were able maintain sound rates of growth. As of mid-1999, the economies of the East Asian countries hit by the financial crisis were slowly recovering while Latin America faced renewed difficulties. For the developing countries as a whole, GDP growth will be barely above 2.5 per cent in 1999.

DEVELOPED ECONOMIES

In recent years, the economic performance of the developed economies can be more readily attributable to some of the structural differences among them than to their being at different phases in a business cycle. Increased global integration, accompanied by rapid technological innovation, has resulted in benefits and losses, not only for developing and transition economies but also for developed economies. Differences in economic structures and in policy responsiveness among these economies have resulted, and will continue to result, in varied performance.

In the last quarter of 1998, the rate of growth in the United States was 6 per cent, while Japan's decline intensified and German and Italian output fell (see table III.1). The action that the United States Federal Reserve Board took in September and October 1998 to restore confidence in domestic and international financial markets was successful. Confidence in the United States economy has been reflected in its rising stock market (see figure III.1) and buoyant domestic demand. In contrast, in Japan, the stock market remained depressed and consumer and business confidence continued to be low and, at least until the first quarter of 1999, frustrated government efforts to stimulate the economy. Monetary policy was loosened to the point where real interest rates were negative. Growth in the euro area was 2.8 per cent in 1998 but there was diversity within the group, which may lead to policy tensions if it persists.[1] Germany and Italy, which together make up half of the euro area economy, had the slowest rates of growth in 1998 among this group of countries (see table A.2) and contracted in the last quarter of 1998. The other members of the euro area grew at rates of about 3 per cent or over in 1998, and Ireland at over 9 per cent. Outside of the euro area, the economy of the United Kingdom of Great Britain and Northern Ireland was moving towards a soft landing.

Contrasts have been drawn between the different ways in which the developed economies organize economic activity and explanations for the differential performance have been sought in various institutional and cultural aspects. For instance, differences in the financial sector can explain some of the recent divergence in economic performance. In the case of Japan, in particular, difficulties in the financial sector were translated into problems in the real sector. Conversely, the United States—the country that had developed the venture capital industry, a part of the financial sector geared to fostering high-risk and high-technology industry—has seen the strongest economic performance in recent years: the United States high technology sector added 1 million high-paying jobs over the previous five years.[2]

There are marked differences also in labour and product markets which can help explain the varied responsiveness of countries to globalization.

It is only through the restructuring of their economies that the developed countries can achieve sustained growth in the twenty-first century. In May 1999, the Organisation for Economic Cooperation and Development (OECD) Council of Ministers, after noting that "growth performance varied considerably across and within OECD countries", asked the Organization "to study the causes of growth disparities, and identify factors and policies (such as rapid technological innovations and the growing impact of the knowledge society and its demands on human capital, the arrival of new service industries, the best framework conditions for fostering the start-up and growth of new enterprises including SME ...) which could strengthen long-term growth performance".[3] The attention to the micro-foundations of growth can be expected to intensify in the coming years.

[1] The euro area is made up of the following European Union countries (EU): Austria, Belgium, Finland, France, Germany, Ireland, Italy, Luxembourg, the Netherlands, Portugal and Spain.

[2] *Financial Times*, 3 June 1999.

[3] Communiqué of the OECD Council Meeting at Ministerial Level, Paris, 26 and 27 May 1999.

Table III.1.
MAJOR INDUSTRIALIZED COUNTRIES: QUARTERLY INDICATORS, 1997-1999

| | 1997 quarters | | | | 1998 quarters | | | | 1999 |
	I	II	III	IV	I	II	III	IV	I
	Growth of gross domestic product[a] (percentage change in seasonally adjusted data from preceding quarter)								
Canada	5.2	5.2	4.4	2.8	3.1	1.4	1.7	4.6	4.1
France	0.8	4.5	3.6	3.2	3.2	3.6	1.6	2.9	1.2
Germany	1.8	4.1	3.2	1.1	5.3	0.0	3.6	-1.8	1.6
Italy	0.1	8.0	2.2	1.0	-0.6	2.3	2.0	-1.1	0.8
Japan	6.6	-9.6	4.1	-3.7	-4.8	-2.9	-1.2	-3.2	7.9
United Kingdom	4.5	4.1	3.6	3.8	1.9	1.2	1.9	0.4	0.4
United States	4.2	4.0	4.2	3.0	5.5	1.8	3.7	6.0	4.3
Total	4.1	0.8	3.9	1.0	2.2	0.6	2.1	1.9	4.2
	Unemployment rate[b] (percentage of total labour force)								
Canada	9.6	9.4	9.0	8.9	8.6	8.4	8.3	8.0	7.8
France	12.5	12.5	12.4	12.3	12.1	11.9	11.8	11.5	11.5
Germany	9.4	9.9	10.1	10.3	9.8	11.0	10.8	10.7	10.5
Italy	12.2	12.1	12.1	12.1	12.1	12.5	11.9	12.6	12.4
Japan	3.3	3.5	3.4	3.5	3.6	4.1	4.2	4.4	4.6
United Kingdom	7.5	7.3	6.8	6.6	6.5	6.2	6.2	6.3	6.3
United States	5.2	4.9	4.9	4.7	4.6	4.4	4.5	4.4	4.3
Total	6.7	6.7	6.6	6.5	6.4	6.6	6.5	6.5	6.5
	Growth of consumer prices[c] (percentage change from preceding quarter)								
Canada	2.1	1.1	1.0	-0.3	2.1	1.4	0.4	0.7	0.0
France	2.1	0.7	0.7	1.1	0.0	2.4	-1.0	0.0	-0.2
Germany	3.8	1.4	3.1	-0.7	0.7	2.0	1.0	-1.3	-1.1
Italy	2.7	2.1	0.6	2.7	2.7	1.7	1.5	0.5	-1.2
Japan	-1.1	8.9	0.0	1.1	-1.8	2.2	-2.2	4.7	-3.5
United Kingdom	2.3	5.3	3.9	3.2	1.3	7.8	1.2	1.9	-3.1
United States	2.7	1.6	1.6	1.6	1.0	2.3	1.6	1.3	0.6
Total	1.8	3.5	1.4	1.3	0.4	2.5	0.4	1.8	-1.0

Source: UN/DESA, based on data of International Monetary Fund (IMF), Organisation for Economic Cooperation and Development (OECD) and national authorities.

[a]   Expressed at annual rate (total is weighted average with weights being annual GDP valued at 1993 prices and exchange rates).
[b]   Seasonally adjusted data as standardized by OECD.
[c]   Expressed at annual rate.

Figure III.1.
TRENDS IN SOME STOCK MARKETS 1985-1999[a]

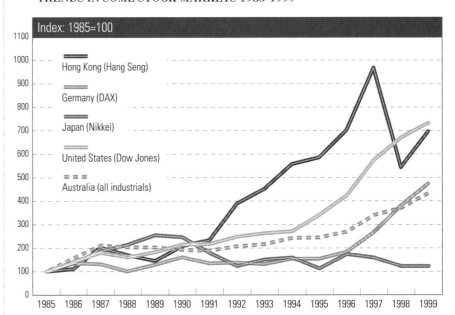

Source: UN/DESA, based on Reserve Bank of Australia Bulletin.

[a]   Figures show end of June except for 1999 which show end of March.

The recent performance of the three major blocs of developed countries, Europe, Japan and North America, will be discussed below, with particular emphasis being placed on their restructuring efforts. Australia is also taken as an example because it thrived in 1998 in spite of its very close trading ties with the Asian crisis countries. Its recent success provides further insights into the importance of policy in determining a country's growth in the globalized economy.

North America: continued strong growth performance

In contrast with slow growth and even decline in many other countries, the United States and Canada continued to enjoy strong growth in 1998.

By early 1999, the United States had sustained its expansion for more than eight years, its longest period of continuous peacetime growth. The current economic expansion has some important distinguishing features. First, it has been accompanied by an improvement in both inflation and unemployment, while the expansions in the 1960s and the 1980s resulted either in a rise in inflation when the economy moved towards high employment or in high levels of both inflation and unemployment. Second, unlike the expansion of the 1980s, which was marked by a large increase in the Federal budget deficit, the current expansion has resulted in the fiscal position's going into surplus for the first time in 30 years. Fiscal policy in the current expansion has been restrictive, whereas monetary policy has been accommodative; in the expansion of the 1980s, however, large deficits resulted from an expansionary fiscal policy accompanied by a tight monetary policy.

Many factors, which may themselves be interrelated, have nurtured this virtuous expansion: sound macroeconomic policy; major technological innovations, especially in the area of information technology where the United State has achieved a leading edge; and increasing global integration, in which the benefits for the United States have far outweighed the costs.

The international financial crises of 1997 and 1998 and the subsequent slow-down in most of the rest of the world had some adverse effects for the United States: a decline in exports, a drop in corporate profits, increased volatility in stock markets, and a sudden deterioration in credit conditions for a few months in the third quarter of 1998. However, the crises also generated benefits for the United States. As its financial markets are much deeper and more liquid than those of other countries, during the crises a large amount of capital from emerging markets moved to the United States in a so-called "flight to quality". Abundant capital further fuelled already strong domestic demand, including through "wealth effects" resulting from the boom in equity prices. Meanwhile, the decline in international commodity prices, particularly of oil, improved the terms of trade for the United States and brought welfare benefits to its con-sumers and producers.

Contributing to the strong growth of GDP were both robust private con-sumption and vigorous business investment, reflecting high levels of consumer and business confidence. Consumer spending rose by about 5 per cent in 1998, supported by a strong labour market and the spectacular surge in the stock mar-ket, exceeding that of other developed countries (see figure II.1). Spending increases were well above the increases in disposable personal income. As a result, the measured saving rate dropped to near zero. Given the already tight labour market and the high valuation of the stock market, the current growth of consumption cannot be sustained indefinitely, and the key policy challenge is to achieve a soft landing.

Business equipment investment has grown at a double-digit annual rate for five years, boosted by the low cost of capital and technological progress, espe-cially in computer-related areas. In contrast, investment in business structures has been flat. The rapid pace of innovation in information technology does not seem to have ended, so the high growth of business investment is expected to continue. However, aggregate figures showing a decline in capacity utilization in 1999 and increasing pressure on corporate profit margins suggest a possible slowdown in investment in some sectors. Meanwhile, residential investment has boomed in recent years, buoyed by low mortgage interest rates, capital gains and increasing real incomes.

Spurred by vigorous economic growth, the labour market has also performed at record levels. In early 1999, the unemployment rate was at a 30-year low, below 4.5 per cent, and real wages, which stagnated in the early years of the expansion, have risen since 1997. Some indicators are now suggesting over-tightness in the labour market: the job searching cycle has shortened consider-ably; business, especially small business, has encountered problems in finding workers; and labour bargaining power is increasing.

In spite of this tightening in the labour market, inflation fell in 1998, with the consumer price index (CPI) increasing by only 1.6 per cent (see table A.8). The drop in import prices, a flexible economic structure, and sound macroeco-nomic policy have all contributed to achieving low inflation.[4] By May 1999, however, there were some ambiguous signs of future inflationary pressures.

[4] The latest methodological changes in compiling the price indices also lowered the measured rate of inflation.

The large and increasing external deficit, which reached $240 billion in 1998, has raised some concern. Many factors have contributed to the increase: declining exports, resulting from weakening demand from the rest of the world, especially Asia; the appreciation of the dollar against other currencies; and strong domestic demand for imports.

Reflecting the strength of the United States economy, Canada is also growing at a fast pace, with exports and business investment in equipment being particularly strong; however, consumption has been weak, partly because the 1998 financial turmoil caused a depreciation of the Canadian dollar and prompted a rise in interest rates to defend the Canadian currency. However, consumer confidence rebounded in early 1999 and spending on durables is recovering, aided by an easing in monetary conditions.

The labour market has improved with the unemployment rate having reached an eight-year low of 7.8 per cent at the beginning of 1999. Meanwhile, inflation has been kept below 1 per cent, as the persistent underutilization of capacity has suppressed domestic prices and international commodity prices have continued to be weak.

Monetary and fiscal policy during the North American expansion

During the long expansion of the United States economy, *monetary policy* has been used actively, and on occasion forcefully. The Federal Reserve has frequently altered interest rates in an attempt to meet the dual goals of price stability and full employment. The many adjustments in monetary policy also reflect, to a certain extent, the increasing difficulties in judging the state of the economy. In particular, advances in technology may have lifted potential non-inflationary growth well above the previously estimated rate of 2.5 per cent. If so, the current high growth rate may not pose as large an inflationary threat as it would have previously. Meanwhile, the sharp contrast between a weakening world economy and the booming economy of the United States has also created a policy dilemma for the Federal Reserve. Although the Federal Reserve's primary concern is the well-being of the domestic economy, in a period of weak global growth policy makers need to take into account the fact that growth in the United States economy has an impact on, and in turn is affected by, the global situation. In addition to this overall impact, the monetary policy of the United States directly affects liquidity in the world economy.

In the second and third quarters of 1998, the Federal Reserve shifted the main focus of its attention from fighting potential inflation to preventing a possible weakening of economic activity. The rapid deterioration in world financial markets produced a sudden shift of investor preferences in the financial markets of the United States. Stock prices dropped steeply, yield spreads between corporate bonds and Treasury bonds widened sharply, and signs of illiquidity in debt markets appeared. Meanwhile, the turmoil took a toll on financial institutions, symbolized by the near collapse of a large hedge fund. Concerned about the "unusual strains" in financial markets and a possible credit crunch, the Federal Reserve cut interest rates three times in the last quarter of 1998, resulting in a cumulative reduction of 75 basis points in the Federal funds rate. At the end of May 1999, the rate stood at 4.75 per cent, the lowest in four years.

With financial conditions improving, the Federal Reserve indicated in May 1999 that its concern had become the possible inflationary implications of continued tight labour markets. It therefore began considering whether it remained appropriate to maintain the policy stance adopted in the last quarter of 1998. As a response to the concern over inflation, the market had by May 1999 pushed up the yield on the benchmark 30-year Treasury bonds to nearly 6 per cent from 5 per cent at the beginning 1999.

Fiscal consolidation, that is to say, reducing the Federal government deficit, has been the centrepiece of fiscal policy in the United States for the past decade and has taken the form mainly of spending restraints in a period when revenues have risen with the level of economic activity, rather than as a result of higher tax rates. As a result, the budget balance turned from a deficit of about 5 per cent of GDP in 1990 into a surplus of over 1 per cent of GDP in 1998.

The Administration of the United States has proposed a plan to use the surplus to strengthen and protect Social Security. Other proposals have included tax cuts and the reduction of existing debts. A large part of the increase in government revenue in the last few years has been generated by unexpected tax revenues from capital gains, which may not continue if stock markets fail to repeat the substantial advances of the last few years. In the short run, fiscal policy is expected to remain moderately restrictive, with expenditure continuing to grow more slowly than GDP and no major tax cut being enacted. The budget surplus is expected to continue for the next few years and the automatic stabilizers in the budget will continue to be an important policy instrument for moderating fluctuations in the economy.

During the international financial crisis of 1998, the value of the Canadian dollar dropped against the United States dollar, reaching a historic low in August 1998. The Bank of Canada decided to stem the fall in the currency by raising short-term interest rates in stages by 100 basis points in the third quarter of 1998. Since late 1998, the Canadian dollar has moved slightly upward, and the Bank of Canada has followed the Federal Reserve in reducing interest rates. With the cut of 25 basis points at the end of March 1999, interest rates were back to their level before August 1998.

Canada has also undertaken fiscal consolidation over the past decade to reduce its large public debt, which now stands at some 60 per cent of GDP. The restoration of stability to government finances was completed in 1997 when a budget surplus was achieved. Fiscal policy afterwards remained conservative. However, Canada's budget plan for 1999 could mark a turning point. It includes a broad relaxation of the fiscal stance, with an increase in the personal tax exemption, the elimination of the 3 per cent surtax for high-income earners, and an increase in spending for health care. Nevertheless, there are some concerns that, by aiming for budget balance, fiscal policy could become pro-cyclical, reducing the effectiveness of the automatic stabilizers. This would shift more of the burden of adjustment to monetary policy, increasing the volatility of interest rates and the exchange rate.

Japan: structural reforms under way?

In marked contrast to Canada and the United States, Japan's economy shrank between the last quarter of 1997 and the end of 1998. This was Japan's longest post-war recession. The economy finally resumed growth in the first quarter of

1999. The boost was provided by a fiscal stimulus package which increased government fixed investment spending by over 10 per cent from the previous quarter and, more unexpectedly in view of low consumer confidence, by private consumption.[5] Corporate investment also rose, partly because of the Government's provision of loan guarantees to small and medium-sized companies which had previously found it hard to obtain credit from the banks.

During the recession, interest rates were driven down to near zero, yet banks still did not extend credit. Some fiscal stimuli even had the contrary effect of depressing confidence because the budgetary costs were felt to be excessive: general government gross financial liabilities rose from 58 per cent of GDP in 1991 to 100 per cent in 1998.[6]

Fiscal consolidation measures in April 1997 brought about a contraction of activity in the second quarter of that year (see table III.1). After the economy had shrunk again in the last quarter of 1997 and the first quarter of 1998, the Government adopted, in April 1998, a Yen (¥) 16 trillion ($133 billion) stimulus package, including government spending on public works and tax cuts. This failed to halt the deterioration in confidence. In November 1998, the Government drafted another stimulus package of ¥17 trillion ($141 billion).

The budget for the fiscal year beginning 1 April 1999 envisaged a spending increase of more than 5 per cent. It included an increase in public works and social security spending as well as tax cuts. Given the sluggish economy and tax cuts, however, the fiscal deficit is expected to widen to nearly 8 per cent of GDP in 1999—the highest among all the developed economies.[7]

To deal with the deficit, a government bond issue of ¥61 trillion ($508 billion) was planned for the fiscal year 1999. Such was the lack of confidence in this proposed issue that domestic long-term bond yields rose from 0.25 per cent in autumn 1998 to 2.44 per cent in early February 1999. To reduce interest rates, the Bank of Japan lowered its overnight call rate from 0.25 per cent to 0.15 per cent in February 1999. In addition, the Ministry of Finance cut its planned March issuance of 10-year government bonds by ¥400 billion ($3 billion) and shifted the issuance to 2-year and 6-year bonds. As a result, the benchmark 10-year government bond yield fell below 2 per cent.

Declining imports and an influx of foreign capital, particularly into the stock market, brought a halt to the decline in the yen/United States dollar exchange rate and the yen appreciated to below 120 in late 1998 and early 1999. The earlier depreciation of the yen, together with sluggish Japanese domestic demand, lowered Japanese imports, impeding the recovery in neighbouring countries and increasing Japan's current-account surplus. In 1999, Japan is still expected to have a substantial current-account surplus.

Japan's banking crisis has been a major contributor to weak growth: saddled with non-performing loans, banks have been cautious in lending. In October 1998, the Government passed a financial revitalization law that would permit ¥60 trillion ($500 billion) to be spent over a period of years to protect depositors, recapitalize banks and deal with the failure of financial institutions. The law envisaged the establishment of a bridge bank to allow failed financial institutions to come under public control, and the Resolution and Collection Organization (RCO) and the Financial Revitalization Commission (FRC) to deal with non-performing loans and to supervise financial institutions, respectively. Yet, even if banks' capital bases were strengthened, the credit crunch

[5] It is difficult to reconcile the increase in consumption expenditure with other data. The Government's real household spending data for the same period registered a 1.5 per cent decline. Declines in spending were shown for the industrial sector: for instance, machinery orders were down 13.8 per cent in April 1999. Unemployment also reached unprecedented levels for the postwar period.

[6] Figures from OECD, *Economic Outlook*, December 1998, p. 224.

[7] Forecast from OECD, *Economic Outlook*, December 1998, p. 220.

would not be completely eliminated as long as banks perceived the risks of lending to be too great.

Bank lending has often been unprofitable because much of Japanese industry has not undertaken the restructuring that would render it competitive. In addition, labour markets lack flexibility. Restructuring will lead to an increase in the number of those losing their jobs and so a resumption of growth will make this process easier. Otherwise short-run increases in unemployment could serve to depress confidence even further and thus could temporarily exacerbate the vicious circle in which the Japanese economy appears to be trapped. However, the Japanese authorities' room for manoeuvre to provide a further stimulus is narrow: given that there is no further room for lowering interest rates, the Bank of Japan may have to shift towards monetizing the fiscal deficit so as to provide a stimulus. This policy, though, would exceed the Bank's terms of reference.[8]

In spite of these adverse considerations, there are some signs that the revival of economic activity in the first quarter could mark a turning point. Even though the unemployment situation is particularly serious in the manufacturing and construction sectors, the service sector exhibited a slight increase in employment late in 1998 and absorbed some of the workers laid off from other sectors in the course of their restructuring.

Government is taking steps to assist restructuring throughout the economy. It is tackling the difficulties of the banking sector. At the end of March 1999, bank restructuring efforts gained new momentum when, under the terms of the October 1998 law (see above), the Government injected ¥7.5 trillion ($62 billion) into the 15 major banks to enable them to dispose of their bad loans. The FRC is to monitor the implementation of the restructuring programmes submitted by these banks.

This caused the major banks to speed up their restructuring efforts. There has been some progress in solving their bad-loan problems and in raising confidence in the banks, as reflected in the rise of their share prices and the fall in risk premiums. Banks have more actively sought alliances with other financial institutions, both foreign and domestic. They also have been trying to cut costs: they plan to reduce their staffs by about 14 per cent, mostly through recruitment reduction and natural attrition, and they have also been scaling down their overseas operations.

Despite the progress in restructuring the financial system, problems remain, as reflected in the failure of two regional banks in April 1999.[9] Other regional banks and other banks may have problems as well. There are also uncertainties about the size of off-the-book liabilities and the amount of loans classified as bad. However, restoring health to the banking system will depend crucially on the performance of the economy and the banks' capacity to implement their restructuring plans.

In June 1999, the Japanese Government introduced measures to promote the restructuring of other sectors of the economy. In light of unemployment's reaching a record high of 4.8 per cent in April, it decided to seek parliamentary approval of a supplementary budget of ¥500 billion ($4 billion) for fiscal year 1999, including measures to boost job growth and industrial competitiveness. It hoped to create more than 700,000 jobs, half of them in local and central government. Subsidies would be offered to industries to employ middle-aged

[8] A law enacted in 1947 prohibits the Bank of Japan from monetizing the government deficit. Any change would compromise the independence of the Bank. The Bank could opt for an alternative way of injecting liquidity, such as purchasing government bonds in the secondary market rather than purchasing them directly from the Government.

[9] On 11 April 1999, Kokumin Bank, Ltd., a regional bank in the Tokyo area, was declared insolvent and placed under government control. Its net worth was estimated to be minus $593.3 million. Kokumin bank will become the first so-called "bridge bank" and will sell its bad loans to the State-run Resolution and Collection Organization. On 12 April, Kofuku Bank, Ltd., in the Osaka area was judged to be below the required 4 per cent asset level and was asked to supplement its capital under the new banking law.

workers forced out of work by corporate restructuring. In this way, it was hoped that 150,000 jobs would be created. The Government also proposed to introduce training schemes and reforms to the pension system to encourage greater mobility of the workforce.

The plan would also include legislation to encourage companies to strengthen industrial competitiveness, as well as to help small and mid-size companies and venture businesses. It would be easier for companies to carry out mergers and acquisitions, and a new bankruptcy law would help ailing companies rebuild. More flexible stock options schemes would be encouraged, a debt-for-equity swap scheme would help banks tackle their bad loan problems, and measures would be enacted to force companies to adhere more strictly to global standards of accounting.

The full reform programme that must eventually be undertaken will entail a move away from arrangements that apparently served the country well for more than 30 years, but had disguised structural faults and by the 1990s had brought the economy to a dangerous state.[10] As the attempts to reform labour markets and the industrial sector indicate, the scope of these arrangements went far beyond the banking sector. Restoring growth and competitiveness to Japan's economy will correspondingly necessitate reforms in many areas.

Western Europe's economic performance after the introduction of the euro

In Western Europe, overall economic activity in 1998 as a whole was stronger than in 1997: the region continued its recovery from the slowdown of 1995-1996 and monetary policy was relaxed in the run-up to monetary union. By 1998, domestic demand had replaced exports as the driving force in the expansion. The acceleration in growth helped reduce unemployment rates which, for the European Union (EU), fell almost to 10 per cent, the lowest rate since 1992 (see table A.7).

In late 1998 and early 1999, however, economic activity in Europe, and particularly in Germany and Italy, slowed down, owing mainly to further deterioration in the external environment after the Russian crisis. The foreign sector's contribution to growth fell and, in some countries, turned negative: the growth of fixed investment decelerated. Inventories, which had made a positive contribution to GDP growth in both 1997 and 1998, were cut to accommodate softer external demand. Weakness in exports and investment was only partly offset by strong consumption, underpinned in many countries by increases in real incomes due to improvements in employment, wage increases and lower inflation.

The deterioration in the external environment hit mainly the manufacturing sector, as a large share of Europe's industrial production is for export. In contrast, service activities, which are influenced mainly by domestic factors, have remained strong.

Consumer-price inflation in EU declined from 2.1 per cent in 1997 to 1.7 per cent in 1998 and, in the euro area, from 1.8 to 1.3 per cent (see table A.8), reflecting the drop in world commodity prices and the slowdown in economic growth at the end of the year. The ongoing restructuring and price deregulation within EU further dampened inflation.

10 T. M. Pempell, "Japan's search for a new path", *Current History* (Philadelphia), vol. 97, No. 623 (December 1998), p. 436. See also Michael E. Porter and Hirotaka Takeuchi, "Fixing what really ails Japan", *Foreign Affairs*, vol. 78, No. 3 (May/June 1999).

Of the countries that slowed down in 1998, Norway suffered from the sharp fall in oil prices in the year, while Denmark and the United Kingdom tightened macroeconomic policy to avoid overheating after their prolonged economic expansion.

Germany and Italy, which have grown more slowly than France since the cyclical upswing began in Continental Europe in 1994, experienced declines in output in the last quarter of 1998. Both were harder hit by the slowdown in some of their export markets. Their manufacturing sectors account for larger shares of GDP,[11] much of their manufacturing output is exported, and they have a higher direct trade exposure to East Asia, Latin America and the transition economies.[12] The strong performance of service activities in France, the Netherlands, Spain and several other countries helped them compensate for weakness in exports. Also, employment growth in Germany and Italy has been much lower than that of other European countries, and so consumer spending provided much less of a cushion against the fall in other components of demand. In the case of Italy, fiscal consolidation to qualify for membership in the monetary union exerted a further large drag on growth: the general government deficit-to-GDP ratio fell from 6.6 per cent in 1996 to 2.7 per cent in 1998. Tax increases accounted for a large part of this decline: they depressed disposable income and resulted in low growth of consumer spending during 1998.

After the end-year deceleration in Europe, there was a turnaround and by spring 1999, there were already tentative signs of some stabilization in industrial production. Consumption expenditure remained resilient. Growth in the Continental European economies is expected to accelerate in the second half of 1999 and into 2000. Growth will be supported by some improvement in emerging markets, subdued inflation, low interest rates, and the more competitive exchange rate of the euro, as well as by policies aimed at stimulating employment and removing impediments to the full exploitation of the opportunities afforded by the single market. When the factors that made Germany and Italy suffer the most at the end of 1998—the decline in their export markets—are reversed, these two countries should have the most to gain.

Though this was not the case in past economic cycles, the United Kingdom appears likely to achieve a "soft landing". The cuts in short-term interest rates and the lagged effects of growth in government spending on infrastructure projects and public services will help offset the impact of the strength of the currency and of sluggish foreign demand. Growth should accelerate in 2000.

Over the past few years, the focus of macroeconomic policies in EU has, to a large extent, been on the introduction of the single currency. This concentration of effort has affected many more countries than those that finally entered the euro area. Efforts to achieve the Maastricht criteria of a maximum fiscal deficit-to-GDP ratio of 3.0 per cent resulted in the fall of the general government deficit in the euro area from 4.8 per cent of GDP in 1995 to 2.1 per cent of GDP in 1998. Outside the euro area, in 1998, budget surpluses were registered in Denmark, Sweden and the United Kingdom, and Greece met the Maastricht budget deficit target.

Monetary easing accompanied fiscal tightening as part of the preparations for the establishment of the euro area. The required convergence of short-term interest rates among the prospective participants in the monetary union took the form of a gradual reduction to below the lowest levels prevailing in the coun-

[11] Industry accounts for 37 per cent of jobs in Germany and 33 per cent of jobs in Italy, but only 25 per cent of jobs in France.

[12] For instance, the share of these three areas in exports of machinery and transport equipment was 21 per cent and 22 per cent respectively for Italy and Germany, compared with 14 per cent for France.

13 During 1998, short-term interest rates declined by 319 basis points in Ireland, 250 basis points in Italy, 230 basis points in Portugal and 175 basis points in Spain.

14 This target rate of inflation does not correspond to that shown in table A.8 (which includes mortgage payments), nor to the Harmonized Index of Consumer Prices (HICP). In 1998, according to the HICP, the United Kingdom's rate of inflation was 1.5 per cent.

15 To achieve this inflation goal, the ECB is to monitor a monetary aggregate and undertake a broad assessment of the outlook for price developments and risks of inflation. The monetary aggregate chosen was M3. Based on the inflation target and assumptions for trend growth in real GDP (2 to 2.5 per cent per annum) and for the velocity of circulation, in December 1998 the reference value was set at 4.5 per cent. It will be reviewed in December 1999.

tries concerned at the beginning of 1998. The euro-area average of short-term interest rates fell by around 100 basis points to 3.0 per cent from January to December 1998. For many countries, the decline was even more pronounced.[13] This was facilitated by a favourable outlook for inflation, by stability in exchange rates among the prospective members of the euro area, and by weakening economic growth.

Outside the euro area, monetary policy was eased, too. In response to the slow growth of the economy, the strengthening of the currency and the reduction of inflation to the 2.5 per cent official target,[14] the Bank of England, in the last quarter of 1998, reversed its policy of raising interest rates and relaxed its monetary stance. Between October 1998 and June 1999, the short-term repurchase (repo) rate was cut from 7.5 to 5.0 per cent, the lowest rate since November 1977.

On 1 January 1999, the EU single currency, the euro, was successfully launched and the new European Central Bank (ECB) took over responsibility for monetary policy in the 11 countries making up the euro area. The ECB is mandated to pursue a target of price stability, which it has defined as inflation of less than 2 per cent, measured by the Harmonized Index of Consumer Prices (HICP), for the euro area as a whole.[15] The Bank has to set monetary policy according to euro-area needs and not those of individual countries. On 8 April 1999, the ECB made its first policy move by cutting the refinancing rate by 0.5 percentage points to 2.5 per cent.

This interest rate cut coincided with an increase in differentials in growth and inflation among the individual euro-area countries. For the euro area as a whole, a relaxed monetary stance may be appropriate, as average inflation is below 1 per cent largely because of the very low rates prevailing in France and Germany. However, some countries such as Ireland, Portugal, and Spain are expanding at rates that would previously have been associated with inflationary pressures, suggesting that a relaxed monetary stance may not be appropriate. On the other hand, these cases bring into question the validity of past relationships of growth to inflation. In the case of Ireland in particular, rapid productivity gains and the labour force's expanding as emigrants return to the country have made possible fast growth. The high, although falling, rate of unemployment in Spain similarly indicates that there is considerable potential for further rapid growth.

In its first four months, the euro depreciated against the dollar by more than 10 per cent. This depreciation can be seen as the natural outcome of the difference in the rates of growth of the United States and euro-area economies. Moreover, interest-rate differentials currently favour the dollar and are expected to continue to do so for some time. A number of political factors have also played a role in the currency's depreciation, including some uncertainty over the future course of European economic policy and the situation in Kosovo.

There has been some concern about the future fiscal positions of the euro-area members. According to the ECB, fiscal performance in 1998, as well as some member States' plans for 1999, and for the medium term, signals a slackening in previous efforts to consolidate public finances. The marginal improvement of budget positions in 1998 was mainly associated with stronger economic growth and lower interest rates. Thus far, those countries that adopted temporary and one-time measures to qualify for entry into monetary union have not yet achieved the permanent and stricter requirement of budget balance over the cycle embodied in the Stability and Growth Pact. The medium-term deficit correction plans in many countries rely mainly on continued economic growth and financial stability, with much less emphasis being placed on the reduction of cyclically adjusted deficits. Hence, in the event of even a normal cyclical downturn, the 3 per cent maximum value for the fiscal deficits would risk being breached.

Despite recent improvements, unemployment in most European countries is still high and its reduction has become the most important objective of the EU's economic and social policy. The consensus is that stronger growth alone will not solve the problem, as weak employment growth primarily reflects labour-market rigidities. This implies that the solution lies in structural policy measures and other microeconomic policies, rather than macroeconomic policies. Structural reforms may gain further momentum as a result of the new initiative for a European Employment Pact adopted by EU in Cologne, Germany, in June 1999.[16]

This will rest on three pillars. One is the Luxembourg process, whereby the employment policies of the Member States are coordinated and subjected to peer review within the framework of the Employment Guidelines[17] and National Action Plans for employment. In the course of 1998, Governments started to implement their National Action Plans. Some of these gave estimates of the expenditures that their implementation would involve—as much as 1.2 per cent of GDP for Spain and 1.4 per cent of GDP for France.

The second pillar is the Cardiff process, whereby member countries have to produce national structural reform reports describing their efforts to improve competitiveness and the functioning of markets in goods, services and capital.

The third pillar will be the Cologne process, introduced at the Cologne European Council in June 1999, to establish a macroeconomic dialogue intended to improve the interaction among wage developments, fiscal policy and monetary policy in the interests of growth and employment.

The Luxembourg, Cardiff and Cologne processes are intended to push forward the necessary structural reforms within Europe that were needed even before the launch of the euro. The success of the launch after so many years of preparation[18] illustrates how, over time, the European process of dialogue and peer review can, starting from small beginnings, produce tangible results.

Australia: reforms and prudent management pay off

The importance of structural reforms was well illustrated by the recent experience of Australia. Despite its close links with Asian economies—about 60 per cent of its total exports go to the region—Australian GDP growth accelerated from 2.8 per cent in 1997 to 4.7 per cent in 1998, continuing the eight-year long expansion (see table A.2). Inflation was kept low (see table A.8). The unemployment rate also fell, to a decade-low level of 7.5 per cent. The contagion effects of the Asian crisis on Australia's financial system were limited and the negative effects on its trade were more than offset by strong domestic demand. This is in striking contrast with other economies that have similarly close links with troubled Asian countries. The impact was smaller in Australia mainly because of its resilient financial system, judicious macroeconomic and exchange-rate policy and rapid switch in export markets.

[16] See Presidency Conclusions: Cologne European Council, 3 and 4 June 1999. These Conclusions describe further the Luxembourg, Cardiff and Cologne processes. They are available at http://europa.eu.int/council/off/conclu/june99/index.htm.

[17] The four pillars of the Guidelines are: improving employability, developing entrepreneurship, encouraging the adaptability of businesses and their employees, and improving equal opportunities for women and men. The Employment Guidelines are available at http://europa.eu.int/com/dg05/empl&esf/empl99.

[18] The progress towards monetary union can be traced to a 1975 report by the Belgian Prime Minister, Leo Tindemans, proposing a set of goals for European Union, including economic and monetary union.

Since the early 1980s, Australia had undertaken a series of reforms, including the adoption of a flexible exchange-rate system, the reform of its financial markets, trade liberalization, the dismantling of the centralized wage bargaining system and the tightening of competition laws. Although some of these measures increased the exposure of the economy to global forces, they strengthened its resilience.

As a result of reforms, the financial system became better supervised and financial intermediaries more prudently managed: the balance sheets of financial institutions were in better shape at the time of crisis than before. The overall exposure of major Australian banks to Asia was only about 5 per cent of their total assets and the share of non-performing loans was small in the fiscal year beginning 1 July 1997. Reflecting the good asset base, robust retail markets and operational efficiency, banks still made profits during the crisis and their capital ratios remained above the minimum requirements.

The Government's efforts at reforming the financial sector continued even after the crisis. A new regulatory structure became operational on 1 July 1998, in response to the 1997 recommendations by the Wallis Committee, which had been set up in May 1996 to assess the financial system and find ways to improve the regulatory environment. Under the new system, the five existing regulatory bodies were consolidated into three. The Reserve Bank of Australia retained its responsibility for monetary policy, the overall stability of the financial system and the regulation of the payments system. The new Australian Prudential Regulation Authority, a single prudential supervisor, became responsible for the supervision of deposit-taking financial institutions, life and general insurance providers, and superannuation funds. Its main functions are to encourage prudent behaviour by financial institutions and to deal with unviable financial institutions. The new Australian Corporations and Finance Services Commission deals with overall market integrity, consumer protection and competition. The Council of Financial Regulators, made up of representatives of these three bodies, was established to provide operational and policy coordination. The new regulatory system does not provide guarantees for deposits.

The flexible exchange-rate system was crucial for Australia's success in defusing the pressure on its currency in 1997 and 1998. When speculative pressures on its currency developed during the initial phase of the crisis, the Reserve Bank of Australia did not attempt to resist market forces but let the Australian dollar depreciate by more than 10 per cent. It intervened infrequently in a well-timed manner, only when the currency depreciation was considered near its nadir. The extent of the currency depreciation was comparable with that of Singapore but less than that of many of the Asian crisis countries. Despite the depreciation of its currency, the Reserve Bank of Australia kept the short-term interest rate (overnight cash rate) low, at 5 per cent. This was in contrast with other central banks that raised interest rates sharply under apparently similar circumstances. Low interest rates played a critical role in offsetting the deflationary forces from Asia. With subdued inflation, the Reserve Bank of Australia lowered the overnight cash rate by 25 basis points to 4.75 per cent in December 1998.

The cycle of panic, massive withdrawals of funds, stock market collapse and a credit crunch that hit many Asian countries did not develop in Australia.

The stock market still increased in 1998 (see figure III.1). Capital inflows continued, particularly from Asia, as Australia was seen as a safe haven and, with the currency depreciation, its assets became even more attractive. As a result, international reserves remained adequate. In mid-1998, when its currency was again under speculative attack as a result of the Russian crisis, Australia's reformed financial system proved its capacity to repel the attack without damage to the economy.

Reflecting the large share of Australia's exports to Asia and the fact that more than 50 per cent of total exports are primary commodities, export earnings suffered from the Asian crisis and the decline in commodity prices in 1998. The value of Australia's exports to East Asia in United States dollar terms fell by about 25 per cent. However, the depreciation of the currency enhanced Australia's export competitiveness against other developed countries and helped effect a switch in exports: the value of exports to other destinations rose by about 5 per cent. Exports to the United States and EU rose particularly rapidly. Nevertheless, total export earnings fell by 15.9 per cent.

In response to strong domestic growth, the volume of imports increased in 1998, but the value of imports in United States dollar terms declined by 4.6 per cent because of the decline in import prices, especially for Asian goods. With the fall in export earnings, the current-account deficit widened from 3.2 per cent of GDP in 1987 to over 5 per cent in 1998. However, the current-account deficit was easily financed with the inflows of capital.

The depreciation caused little inflationary pressure not just because import prices fell, but also because Australia has a very competitive pricing environment. Budgetary consolidation (including spending cuts) also helped contain the inflationary pressures from depreciation and in turn allowed interest rates to remain at a low level at the critical moment. A surplus was achieved in fiscal year 1997/98.

The strength of domestic demand in Australia stands in sharp contrast to that in many of its Asian neighbours, including Japan. Domestic demand's contribution to GDP growth was about 6.4 percentage points which more than offset the negative contribution of net exports. Private consumption was supported by employment gains, low interest rates, increased asset values, demutualization[19] and strong consumer confidence. The wealth effect from increasing asset values played an important role in boosting spending. The steady increase in house prices, combined with the increased availability of credit and low borrowing costs, encouraged private consumption. However, household debt grew by more than 10 per cent and the savings ratio fell to 0.8 per cent in late 1998.

Housing and business investment was buoyant. In addition, construction projects related to the Games of the XXVII Olympiad in the year 2000 and the mining sector have provided a stimulus to growth in the past few years.

A slowdown in investment and exports is expected to lead to slower growth in Australia in 1999—but still at a brisk rate of 3.0-3.5 per cent. In all, the structural reforms undertaken by the Australian authorities before the Asian crisis and prudent and unpanicked management during the crisis served the country well.

[19] With demutualization, members can realize the value of a mutual fund's accumulated surpluses by surrendering their non-tradable interest for publicly listed shares. In many cases, the result is a windfall gain to members.

ECONOMIES IN TRANSITION

In 1998, there was a deceleration in growth in the majority of the economies in transition, with recession in some. Many suffered a deterioration in the macroeconomic stability that they had been building. Although most were not immediately or directly affected by the Asian financial crisis, they suffered the consequences of the subsequent reverberations. The fall in commodity prices benefited the Central and Eastern European and Baltic economies but adversely affected many members of CIS, most notably the Russian Federation where the fall in export earnings was one of the factors contributing to the financial crisis in August 1998. Directly and indirectly, that event had negative consequences for most transition economies. The other members of CIS and the Baltic countries were confronted with a decline in Russian imports and were also affected by the turbulence in international financial markets; for the Central and Eastern European countries the trade consequences were negligible, but most were affected by the financial fallout. In the last quarter of 1998, the slowdown in Western Europe, particularly Germany, had a further negative effect, particularly on the Central and Eastern European countries. The external consequences of the crisis in Kosovo subsequently compounded the economic difficulties for the countries in that subregion.

Commonwealth of Independent States (CIS): revival derailed

In 1998, aggregate GDP for the CIS region contracted by 3.4 per cent (see table A.3), more than reversing the modest gain of the previous year. The crisis in the Russian Federation was the main reason for the decline, both in respect of producing a fall in output in that country and in having negative spillover effects on other CIS economies: output declined in the Republic of Moldova, Kazakhstan and Ukraine and growth decelerated in Belarus, Georgia and Kyrgyzstan. Only Armenia, Azerbaijan, Tajikistan and Turkmenistan had higher growth rates in 1998 than in 1997, the second on the strength of oil-related foreign investments and the other three largely because of the recovery from previous disruptions.

Russian Federation and Ukraine: renewed and protracted recession

For the Russian Federation, 1998 was one of the most difficult years since the start of the transformation in 1991. The macroeconomic stability and growth that finally began to emerge in 1997 were lost: the formal banking system almost ceased to operate and GDP fell by more than 4 per cent.

By the end of 1997, the Russian Federation had achieved relatively low inflation, a stable exchange rate, some improvements in the real sector, and some growth of consumption and income. Tight monetary policy had reduced inflation and stabilized the exchange rate, but the fundamental fiscal problem had not been solved: public debt was rising and servicing it was assuming an increasing proportion of the government budget, reaching almost one third of government expenditures by August 1998. Moreover, reforms had been slow: the country still lacked the institutional infrastructure of a market economy, including property laws and creditor rights. It also suffered from a huge accumulation of wage and inter-enterprise arrears and a demonetization of the real sector (which, together with a desire to avoid taxation, induced firms to increase barter trade). The situation was tenable largely because revenues from exports of primary commodities alleviated the internal and external financial pressures: the Russian economy had a trade surplus of $17.6 billion in 1997.

The drop in the prices of commodities, particularly oil,[20] turned this surplus into a deficit in 1998. This deterioration was largely responsible for triggering the financial crisis of mid-August. However, the trade deficit alone might not have prompted the collapse of the currency. The additional contributing factor was the weak fiscal position. Critically, about 30 per cent of the short-term debt that had been used to cover successive budget deficits was held by non-residents. With the disappearance of the trade surplus, foreign lenders realized that it would be difficult for the Government to service these loans. This international loss of confidence provoked massive capital outflow.

In an attempt to restore investor confidence and avoid devaluation, the Russian Federation agreed in mid-July 1998 with the International Monetary Fund (IMF), the World Bank and Japan to borrow $22.6 billion in 1998 and 1999. Although, the legislation necessary to implement stabilization measures agreed with IMF failed to gain parliamentary approval, IMF provided an immediate infusion of $4.8 billion. Nevertheless, investor confidence did not recover; stock prices plummeted and interest rates on Russian government short-term borrowing rose sharply. The Russian Government was forced to devalue the ruble on 17 August 1998; it also announced a unilateral rescheduling of most of its short-term debt into long-term securities and the imposition of a 90-day moratorium on payments by Russian banks and enterprises on much of their foreign debt.

Other measures included some return to controlled prices at the local level, the retention of foreign exchange controls, financial austerity and remonetization of the real sector. In the short term, the Government succeeded in preventing hyperinflation and in avoiding a complete breakdown of financial institutions. The consequences were a sharp reduction in imports and a fall in real incomes, to some small extent alleviated by the increase of the value in real terms of the foreign exchange holdings of the population at large.[21]

Fiscal adjustment remains a priority for the Russian Federation because there is now almost no government bond market and no scope for commercial foreign borrowing. Any budget deficit can be financed only by official lending or by being monetized, one negative effect of which is to further discourage foreign capital inflows. Reflecting the imperative to tighten fiscal policy, the budget for 1999 is the most stringent since the beginning of the transition period.[22] Priority has also been given to the restructuring of the banking sector. However, many other key institutional reforms have been postponed, partially because some of the necessary structural changes are likely to have negative effects on enterprises in the short term and to create additional social problems. Nevertheless, as 1998 demonstrated, their postponement increases the difficulty of achieving sustainable growth, over the longer term.

The country's economic situation, particularly its current-account balance, would improve if oil prices sustained the levels they reached in the first half of 1999. Even so, the external situation will continue to be a constraint on growth. Domestically, credit will continue to be tight. Investment will be restrained by low levels of foreign direct investment (FDI) and the lack of

[20] Raw materials account for almost 80 per cent of Russian exports.

[21] It is estimated that about $50 billion in foreign currency, primarily in dollars, is held by citizens within the Russian Federation.

[22] The target budget deficit for 1999 of 2.5 per cent of GDP is based on the assumption that tax collection will be substantially improved and that there will be no shocks to the inflation rate or to the exchange rate.

domestic finance. Because enterprises are having difficulties mobilizing financial resources, the Government has introduced measures to attract foreign direct investors, for example, by creating a legal basis for production-sharing agreements in the raw materials sector. It is hoped this will attract FDI to the energy sector, possibly starting a recovery in investment. In particular, many oil deposits are depleted and large capital inflows will be required to develop new production capacity.

In the meantime, the Russian oil sector is working at full capacity and is unlikely to be able to increase output significantly in the short run. Nevertheless, in the first few months of 1999, overall industrial production was recovering, largely in response to the devaluation. Imports were being replaced by domestic goods and there were also increases in exports in some sectors (such as pulp and paper). The financial situation of some enterprises was also improving. Despite these signs of recovery in some areas, much of the economy faces severe difficulties and early forecasts were for a further contraction of GDP in 1999.

Given that the Russian Federation is a neighbour with extensive economic ties to Ukraine, the Russian crisis had immediate and large negative effects on the struggling Ukrainian economy. Ukraine shares many of the economic problems of the Russian economy, including large foreign debt and external payments obligations, a low level of foreign exchange reserves, poor fiscal performance and accumulated public sector wage arrears. In 1998, the repercussions of the Russian crisis were added to these difficulties and GDP fell by 1.7 per cent. The Russian Federation accounts for more than a quarter of Ukraine's exports and the strong association in the eyes of foreign investors of the Ukrainian currency with the ruble put the hryvnia under pressure. As result and in order to retain the Russian export market, Ukraine devalued its currency shortly after the Russian crisis broke. Subsequent support of the hryvnia reduced reserves to critically low levels and in September 1998 the Government obtained some $3 billion in loans from IMF and the World Bank. Even with these loans, the external financial position of the country is weak.

With suppressed domestic demand, a cut in government spending and the recession in the Russian Federation, Ukraine is expected to suffer a decline in GDP of a further 3 per cent in 1999, with inflation as high as 50 per cent. As for the Russian Federation, a recovery depends in large measure on the prices of key exports, which, for Ukraine, are unprocessed metals and chemicals; these have not yet shared in the recovery enjoyed by oil prices. Ukraine's prospects also depend on a revival of the Russian economy and that remains uncertain.

Other members of CIS: stricken by contagion

As 1998 progressed, many of the CIS countries other than the Russian Federation and Ukraine suffered from soft world prices for the exports of primary commodities on which they are so dependent (such as metals and oil in Kazakhstan; gold in Kyrgyzstan;, aluminium in Tajikistan; gas and cotton in Turkmenistan; and cotton, gold and hydrocarbons in Uzbekistan).[23] Partially because of these lower prices, foreign investor interest in these economies weakened. Their external environment deteriorated even further in the second half of 1998 with the crisis and recession in the Russian Federation and

23 Overall, the terms of trade of this group of countries are estimated to have worsened by 13.5 per cent in 1998.

Ukraine. Especially hard hit were neighbouring countries with strong trade links and other ties with these two countries. The fact that these economies are closely integrated among themselves and with the Russian Federation makes them extremely vulnerable to recession in that country. A downturn in one affects the rest through a multitude of channels, including such infrastructure as the common energy network and transportation links. Following the Russian crisis, intra-CIS trade plummeted by almost half in one month alone, including declines of about two thirds in exports from Armenia and the Republic of Moldova. In addition, the currencies of the region depreciated substantially following the Russian devaluation.

One result was a drop in industrial output in the last part of 1998. Following an increase of 2.3 per cent in the first half, industrial output in the Republic of Moldova fell by 11 per cent over the year as a whole; the corresponding figures were 0.8 per cent and -2.5 per cent in Armenia and 23.5 per cent and -4.6 per cent in Kyrgyzstan. Industrial output for the year increased only in Azerbaijan, Turkmenistan and Uzbekistan. Except in Armenia and Turkmenistan, agriculture did not fare well either, with bad harvests in major producer countries. Agricultural production fell by about one fifth in Kazakhstan, one tenth in the Republic of Moldova and 8 per cent in Georgia. The service sector failed to compensate for the decline in the other sectors because of weakened domestic demand.

The sharp fall in export revenues and the general economic slowdown caused fiscal balances to worsen.[24] Export revenues have continued to fall in 1999 and further increases in deficits are likely unless Governments revise their budgets. Because domestic capital markets are underdeveloped, these budget deficits have to be financed externally or monetized. In the absence of corrective policies, the deficits would pose the threat of increasing inflation and would erode the gains in competitiveness from the recent devaluations, further worsening the external situation.

On average over the year, inflation continued its previous widespread downward trend in 1998. However, this annual average hides widespread differences within the year. Although few currencies (other than that of Belarus) fell by as much as the ruble, the depreciations in the latter part of 1998 more than offset the lower prices of imported energy and raw materials and, reinforced by the monetization of the fiscal deficits, caused inflation to increase. The deterioration was particularly bad in Belarus where, on a year-on-year basis, prices rose almost 200 per cent in 1998, compared with some 60 per cent in 1997; in the Republic of Moldova, the increase was from about 10 to over 80 per cent. Inflationary pressure appear to be increasing further in 1999, especially in such countries as Georgia, Kazakhstan and Kyrgyzstan.

There was a general weakening of investment and of the external sector in 1998. The broad picture of falling or stagnant investment continues to characterize most countries. In most CIS countries, an unrestructured real economy coexists with an underdeveloped financial sector, itself dominated by a few government-owned banks that are burdened with non-performing loans and lend mostly to the public sector. Under these circumstances, growth is heavily dependent on foreign demand and financing and is vulnerable if either falters.

The increase in trade imbalances caused these countries' current-account deficits to widen in 1998. With their rich mineral resources and potentially high

[24] The share of the Russian Federation in total merchandise exports was around 60 per cent in Belarus and the Republic of Moldova, 40 per cent in Kazakhstan and 30 per cent in Georgia.

marginal productivity of capital (on the assumption of systemic reform and technological catch-up), it is natural that external resources should be readily available to finance those deficits. However, those external resources are currently being used predominantly to finance private and public consumption rather than to finance investment that would create the ability to service such inflows in the future. Private savings have fallen and, as noted, government deficits are large, while output is falling or stagnant. Such countries as Armenia, Georgia, the Republic of Moldova and Turkmenistan have fiscal and current-account deficits that are predominantly financed by official sources, making these countries particularly vulnerable to changes in these inflows. Meanwhile, the Republic of Moldova, Turkmenistan and Uzbekistan are already experiencing debt-servicing difficulties.

In 1998, there was a slowdown in the reform process in the region, including increased resort to administrative controls in such countries as Belarus, Turkmenistan and Uzbekistan. There was also pressure for protectionism in many countries. The slow restructuring of the real economy is a constraint on recovery and growth, and renewed efforts are required to intensify structural change on a broad front. This need is compounded by the lack of effective corporate governance and the lack of FDI (except in countries like Azerbaijan, Kazakhstan, Kyrgyzstan, Turkmenistan and Uzbekistan, where resource-related investment has been high).

The recession in the Russian Federation and continued low prices for their main export commodities will make 1999 a difficult year for the CIS countries. Their undiversified export structures and, in some cases, their heavy dependence on official financing make them vulnerable to balance-of-payments constraints and they are likely to have to reduce domestic absorption. A contraction in GDP in 1999 is anticipated in Belarus, Kazakhstan and the Republic of Moldova. The Transcaucasian region is likely to fare better than the rest, with the partial recovery of world oil prices, the opening of an oil pipeline and a new Black Sea rail ferry route connecting the Caspian basin to the West. The Caucasus subregion as a whole is forecast to achieve growth of about 5 per cent, with relatively low inflation and stable external financing, but growth in Georgia and Azerbaijan is expected to slow in 1999.

The mineral-rich Central Asian countries will continue to suffer from depressed commodity prices (which in turn may reduce foreign investment), but are likely to achieve modest increases in GDP. A more substantial improvement may be possible for Turkmenistan if gas exports to Ukraine prove to be more successful than currently anticipated. On the other hand, the possibility of permanently lower commodity prices will require a revision of development strategies in these economies.

Central and Eastern Europe

With the exceptions of the Czech Republic and Romania, where output declined, most of the Central and Eastern European economies grew by 3 per cent or more in 1998. Nevertheless, the rates of growth were generally less than in the previous year. The exceptions were Albania and Bulgaria, which rebounded from their declines of 1997, Hungary and the former Yugoslav Republic of Macedonia.

Most Central and Eastern European countries largely withstood the first wave of the international financial crisis in 1997. The crisis even had some positive effects; for example, the Czech Republic attracted some of the funds withdrawn from other countries and, with primary commodities being an important part of their imports, these countries were among those that benefited from the price fall. Moreover, the trade effects of the Russian crisis were generally small for these countries. During the transition, most reoriented their trade and EU has become their major trading partner. Bulgaria and Poland are those most dependent on trade with the Russian Federation, but such trade accounts for only about 8 per cent of their exports.

The region was more affected by the financial fallout from the crisis. After the default on Russian foreign debt, investors not only disposed of Russian assets, but also sold holdings in other countries, among them Eastern European bonds.[25] There was also strong pressure on many Central and Eastern European currencies. The Slovak central bank abandoned the fixed exchange rate on 1 October 1998 and the Hungarian and Slovak central banks intervened in the foreign exchange markets, using a substantial proportion of their foreign exchange reserves to support their currencies.

Despite these external influences, domestic factors were important in determining performance in 1998. For example, the turnaround in Bulgaria could be attributed to a good harvest but also to improved macroeconomic stability: the adoption of a currency board and tight fiscal policy reduced inflation and improved domestic confidence. The recession in the Czech Republic was partially attributable to a decline in exports but there was also a slowdown in both domestic consumption and, particularly, investment, mainly because of a shortage of credit resulting from the high level of non-performing loans in the financial sector. In Slovakia, tight monetary and fiscal policies reduced domestic demand, particularly investment, exacerbating the effects of the external shocks. Poland had previously experienced a period of high growth, and a slowdown to a more sustainable level was only to be expected.

Most of these countries faced an increase in the cost of capital in 1998, both domestically and in foreign markets. Inflation in these countries was generally lower than targeted, partially because of the fall in commodity prices. Nevertheless, in many cases, central banks were reluctant to reduce nominal interest rates because of the possible pressure on their currencies.[26] The result was that real interest rates rose high in most Central and Eastern European countries in 1998, dampening investment and slowing growth. After October 1998, interest rates began to be reduced, but they remained high.

FDI flows to the Czech Republic, Hungary and particularly Poland increased in 1998, largely because of some major privatizations. In addition, investors are already returning to other countries, with Hungary and Slovenia having regained access to capital markets. Investors apparently have less concern about Central and Eastern European countries than about many Asian and Latin American economies and are attracted by high expectations regarding corporate earnings and by the benefits of the actions necessary for future access to EU.

There is no indication yet of a realistic date for admission of the first Central and Eastern European countries to EU. The first round of the negotiations with the Czech Republic, Hungary, Poland and Slovenia was completed in 1998[27]

[25] Many foreign portfolio investments in the Russian Federation were leveraged. After the Russian crisis, leveraged investment funds were pressed to sell assets to raise cash balances.

[26] In a few cases, real exchange rates appreciated because of large inflows of foreign direct investment (FDI).

[27] Cyprus and Estonia are also negotiating accession to EU.

and, at the beginning of 1999, the discussions moved to issues of capital movements and agricultural policy. The negotiations might be protracted because candidate countries need to complete major structural adjustments and to improve macroeconomic performance. They also have to adopt an entire body of law of European union prior to their admission. EU, in turn, has to adjust its agricultural policy and structural funds arrangements and its internal arrangements to prepare for the admission of new members.

As was the case for most other transition economies, one of the features of the Central and Eastern European countries in 1998 was the widening current-account deficit. For some countries, like Hungary and Poland, this deficit was mainly the result of an increase in investment, while for other countries its origin was a decrease in domestic savings and an increase in domestic consumption. In the former cases, capital inflows largely took the form of FDI which both complemented domestic investment and contributed to the financing of the current-account deficit. However, other countries have had to resort to international borrowing to finance their deficits.

Because of strong domestic demand, trade and current-account balances are generally expected to deteriorate further in 1999, especially in Hungary, Poland and Romania. Although the more advanced countries of the region do not have great difficulties in mobilizing foreign capital, the costs of borrowing on international capital markets—including being subject to the volatility of short-term capital—have risen sharply. There are therefore pressures on these countries to reduce the current-account gap by slowing import growth and increasing the quality and competitiveness of domestic goods for export.

Growth in most of the economies of Central and Eastern European is expected to decelerate further in 1999. The lagged consequences of the slowdown in Western Europe at the end of 1998 and of the financial crises will continue to be felt and difficulties created by the universal current-account deficits will also be a constraint on growth. The Czech Republic, Romania and Slovakia are forecast to remain in recession and Bulgaria and Croatia are also expected to register negative growth in 1999, with GDP contracting by up to 3 per cent in some cases. In Bulgaria, the closure of some privatized loss-making enterprises will result in a fall in output in the short run. Hungary, Poland, and Slovenia are expected to continue to achieve positive growth, but only of about 3.5 per cent. The fallout from events in Kosovo and other conflicts in the Balkans will continue to affect economic prospects in that subregion: in Albania, the need to correct the fiscal imbalance resulting from the refugee crisis is likely to restrict growth to less than 3 per cent in 1999 and similarly modest growth rates are expected for Bosnia and Herzegovina and the former Yugoslav Republic of Macedonia.

The Baltic States

In the Baltic countries, the economic overheating and sizeable capital inflows that characterized 1997 were replaced by deceleration and a tightening of external finance in 1998. These countries are more open and integrated into international financial markets than the CIS countries and were already pursuing tight macroeconomic policies in order to reduce overheating and their consequent current-account deficits. They were correspondingly more affected by both the trade and financial effects of the Russian crisis. About 20-25 per cent of Baltic exports are to the Russian Federation and regional exports declined by 5 per cent in 1998, after increasing by 13 per cent in the first half of the year. Estonia lost 6-8 per cent of its total exports and Latvia and Lithuania 7-10 per cent. Especially hard hit were food exports, which account for about 40 per cent of manufactured exports in Latvia and for half of Estonian exports to the Russian Federation. The service sector was particularly adversely affected because trans-shipment of goods to and from the Russian Federation is a major activity in all three countries. Financial contagion was also strong, especially in Latvia where banks had invested heavily in Russian securities.

The aggregate GDP growth rate for the three countries dropped by about 4 percentage points in 1998 from almost 8 per cent in 1997 (see table A.3). Industrial production barely grew in Estonia and Latvia, although it increased in Lithuania by 7 per cent. Unemployment in the region, which had previously been falling gradually, rose from 5.9 to 7.3 per cent in the second half of 1998.

Current-account deficits for the year increased by over 4 per cent of GDP in Latvia and Lithuania, while falling by 3 per cent in Estonia. Despite the external difficulties there was a high degree of business confidence and both domestic and foreign investment were strong. Net financial flows to the Baltic countries again increased in 1998, predominantly in the form of FDI.

Inflation in the Baltic countries is the lowest among the transition economies and is likely to remain so, aided by lower prices for imported energy and raw materials. Nominal wage increases decelerated in 1998, but there was an even faster deceleration of producer prices, weakening these countries' competitive position at a time when trade deficits have become large. The Russian market is not likely to be restored soon and it will be difficult to shift low-value exports to other markets, particularly when demand in Western Europe is weakening and competition from other markets, such as those of the crisis countries in Asia, has increased. In order to increase exports under their fixed exchange-rate regimes, it is vital for these countries to control wage growth and further boost productivity through continued reforms.

The impact of the recessions in the Russian Federation and Ukraine on these countries was proving to be stronger than initially anticipated and was being compounded in early 1999 by the sluggishness of the EU market. The first few months of 1999 have shown continued weakening of economic activity in all Baltic countries, with Estonia likely to see a contraction of GDP in the first half of the year, and a recovery thereafter. The resulting contraction in imports is expected to reduce the regional current-account deficit to 5-6 per cent of GDP. Given the increasing differentiation of investor perceptions in their favour because of their progress in transition, their strong macroeconomic policy framework and their sound financial systems, it should not be difficult to finance deficits of this magnitude. All three countries are forecast to have GDP growth of between 1 and 1½ per cent in 1999. This will be followed by a recovery in 2000, the strength of which will be determined largely by developments in Western Europe.

Box III.1.

THE ECONOMIC CONSEQUENCES OF THE KOSOVO CONFLICT FOR NEIGHBOURING COUNTRIES

It is difficult to assess at this point in time the economic dimensions of the fallout of the Kosovo conflict on neighbouring countries, especially Albania, Bosnia and Herzegovina, Bulgaria, Croatia, Hungary, Romania and the former Yugoslav Republic of Macedonia, but also Greece and Turkey. The direct costs for these countries comprise not only the expenditures required to care for the refugees and to repatriate them, but also the immediate financial and related economic losses sustained by the countries in the region on account of lost trade, capital flows and tourism earnings and the longer-term economic costs arising from delays in structural reforms.

In the first half of 1999, sizeable economic losses and additional expenditures were incurred by neighbouring countries to provide care for the Kosovar refugees. These put increasing pressure on the internal and external balances of these countries, none of which were in a position to bear such outlays, neither on a current basis nor in terms of the setbacks to the stabilization and reform efforts that they had been undertaking.

In addition, a number of Yugoslavia's neighbours have been physically cut off from their principal markets in Western Europe. They can circumnavigate the closed and damaged traditional land, river, railroad and related routes only at great expense and with a great loss of time. For example, Bulgaria used to ship 60 per cent of its trade with the European Union (EU) via Yugoslavia.

The crisis in Kosovo has also negatively affected investors' sentiment for countries that, prior to the crisis, had been poised to enjoy increased net capital inflows. For example, Albania's privatization programme has been delayed and the risk premiums on bonds issued by Bulgaria, Croatia and Hungary rose following the eruption of the crisis. Likewise, the ability of some of these countries to earn normal tourism revenues has been compromised: tourism in Croatia and Slovenia (where it accounts for 12 per cent of gross domestic product (GDP)) has reportedly been severely hit. These setbacks to financial flows and tourism apply in particular to the countries of south-eastern Europe that have only recently recovered a measure of economic and political stability.

In recognition of the costs they were incurring because of the crisis, the Paris Club has agreed to ease the debt-service obligations for Albania and the former Yugoslav Republic of Macedonia for 1999. The multilateral financial institutions have been revising their programmes with these countries and appear prepared to increase lending. In the first instance, balance-of-payments support will be provided.

The immediate priority is to address the problems of the refugees in these countries. However, it is also necessary to reverse the slowdown in their restructuring efforts caused by the crisis. This requires a strategy for catch-up growth involving integration into EU and greater interaction with the rest of the world. This, in turn, will need coherent, comprehensive and long-term support for structural change in the region over a protracted period of time.

THE DEVELOPING ECONOMIES

Economic growth in developing countries decelerated sharply in 1998 from 5.5 per cent in 1997 to an average 1.7 per cent (see table III.2). The financial crisis in Asia and its spillovers and after-effects were the main cause of the slowdown. Private capital flows became unavailable or scarce, restricting growth in a number of ways. Net long-term private flows in 1998 declined by about $72 billion in relation to 1997, almost all of which was accounted for by reduced flows from banks and capital markets. For most countries, the cost of borrowing, both abroad and in the domestic market, increased substantially. In addition, export revenues fell substantially as a result of both a decline in the volume of exports and lower international prices (see chap. II).

These factors imposed a severe toll on economic activity in most developing regions in 1998. South-East and East Asia was the most adversely affected. Several countries of the region experienced a deep economic recession—a marked contrast to the fast rates of growth these economies had registered in the past. China, on the other hand, continued to record an impressive growth. In Latin America and Western Asia, economic growth receded substantially and

Table III.2.
DEVELOPING COUNTRIES: RATES OF GROWTH OF GDP, 1991-1999

Annual percentage change							
	Annual average 1991-1998	1994	1995	1996	1997	1998[a]	1999[b]
Developing countries of which:	4.6	5.7	4.8	5.7	5.5	1.7	2½
Africa	1.8	2.0	2.8	4.5	2.7	2.5	3
East and South Asia	6.8	8.6	8.2	7.4	6.2	1.2	4¾
Region excluding China of which:	5.2	7.0	7.3	6.5	5.0	-1.9	3¼
East Asia	5.3	7.6	7.6	6.6	5.2	-4.1	2½
South Asia	4.8	5.2	6.2	6.0	4.6	5.5	5½
Western Asia	2.4	-0.9	4.1	4.8	5.2	1.3	½
Latin America and the Caribbean	3.4	5.8	0.4	3.8	5.4	2.4	0
Memo items: Sub-Saharan Africa (excluding Nigeria and South Africa)	1.7	1.8	4.2	5.0	4.0	3.1	3¾
Least developed countries	2.1	1.8	4.1	4.7	4.4	2.8	3
China	10.8	12.6	10.5	9.6	8.8	7.8	7½

Source: UN/DESA.

[a] Preliminary estimates.
[b] Forecast, based in part on Project LINK.

in Africa it declined marginally. South Asia was the only region where economic growth accelerated in 1998: it became the fastest growing region in the world in 1998 thanks to its less-than-full integration in international private capital markets and its limited reliance on exports as a source of growth.

Economic growth is expected to pick up somewhat in 1999 but, at 2.5 per cent, it will remain substantially below the average for the period 1991-1997. South-East and East Asian economies are expected to slowly overcome their financial crises as domestic demand, supported by fiscal measures and a relaxation of monetary policy, recovers. Latin America, on the other hand, will slide into a moderate recession as it continues to confront the negative effects of low commodity prices and reduced capital inflows, and the adjustment measures they necessitate. Developments in Brazil in early 1999 have aggravated the situation. Barring additional external shocks and adverse weather conditions, economic growth will improve slightly in Africa, but its pace will continue to be insufficient to make any dent in poverty.

Africa

Real GDP growth in Africa decelerated from 2.7 per cent in 1997 to 2.5 per cent in 1998, an outcome that represented another year of decline of growth from the peak rate of 4.5 per cent attained in 1996. Per capita GDP growth was negative in 1998, as it has been for most of the decade. Africa's annual average increase in real GDP from 1991 to 1998 amounted to just 1.8 per cent. With population growing at an average of 2.7 per cent per year, Africa needs to grow much faster to prevent further declines in GDP per capita and to improve the welfare of its people.[28]

Growth decelerated in Nigeria and South Africa, among the largest economies in the region, as well as in other countries such as Ethiopia, Kenya and Uganda, that had performed well during the past three years. The Libyan Arab Jamahiriya and Zambia experienced a year of negative growth in 1998, while the Democratic Republic of the Congo lapsed into a second consecutive year of recession. Despite the slowdown in most of the region, 12 out of 38 countries regularly monitored by the Department of Economic and Social Affairs of the United Nations Secretariat attained growth rates of per capita GDP of 3 per cent or higher, compared to 11 countries in 1997.

Most countries that belong to the CFA franc zone[29] maintained the relatively strong economic performance they had achieved since 1995 and did relatively well in 1998, despite the overall depressed international economic conditions. Preliminary estimates indicate that the Union économique et monétaire ouest africaine (UEMOA) subregion grew by 5.5 per cent in 1998, compared with 5.9 per cent in 1997. The combined GDP of countries belonging to the Communauté économique et monétaire de l'Afrique centrale (CEMAC) increased by 4.9 per cent in 1998. In a year marked by a sharp deceleration in output growth in many developing countries, such outcomes place these regional groupings among the best performers in 1998. However, several CFA countries are still classified as least developed, that is to say, as low-income economies facing substantial structural developmental constraints. This implies that recent economic performance will have to be sustained for some time if these economies are to address their many socio-economic challenges.

[28] According to the Economic Commission for Africa (ECA), growth of 7 per cent is required to achieve significant reductions in poverty levels in the region. See ECA, *Economic Report on Africa 1999: The Challenge of Poverty Reduction and Sustainability*, May 1999 (available on the ECA Web site at www.un.org/depts/eca/divis/espd/ecrep99.htm).

[29] The CFA zone comprises two regional integration schemes: the Union économique et monétaire ouest africaine (UEMOA) and the Communauté économique et monétaire de l'Afrique centrale (CEMAC). UEMOA member States are: Benin, Burkina Faso, Côte d'Ivoire, Guinea-Bissau, Mali, the Niger, Senegal and Togo. CEMAC member States are Cameroon, the Central African Republic, Chad, the Congo, Equatorial Guinea and Gabon. In UEMOA countries, CFA stands for "Communauté financière de l'Afrique", while in CEMAC countries, it stands for "Coopération financière africaine". Additionally, the Comoros used to peg its currency to the French franc; now the Comorian franc is pegged to the euro.

The slowdown in Africa's output growth in 1998 can largely be attributed to external factors: a sharp drop in export earnings, amounting to $18 billion (roughly 15 per cent of the value of exports in 1997), owing to lower international demand. Lower commodity prices and the plunge in oil prices for net energy exporters were only partially mitigated by a corresponding decline in import prices of manufactured goods. Although the value of imports contracted by less than 1 per cent, Africa's overall merchandise trade deficit deteriorated sharply from less than $5 billion in 1997 to $22 billion in 1998.

Besides negatively affecting African export earnings, the Asian crisis also led to a reduction of FDI from Asia to several African countries as projects were cancelled or postponed. Yet, financial contagion as a result of the Asian crisis was largely limited to direct effects on the South African economy. Africa as a whole is still far from integrated into international capital markets and usually attracts a limited share of private capital flows to developing countries. Moreover, such flows are highly concentrated in a few countries of the region, with South Africa being one of them. South Africa received record levels of portfolio investment in late 1997 and in early 1998 as the crisis unfolded. However, between May and August 1998, the South African rand came under speculative attack while the financial sector suffered from the "flight to quality" of portfolio investment which affected other emerging markets worldwide, resulting in the depletion of the country's reserves. Higher interest rates in response to the speculative attacks on the currency led to a slowdown in economic growth, which spread to neighbouring countries.

Africa's growth performance in 1998 can also be attributed to a variety of factors. Adverse weather conditions in several countries depressed agricultural output and slowed economic activity in other sectors. Heavy rains and flooding associated with the El Niño weather conditions in late 1997 and early 1998 led to reductions in agricultural production in Kenya, Rwanda, the United Republic of Tanzania, Uganda and several other countries in Eastern and Central Africa. More favourable weather and improved growing conditions in the second half of 1998 led , however, to partial recovery of output. Nonetheless, the disruptions in production, in transportation and in processing of agricultural output earlier in the year resulted in below-normal output for the entire year.

Northern and Western Africa similarly benefited from favourable weather conditions. In Northern Africa, particularly in Algeria and Morocco, agricultural output recovered from the drought in 1997. Record cereal crops were registered in Chad, Mali and the Niger. Cereal output was above normal levels in Burkina Faso and Senegal. Strong growth in agricultural output also contributed to GDP growth in Madagascar, Malawi, Mauritius and several other countries that experienced good weather and favourable growing conditions.[30] In several other countries, however, agriculture performed rather poorly, thus contributing to slower GDP growth, higher inflation and increased food imports. In Ethiopia, drought in the early months of 1998 affected agricultural output, although food production recovered in the second half of the year. Substantial inflows of food aid were required to cover food deficits from production shortfalls earlier in the year. Emergency food assistance was also needed in the Sudan as inadequate rainfall and the effects of the long-running civil war caused the collapse of local food production. Agricultural output fell below normal levels in Botswana, Namibia and

[30] In 1998, Mauritius was able to fulfil its sugar export quota to EU and the United States of America for the first time since 1992/93. However, crop damage from drought in January 1999 and a cyclone in March in 1999 are expected to contribute to a 25 per cent decline in sugar output in the 1998/99 crop year.

Zambia and in several other countries in Southern Africa affected by drought, but food output shortfalls were adequately covered by imports through normal commercial transactions. In Zimbabwe, an unexpected shortfall in maize production and in other food crops led to severe shortages, to substantial price increases of food staples and of other consumer goods, and to food riots in January and September 1998.

Armed conflicts, civil disturbances and political instability disrupted normal economic and commercial activities in several countries. The civil war in the Democratic Republic of the Congo has prolonged the economic decline of the country and undermined prospects for recovery. At least six other countries have been drawn into the conflict at considerable costs and with significant diversion of scarce resources from expenditure on development to increased military spending.

The border dispute between Ethiopia and Eritrea that erupted in armed conflict in May 1998 and in February 1999 was similarly disruptive to economic activities in both countries. Continuing civil wars in Somalia and the Sudan; the resumption of full-scale civil war in Angola; and outbreaks of armed conflicts in Burundi, the Comoros, Guinea-Bissau, Lesotho, Rwanda, Sierra Leone and Uganda during the year undermined progress in economic and social development in those countries. Civil strife and the fighting that erupted at the beginning of the planting season disrupted agricultural activities in Guinea-Bissau. Unstable security conditions limited mining operations in some countries. In the Democratic Republic of the Congo, for example, negotiations for a major joint-venture investment project in copper and cobalt mining were halted because of the civil war. Similarly in Angola, the rapid deterioration of the security situation in some parts of the country, with the resumption of the civil war in late 1998, impeded progress with respect to the exploitation of the country's vast reserves of diamond deposits. Angola's official diamond exports nevertheless jumped from $119 million in 1997 to over $1 billion in 1998 as more diamond mines were turned over to State control in the beginning of the year. In contrast, in several post-conflict economies (Burundi, Mozambique and Rwanda), GDP growth was fuelled partly by a revival of farming activities. In Burundi and Rwanda, successful resettlement of large numbers of displaced persons was instrumental in restoring peasant and commercial farming.

The mining and minerals subsectors of economies in the region provided little stimulus to GDP in 1998, primarily because of the collapse of commodity prices and weak global demand. Depressed global demand for diamonds, for instance, contributed to lower GDP growth in Botswana. Mining output in Zimbabwe declined by 3 per cent in 1998, while earnings from minerals exports decreased by over 20 per cent. Except for Angola, oil output fell in all major African oil-exporting countries (Algeria, Egypt, Nigeria and the Libyan Arab Jamahiriya) in 1998. In Nigeria, the decline in GDP growth was also brought about by a prolonged energy crunch that has depressed the economy since 1997, as well as by uncertainties surrounding political developments in the country. Conversely, crude oil output increased in other oil-exporting countries such as Cameroon, the Congo and Equatorial Guinea in 1998.

Inadequate investment in countries' mining sectors in need of repair, upgrading and modernization of production and operational facilities also contributed to the decline of mining output. In Zambia, for instance, delays in the completion of the privatization of Zambia Consolidated Copper Mines stalled badly needed investment activity to upgrade and modernize two mines that account for 65 per cent of the country's copper assets. The sales were finally completed only in December 1998 after negotiations that had lasted the entire year. The collapse in copper prices and lower export volumes contributed to the delay in the privatization.

Growth in the manufacturing sector, which depends to a large extent on food processing, was weak in most countries where the agricultural sector had performed poorly. Additionally, manufacturing industries in several African countries continue to be constrained by the lack of foreign exchange needed to import essential raw materials and intermediate inputs. In countries such as Kenya, Mauritius and Zimbabwe, with relatively large manufacturing sectors, the sector faced the additional challenge of increased competition of low-cost imports from Asian countries in 1998. Mauritius, however, used the opportunity to streamline operations in its export-processing zone so as to achieve significant productivity and efficiency gains and moderate growth in that sector. In Malawi, sizeable currency devaluations improved the domestic competitiveness of its textile industry, contributing to moderate growth in output of its manufacturing sector. Similarly, manufacturing—albeit from a small base— expanded in most countries belonging to the CFA zone in 1998. Manufacturing in both Benin and Togo recovered during the third quarter of 1998 after having suffered from severe power shortages associated with the drought in Ghana.[31] Nonetheless, energy supply disruptions contributed to curtailment of growth in both countries in 1998. Manufacturing in CFA countries continues to benefit from the devaluation of the currency in 1994.[32] Although the real effective exchange rate has appreciated somewhat in some countries since 1994, imported manufactures remain costly, and this has provided a boost for local industry.

Macroeconomic policy. The majority of African countries succeeded in maintaining macroeconomic stability in 1998. Twenty-two African countries were recipients of Enhanced Structural Adjustment Facility (ESAF) loans from IMF in 1998 under conditions that committed those countries to tight fiscal and monetary policies. Government budgets, however, continued to be heavily constrained by the small size of the formal economy and by the predominance of subsistence activities in several countries. Weaker economic growth and lower export earnings adversely affected fiscal revenues in 1998. Additionally, the region is still plagued by largely unsustainable debt-service obligations, despite the recent initiatives on this front. The year 1998 therefore provided little room for increased investments in human capital, in physical infrastructure and in institutions—all so necessary to remove some of the growth constraints that the continent currently faces.

Among the CFA countries, monetary arrangements of the franc zone— such as ceilings on government borrowing from the regional central banks— contributed to maintaining fiscal and monetary discipline. Public finances, however, remain under strain and some Governments have resorted to less orthodox practices, such as the accumulation of arrears in paying civil service and domestic suppliers. Privatization programmes have been launched and public divestiture has progressed well in most countries.

[31] Rapport du Gouverneur de la Banque centrale des États de l'Afrique de l'Ouest (BCEAO), *Situation Économique des États de l'UEMOA au Cours du 3ème Trimestre 98* (http://www.195.25.42.149/izf/Documentation). Accessed on 15 April 1999.

[32] See *World Economic and Social Survey 1994* (United Nations publication, Sales No. E.94.II.C.1), box II.3.

The CFA institutions have a great influence on the design of monetary and fiscal policies in member countries. Control over inflation is a priority due to the fixed exchange-rate regime. As a result, given inflationary pressures, the Banque centrale des États de l'Afrique de l'Ouest (BCEAO) tightened monetary policy and raised the reserve requirements of banks in August 1998. The latter were lowered for both Senegal and Côte d'Ivoire in December 1998 but maintained for the other countries. Additionally, uncertainties surrounding the peg of the CFA franc to the euro in January 1999 triggered BCEAO's raising both the repurchase rate and the discount rate in August 1998. The rates were lowered in January 1999 when the CFA franc was pegged to the euro—without a devaluation—at a rate of 655.957 CFA francs per euro.

Tight monetary and fiscal policies and generally stable exchange rates contributed to lower inflation in Africa. Most countries also benefited from lower domestic food prices with the turnaround in agricultural output and lower import prices for food and fuel. The average rate of inflation for Africa fell to 9.3 per cent in 1998, which was the lowest level in over two and a half decades, and is projected to fall further in 1999. Despite the favourable overall trend, however, inflation rates rose in countries where food shortages persisted throughout the year and in countries where large currency depreciations fuelled substantial domestic price increases. Increased government spending, attributed to large increases in public sector wage bills in Botswana and Mauritius, and widening fiscal deficits in Angola, the Democratic Republic of the Congo, Madagascar and Zimbabwe contributed to higher inflation in these countries. Consumer prices rose sharply after the introduction of a value-added tax (VAT) in Mauritius and the United Republic of Tanzania.

Regional integration. Economic integration policies and strategies designed to complement the potential trade- creation benefits of the main subregional organizations were also instrumental in shaping economic policies in several countries in 1998. Egypt was admitted as a new member of the Common Market for Eastern and Southern Africa (COMESA) in June 1998, with the aim of enlarging and diversifying the regional market for member States. COMESA's effectiveness in implementing regional strategies for economic and social development was, however, severely limited by the destabilizing effects of the various domestic conflicts in which a large number of member States were involved.

Kenya, the United Republic of Tanzania and Uganda, in pursuit of coordinated regional economic development, completed the review of a draft of the East African Cooperation treaty, scheduled to be ratified in July 1999. The treaty will transform the cooperation arrangement between the three countries into a formal economic community. The latter will adopt the name of a similar arrangement among these countries, the East African Community, which existed from 1967 to 1977. The draft treaty builds on the considerable progress that the three countries have made in recent years in harmonizing fiscal, monetary and other economic policies—as well as in developing various political, legal and administrative institutions—to strengthen the integration process. Cooperation in the development of infrastructure (rail, road and port facilities), telecommunications facilities and energy resources on a regional basis have been high in the agenda of the agreements between the three countries. Nonetheless, implementation of the treaty may take longer than anticipated.

Plans to eliminate tariffs between the three countries are likely to be postponed to July 2000 owing to the need to finalize underlying technical work.

The Southern African Development Community (SADC)[33] also made significant strides in furthering coordinated economic and social development objectives among its member States in 1998. Despite an expanding mediation and peacekeeping role in several armed conflicts in the region (civil wars in Angola and in the Democratic Republic of the Congo, for example), SADC concluded an important protocol on tourism at the organization's annual summit in September 1998. The organization also made progress in finalizing other regional agreements covering other sectors such as transportation, energy and shared watercourses. Additionally, SADC is negotiating other agreements that will eventually lead to dual listings on seven regional stock exchanges. Listings of SADC depositary receipts are expected to boost cross-border investments between SADC countries, especially South African investment in neighbouring countries, and investment from outside the region.

Countries within the UEMOA area are pursuing increased economic integration. UEMOA countries are to eliminate trade and non-tariff barriers on certain products (local agricultural products and approved industrial products of origin with a minimum local content of 40 per cent) among themselves by January 2000. They have also agreed to rationalize and harmonize their trade policies vis-à-vis third countries. Non-tariff barriers will be eliminated and a common external tariff will be adopted. The latter envisages four rates, with a maximum tariff of 20 per cent. The new common tariff structure is currently being implemented, according to an agreed schedule, and should be in place also by January 2000.[34] The impact of such measures on fiscal revenues can be significant given the relatively high import duties in some countries (Burkina Faso and Senegal, for instance) and their importance for the generation of fiscal revenues. As a result, countries have been active in broadening their fiscal base and in improving their tax collection systems. In Mali, for instance, the VAT will be raised from 15 to 18 per cent and applied to areas that had previously enjoyed reduced rates or were exempted.

UEMOA countries are also pursuing a gradual convergence of their economies. Common guidelines for the execution of their fiscal policies have been adopted. These include the following: (a) the share of the civil service wage bill is to be kept below 40 per cent of total tax revenues; (b) tax revenues should contribute to at least 20 per cent of the domestic financing of public investment; (c) the primary budget surplus should be equivalent to at least 15 per cent of tax revenues, thus actually reserving 15 per cent of the tax revenue for servicing their large external and domestic debts; and (d) the level of domestic and external arrears is to decline or remain unchanged. According to UEMOA, convergence progressed in the region in 1998 though final data are not yet available. For the region as a whole, the wage bill ratio declined from 38 per cent in 1997 to 36 per cent in 1998, fiscal revenues financed about 20 per cent of public investment in 1998, and external and domestic arrears, for the group as a whole, were reduced from 1997 levels.[35]

Integration took a step further with the opening of the Bourse régionale des valeurs mobilières—a regional stock exchange—in Abidjan (Côte d'Ivoire) in September 1998. Trading volumes are, however, small and dominated by a few companies. It is expected that as privatization progresses in the region, stock

[33] Southern Africa Development Community (SADC) members are: Angola, Botswana, the Democratic Republic of the Congo, Lesotho, Malawi, Mauritius, Mozambique, Namibia, Seychelles, South Africa, Swaziland, the United Republic of Tanzania, Zambia and Zimbabwe.

[34] E. Hernandez-Cata, *The West African Economic and Monetary Union: Recent Developments and Policy Issues*, IMF Occasional Paper, No. 170 (Washington D.C., IMF, 1998).

[35] UEMOA, *Rapport d'Exécution de la Surveillance Multilatérale, December 1998* (http://195.25.42.149/izf/Documentation/Rapports/uemoa/resumeUEMOA.htm). Accessed on 14 April 1999.

trading will pick up. CEMAC countries have similar plans, but integration is advancing more slowly in the subregion.

Regional outlook for 1999. The region's output is likely to accelerate to 3 per cent in 1999 and to 3.5 per cent in 2000 from weak growth of about 2.5 per cent in 1998. At only 1.3 per cent in 1999, growth in South Africa—the largest economy in the region—will remain weak, but it might accelerate to about 2.8 per cent in 2000, thus recovering from zero growth in 1998. Economic growth in Nigeria—the second largest economy— is expected to recover somewhat and remain at about 3.4 per cent for both 1999 and 2000. In addition to a recovery in oil prices, the Nigerian economy will benefit from policy measures recently implemented such as the removal of the dual exchange rate and the granting of autonomy to the central bank. Additionally, the energy crunch will ease as domestic refineries resume production and investors' confidence will improve given the favourable developments in the political arena.

Countries will continue to pursue tight monetary and fiscal policies in 1999 and to advance with the implementation of structural reforms. Among the CFA countries, efforts to broaden their fiscal base and control current spending, especially the wage bill, will continue. Great emphasis will be placed on sectoral reforms, particularly in agriculture, and on public investment in physical infrastructure and in the development of human capital. Improved producer prices are expected in CEMAC countries, which will contribute to higher agricultural output and domestic demand, given higher earnings. The development of new oil fields in the Congo and Equatorial Guinea will increase oil production in these countries.

The introduction of the euro in January 1999 may bring advantages as well as additional challenges for CFA countries in terms of achieving greater control of inflationary pressures and additional gains in productivity. If the euro strengthens vis-à-vis the dollar during the year, CFA countries may lose competitiveness in major commodity markets. This is a problem these countries have already been facing owing to the deep devaluation of the currencies of the Asian crisis countries.

Notwithstanding the above, Africa's exports are expected to remain depressed in 1999; but they should sharply increase in 2000 if oil prices recover and non-oil primary commodity prices improve together with external demand. Meanwhile, the region's import demand may increase, responding to tariff cuts on intermediate and capital goods, and also to food emergency needs. As a result, the trade deficit is likely to widen, as is the current-account deficit, given the chronic deficits in invisibles. Financing the current-account deficit remains the major challenge faced by African countries. FDI might relieve external payment pressures, but such investment goes to only a few countries, mostly energy and mining producers.

Many African countries have suffered from debt overhang and the heavy burden of debt servicing for quite some time, and the near future will not be different. The total external debt of many countries is well above 400 per cent of GDP. Although many qualify for relief with the framework of the Highly Indebted Poor Countries (HIPC) initiative, so far only Burkina Faso, Côte d'Ivoire, Mali, Mozambique and Uganda have advanced in the process and obtained a commitment of assistance. Among the countries in this group,

Uganda is the only country that has received the promised debt relief through the initiative. In addition to the external debt, economic diversification is another challenge that still must be addressed if rates of output growth for sustaining increases in per capita incomes are to be attained in many countries.

Asia and the Pacific

East Asia

The region experienced its worst economic performance in decades. Its aggregate GDP growth contracted by over 4 per cent in 1998, after having grown by 5.2 per cent in the previous year and by an annual average of 7 per cent during the period 1980-1996.[36]

The Thai currency crisis that started in mid-1997 rapidly spread to other countries in the region. The fact that several countries, particularly those with a relatively liberalized capital account, but with a less-than-robust domestic financial system, were severely affected by the crisis necessitated drastic adjustment measures to regain stability. As private capital fled these countries owing to the rapid deterioration of investor sentiment, stock markets collapsed, national currencies plummeted and interest rates skyrocketed. Debt-servicing obligations suddenly ballooned. Given the high indebtedness of corporations and domestic banks, bankruptcies mushroomed. Financial institutions were faced with an increased amount of bad loans and depreciated assets, thus exposing the inadequacy of local supervisory and regulatory systems. Under a tight adjustment policy and a severe credit crunch, domestic demand and production contracted sharply and unemployment surged. This, combined with acute foreign currency constraints, led to a sharp contraction of imports. Given the significant weight of these countries in the region's total trade, the import retrenchment had substantial effects on neighbouring countries.

GDP contracted in 6 out of the 11 countries in the region. The sharpest contraction was in Indonesia where GDP declined by over 13 per cent in 1998. Also the Republic of Korea, Malaysia and Thailand experienced recessions (see table A.4). Output declined in virtually all non-agricultural sectors, particularly in manufacturing, construction and financial-service sectors. Labour strikes and riots also interrupted production in Indonesia and the Republic of Korea. In Indonesia, adverse weather conditions brought about by El Niño curtailed agricultural output, particularly food output.

Despite the sharp depreciation, export volume gains were insufficient to offset the setbacks in domestic demand. Export earnings in crisis-hit countries declined in 1998. The suspension of trade credit and the overall lack of financing to import required inputs limited export growth. Regional markets, which are major sources of external demand for these countries (see table III.3), contracted, reducing export opportunities; the deepening economic recession in Japan further aggravated the problem. Moreover, much of the gain in competitiveness brought about by the devaluations in the crisis-hit countries has been eroded by the subsequent partial recovery of their currencies (see figure III.2), domestic inflation and the depreciation of their competitors' currencies vis-à-vis the dollar. Additionally, some countries, such as Indonesia and Malaysia, suffered significant terms-of-trade losses because of weak commodity prices. Nonetheless, countries succeeded in generating trade surpluses, mainly through

[36] These figures do not include China, which is considered separately in a section below.

Table III.3.
SELECTED ASIAN COUNTRIES: DESTINATION OF INTERREGIONAL EXPORTS, AVERAGE 1995-1997

Percentage of total exports									
				To					
Exports	Chinaª	Indonesia	Japan	Republic of Korea	Malaysia	Philippines	Singapore	Thailand	Totalᵇ
From									
Chinaª	-	1.1	17.2	4.4	5.4	1.3	3.6	1.3	34.4
Indonesia	7.6	-	25.4	6.5	2.4	1.4	9.3	1.6	54.2
Korea, Republic of	17.3	2.5	12.2	-	3.0	1.5	4.8	1.9	43.6
Malaysia	8.1	1.5	12.8	3.0	-	1.2	20.3	3.9	50.7
Philippines	5.4	0.3	16.3	2.2	2.7	-	6.0	3.1	36.1
Singapore	11.6	0.0	7.7	3.2	18.2	2.0	-	5.4	47.9
Thailand	8.7	1.8	16.2	1.7	3.6	1.0	12.4	-	45.2

Source: IMF, *Direction of Trade Statistics* (various issues).

a   Including Hong Kong Special Administrative Region (SAR).
b   May not add up due to rounding.

Figure III.2.
SELECTED ASIAN COUNTRIES: REAL EFFECTIVE
EXCHANGE RATES, JUNE 1997-APRIL 1999

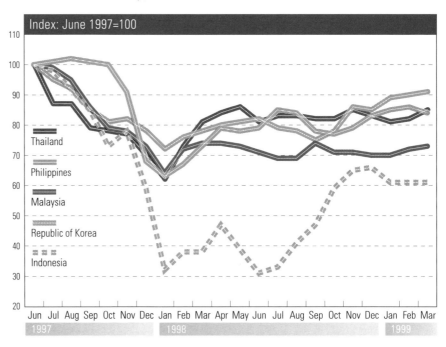

Source: Morgan Guaranty Trust Company, *World Financial Markets*.

the drastic contraction of imports. In the Republic of Korea, for instance, the trade balance shifted from a deficit of about $3.2 billion in 1997 to a surplus of about $41 billion in 1998.[37]

Inflationary pressures increased in crisis-hit countries in early 1998 as a result of depreciation, the shortage of imports, the easing of price controls, the elimination of subsidies and poor agricultural production. In Indonesia, for instance, food prices increased as a result of poor agricultural output and problems in the rice distribution systems; annual inflation reached 77.6 per cent by the end of 1998. For the other crisis-hit countries, annual inflation was below 10 per cent in 1998, which was nonetheless nearly twice as high as in 1997 (see figure III.3).

Countries with more resilient financial systems and adequate reserves withstood the initial contagion dangers well, but even they could not escape a slowdown as the effects through trade and investment unfolded. These countries were also negatively affected by steep declines in stock market values, which led to significant wealth losses, speculative attacks on their currencies, and the need to maintain relatively high interest rates. The last-mentioned contributed to a choking of domestic demand and a weakened ability of debtors' to service their debts, which in turn led to an increase in non-performing loans, growing bank insolvencies and the emergence of problems in the financial sector of some countries.

In Hong Kong Special Administratives Region (SAR), GDP was severely affected by the regional crisis. The Hong Kong dollar, which is pegged to the United States dollar through a currency board, was under severe speculative attacks off and on. Stock and real estate prices plummeted. Interest rates were

[37] The Bank of Korea, *Quarterly Economic Review*, March 1999.

Figure III.3.
SELECTED ASIAN COUNTRIES: CONSUMER PRICE
INDICES, JANUARY 1997-MARCH 1999

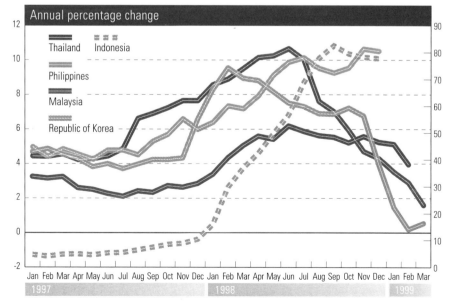

Source: IMF, *International Financial Statistics* (various issues).

Note: Indonesia on the right axis.

increased drastically to defend the currency. The exchange rate was maintained, but the economy contracted by 5 per cent. Both private consumption and investment fell sharply, unemployment rose significantly, real wages shrank and exports fell 7.3 per cent in nominal terms in 1998.

In Singapore and Taiwan Province of China, GDP growth decelerated markedly. Singapore slipped into a mild recession in the second half of the year—for the first time in more than a decade—as a result of the collapse in regional trade and the sharp decline in domestic investment. The service and manufacturing sectors were adversely affected by the crisis and contracted. Reflecting the excess capacity in business property, construction was sluggish. On the other hand, Taiwan Province of China experienced financial difficulties and two banks had to be placed under the control of the Central Deposit Insurance Company in November 1998.

Output growth also declined in the Philippines, despite impressive growth in electronics' exports to countries outside the region. Agricultural output suffered the worst setback in decades as a result of both the El Niño and La Niña phenomena during 1998, but non-agricultural output grew in 1998. Tight credit and a deteriorating business climate adversely affected the industries catering to the domestic market.

The turmoil in Asian financial markets has apparently been weathered as signs of improvement began to emerge in an increasing number of countries towards the end of 1998 and in early 1999. In the case of the Republic of Korea, there were ample signs of incipient recovery in domestic demand as well as in production at the beginning of 1999. Consumer confidence improved and the upturn in private consumption was spreading to a broader spectrum of consumer goods. Although overall investment is still weak, investment in a number of major sectors has been expanding. Led by output of semiconductors, computers, automobiles and office equipment, overall manufacturing production has been slowly increasing since late 1998 owing to the increase in export demand.

Thailand is also starting to show some signs of recovery as the contraction in domestic demand has moderated since late 1998. In Malaysia, industrial output growth, although still low, picked up somewhat in early 1999. On the other hand, the recovery in Indonesia is lagging behind that in other crisis-hit countries because of the political and social tensions in the country as well as delays in the implementation of stabilization and restructuring measures.

Macroeconomic policies: easing the crunch. Initial policy responses in the crisis-hit countries included austere monetary and fiscal adjustment, financial sector consolidation and other structural reforms. These programmes were supported by the international financial institutions and involved considerable amounts of official financing. The original combined financing package for Indonesia, the Republic of Korea and Thailand amounted to $111.7 billion—an unprecedented amount.[38]

The main initial policy measures included a tight monetary policy (interest rates, in particular were raised sharply) and a restrictive fiscal policy. While monetary policy aimed at stemming capital outflows, restoring international confidence, and stabilizing exchange rate and inflation, fiscal policy focused on reducing current-account imbalances, rebuilding international reserves and financing adjustment costs, including funds required for bank restructuring.

38 T. Lane and others, *IMF-Supported Programs in Indonesia, Korea and Thailand: A Preliminary Assessment* (Washington, D.C., IMF, January 1999).

However, the programmes failed to stop the panic and break the cycle of capital outflows, exchange-rate depreciation, and deterioration in financial markets. Market sentiment worsened further owing to delays in restructuring financial systems and political uncertainties. In all these countries, the slowdown in economic activity was much sharper than anticipated and, together with restructuring, generated large unemployment, causing serious social pains and political strains (see box III.2). The programmes were subsequently revised to alleviate those strains.

Since the second half of 1998, macroeconomic policy has been relaxed in an increasing number of countries. By early 1999, most crisis-hit countries had eased their fiscal and monetary policies substantially from the initial extreme stringency. Interest rates have declined in several countries (see figure III.4) as exchange rates stabilized. This policy shift was crucial in order to reverse the deflationary tide and to support economic recovery.

The original IMF programme for Thailand, for instance, envisaged a public sector surplus equivalent to 1 per cent of GDP in fiscal 1997/98 (October-September). Revisions to the programme included replacing the initial target of a surplus by a deficit target of 3 per cent in fiscal 1997/98, not including the costs of financial sector restructuring. For fiscal year 1998/99, the deficit target has been established at 6 per cent of GDP.

Indonesia and the Republic of Korea enacted similar revisions of the fiscal-balance target. The original programme for the Republic of Korea envisaged a small budget surplus in 1998 (0.2 per cent of GDP). The target was subsequently revised to a deficit of 5 per cent of GDP in 1998 and 1999. In the case of Indonesia, the fiscal-deficit target was readjusted several times and expected to exceed 8.5 per cent of GDP the fiscal 1998/99. Malaysia's fiscal balance also shifted from a surplus in 1997 to a deficit of 6 per cent of GDP in 1998.

Several other East Asian countries have cautiously cut interest rates, lowered reserve requirements, and increased fiscal spending to revitalize the domestic demand. For instance, in November 1998, Taiwan Province of China lowered interest rates and increased spending on infrastructure projects. The Government also introduced measures to support the local stock market, including an injection of $6 billion through a stock price stabilization fund.[39] These measures seem to have exerted a positive impact on the economy. GDP growth in the first quarter of 1999 accelerated to 4.3 per cent from 3.7 per cent registered in the last quarter of 1998.

Singapore, in turn, introduced a fiscal stimulus package valued at $6.3 billion to improve competitiveness of the economy. This package supplements the $1.2 billion off-budget measures announced already in June 1998. The new measures include halving the employers' contribution to the central providence fund from 20 to 10 per cent, for a period of two years (effective 1 January 1999). The package also reduced certain government charges and fees. Voluntary wage reduction and a cut in rent on government land will also be conducive to lowering costs.

Structural reforms: mixed progress. Structural reforms are a central component of the programmes being implemented by the Asian-crisis countries. These reforms range from financial sector restructuring, to the consolidation and restructuring of corporations, the introduction of improved prudential regulations

[39] Pension funds, postal saving funds and other publicly run institutions bought blue chips listed on the stock exchange under the instructions of the Finance Department.

Box III.2.
SOCIAL IMPACT OF THE ASIAN CRISIS

a   ILO, *Supplement of the Bulletin of Labour Statistics 1998-4* (Geneva, ILO, 1999); and *Economic and Social Survey of Asia and the Pacific 1999* (United Nations publication, Sales No. E.99.II.F.10).

b   Eddy Lee, *The Asian Financial Crisis: The Challenge for Social Policy* (Geneva, ILO, 1998), p. 41.

The Asian crisis has had severe social consequences for the affected countries. As economic activity contracted, unemployment soared in countries that had previously faced tight labour-market conditions. Increases in the number of bankruptcies, retrenchment and recruitment freezes led to a collapse in the demand for labour. In the Republic of Korea, the unemployment rate jumped from 2.3 per cent in October 1997 to 8.2 per cent in November 1998, while in Hong Kong Special Administrative Region (SAR) it increased from 2.2 per cent in 1997 to about 5 per cent in 1998. Estimates of the open urban unemployment rate for Indonesia are less precise and range from 15 to 20 per cent by the end of 1998. The unemployment rate at least doubled in Malaysia and in Thailand from 1997 to 1998.[a]

These statistics fail to give a complete picture of the unemployment problem. They do not take into account, for instance, the increase in the number of discouraged workers—those who withdraw from or decide not to join the labour force. In the Republic of Korea, for instance, the labour force participation rate fell from 63.1 to 61.5 per cent between the second quarters of 1997 and 1998. If the pre-crisis participation rate had prevailed, an additional 1.6 million workers would have been in the labour force and the unemployment rate would most likely have been even higher.[b] Additionally, the unemployment rate does not include those who are underemployed, working fewer hours than they would like, or engaged in the informal sector.

The informal sector, an important source of employment in countries such as Indonesia and Thailand even before the crisis, is estimated to have expanded in the crisis-hit countries as the unemployed searched for alternative sources of survival. The switch to informal activities, however, is often done at considerable loss of income. This is in part due to the fact that earnings in the informal sector are usually lower and more volatile than in the modern sector. Moreover, the dynamism of the informal sector itself is dependent on the overall demand conditions in the economy as well as on its links with the formal sector. As aggregate demand contracts and links are interrupted, the income-generating potential of the informal sector is severely curtailed. Hence, the swelling of its ranks by displaced workers in such conditions can only imply declines in income. This affects not only the new entrants to the sector but also those who were there before the crisis. Additionally, increased inflation brought about by devaluation and reduced subsidies of essential goods results in a further deterioration in purchasing power, relegating a great number of people to poverty. In Indonesia, these problems were compounded by a severe drought which curtailed food production. Supply problems soon emerged because of crop failure and the country's reduced capacity to import food. This, in turn, contributed to social tensions and disrupted ethnic relations.

The negative impact of the crisis has been more severe in urban than in rural areas. Most of the economic contraction took place in the modern sectors such as manufacturing, construction and financial services, which are usually located in urban areas. Rural areas should have fared better, particularly those geared to producing cash crops, given the devaluation of the currency. However, adverse weather conditions (in Indonesia) and weaker international demand (and therefore lower commodity prices) imposed a toll on rural areas as well. Moreover, they were negatively affected by the decline of remittances from the cities and by reverse migration. Nonetheless, subsistence activities did provide some cushion, as is usually the case during such a crisis.

Box III.2 (continued)

The incipient and limited social security and welfare systems of the affected countries could do little to shield people against a drastic fall in their living standards. Unemployment insurance, for instance, is unavailable in most countries of the region. The exceptions are the Republic of Korea, which had recently introduced—albeit with restricted coverage—an unemployment compensation scheme, and Hong Kong SAR. While most countries have provisions for severance payments, compliance has been undermined by the economic crisis as bankrupted enterprises failed to honour these obligations. Informal social-protection systems, given the generalized deterioration of economic conditions, were unable to provide meaningful economic security. The unemployed therefore had limited fallback options.

While the crisis affected both the poor and the rich, it is the poor and the more vulnerable segments of the society that are less well prepared and have fewer means to cope with impoverishment. Migrant workers are usually the first to lose their jobs when labour-market conditions tighten. In the Republic of Korea, for instance, efforts were made to improve working conditions in small and medium-sized enterprises with the objective of attracting nationals to replace foreign workers.[c] Other countries announced repatriation of migrant workers. According to the International Labour Organization (ILO), by mid-1998 the number of migrant workers had declined in Thailand by 460,000, in Malaysia by 400,000 and in the Republic of Korea by about 117,000.[d]

Lower household income has led some families to delay their children's entry into the educational system or to withdraw them from school. In some instances, families cannot afford tuition fees and the cost of materials. In other cases, they need the extra, although meagre, income the child can potentially bring back home. Preliminary estimates indicate that enrolment rates declined in Indonesia between 1997 and 1998. Enrolment of older children (aged 13 years and over) is usually more adversely affected than that of younger ones.[e] In Thailand, child labour is estimated to have increased as well. Another negative effect is the increase in prostitution. The poor are also likely to adapt their eating habits to their decreased means. Both the quality and the quantity of their food intake worsen, lowering their resistance to diseases, reducing their productivity and, in the case of children, impairing their development. In Central Java, Indonesia, the prevalence of wasting (low weight per height) among children below 35 months of age increased from 8 per cent in 1996 to 14 per cent in 1998. Anaemia now affects 65 per cent of children (up from 40 per cent) in the same age group in that region.[f] Considering the nature and magnitude of these effects, countries will continue to face the social consequences of the crisis, long after the apparent return of economic "normalcy".

The original stabilization and structural adjustment programmes applied in affected countries had few, if any, provisions for dealing with the social consequences. Fiscal austerity was recommended so that it would be possible to accommodate the additional expenditure required for the restructuring of the banking system and, in the case of the Republic of Korea, for the increased outlays of the Employment Insurance System without incurring a large deficit. In Indonesia, for instance, fiscal policy was designed to maintain the budget surplus (about 1 per cent of gross domestic product (GDP)). It included measures such as

c   ILO Regional Office for Asia and the Pacific, *The Social Impact of the Asian Financial Crisis* (Bangkok, ILO, 1998).

d   ILO, *Evolution of the Asian Financial Crisis and Determination of Policy Needs and Response*, presented to the Governing Body, 274th Session, Geneva (March 1999) (http://www.ilo.org/public/english/20gb/docs/gb274/gb-4-2.htm). Accessed on 29 April 1999.

e   Jessica Poppele and others, *Social Impacts of the Indonesian Crisis: New Data and Policy Implications* (http://www.smeru.or.id/report/datapoli2.htm). Accessed on 30 April 1999.

f   World Food Programme, *Special Report FAO/WFP Crop and Food Supply Assessment Mission to Indonesia* (http://www.fao.org/WAICENT/faoinfo/economic/giews/english/alertes/1998/srin9986.htm). Accessed on 30 April 1999.

Box III.2 (continued)

the removal of government subsidies, a new tax on gasoline, the elimination of value-added tax (VAT) exemptions, and adjustment of administered prices for electricity and petroleum products. Thailand's original letter of intent with the International Monetary Fund (IMF), while stating that sufficient resources would be allocated to basic health and education, contained measures to reverse the fiscal deficit into a surplus through reduced spending and increased taxation. In the Republic of Korea, the fiscal position was to have been supported by widening the tax base, as well as by reducing fiscal support to the corporate sector and to low-priority capital expenditures.

As the crisis manifested itself in increased unemployment and mounting social discontent, these programmes were revised and provisions for social protection, according to each country's particular need, were added. In Indonesia, for instance, the sharp depreciation of the currency implied delays (or a slower phasing out) in the adjustment of the administered prices and the removal of subsidies. Drought compounded the problem as the price of rice soared. Initially, price subsidies absorbed most of the safety net spending in Indonesia (about three quarters of it).

Indonesia's safety net programme evolved slowly. It includes, among other things, an increase in health expenditures for vulnerable groups, aid to students (such as grants and scholarships to support children enrolled in primary and junior high schools) to replace existing fees, microcredit, and public works' programmes. Additionally, there is distribution of rice at highly subsidized prices (about one third of the market prices) to needy families. The rice programme reached about 5.9 million by September 1998 and it has been expanded since then by including additional beneficiaries and increasing the size of their rations.

Notwithstanding the above, implementation of the safety net programme, particularly the job-creation, health and education components, has been slow in Indonesia. Because of delays due to targeting difficulties and the need to prevent leakage and corruption, Indonesia achieved a stronger-than-expected fiscal balance in 1998.[g]

The programme of the Republic of Korea, on the other hand, has a strong unemployment-insurance component. As the crisis developed, the Government increased the coverage, the duration and the minimum benefits of this scheme. It originally covered employees of firms with more than 30 workers, while as of April 1999 it extends to all firms, as well as to temporary and part-time workers.[h] Additionally, the programme of the Republic of Korea includes a public works component, increased social welfare spending (livelihood protection and cost-of-living subsidies), start-up loans to the unemployed, and job training.

While these and other programmes have mitigated some of the adverse social impacts of the crisis, they have been able to provide support to only a small proportion of those in need of assistance. This highlights the need to take a more comprehensive approach when economic reforms are considered. The introduction of social protection mechanisms is usually implemented only when a given developing economy is experiencing a severe recession. Relief often comes too late and benefits just a few. Social reforms should precede or at least accompany economic reforms so that formal safety nets may be already in place when most needed, thus averting unnecessary human suffering.

[g]   The overall budget deficit was estimated at about 4 per cent in fiscal year 1998/99, well below the deficit target of 8.5 per cent.

[h]   About 570,000 individuals will receive unemployment benefits in 1999 (see Letter of Intent of the Republic of Korea, 10 March 1999 (http://www.imf.org/external/np/loi/1999/031099.htm). Accessed on 26 March 1999.

Figure III.4.
SELECTED ASIAN COUNTRIES: LENDING RATES,
JANUARY 1997-MARCH 1999

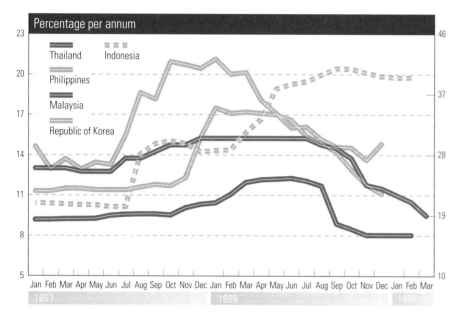

Source: IMF, *International Financial Statistics* (various issues).

Note: Indonesia on the right axis.

and supervision in the financial sector, the liberalization of the domestic economies, and the strengthening of social protection systems. These broadened structural initiatives aim at enhancing efficiency and transparency, deepening the role of the private sector, and reinforcing its outward orientation, thus strengthening the foundations for market-oriented and self-sustained growth.

A key objective is to free the financial and corporate sector from its heavy debt burden, particularly non-performing loans. The large indebtedness and the deterioration of debt structures were caused by both domestic and external factors. The accumulation of domestic debts resulted from the financing of investment through credit expansion and through financial inflows, rather than by raising equity, leading to unusually high debt-to-equity ratios. Lax supervision, inadequate prudential regulations and lack of accountability contributed to this outcome as well, especially since the capital account has been liberalized. Large bubbles and excess capacities built up. Many financial institutions and firms borrowed heavily abroad because of the interest-rate differential and because the exchange rate was assumed to be fixed. These loans were usually short-term and unhedged and were often invested in local currency loans in projects with a long gestation period and uncertain pay-off, such as for real estate developments in Indonesia, Malaysia and Thailand and excessive expansion of manufacturing capacity in the Republic of Korea.

Externally, massive capital inflows during this period were facilitated by the liberalization of the capital account and the deregulation of the domestic financial market during the past decade or so. These countries were encouraged to open their financial markets without adequate domestic institutional preparation and experience. The low rate of return in developed countries during this period also drove fund managers to seek higher returns elsewhere, and the Asian emerging economies offered an attractive opportunity. The high confidence in the Asian economies, given their remarkable economic performance, and the belief in the stable link of most Asian currencies to the United States dollar were also a factor.

Once the crisis was triggered, the almost simultaneous developments of capital outflows, currency depreciation, stock market collapse, liquidity squeeze, higher interest rates and cooled domestic demand led to a surge in non-performing loans, which in turn worsened the balance sheets of financial institutions. Banks became unable to extend new loans, or renew old ones, and firms found it increasingly difficult to obtain credit even for working capital and to repay their debts. The tightening of credit and the high return-rate policies are therefore a major factor behind the sharp contraction of domestic demand. Without addressing the origin of the credit crunch by including structural reforms in the financial and corporate sectors, the effectiveness of policy stimuli to boost domestic demand is compromised.

The Republic of Korea has advanced expeditiously with the restructuring and consolidation of financial institutions and corporations. Implementation of the first phase of restructuring—banking reconstruction, including the sale of two major local banks to foreign investors—has progressed well. Most of the 64 trillion won (about $45 billion) committed to bank recapitalization has already been disbursed. More recently, policy in the country has focused on the restructuring of the corporate sector. The central issue is the implementation of the broad agreement reached among conglomerates, domestic creditors and the Government at the end of 1998. It includes, among other things, the so-called Big Deals (asset swaps) and the establishment of joint ventures in eight industries among the five largest conglomerates (*chaebols*) so that they can concentrate on their core businesses, improve their corporate governance systems, reduce indebtedness and attract FDI. Practices such as cross-subsidies and credit guarantees among affiliates are no longer allowed. Smaller *chaebols* are also under pressure to restructure their liabilities and reduce their overall level of indebtedness. Given the complexity of the issues involved, there has been some delay in implementation, particularly in the semiconductor and automobile industries.

In the process of carrying out corporate restructuring and labour-market rationalization, a negotiation forum for the tripartite accord among business, labour and government was formed to open communication channels among the major actors concerned, so as to reduce the transitional burdens and to strengthen the social safety net. Additionally, the country has proceeded with the liberalization of the economy. On 1 April 1999, for example, the Government abolished all foreign exchange controls except for measures that aim to prevent currency speculation.

Thailand has also been pursuing financial sector reform and the restructuring of corporate debt. Progress on these fronts is advancing, albeit slowly.

Efforts to restructure bad debts (estimated at 44 per cent of all total commercial bank lending, which amounts to $64 billion, at the end of 1998) have been constrained by the lack of adequate legislation. In February 1999, however, the Thai Senate approved new bankruptcy and foreclosure laws. These are expected to enable banks to speed up the process of debt restructuring and to resume normal lending.

Indonesia, on the other hand, has been facing great difficulties in implementing financial restructuring and other structural reforms. The large external debt (estimated at about $80 billion) owed by private firms compounds the problem, as most of them, having stopped servicing their external debt, seek direct solutions with their creditors.

Indonesia established the Indonesian Debt Restructuring Agency (INDRA) in August 1998 to coordinate the negotiations between the private domestic debtors and foreign creditors. Nonetheless, debtors in the private sector were reluctant to participate in the debt-restructuring scheme and pressed for debt forgiveness, while foreign creditors demanded comparable treatment on the part of domestic creditors. Debt-restructuring negotiations between private lenders and Indonesian firms remained stalled, as neither the lenders nor the debtors would come forward to shoulder the large losses brought about by the depreciation of the roupiah. In March 1999, however, Indonesia closed down 38 banks and nationalized 7 more, thus paving the way for an envisaged $34 billion bank recapitalization (about 15 per cent of GDP).

In Malaysia, which was initially believed to have a relatively more resilient financial system, the sharp economic downturn created difficulties for the banking system as well. Although relatively small in comparison with the problem in the countries discussed above, there was the matter of non-performing loans (mainly property-related) which increased from 2.1 per cent of total loans at the end of June 1997 to 7.3 per cent by June 1998. Consequently, Malaysia established two agencies to restructure the financial system. On the one hand, *Danaharta* will purchase non-performing loans from financial institutions and manage some of the non-performing loans for the banks without outright purchase. On the other hand, *Danamodal*, a funding agency, will assist banks to meet their capital adequacy requirements. It will also facilitate the process of consolidation and mergers among financial institutions. The purchase of non-performing loans through *Danaharta* and the injection of liquidity through *Danamodal* are expected to ease the credit crunch in the banking sector. In February 1999, Malaysia also introduced new regulations to replace the 12-month ban on the repatriation of the proceeds of share sales by foreign investors imposed in September 1998. The new measures subjects the repatriation of principal and profits on portfolio investment to an exit tax.

Emerging from the crisis. GDP growth in the region is expected to recover slowly to about 2.5 per cent in 1999. With expansionary macroeconomic policy in place and slowly improving credit conditions, a modest upturn in the second half of 1999 is likely. A recovery in intraregional trade in response to the mild upturn in domestic demand and the need to replenish input stocks will also be conducive to a recovery. In most of these countries, both private consumption and investment are expected to exhibit modest growth, with public investment taking the lead. Fiscal policy emphasizes strengthening the social safety net, which will stimulate private consumption. Stabilized financial markets and increasing—albeit limited—foreign-capital inflows will help boost the supply of investor funds and overall demand. On the supply side, most industries will grow, except for those beset by large redundant capacity, such as construction. The recovery, however, is likely to be modest and considerably differentiated among countries. The Republic of Korea is expected to lead the recovery. In Indonesia, among the crisis-hit countries, growth recovery will be slower.

Policy stimuli, buoyancy in certain segments of the world electronics products market and an upturn in intraregional trade will be the main driving forces of growth in Hong Kong SAR, the Philippines and Singapore. In the case of the Philippines, the rebound in agricultural production following drought will play a major role in its modest recovery by the middle of 1999.

There are several downside risks to this outlook. First, the effectiveness of the policy measures to stimulate the domestic economy, particularly in crisis-hit countries, depends on the successful restructuring of the banking and corporate sectors and the resumption of normal bank lending. Reforms to tackle structural weaknesses in Indonesia and Thailand have not progressed as fast as policy makers had hoped. Difficult problems, such as huge adjustment costs, high unemployment and conflict of interest among major actors, remain to be overcome. Moreover, political uncertainties related to the coming elections in these countries could impede reforms. Even if the private debt overhang were reduced and credit conditions improved, the demand responses of private consumers to policy stimuli might remain below expectations owing to weak confidence, given high unemployment. In countries such as Singapore, where physical infrastructure is already in place and import leakage is large, the effectiveness of the measures adopted will be smaller than in other countries.

Foreign investors' behaviour represents another source of uncertainty. It is still not clear how much capital will return. As the economy recovers, financial markets remain stable and confidence in these economies is restored, there may be some increase in capital inflows.[40] However, massive inflows are unlikely for a while. Moreover, any further turmoil in the world financial markets, such as a major correction in United States financial markets or a new currency crisis, could be disastrous to the recovery in Asia.

Third, the export performance of these countries in 1999 is also somewhat uncertain. Despite the sharp depreciation, the strength of exports has lagged behind expectations. Exports will depend on four major factors: the rate of economic growth in developed countries, particularly the United States; the upturn of demand in the region; the exchange rate of the yen to the United States dollar; and developments in the world market for electronics. The implications of these factors differ among countries depending upon the composition of their exports and their major export markets. The sustainability of demand in the United States and other developed countries is particularly important. The favourable situation in semiconductors, if sustained, will benefit many exporters. On the other hand, over-reliance on one single product brings additional risks, such as increased vulnerability to the industry cycle in world markets.

[40] The sovereign credit rating for the Republic of Korea was recently raised to investment grade, while the risk premium has declined. Stock prices have also increased.

Fourth, the weakening of the yen is a concern for a number of countries, such as the Republic of Korea and Taiwan Province of China, both of which compete against Japan in many third markets. If the exchange rate of the yen to the dollar was to rise above 145, the impact on neighbouring countries would be serious, possibly entailing competitive devaluations. This in turn might set off another currency crisis.

Finally, the recovery of oil prices since the Organization of the Petroleum Exporting Countries (OPEC) agreement in March 1999, if sustained, can have serious implications for inflation and the balance of payments of vulnerable oil-importing countries.

Whereas many of the fundamentals underlying the former "Asian miracle" countries remain valid, a return of these countries to the pre-crisis high-growth path is not forecast in the near term. Owing to intensifying competition in the globalizing world, the promotion of fast export growth at favourable prices has become more difficult. With the entry of new large suppliers like China, world markets for cheap labour-intensive goods are increasingly subject to excess capacity. The more advanced countries in the region have fewer opportunities for growth. Productivity gains will increasingly have to come through indigenous technological change, as cheap unskilled labour is no longer abundant in these economies. Countries will have to upgrade or reorient their production base and trade structure towards high value-added, high-tech and knowledge-intensive products. This requires considerable efforts, including the development of human capital by encouraging highly trained managers, scientists and researchers, the development of more sophisticated core technology, and the establishment of a technology-intensive production base.

China

China's economic performance in 1998 was in marked contrast to that of many neighbouring countries. In spite of many unexpected difficulties, both exogenous and endogenous, GDP grew by 7.8 per cent in 1998,[41] close to the target of 8 per cent set at the beginning of the year. This was, however, China's lowest rate of growth since the early 1990s. The weakening of domestic demand due to the restructuring of State-owned enterprises (SOEs), a severe flood and the impact of the Asian economic crisis were the three major constraints on growth in 1998.

Domestic demand started to decelerate at the end of 1997, and this trend continued into the first half of 1998, owing largely to the restructuring of SOEs. The increasing number of lay-offs curbed growth of private consumption and uncertainties surrounding the State firms themselves reduced the growth of investment.

In order to reverse the downturn in domestic demand, China has applied a strong fiscal stimulus since mid-1998. Government spending on infrastructure has increased significantly, financed by bond issues of about 100 billion yuan (Y) ($12 billion) in 1998. Monetary policy has also been accommodative, with interest rates lowered by an average of 300 basis points in several stages during 1998. As a result, total fixed investment increased by 14 per cent in 1998, raising industrial production by about 9 per cent. Private consumption, however, grew by only 5 per cent in 1998. Lay-offs from the SOEs are still growing, although 6 million workers were re-employed in 1998. Weak consumer

41 Data and discussions of the performance in 1998 draw partly from China State Statistical Bureau, *Statistical Bulletin on China's Economic and Social Development in 1998* (Beijing, February 1999).

spending has led to a mild deflation in retail prices. Despite some direct intervention to control the slide in prices, the retail price index dropped by 2 per cent in 1998.

In the summer of 1998, one of the most severe floods devastated a large area of China, with the direct loss estimated to be equivalent to 2 per cent of GDP. Nevertheless, the agricultural sector grew moderately, with grain production of 490 million tons exceeding the annual average for the 1990s.

Surviving the contagion. More than one third of China's total exports used to go to Japan and the Asian crisis countries (see table III.3). These countries cut their imports dramatically, with the result that China's exports to Asia declined by 9 per cent in nominal terms in 1998. Exports to Japan, to the Republic of Korea and to the Association of Southeast Asian Nations (ASEAN) countries shrank by 7 per cent, 31 per cent and 14 per cent, respectively. The impact both on export revenue and on industrial production has been significant.

Other negative effects of the Asian crisis have not been very marked so far, but may unfold gradually in the future. For example, because China maintained its exchange rate to the United States dollar, the devaluations of many currencies during the crisis led to appreciation of the yuan vis-à-vis other currencies of the region. This would normally have caused a decline in the international competitiveness of China's exports and to a loss of market shares. China, however, was able to increase exports to most regions other than Asia in 1998.[42] Nonetheless, export earnings grew by only 0.5 per cent in 1998, in marked contrast to the 21 per cent increase observed in 1997 (table A.13). On the other hand, the value of imports fell by 1.5 per cent in 1998 because of sluggish domestic demand and, despite lower tariffs, the trade surplus reached $40 billion, about the same as in 1997, while the current-account surplus was $45 billion (3 per cent of GDP).

The effects on exports of the devaluations elsewhere have recently become more apparent in bilateral trade between China and the crisis-hit Asian economies. As a general measure to alleviate this problem, tax rebates on exports have been increased. Although the devalued currencies have rebounded and stabilized to some extent, China's exporters are now struggling to remain competitive. For example, increased competition from the Republic of Korea's iron and steel producers has created pressures on China's producers. These new competitive pressures partially explain why China's exports declined by about 8 per cent in nominal terms in the first quarter of 1999.

Contagion through financial channels has been relatively small. Total foreign capital inflows declined by about 8 per cent in 1998, owing to a drop in bank loans and portfolio investment. On the other hand, FDI, which accounts for 80 per cent of total foreign capital inflows, increased slightly to $45 billion. Declines in foreign capital inflows from the Asian region were largely offset by increased inflows from the United States and Europe.

The Asian crisis has also revealed some weaknesses in China's financial sector.[43] However, these are not a direct consequence of the Asian crisis because China's controls on capital flows limit the exposure of the domestic capital market to external forces. Nevertheless, the crisis has highlighted the need to strengthen China's domestic financial structure. In October 1998, for example, the closure of a heavily indebted provincial International Trust and Investment

42   In 1998, China increased its exports to the United States by 16 per cent, to Europe by 18 per cent, to Africa by 27 per cent and to Latin America by 16 per cent.

43   On China's financial sector developments, see chap. VI in part two of the present Survey.

Company (ITIC) caused concerns about the solvency of other ITICs (of which there are 239 in China). Moreover, concerns about the high level of non-performing loans of the State banks (estimated to range from 15 to 25 per cent of total loans) have prompted international rating agencies to downgrade a few State-owned banks to the lowest investment grade while the rating for ITICs has been lowered to below investment grade.

China's exchange-rate policy has been a core issue throughout the crisis. China has maintained an exchange rate of about 8.3 yuan per dollar since 1994. Speculation over a possible devaluation of the yuan emerged when other Asian countries devalued their currencies from mid-1997 onwards. This fear was rekindled at the beginning of 1999 when Brazil devalued the real (discussed below). The inconvertibility of the yuan and other capital controls have protected the currency from direct speculative attacks. They have also prevented the Chinese financial institutions from borrowing excessively abroad, thereby reducing the vulnerability of the currency to external forces.

At the present time, a devaluation of the yuan does not appear necesssary for policy reasons. China is running a sizeable current-account surplus and its foreign reserves reached $145 billion at the end of 1998, a slight increase over the previous year. The country has an external debt of $140 billion, of which 80 per cent is long-term. Given these sound fundamentals, a devaluation of the currency is not warranted. The only argument for devaluing at present is to stimulate exports in order to enhance overall economic growth. However, a devaluation of the yuan would increase uncertainties and produce negative shocks for other sectors of the economy, possibly offsetting the benefits to the export sector. Considerations have prompted policy makers in China to stimulate domestic demand, rather than bolster exports, in order to sustain economic growth. From a global point of view, this has the added advantage that it does not aggravate the existing global imbalances.

China has adopted many policy measures to prevent contagion from the Asian crisis, and these measures are expected to continue in the coming years. Several administrative measures have been adopted to prevent capital flight, to crack down on the black market for foreign exchange and to curb smuggling. Additional efforts have been made to improve prudential regulations and surveillance of the banking and the non-banking financial sectors. For instance, at the beginning of 1999, the Central Bank of China replaced its 30 provincial branches by 9 regional branches to make them more independent from local governments. A national securities law was also passed and will take effect in July 1999.

Growth challenges. The outlook for China is for GDP to grow by about 7.5 per cent, with economic policies continuing to focus on stimulating domestic demand. Reflecting a positive response to these policies, GDP grew by 8.3 per cent during the first quarter of 1999. The expansionary fiscal policy will continue. Although the government deficit will increase, it will remain below 2 per cent of GDP, while the ratio of public debt to GDP is expected to reach 10 per cent. Both ratios are modest by international standards, but there have been concerns about the strain on public finances because central government revenue amounts to only 12 per cent of GDP, owing to decentralization measures implemented over the past decade. Chinese monetary policy is also expected to remain accommodative. In order to stimulate consumer spending, consumer loans, which have been limited in the past, will be encouraged. While inflation is expected to remain low, unemployment, especially the lay-offs from SOEs, will continue to be a key policy concern.

The restructuring of SOEs will remain a major policy concern, albeit one beset with major internal uncertainties. With weakening domestic demand, the pace of some reforms has slowed.[44] Rapidly closing down loss-making SOEs would increase the already large number of unemployed and thus further depress demand and heighten the risk of social turmoil. The balance between economic efficiency and social stability poses difficult dilemmas for Chinese policy makers, but they are nonetheless expected to forge ahead with enterprise reform while at the same time enhancing the social safety net.

The gains in competitiveness by crisis-hit countries and slow overall external demand are expected to cause the value of Chinese exports to stagnate in 1999, before rebounding modestly in 2000. The trade surplus is forecast to decline to about $30 billion in 1999-2000, as further trade liberalization and the acceleration of domestic investment increase import demand. China is expected to continue its trade reforms. These include a further reduction of tariffs and additional liberalization of trade-related services in line with the country's persistent efforts to meet the criteria that will enable it to join the World Trade Organization.

Major external risks for China include a possible slowdown in foreign investment, which is an important source of finance for the dynamic non-State sector. A sudden large drop in foreign investment would exacerbate weak domestic demand and aggravate unemployment. This might lead policy makers to promoting exports more vigorously and it might then be necessary to use a devaluation of the yuan as a policy tool.

South Asia

The financial crisis had only a limited negative impact on South Asian countries. They have been shielded by their non-convertible currencies, low inflows of short-term private capital, limited trade openness and relatively small external commercial indebtedness. They did, however, experience some adverse consequences in the form of reduced competitiveness vis-à-vis the crisis countries, lower commodity prices, and weaker international demand. Although export revenues declined in most countries, GDP growth exceeded or was close to 5 per cent in 1998 in all countries of the region, except Nepal. Nepal's GDP grew at only 2.1 per cent in 1998, largely as a result of the effects of adverse weather conditions on agricultural output; in the other countries, growth was often supported by strong agricultural performance.

Some South Asian countries suffered additional exogenous shocks during 1998. Monsoon floods hit Bangladesh for about two months during the summer and caused damage to infrastructure and agriculture estimated at over $2 billion. The negative impact of the flood on GDP growth, however, will become evident in fiscal 1998/99 (July-June). During fiscal 1997/98, Bangladesh recorded strong growth with its industrial sector having expanded by 8.1 per cent.[45]

Several developed countries imposed economic sanctions on India and Pakistan, following their nuclear tests in May 1998. These sanctions involved

[44] Total profits from SOEs dropped by 17 per cent in 1998, while the total loss from the deficit SOEs increased by 22 per cent. Moreover, the recent government stimulus package has directed more investment spending into the less efficient State sector than into the more efficient non-State sector. Fixed investment in SOEs increased by 19 per cent in 1998, compared with the 14 per cent increase in total fixed investment.

[45] *Economic and Social Survey of Asia and the Pacific 1999* (United Nations publication, Sales No. E.99.II.F.10).

the suspension of loans to official agencies in these countries, the withdrawal of trade finance and official development assistance flows, as well as a moratorium on non-humanitarian loans by international financial organizations. Investors' confidence was negatively affected.

The impact of the sanctions was more severe in Pakistan than in India, given the former's dependence on official flows and its limited international reserves. The country's external problem was compounded by a decline in workers' remittances, an important source of foreign exchange. The foreign exchange constraint led to balance-of-payments difficulties, in spite of the severe import compression, and the accumulation of arrears on the servicing of its external debt. Sanctions were suspended towards the end of 1998 and the external constraints eased somewhat as a result.

Inflation accelerated in some countries of the region in 1998. In India, for instance, consumer prices rose by about 18 per cent late in the year owing largely to shortages of staple food and increases in certain administered prices. The fact, however, that inflation was quickly brought down and stabilized below 10 per cent in early 1999, allowed India to relax its monetary policy. Inflation also increased in Sri Lanka in 1998 owing to food shortages induced by bad weather.

In most of the South Asian countries, large fiscal deficits, usually above 5 per cent of GDP, have been a major factor underlying inflation in the region. Such deficits have also raised the debt-service burden. As a result, countries have been under pressure to pursue reforms, including the privatization of public enterprises. In India, for example, the central government deficit was estimated to have reached 6.5 per cent of GDP in fiscal 1998/99 (April-March), thus surpassing the target of 5.6 per cent. In Sri Lanka, the public deficit was about 8 per cent of GDP in 1998 despite fiscal consolidation efforts.

South Asia is expected to grow by 5.6 per cent in 1999, thus maintaining the growth performance exhibited in 1997. Whereas India and Nepal will witness a modest recovery, Bangladesh, Pakistan and Sri Lanka will slow down somewhat in 1999. With good crops and a relaxation of monetary policy, growth in India is expected to recover slightly this year. The 1999/2000 budget envisaging fiscal consolidation allowed the Reserve Bank of India to lower the cash reserve ratio (CRR) and interest rates recently. These measures are expected to boost the industrial output and to moderate the dampening effects on domestic demand from the fiscal side.

Pakistan's economic prospects in 1999 depend on the implementation of the programme agreed with IMF, which will constrain government spending. The tight fiscal situation, together with business pessimism and low FDI (given the low credit rating), will restrain investment and industrial output. Growth in Bangladesh, on the other hand, will be hampered by the negative lagged effects of the severe damage from the previous summer's monsoon flood and the subsequent long drought. As the rehabilitation progresses and the normal monsoon returns, recovery, particularly in construction and service sector, is expected in the next fiscal year.

Beyond 1999, barring adverse weather conditions and political disturbances, the economic performance in these countries may register a moderate improvement. Region-specific downside risks include a possible deterioration of the balance of payments in Pakistan due to the recent poor crops. Cotton production has suffered significant damage from adverse weather, which will negatively affect the textile industry and exports.

Western Asia

Economic growth in Western Asia, with some exceptions, is strongly influenced by the behaviour of oil prices in international markets. For all oil-exporting countries in the region, oil is the major export product and the most important source of government revenues. Additionally, government activity dominates investment and the generation of employment in these economies. The economics of oil also affects the oil-importing countries (less so Turkey and Israel) in the region owing to the importance of regional trade, financial and labour flows for their economies. In many instances, the benefits of lower oil prices are usually not sufficient to offset the negative impacts of lower exports to, and the decline in workers' remittances and in official flows originating from, the oil-exporting countries.

Other factors significant for economic growth in the region include the Middle East peace process and the situation of Iraq. A perception of increased political instability discourages flows of trade and investment. In 1998, weaker external demand for other exports and tight external financial conditions compounded the economic difficulties that these countries experienced as a result of plummeting oil prices.

The annual rate of growth of the region's GDP fell from 5.2 per cent in 1997 to 1.3 per cent in 1998 (table A.4). GDP contracted in 7 out of the 15 countries that make up the region, and the positive rate of growth for the region was largely due to the fact that Iraq's GDP, which generates about 8.5 per cent of the regional GDP, was estimated to have grown by 15 per cent. This was possible only because of the resumption of oil production within the framework of the United Nations oil-for-food programme. In more normal circumstances, Iraq might have been expected to record an economic performance similar to its neighbours, in which case the region's GDP would have contracted by 0.2 per cent in 1998.

Most countries of the region experienced a deterioration in their current-account balances. This is particularly true for the oil-exporting countries, although some, such as Kuwait, registered a surplus. Most oil-exporting countries financed their deficits by drawing upon their international reserves and foreign assets. The oil-importing countries benefited from lower prices for both oil and other commodities and their demand for imports was reduced by slower economic growth. Hence, these countries were able to improve their current-account balances in 1998.

Domestic demand declined in several oil-exporting countries. As investment expenditures were cut, multiplier effects led to a rapid deceleration of growth. In the Islamic Republic of Iran, for instance, austerity measures led to a contraction of 10 per cent in the construction sector, one of the main engines of growth in that country. Elsewhere, anaemic external demand constrained the growth of the manufacturing sector, in such areas as petrochemicals and aluminium. Unemployment increased, further weakening domestic demand. The plunge in oil prices and the economic slowdown in the region caused a deceleration in growth even in countries with more diversified economies, such as Bahrain and the United Arab Emirates.

Lower oil prices implied severe shortfalls in fiscal revenues. Public expenditures, including for defence, had to be curtailed. Public investment, particularly in infrastructure, took most of the brunt as new projects were frozen or postponed in several countries. On the other hand, reductions in current expenditures (basically wages) and in transfers (especially price subsidies) have been more difficult to implement. Such measures usually meet strong resistance. In Yemen, an increase in the prices of subsidized goods in June 1998 led to widespread rioting and attacks on the country's oil installations. The Government of Kuwait, on the other hand, proposed to create additional sources of fiscal revenue by raising existing fees and by introducing user charges to services previously provided for free. The National Assembly, however, has not endorsed these measures. Elsewhere, countries resorted to other alternative initiatives. Saudi Arabia, for instance, halted public sector hiring in May 1998. Some countries have also considered privatization as a means to raise additional finance. Qatar, for instance, partially privatized its telecommunication company. Nevertheless, progress in privatization remains slow in the region.

Given the lower oil prices and the difficulties of cutting public expenditures and of expanding the fiscal base, public sector balances deteriorated sharply in several countries. In Kuwait, the budget surplus of about 17 per cent of GDP in fiscal 1997/98 (July-June) is expected to turn into a deficit equivalent to 7 per cent of GDP in fiscal 1998/99. In Yemen, the public deficit rose from less than 1 per cent of GDP in 1997 to an estimated 6 per cent of GDP in 1998, while in Saudi Arabia and the Islamic Republic of Iran, the public deficit is expected to reach 8 per cent of GDP in fiscal year 1998/99. Most countries financed their budget deficits domestically through the issuance of government paper to the local banking system and government agencies such as those administering pension funds.

In Jordan, workers' remittances were estimated to have fallen during 1998, thus negatively affecting domestic consumption. Exports have been constrained by weaker international demand and by the political and economic difficulties in the region. In Lebanon, on the other hand, economic growth has been dominated by reconstruction efforts, and the country was able to record a positive, albeit modest, rate of GDP growth in 1998. Lebanon, however, had a public deficit estimated at 43 per cent of GDP by the end of 1998, one of the highest in the developing world.

Israel's growth rate declined in 1998 owing to the continuous erosion of consumer demand and the slump in the construction sector. Furthermore, the tourism industry was negatively affected by the uncertainties surrounding the Middle East peace accord. Exports continued to grow, albeit at a slower pace than in 1997, as the country was able to compensate for the lower exports of diamonds to Asian countries with a rise in exports of industrial goods to Europe and the United States. The boost in domestic consumption and in construction previously brought about by the large inflows of Russian immigrants has subsided with the decreasing number of immigrants. More important, private consumption and investment, as well as exports, have been constrained by the anti-inflationary policy.

Annual inflation in Israel declined from 10.2 per cent in January 1997 to 3 per cent in July 1998, as both nominal and real interest rates were kept high. Besides curtailing domestic demand, high interest rates increased the gap

46   Given the strong fundamentals of the Israeli economy, capital flows to the country are mainly determined by the monetary policy followed by the Central Bank. Contagion from the Russian crisis is not considered to have been a major factor underlying financial outflows that occurred after August. Lower interest rates, on the other hand, had a more significant impact on these flows.

between domestic and international interest rates. This attracted foreign capital, but it also led to an appreciation of the new sheqel. As a result, exports slowed, increasing the pressure on the Central Bank to review its monetary policy. Nominal interest rates were cut by 150 base points in August 1998, narrowing the interest-rate differential. Foreign capital left the country and the value of the currency fell against the dollar by about 16 per cent from the end of July to the end of October 1998.[46] Given the large ratio of imports to GDP (about 50 per cent), such a devaluation has an important inflationary effect on the economy. Monthly inflation rates quickly accelerated after August. Consequently, interest rates were raised again in October, thus further constraining domestic demand.

Economic growth in Turkey in 1998 was characterized by weak domestic demand, a fall in investment and lower exports. The economy slowed down during 1998, particularly after the Russian crisis. The manufacturing sector was affected by the collapse of the Russian market and by increased competition from Asian producers in both the domestic and the external markets. Preliminary data indicate that the deceleration of the economy intensified at the beginning of 1999.

The fact that interest rates were kept at very high levels and the financing of the domestic debt consumed much of the available credit contributed to a choking of economic activity in 1998. Higher interest rates also created additional difficulties for the management of public finances. Interest payments on public debt rose. The overall fiscal deficit relative to GDP widened from 7.3 to 7.7 per cent in 1998, despite sizeable privatization proceeds and a substantial improvement (about 3 per cent of GDP) in the primary surplus. The latter was the result of improved tax collection and the slowdown in government spending.

Unemployment is a major problem in Western Asia. Fast population growth and/or slowdown in economic growth have/has led to an increase in unemployment in most countries. In Israel, unemployment inched up slightly to 8.8 per cent in 1998. In Jordan, unemployment is estimated to be about 25 per cent and is an important factor underlying poverty in the country. In January 1999, the Jordanian Government launched the Social Productivity Programme, which aims at increasing the support for the poor, including the upgrading of infrastructure in poor urban and rural areas and the provision of gratis school meals. Against the background of increasing poverty, the school drop-out problem is a serious one in Jordan, as it compromises the Government's effort to upgrade the skills of the labour force and to enhance their earning opportunities.

In the oil-exporting countries, the unemployment problem is compounded by the limits in respect of hiring by the public sector, which have been renewed by weak conditions in oil markets. This has imparted additional urgency to the need to undertake structural reforms in these economies. Some countries have been trying to encourage greater involvement of domestic and foreign private investors as a means to accelerate growth and increase employment. Others have attempted, with limited success, to replace the relatively large expatriate labour force by their nationals. Nevertheless, if efforts persist and migrant workers are forced to return to their homes, the employment problem of the labour-exporting countries of the region (Jordan, Lebanon, the Syrian Arab Republic and Yemen) will mount.

Economic prospects for 1999. As mentioned, the region's economic growth depends to a large extent on the fortunes of the oil market. Whereas improved oil prices may bolster economic activity in the short run, provided the gain is not offset by volume cutbacks, the longer-term implications need to be borne in mind: improved oil prices may weaken policy makers' commitment to structural reforms. Overall international demand is forecast to be sluggish in 1999, and hence it will not be a relevant source of growth for the group as a whole.

If there is only a modest recovery of oil prices on average in 1999, prospects for the region are poor, with GDP growth rates in most oil-exporting countries expected to decline further. Fiscal consolidation, with further expenditure cuts and other measures aimed at diversifying government revenues, is expected to intensify and will constrain demand. While some oil-exporting countries accept that there is a need to streamline their welfare systems, fiscal deficits will nevertheless remain because the complete dismantling of subsidies—or the levying of new taxes—remains politically difficult. An acceleration in these countries' privatization programmes and increased borrowing might help to cushion, but would not offset, the impact of lower oil-tax revenues.

Current accounts are likely to remain under pressure, particularly for the oil-exporting countries. Additionally, other countries in the region have heavy external debt-servicing obligations to meet during the first half of 1999. Similarly, the decline in agricultural output in countries such as Jordan and the Islamic Republic of Iran because of drought in the beginning of 1999 may exert further pressure. The persistence of tight conditions in international financial markets and slow growth in external trade may pose additional difficulties. The external debt will continue to divert resources from productive uses. [47] Aid, soft loans and workers' remittances are also expected to decline in 1999.

[47] Jordan is the only country in the region that benefited from debt cancellation in 1998: around $300 million was written off by the United States and Western European and neighbouring countries.

Latin America and the Caribbean

Latin America was affected by severe shocks in 1998, economic and otherwise. The year started with the region's economies being still shaken by the contagion from the Asian crisis and the measures adopted to address it. As the year progressed, Latin American countries faced a continuous deterioration of commodity prices, sluggish demand and increased competition in their export markets, renewed speculative attacks on their currencies after the Russian crisis, capital outflows and scarce and expensive external finance. Economic difficulties persisted and intensified in early 1999 with the emergence of another, but now local, currency crisis—the crisis of the real in Brazil. Additionally, Latin America has been hit by a series of adverse natural phenomena ranging from floods to drought, hurricanes and earthquakes.

External vulnerability exposed. A significant slowdown spread over the region in 1998, thus exposing once again the region's external vulnerability, in terms of the reliance on foreign capital as a source of finance and the relevance of commodities for the generation of export revenues. The annual rate of growth of the regional GDP declined from 5.4 per cent in 1997 to 2.4 per cent in 1998. The deceleration was marked in the largest economies of the region, particularly those countries exposed to the volatility of short-term financial flows.

Monetary conditions had to be tightened throughout the region in the wake of the Russian crisis. The increased restrictions on credit and higher interest rates (see figure III.5) constrained domestic demand and overall GDP growth in Argentina, Brazil, Chile, Colombia, Ecuador, Mexico, Peru and Venezuela. Manufacturing output decelerated sharply in the last two quarters of 1998 (see table III.4), particularly in countries with a large manufacturing sector. Mexico was an exception: it sustained positive growth of manufacturing output through-out 1998, mostly due to the strong performance of the *maquila* (in-bond assembly) industry, which was supported by strong demand from the United States. Industrial output growth, however, decelerated abruptly towards the end of the year. Mexico's experience in 1998 indicates that its economic performance has become more associated with that of its NAFTA (North American Free Trade Agreement) partners than with the rest of Latin America.

In the oil-exporting economies, such as Colombia, Ecuador, Mexico and Venezuela, lower oil prices compounded the problem of declining domestic demand as the fiscal position deteriorated and austerity measures were adopted. By the end of 1998 and early 1999, Colombia, Ecuador and Venezuela were in severe recessions. These countries have also faced delicate domestic political situations, which have temporarily undermined investors' confidence in the stability and future prospects of their economies.

In Chile and Peru, lower metal prices and reduced imports by Asian countries negatively affected domestic disposable income and posed additional challenges to policy makers. Reduced export earnings and lower capital inflows led Chile and Colombia to revoke or ease measures aimed at discouraging short-term inflows. Chile suspended reserve requirements on capital inflows in September 1998 while Colombia reduced both the tax on inflows and the required minimum-holding period.

Economies with relatively insulated or incipient capital markets and/or strong trade links with the United States performed better, maintaining or even improving upon their 1997 performance. In the Caribbean region, for instance, most countries recorded moderate rates of growth, with output in the Dominican Republic and Trinidad and Tobago increasing at rates well above the regional average. Costa Rica had a particularly good year—growth of over 6 per cent—thanks to substantial foreign investment and a strong export performance. In Guyana and Jamaica, on the other hand, output contracted in 1998. Central American economies achieved moderate rates of growth in 1998.

Latin American countries have been adversely affected by weather conditions. El Niño's negative impact on the region began in 1997 and brought drought and floods in early 1998. It caused an estimated $15 billion in damage and production losses, half of which were in the Andean subregion. Agriculture was particularly affected. Vulnerability to natural disasters has become pertinent again in 1999, as a severe earthquake hit Colombia in the beginning of the year. The Caribbean and Central American countries were hit by hurricanes Georges and Mitch in late 1998. The winds and rains were among the worst experienced in the Caribbean region this century and resulted in severe and extensive damage to crops and infrastructure, particularly electricity and telecommunications facilities. There was also a significant loss of lives. In Honduras alone, nearly 6,000 people are believed to have died owing to hurricane Mitch. The destruction of residential buildings left hundreds of thousands of people homeless.

Figure III.5.
SELECTED LATIN AMERICAN COUNTRIES:
LENDING RATES, JANUARY 1997-MARCH 1999

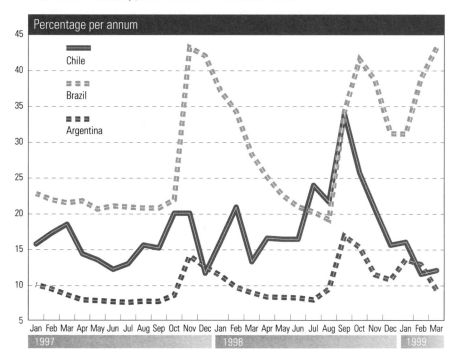

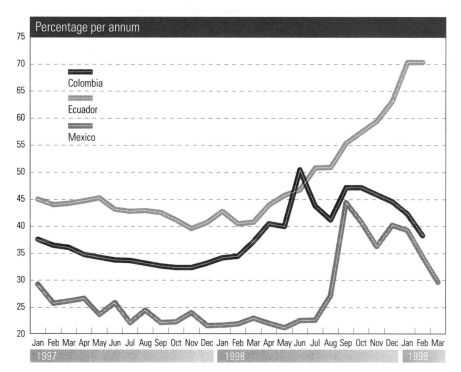

Source: IMF, *International Financial Statistics* (various issues).

Table III.4.
SELECTED LATIN AMERICAN COUNTRIES: GDP AND
MANUFACTURING QUARTERLY RATES OF GROWTH, 1998

Annual percentage change				
	Quarter			
	I	II	III	IV
Argentina				
GDP	7.2	7.4	3.2	-0.5
Manufacturing	8.8	8.1	2.4	-1.7
Brazil				
GDP	1.1	1.6	-0.1	-1.9
Manufacturing	1.7	1.0	-1.9	-4.5
Chile				
GDP	8.0	5.9	2.9	-2.8
Manufacturing	2.6	-2.4	0.4	-6.4
Mexico				
GDP	7.5	4.4	5.0	2.6
Manufacturing	12.7	6.1	7.1	4.2

Source: UN/DESA, based on international and national sources.

Most Latin American economies have been facing a deterioration of their fiscal positions, due to lower economic growth, increased spending on interest payments and lower commodity prices. In such countries as Brazil, Ecuador and Venezuela, fiscal deficits exceeded 5 per cent of GDP by the end of 1998. Fiscal policy in the region has been tightened. Argentina, Brazil, Colombia and Venezuela raised taxes and improved their tax collection systems. Countries have also made adjustments on the expenditure side by reducing spending on infrastructure and other investment outlays. These efforts failed to improve the fiscal balance, however, as they were offset by higher interest payments. Moreover, austerity measures are not always easily implemented and entail considerable costs for all involved. In Jamaica, for example, policy makers attempted to boost fiscal revenues by sharply increasing the consumption tax on petroleum products and the user fees for a variety of government services. The increases were met with violent street demonstrations and riots in April 1999, resulting in nine deaths. This prompted the Jamaican authorities to scale back the tax increases.

Monetary policies have also been restrictive. In many countries in the region, there was slower or even negative growth of real money supply in 1998 and, as mentioned earlier, interest rates were raised in several countries. The tight monetary policies and worldwide deflationary pressures caused the average regional inflation rate to fall from 11.7 per cent in 1997 to 9.0 per cent in 1998 (see table A.10). Ecuador was one of the few countries where inflation increased in 1998.

High interest rates curbed demand and controlled inflationary pressures, but they also weakened financial sectors in some countries by causing the volume of non-performing loans to increase, undermining the quality of bank assets.

Ecuador faced severe banking difficulties in the beginning of 1999 (see below). Most Latin American banks, however, have shown resilience in the face of the recent financial crises, mainly owing to the prior implementation of structural reforms in the sector and improvements in regulatory frameworks, particularly after the Mexican crisis in early 1995. Nevertheless, the share of non-performing loans has been increasing in several countries.

Open unemployment rates have remained high in Latin America, despite faster growth in the earlier 1990s. In several countries, trade liberalization and restructuring of the domestic economy have contributed to the lowering of demand for labour by the modern sectors, particularly manufacturing. Mexico is one exception to this trend, as employment in manufacturing has grown. However, such growth has taken place mostly in the *maquila* sector; employment in industries catering to the domestic market has declined.[48] Additionally, most of the new jobs created in the region are in low-productivity and non-tradable sectors and increasingly outside the protection of formal social security programmes. On the supply side, the Latin American labour force is expanding at over 3 per cent per year because of the region's young population and increasing female participation in the labour market. Several countries (Argentina, Barbados, Colombia, Jamaica, Nicaragua, Panama and Venezuela, among others) registered open urban unemployment rates well above 10 per cent in 1998.

The external balance deteriorated in most countries in 1998. The region's current-account deficit widened to 4 per cent of GDP, up from 3 per cent in 1997. Official financial inflows to the region increased through support provided by the international financial institutions and bilateral sources (see chap. II). In contrast, net private flows dropped in 1998, and may decline even further in 1999. FDI, however, has been relatively stable and even increased in some countries, such as Brazil, owing to large privatizations. Portfolio investment and bank loans, on the other hand, experienced sizeable declines. Because of the net reduction in capital inflows, several countries, notably Brazil, Chile and Venezuela, had to draw on their international reserves in order to finance their current-account deficits.

The Brazilian currency crisis and financial contagion. The "peg" of the Brazilian currency (the real) to the dollar under the 1994 Real Plan had successfully been used as an "anchor" to eliminate Brazil's hyperinflation: annual inflation fell from almost 2,200 per cent in 1993 to about 6 per cent in 1997.[49] Nevertheless, because of the inflation differential between Brazil and its main trade partners, the real became overvalued. This in turn hurt exports, because it exposed the tradable sector to additional foreign competition amid increased trade liberalization. As a result, Brazil's trade balance changed from a surplus of $13.3 billion in 1993 to a deficit of $8.6 billion in 1997. In 1998, the deficit decreased (to about $6.4 billion) but this was not enough to reduce the current-account deficit, which reached 4.5 per cent of GDP.[50]

Devaluation pressures escalated with the emergence of the Asian crisis in the summer of 1997 and were renewed with the Russian crisis in August 1998. In addition to the current-account deficit, Brazil registered large and increasing fiscal deficits, even though the Government had been struggling to keep public

[48] Employment in the *maquila* (in-bond assembly) sector increased by 90 per cent during 1994-1998, while the number of employees by the rest of the manufacturing sector declined by 2.7 per cent. Employment in the *maquila* sector expanded even during the economic recession following the devaluation of the peso in December 1994 (see Instituto Nacional de Estadística, Geografía e Informática (http://www.inegi.mx)).

[49] December-to-December inflation. On the Real Plan, see *World Economic and Social Survey 1995* (United Nations publication, Sales No. E.95.II.C.1), Chap. V, subsect. entitled "Brazil's innovative attack on inflation".

[50] Instituto de Pesquisa Economica Aplicada (IPEA) *Boletim Conjuntural Trimestral, No. 45* (April 1999).

finances under control in order to sustain the success on the inflation front. On the revenue side, there had been increasing dependence on extraordinary revenues, such as the tax on financial operations and the proceeds from the privatization of public utilities. On the expenditure side, proposals for reforming the social security system and the civil service had met strong opposition and had to be scaled down. Costly banking rescues and the restructuring of the debt that local governments owed to the central Government raised the public debt. The cost of servicing this debt rose because the Government was required to increase interest rates to prohibitive levels in order to defend the exchange rate, the anchor of the stabilization plan, against speculative attacks. The fiscal deficit and the public sector borrowing requirement increased sharply as a result (see figure III.6).

In November 1998, Brazil finalized an agreement with IMF and several other multilateral and bilateral lenders to provide $41.5 billion in financial assistance. The agreement included a three-year programme of economic measures to be taken by Brazil that combined a fiscal adjustment of over 3 per cent of GDP with reforms of the public sector and changes in fiscal policy. The overall programme aimed at supporting the exchange rate, while safeguarding international reserves, which had fallen to $39 billion from $72 billion in April 1998.

The programme, however, did not restore market confidence. Among other things, it faced strong domestic political opposition, which blocked implementation of several of the measures envisaged. In January 1999, the decision of the State Governor of Minas Gerais to suspend payment for 90 days on debt owed

Figure III.6.
BRAZIL: PUBLIC SECTOR BORROWING REQUIREMENTS,
DECEMBER 1996-FEBRUARY 1999

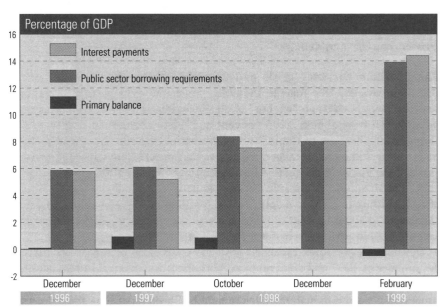

Source: Instituto de Pesquisa Econômica (IPEA), *Boletim Conjuntural Trimestral* No. 45 (April 1999).

Note: Negative values represent a surplus.

to the federal Government further eroded confidence. Initially, the Central Bank attempted to defend the country's international reserves and keep its foreign exchange policy by widening the real's band. The new band implied a devaluation of the real by about 8 per cent. The band could not be held, however, as capital continued to flee the country, depleting international reserves even further. Therefore, the Central Bank let the real float freely on 15 January 1999. By the end of that month, the real had fallen by more than 70 per cent relative to the dollar, although it has recovered since (see figure III.7).

A revised programme envisaging further fiscal adjustments was negotiated with IMF to take into account the change in foreign exchange policy. Monetary policy was made extremely restrictive with interest rates raised as high as 45 per cent. The objective was not only to stabilize the currency, but also to curb domestic demand and minimize price increases.

Given the country's past record of high inflation, there was great concern that the abandonment of the exchange-rate anchor against inflation, reinforced by the magnitude of the devaluation, would unleash an inflationary spiral. In the event, inflation accelerated sharply in February, but receded quickly thereafter. One reason why inflationary pressures could be contained was that Brazil entered the crisis while already in recession. This reduced pressure on prices in general but, in particular, labour was extremely cautious in its demands for higher wages because of the increase in unemployment during the past few years. As inflation declined, the monetary authorities could reduce the high interest rates, which were compromising the fiscal adjustment. With the sharp devaluation of the real and the interest-rate hike, public spending on interest

Figure III.7.
SELECTED LATIN AMERICAN COUNTRIES: REAL EFFECTIVE
EXCHANGE RATES, JUNE 1997-APRIL 1999

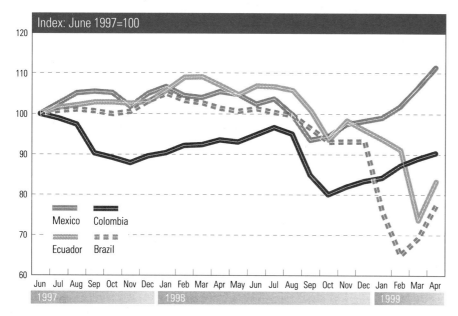

Source: Morgan Guaranty Trust Company, *World Financial Markets.*

payments shot up from about 8 per cent of GDP in December 1998 to over 14 per cent of GDP in February 1999 (see figure III.6).

These events highlighted the fact that the policy instruments available to the Brazilian authorities were limited. Any further devaluation of the currency could lead to inflation, which all concerned were anxious to avoid. International reserves are limited and cannot be used indefinitely to sustain the currency. Monetary tools (namely, higher interest rates) can be used to temporarily control or decelerate the fall of the currency. However, this has negative implications for the fiscal balance because of the increase of interest payments on the domestic debt. A deterioration of the fiscal position, in turn, may renew pressures on the exchange rate, possibly triggering a new round of interest-rate hikes and setting in motion a vicious circle.

The real crisis shows the limits of stabilization efforts based on a fixed or pegged exchange-rate regime within a framework of liberalized capital flows. There is usually an inflation differential between an adjusting country and its trade partners, particularly when inflation in the former is still converging to—but has not yet reached—the latter's levels. The currency therefore becomes overvalued. The peg can be maintained, however, if productivity increases and the country remains competitive in international markets, or if the country is able to keep foreign capital flowing into the economy. Nonetheless, there comes a crucial moment in the stabilization effort when the peg needs to be revised and the currency devalued because high interest rates—the typical answer to devaluation pressures—alone cannot sustain a given exchange rate indefinitely. Countries usually delay abandoning the peg until it is too late for an orderly devaluation to occur. Eventually, reserves having been depleted, a devaluation far larger than necessary, given fundamentals, is imposed upon the country, throwing the economy into disarray.

Contagion effects of the Brazilian crisis. The immediate impact of the Brazilian crisis on the external financial conditions of the region has so far been less severe than the corresponding spillovers from the Asian and Russian crises. However, as in these two previous cases, it is too early for the impact on the real sector to have been fully felt.

The devaluation of the real exposed the vulnerability of the Ecuadorian currency, the sucre, which had arisen because of lower oil prices and the adverse consequences of El Niño. Oil exports provide about 40 per cent of government revenue and the fiscal deficit increased to 5.9 per cent of GDP in 1998 as a consequence of the price collapse. Meanwhile, the current-account balance widened to 9.6 per cent of GDP. The sucre had been under devaluation pressure even before the emergence of the crisis with the real and, even though interest rates were raised as high as 180 per cent, the exchange rate could no longer be maintained. Accordingly, Ecuador abandoned its four-year-old crawling-peg exchange-rate band in February 1999 and allowed the sucre to float freely. Within a month, the sucre lost 40 per cent of its value against the United States dollar. In order to avoid a run on banks, the Government shut down the country's banks for a week in March, froze access to most deposits, and declared a state of national emergency.

The impact of the Brazilian crisis on the availability and cost of external finance for the countries in the region over the medium term is unclear. The Asian and the Russian financial crises dramatically increased the cost of external financing for all Latin American economies, as international investors indiscriminately raised their risk premiums on borrowing by developing countries in general. For Latin America, the yield spreads between the region's sovereign debt and the United States Treasury bonds were pushed up from a range of 5 to 7 percentage points to a range of 15 to 20 percentage points by the Russian crisis in August 1998. Spreads then declined until the Brazilian devaluation, when they rose again.

Historically, risk premiums have been highly correlated across Latin American countries, but the pattern of these spreads since the Brazilian crisis suggests a change in the way international investors assess the risks for emerging markets. The movement of the spreads after the Brazilian crisis shows that international investors are now more likely to take into account macroeconomic fundamentals and other relevant factors and to differentiate among countries in setting risk premiums. The spreads for Argentina, Chile and Mexico since the Russian crisis, for example, have been much smaller and less volatile than that of Brazil.

Additionally, countries that had access to international capital markets before the Brazilian crisis were able to return to those markets quickly. Within days of the Brazilian devaluation, Argentina and Mexico, for instance, were able to raise more than $1 billion in sovereign issues in international capital markets. After the 1994 Mexican crisis, it was more than four months before international investors bought any Latin American debt instrument and, after the Asian and the Russian crises, about two months. Even these outcomes were considered remarkable at the time, since it had taken years after the debt crisis of the early 1980s for any Latin American country to have access to international capital markets. Following the devaluation of the real, Brazil was able to return to the market—albeit at the high cost of paying 6.75 percentage points over comparable United States treasury bills in April—just three months after the crisis.[51]

Overall, international financial markets have recovered from the Brazilian crisis with unprecedented speed. Nevertheless, external borrowing for Latin American economies is still constrained compared with 1996 and early 1997, and it is expected that foreign investors will remain cautious in 1999. Moreover, as the Asian economies recover, Latin American countries will face strong competition from Asia in raising external funds.[52]

Outlook for 1999: recovery challenges. Despite some notable signs of improvement in the region's financial markets and in some commodity prices, the downward adjustments in the real sector of many economies, which started in 1998, will continue. Several countries are expected to register a recession or no growth in GDP for 1999.

One reason for this is that fiscal policies will continue to remain tight in an effort to correct fiscal imbalances. In Brazil, for example, the revised programme with IMF calls for the primary budget surplus to be raised by an additional 0.5 per cent of GDP per year between 1999 and 2001. This is to be attained mainly through expenditure cuts, whereas further tax increases are likely in such countries as Colombia, Ecuador and Venezuela.

[51] Latin America's bond issues reached $9.2 billion during the first quarter of 1999, well above the $3.7 billion issued during the last quarter of 1998 and equivalent to the amount issued a year earlier (*Financial Times*, 14 May 1994, p. III).

[52] For example, Mexico's spread was about 260 basis points above Thailand's, which was 209 in mid-May 1999.

Monetary policy is likely to continue to be restrictive in some countries, whereas an easing of policy has recently been implemented in others, especially those countries with stronger fiscal positions. Such countries as Argentina, Chile, Colombia and Mexico have begun to cut interest rates substantially. Even Brazil has been able to reduce interest rates although they remain high in real terms.

Brazilian economic performance is central to the region's economic outcome in 1999, as the country accounts for about 40 per cent of the region's GDP. If the Government applies fiscal austerity and high interest rates, Brazil's GDP is likely to contract in 1999.[53] The planned fiscal spending cut will lead to a decline in public consumption, and fixed investment will also decline because of external-financing constraints, tight monetary policy and unused capacity. With the depressed domestic demand and the devaluation of the currency, Brazilian import demand is likely to drop, transmitting a negative shock to the region.

However, these regional spillover effects are expected to be limited to a few economies—those, particularly its Southern Cone Common Market (MERCOSUR) partners, that have strong direct trade links with Brazil. Argentina is a case in point, as Brazil absorbs about 30 per cent of its total exports. The Brazilian crisis and weakened domestic demand, due to credit tightening and high unemployment, will cause Argentina to have a mild recession in 1999. Paraguay and Uruguay have strong trade links with both Argentina and Brazil (see table III.5) and will be negatively affected by the economic difficulties in these countries. The direct effects of the Brazilian crisis on other Latin American economies will be less significant, except for those countries that compete with Brazil in international markets where the devaluation of the real will allow Brazilian producers to cut prices.

The outlook for several other Latin American countries does not give cause for optimism. Prospects for most oil-exporting countries in the region are not encouraging. Lower oil prices sent the Venezuelan economy into a mild recession in 1998 and this is expected to deepen in 1999. Economic difficulties will continue in Ecuador owing to austerity measures introduced in the aftermath of the devaluation of the sucre.

In contrast, in the absence of any major natural disaster, economic prospects for the Caribbean region are expected to improve in 1999. Results for the first

[53] Brazilian GDP increased by 1 per cent in the first quarter of 1999 because the agricultural sector grew by almost 18 per cent in relation to the last quarter of 1998. This performance is unlikely to be sustained and both manufacturing and services remain depressed.

Table III.5.

SOUTHERN CONE COMMON MARKET (MERCOSUR): PERCENTAGE SHARE OF INTRAREGIONAL EXPORTS IN TOTAL EXPORTS, AVERAGE 1995-1997

| | To | | | | |
	Argentina	Brazil	Paraguay	Uruguay	Total[a]
From					
Argentina	-	28.3	2.5	2.9	33.6
Brazil	11.2	-	2.7	1.7	15.6
Paraguay	10.6	43.4	-	2.9	59.9
Uruguay	12.3	34.1	1.9	-	48.3

Source: IMF, *Direction of Trade Statistics* (various issues).

[a] Totals may not add up due to rounding.

quarter of 1999 indicate that agricultural production throughout the region improved, most notably in Cuba, where sugar production has recovered owing to better weather conditions. Strong growth in the United States will benefit the region by supporting export growth and the tourism industry in these countries. Similarly, Mexico and the economies in Central America will perform better than the South American countries. Honduras, however, is an exception because of the devastation of its economy by hurricane Mitch.

The slowdown of economic growth in the region is likely to impose a toll on employment. Such an outcome is already visible in some countries. In Brazil, for instance, the open unemployment rate for the six major metropolitan areas increased from about 7 per cent in November 1998 to 8.15 per cent in March 1999. In the metropolitan region of São Paulo, the largest in Brazil, open urban unemployment reached 12.9 per cent in March 1999 and total urban unemployment—that is, including hidden unemployment—was 19.9 per cent. Similarly, open unemployment in Colombia's seven largest cities increased to 19.5 per cent in March 1999 from 14.4 per cent a year previously. Despite these increases in unemployment, several countries are attempting to offset the lower fiscal revenues brought about by the economic slowdown by reducing expenditures. Social spending is likely to decline. Increased unemployment and lower earnings, on the one hand, and reduced government expenditures in social sectors, on the other hand, will combine to lower living standards for many in the region and will reverse some of the recent reductions in poverty.[54]

Finally, domestic saving rates in most Latin American economies remain low and the region's growth depends heavily on external financing. Unless this dependency is reduced, many economies in the region will remain vulnerable to the volatility of capital markets and related external shocks.

[54] The percentage of households living in poverty in the region declined from 41 per cent in 1990 to 36 per cent in 1997, mirroring the acceleration of growth the region experienced during this period (*Panorama Social de América Latina 1999* (United Nations publication, Sales No. S.99.II.G.4)).

PART TWO | # FINANCIAL DEVELOPMENT IN THE GLOBALIZING WORLD

IV   FINANCIAL ACTIVITY AND DEVELOPMENT IN A GLOBALIZING WORLD

In recent years, in one developing or transition economy after another, financial systems seemed suddenly to fail. Instead of smoothly funding production, trade and investment, they became channels of financial instability. Something changed in the financial sectors. Was it financial liberalization? Was it technology? Were the weaknesses always there, hidden below the surface? Or were they new? Were financial systems putting funds in the hands that warranted them? Or just financing the well connected?

Some of these concerns are long-standing ones. But their salience was underlined by the unfolding crises of the banks and the frenzied instability in the currency and financial markets in several emerging economies. Distinct weaknesses in the financial systems of several countries in Latin America had been accentuated by the Mexican peso crisis of 1994-1995, and in East Asia by the crisis that began in Thailand in 1997 and spread to other countries in 1997 and 1998. In the transition economies, reform of the financial sector had been high in the agenda since the beginning of the transition period in the early 1990s. However, the crisis that erupted in the Russian Federation in August 1998 highlighted the fact that many financial sector shortcomings remained to be addressed. The unexpected repercussions in September and October 1998 in financial and currency markets of developed countries then showed that there were important reform issues even in those countries. And observers noted that, in Africa, countries were spared contagion owing not to the strength of their financial sectors but to a kind of financial marginalization which was part and parcel of the underdeveloped state of most African financial systems.

When financial crises occur, they wreak extensive damage. On average, they take over three years to overcome and cause an economic loss of over 10 per cent of gross domestic product (GDP).[1] Their fiscal impact can be especially severe; for example, the fiscal cost of the banking crisis in Chile in 1981-1985 was 41 per cent of GDP.[2] While this was an extreme case, even in the United States of America, the savings and loan crisis of 1984-1991 raised fiscal expenditures by 7 per cent of GDP. The current financial crises in Japan and in the emerging economies of East Asia are also going to be very costly.[3]

These crises are messengers that have directed attention to the evolution of the financial system. And thus it has been realized increasingly that the policy and technology changes, which are often called "globalization" for short, have been revolutionizing domestic financial sectors and their international linkages. The changes have gone furthest in developed economies,

---

[1] Based on "currency and banking" or "banking" crises of 86 developed and emerging market economies; cost defined as difference between trend and actual gross domestic product (GDP) from the onset of crisis until the return to the trend growth rate (see International Monetary Fund, *World Economic Outlook* (Washington, D.C., May 1998), p. 79).

[2] *World Economic Outlook...*, p. 78.

[3] Although comprehensive estimates of fiscal cost are unavailable, it has been estimated that $90 billion in "bad loans" had yet to be dealt with in early 1999 in the three worst-affected Asian emerging markets, representing 26 per cent of GDP in Indonesia, 19 per cent of GDP in Thailand and 17 per cent of GDP in the Republic of Korea; this was a considerable improvement, however, over the earlier peak level of bad debt, which had totalled $279 billion for these three countries taken together (data of Warburg Dillon Read, New York, April 1999). There are varying estimates of the amount of bad loans in Japanese banks, but the Government in October 1998 approved 60 trillion yen (¥) (about $500 billion) for a new bank safety net, of which ¥25 trillion was for the recapitalization of "healthy banks".

but the developing and transition economies are also feeling their effects. The result is that the strengthening and reform of the financial sector have taken on new urgency in developed, developing and transition economies. So, too, have strengthening and reform of mechanisms for international cooperation in oversight of financial institutions and markets. At the same time, reflecting the greater international attention given to social dimensions of development, questions of equity and development in the financial system are rising in visibility next to the questions of stability.

Much of the discussion of financial evolution and reform is highly technical; but as there are important developmental implications of the work, it is important to gain a perspective on how financial systems work, the directions of their change and how the weaknesses and biases can be reduced. The aim of the present part of this *Survey* is to contribute to such an effort.

Because the financial sector has changed so dramatically in recent years, the next section outlines the main institutions and functions of a contemporary financial sector as it may be found in some large developed economies. Financial sectors in other countries, especially developing and transition economies, may have some elements of the financial sector described below, and in the future they will have more of them. Ensuing chapters discuss some of the institutions and markets and related policy concerns in more detail.

CHARACTERISTICS OF A MODERN FINANCIAL SECTOR

The financial sector has always been an unusual industry in a number of respects. First, a special feature characterizes many of its transactions. In a typical business, when a purchase is made, a good or service changes hands and money is exchanged in the opposite direction. When a comparable transaction takes place in the financial sector, money is transferred and the provider of the money receives either an ownership share or a promise to repay borrowed funds plus interest. Only the recipient of the funds knows what he really intends to do with them and therefore the provider has to monitor the user. This difference between what the two sides of a financial contract know creates the "asymmetric information" problem and various methods have arisen for coping with it.

A second unusual feature of the financial sector—one that in part grows out of the first—is that it is under a high degree of government oversight because the sector is susceptible to catastrophic failure and abuses of the public trust. The commercial banking sector, in particular, is heavily regulated by the government. Other parts of the financial sector are also subject to varying degrees of official oversight. In addition, the central bank engages in financial interactions with the commercial banks, adding and subtracting liquidity to control the money supply and making sudden infusions of liquidity in crisis situations.

A third characteristic of the financial sector is that it comprises a collection of very different institutions and markets. Some evaluate clients and make loans to them, others buy the loans and turn them into securities, and still others create contracts that mimic securities with no paper changing hands. Ultimately, the diversity of the financial sector arises because it intermediates between suppliers and users of financial resources and there are multiple ways in which this can be done.[4]

[4] While comprising a complicated set of institutions, the financial sector is usually not a large source of employment. In the United States of America in 1997, for example, the finance and insurance sector accounted for 8 per cent of GDP, while providing only 4 per cent of employment (see United States Department of Commerce, *Survey of Current Business*, February 1999, pp. D-28 and D-32).

Commercial banks and the dual financial function

Commercial banks are the core of every financial system. They supply the largest part of the means of payment of a monetized economy and operate the payments system. Sometimes joined by other financial institutions, commercial banks make available demand deposits to firms and households, and through their interbank networks—with some transactions passing through the central bank—they clear the payments transactions that are carried out with cheques or other methods of payment.[5]

While operation of the payments system is a key activity of banking, it is not traditionally the main source of income of banks. That arises from financial intermediation: funds that firms and households hold as deposits in their bank accounts are lent out to other firms or households as bank loans. The main income for the bank is the difference between the interest it pays its depositors and the interest it charges on its loans. Through most of the modern industrialized period, banks' main operation was this transformation of deposits into loans. However, this is one of the functions that has been changing dramatically (see chap. V).

Banking has been a viable business because a bank takes in the deposits of many depositors and lends to many borrowers. Lending takes the form of creating a deposit or adding to the account of a borrower. In the process, banks create most of an economy's money supply. If for no other reason, this brings them under government supervision and control.

To the extent that deposits are in the form of chequing accounts against which customers can write cheques at any time or from which they can make cash withdrawals on demand, the bank needs to have a large number of depositors so as to reduce the probability that a large part of its deposits will be withdrawn at one time. By the same token, in order to reduce the potential impact on the bank of a default by any single borrower, it needs to have a large portfolio of borrowers, which diversifies the risk.

This also means that banks have to be of a certain minimum size to be viable, and thus small markets might be able to support only one bank. In this case, the bank would be a "natural monopoly"; that is to say, left to itself and facing no competitors, the bank might maintain an excessively high margin between the borrowers' and depositors' interest rates. As a result, Governments have intervened in various ways. They decided that the interest rates on loans and deposits needed to be regulated or that the bank could be run as a State enterprise or that the Government could seek to introduce competition from other financial intermediaries. Each has happened, although under current policy approaches, the first two types of response would now be less common. Moreover, technical change and financial sector liberalization have made small markets more contestable.

Financial sector allocation of funds

The basic activity of a financial sector is to move funds from those who have more than they need to those who need more than they have and can pay for the use of the funds. There is, as already noted, a diverse set of institutions and markets that carry out this function. The role of some of the institutions is changing, as technology, policy and competitive forces evolve.

[5] The interbank network also makes direct transfers between banks. In addition, already in some countries—and this will be increasingly the case in the future—electronic funds transfers partially substitute for the physical movement of paper cheques.

Banks and other deposit-taking institutions

Because most deposits at commercial banks can be cashed on demand, commercial banks tend to specialize in short-term credits, such as working capital to finance a firm's operating costs or commercial credits to help firms while they wait to collect on their accounts receivable or loans to cover the expense of carrying inventories. Commercial banks typically also lend short-term to other banks to cover their temporary funding needs and to the government, through, for example, the purchase of treasury bills that are issued to allow smooth public expenditure operations when tax revenues follow, say, quarterly cycles.

Banks also engage in some medium-term lending.[6] They can do this, first, because banks take in some funds that are less liquid than demand deposits (such as six-month or even multi-year certificates of deposit); and second, because most holders of demand deposits will roughly maintain the size of their account balances, regularly replenishing deposits after they are drawn down. Thus, the bank can count on having a certain stock of funds on deposit and can safely tie up some of its funds in less-than-liquid uses.

Loan officers are expected to assess credit applications and the borrower's repayment capacity and to form a judgement about the planned use of the funds. Larger loans are generally extended to clients with which banks have a continuing business relation and whose management ability is known personally to the bank officers.

The essence of a commercial bank's relationship with its client is trust and monitoring: trust that the borrowed funds will be used for the intended purposes and will be repaid on schedule, as contracted; and monitoring to ensure that this happens. The distinguishing feature of traditional bank lending is the presence of imponderables (such as the outcome of a planned marketing campaign, smoothness of future labour-management relations or prices to be received for goods sold) which in the end make the loan decision rest on the banker's judgement. The borrower has to be trusted to carry out the contract, although the trust is limited.[7]

The bank thus demands transparency and reliability in respect of the information provided to it by the client and monitors the borrower's use of the loan. The bank also demands collateral as security for its loans.[8] Collateral reduces the bank's net exposure to the borrower and thus its risk, although realizing the collateral in the event of default can be expensive and time-consuming. And, as Japanese banks discovered in recent years, what appears to be prime collateral, such as high-priced real estate, can turn out to be very poor collateral for defaulted loans after a real estate bubble collapses.

Commercial banks are not the only "financial intermediaries", that is to say, the only deposit-taking and lending institutions. In many countries, other institutions offer time deposits, including "savings accounts" in which withdrawals may be formally subject to a 30-day delay, which is rarely invoked. Also, minimum deposit balances are often smaller than in commercial banks. As a group, the institutions offering such accounts are called "thrifts" and include savings banks, savings and loan associations, building societies, *caisses d'épargne*, *sparkasse* and so forth. Such institutions have historically specialized in housing finance, a very long-term form of lending, which was made feasible by the fact that the deposit base of the lending institution is less liq-

[6] Sometimes banks issue short-term credits in lieu of medium-term credits, that is to say, with the understanding—but not the commitment—that the credits will be rolled over on a regular basis. This is an old but dangerous practice: when the borrower seeks medium-term finance because the project to be financed will not generate income for some time, a refusal of the bank to roll over the loan could create a liquidity crisis for the borrower.

[7] "Trust" here does not refer to the human feeling arising from a personal relationship, although the banker may have long-standing social contacts with the client (on the golf course, at the "club" and so forth). It is, rather, the acceptance by banker and client that a contract embodies expected behaviours and that there are rewards for fulfilling such expectations (such as new loans on better terms) and sanctions for not doing so. In some societies (for example, in some Asian countries), trust is accorded a larger role in a complex web of relationships and implicit contracts that develop in a business community, although the meaning of trust is itself not necessarily transparent (see Mark J. Scher, "Japanese interfirm networks: 'high-trust' or relational access?" in *Interfirm Networks: Organization and Industrial Competitiveness*, Anna Grandori, ed. (New York, Routledge Publishing, 1999), pp. 303-318.

[8] The main exception is lending to a Government, which is deemed to be less uncertain and is referred to as "sovereign risk", which is to say that it relies on the Government's promise to repay (the promise is credible because of the Government's ability to tax its citizens).

uid than that of a commercial bank. This notwithstanding, thrifts long ago began offering chequing accounts that can compete with household demand deposits at commercial banks.

In addition, credit unions are deposit-taking institutions that are cooperative undertakings of members in specific groupings, such as employees in a large firm or government agency or members of a professional association. The credit union takes deposits from and lends exclusively to its members. Also, profits are divided among the members of the union, who are its shareholders.[9]

Today, in developed countries, thrift institutions and commercial banks have each so evolved that they are barely different from each other. Banks, like thrifts, offer a range of long-term deposits and mortgage loans. Moreover, neither banks nor thrifts need keep their mortgage loans on their books, particularly in the United States, which pioneered the securitization of mortgages; that is to say, a special government-backed securitizing agency will issue a bond on the financial market and with the proceeds buy a number of mortgages, using the interest received from the mortgages over time to pay the interest on the bond. In this manner, long-term credits can be moved off the books of banks and thrifts, thereby increasing their liquidity, while providing a long-term savings instrument in the financial markets in the form of the bond. Indeed, banks can also borrow funds outside the deposit nexus, directly from other banks or even by issuing certain types of debt instruments, such as debentures, which are a type of bond.

Development banking

There is an additional category of financial intermediaries that have a public purpose and are usually government-owned. These institutions have been called "development banks", although their aim could be more narrowly focused than that encompassed by the term. The largest of the institutions are international in scope and exist to promote the development of developing and transition economies, notably the World Bank and the regional development banks. Five of the 15 largest institutions in the world that are so classified, however, serve developed economies (see table IV.1).

The modus operandi of all these institutions is to raise funds through the issuance of bonds or medium- and long-term borrowings from banks or loans or transfers of government resources for onlending in policy-determined programmes. The fundamental role of such institutions is to lend to population groups or for uses that the government wishes to promote but that private financial institutions eschew. Even with all the opportunities for private funding that have arisen in the developed financial systems, the public financial institutions still have a niche to fill (albeit oftentimes a smaller one than in earlier decades).

Typically, the institution makes an outright loan to a project, or in some cases takes an equity share. Private lenders may co-finance the project, drawn by the reputation of the public institution for high-quality project appraisal and the financial protection from cross-default clauses in lending agreements. In many cases, the financial resources provided are derived entirely from the private sector, with the public institution guaranteeing some or all of the private risk. Moreover, the lending or guaranteeing agency need not even be a free-standing financial institution, but can be part of a larger agency, as is the case

[9] Some financial intermediaries are organized as mutual associations, where depositors and borrowers are treated as owners with respect to profit-sharing (and sometimes they vote for the board of directors) rather then purely as customers purchasing services. A third category of financial intermediary comprises the Islamic banks, which in an Islamic country may operate the payments system and perform as a financial intermediary. As the shariah prohibits the taking of interest, the users of funds from Islamic banks in essence share their profits from the use of the funds with the depositors (see Zubair Iqbal and Abbas Mirakhor, *Islamic Banking*, Occasional Paper, No. 49 (Washington, D.C., IMF, March 1987); and Luca Errico and Mitra Farahbaksh, "Islamic Banking Issues in Prudential Regulation and Supervision", *IMF Working Paper*, No. 98/30 (March 1998)).

Table IV.1.
FIFTEEN LARGEST DEVELOPMENT BANKS, 1998

	Name	Location	Equity	Assets
			(billions of dollars)	
1	World Bank	United States	26.5	205.0
2	European Investment Bank	Luxembourg	22.6	206.0
3	Inter-American Development Bank	United States	11.0	54.6
4	Export-Import Bank of Japan	Japan	10.9	78.1
5	Asian Development Bank	Philippines	10.1	41.7
6	Japan Development Bank	Japan	9.9	127.6
7	European Bank for Reconstruction and Development	United Kingdom	5.8	18.7
8	Korea Development Bank	Republic of Korea	3.6	66.3
9	Islamic Development Bank	Saudi Arabia	2.3	2.5
10	Industrial Development Bank of India	India	2.0	15.2
11	African Development Bank	Côte d'Ivoire	1.9	6.5
12	Export-Import Bank of Korea	Republic of Korea	1.7	14.9
13	Export-Import Bank of the United States	United States	1.6	13.5
14	Mediocredito Centrale	Italy	1.5	8.7
15	Industrial Credit and Investment Corporation	India	1.3	11.6

Source: "Top 50 development banks", *The Banker* (London), May 1999, pp. 41-42 (data pertain to closing dates of fiscal years ending during 1998, except for Japan Development Bank, for which data are as of 31 December 1997).

for the direct lending and loan guarantee programmes of the Small Business Administration of the United States Government.

None of these public providers of financing are themselves deposit-taking institutions. In some countries, however, fully or partially State-owned banks combine a public purpose with a mandate to provide commercial banking or savings services. In addition, in some countries the national postal system offers savings accounts and other financial services. These are utilized mainly by middle- and lower-income households. The range of national experiences in operating postal savings systems is wide: in several countries, "postbanks" have been privatized or abolished, but the Japanese postal savings system has become the largest financial institution in the world. This reflects in part the "flight to safety" of household accounts in the context of Japan's current banking crisis.[10] Revenues accumulated in most postal systems are transferred to the government treasury or placed in the wholesale banking sector, although they also can be transferred to development-oriented financial intermediaries, as in Japan.

Institutional investors

Pension funds and insurance companies are two of the most familiar examples of non-bank financial institutions.[11] Household or enterprise accounts in pension funds differ from those in banks in that they are contractual in nature, requiring a schedule of payments into the accounts, typically over many years. Purchases from an insurance company, in particular casualty insurance, are of a different nature, as the insured buys a contingent claim for a particular amount of money that lasts a specified length of time. The claim is realized if some named event occurs, such as a death or injury (although life insurance

[10] Much the same occurred in the United States at the start of the Great Depression (the United States system was abolished in 1967).

[11] The discussion in the present section does not seek to be exhaustive, as the variety of non-bank financial institutions is vast. Certain institutions are more important in some countries than others, such as factoring companies in Europe (for inventory financing) and finance companies in North America, including consumer credit and household finance companies, and small business loan and leasing companies.

companies offer policies that have contractual saving as well as insurance components). Both contractual saving and insurance purchases lead to the accumulation of large pools of funds in the hands of institutions, which makes them major "players" in the financial sector. In both cases, the pool of funds needs to be large to ensure that the prospective claims can be paid without difficulty. However, the funds do not need to be as liquid as those of banks, as the probability that they will be drawn can be estimated with greater certainty than in banks.[12]

Institutional investors, particularly insurance companies and pension funds, purchase government bonds, corporate bonds or equities, and make investments directly, as in large-scale real estate developments. The securities that they hold may be purchased on an organized exchange, but they are often obtained in "private placements"; for example, a bond issue might be negotiated directly between the issuer and a set of institutional lenders.

A small part of the funds of institutional investors may be placed with firms that in turn invest directly in a selection of high-risk endeavours, in particular the supporting of start-up firms led by innovative entrepreneurs. These "venture capital" funds are usually private sector activities. Venture capitalists become closely involved in the business strategy of the firms in which they invest, bringing management skills as well as financial resources to the operation. The venture capitalist intends to stay with a company until it reaches a stage of success and maturity at which the firm can be "taken public" (shares can be sold on a stock market) or become attractive to another corporation which buys it. Most investments do not reach that stage, but the venture capitalist engages in the activity because profits from those that do can make up for all the losses incurred (see chap. VIII).

Markets and market-related institutions

In financial markets, transactions entail a very different relationship between supplier and user of funds than in financial institutions. A buyer in a financial market makes a one-off purchase of a security representing a share of the equity of a firm or a debt obligation. In "secondary market" purchases, the original issuer is not even party to the transaction (it is merely notified that ownership has changed hands).

Securities purchasers, however, face the same asymmetric information problem as loan officers in banks, but without the continuing relationship that makes bank monitoring feasible.[13] Instead, most securities purchasers rely on specialists to monitor the companies whose securities trade in the market and to advise them when to buy or sell a particular security. Indeed, one requirement of a well-functioning securities market is that there be a competitive market of securities analysts.

Managers of corporations nevertheless have an advantage over outside investors in respect of access to information about their companies, and it may be in their interest not to disclose all relevant information. Thus, incentives and regulations to ensure proper disclosure are needed. Government policies and market institutions, including a system of supervision and regulation, can create the incentives to ensure an accurate, timely and easily available flow of such information. Appropriate standards for supporting legal and accounting systems are also needed for adequate information disclosure.[14]

[12] This notwithstanding, the uncertainty has been growing, particularly as life insurance companies introduce new products for their customers and as customers increasingly avail themselves of liquidity options, such as borrowing against the value of an insurance policy.

[13] Shareholders have a continuing relationship with their firm in that they vote for members of the board of directors and on proposed changes in the corporation's by-laws; nevertheless, most shareholders hold a small stake in any single firm and do not take an active interest in monitoring the management.

[14] See Joseph Stiglitz, "The role of the state in financial markets", in *Proceedings of the World Bank Annual Conference on Development Economics, 1993* (Washington, D.C., World Bank, 1994), pp. 19-52.

Thus armed, the secondary market may be said to serve a monitoring function, with the price of a security rising or falling, *inter alia*, as market assessments of the profitability of the firm change. To the degree that management of a company is judged by the performance of its share price—and compensated accordingly—the market can be said even to discipline management. However, the market is not innocent of fads and is not necessarily a fully informed monitor, so that the firms that are rewarded or punished by the market are not always the most deserving ones. It has also been argued that the monitoring and control of corporations by the market encourage management to focus on short-term profits at the expense of long-term productivity and earnings.[15]

These are usually considered relatively minor concerns set next to the overall advantages of securities markets. The principal attraction to buyers of securities is that they enable diversification of assets into a variety of financial instruments with a wide range of risk and return trade-offs. To the degree that the market is liquid, these securities can be bought and sold at will, albeit at varying prices. For the user of funds, securities markets enlarge the variety of funding alternatives; for example, bonds offer longer original maturities than those banks are usually willing to give on loans.[16]

Securities traded on the secondary market first have to be floated on the "original issue" or primary market and this requires the services of a specialist institution, the investment (or "merchant") bank. These institutions help corporations to prepare a public stock issue or help corporations or Governments to issue bonds, bring them to market and underwrite them (in other words, they promise to buy any shares or bonds in the issue that are not purchased by the public). They are intermediaries in the literal sense of the term, bringing large-scale users and suppliers of funds together for a transaction, but not themselves making the long-term investment. They also arrange private placements of securities, such as with institutional investors, as noted above, and facilitate mergers and acquisitions.

Investment banks thus arrange the supply of securities that are traded on organized bond and stock exchanges or that trade on the "over the counter" market—formerly a telephone but now a computer screen. Brokers and dealers affiliate with these securities exchanges and facilitate transactions between buyers and sellers of the securities traded on the floor of the exchange (or increasingly in an electronic market).

The original issuer receives no funds from the trading of its shares on the secondary market. The benefit of the secondary market to the issuer of publicly traded shares is, rather, twofold. First, when the shares are initially sold to the public, their value is raised by the knowledge of potential buyers that the securities can be later sold on the secondary market (liquidity). Second, when the secondary market raises the price of a firm's shares, it signals endorsement of management and raises the creditworthiness of the firm (it lowers the debt-to-equity ratio).[17]

Finally, another set of institutions has become important in recent years. These are "mutual funds" or "investment trusts" or "unit trusts" and related vehicles whose modus operandi is to sell shares in their funds and combine the proceeds into large pools of resources for placement by professional portfolio managers in any of a variety of financial market instruments. While some such funds cater to corporations and wealthy individuals with an inter-

[15] See Ajit Singh, "Financial liberalization, stockmarkets and economic development", *The Economic Journal*, vol. 107 (May 1997), pp. 771-782.

[16] See J. C. Berthélemy and A. Varoudakis, "Models of financial development and growth: a survey of recent literature", in *Financial Development and Economic Growth: Theory and Experiences from Developing Countries*, N. Hermes and R. Lesink, eds. (London and New York, Routledge, 1996); and R. Levine and S. Zervos, "Stock markets, banks and economic growth", *American Economic Review*, vol. 88, No. 3 (June 1998), pp. 537-558.

[17] Also, high share prices reduce the cost in terms of dilution of the ownership of existing shareholders when additional capital is raised through a new share issue by the firm.

est in particular types of transactions (such as "hedge funds"), others serve the small-scale market.

They all offer investors the opportunity to diversify their holdings and risks. Mutual funds give small investors opportunities to buy shares in portfolios of securities that meet a wide variety of needs and interests, ranging from the equity shares of high-risk, high-volatility companies to low-risk pools of short-term government treasury bills. Mutual funds have been set up to pursue an ever-widening range of investment goals (such as appreciation of stock prices, income from dividends and tax-free income). There are also mutual funds designed to purchase securities of particular countries or particular industries, large companies or small ones, equity shares or bonds alone, or even mixtures of types of financial instruments. Some mutual funds even offer a "social screen", buying the securities only of firms that meet such criteria as abiding by voluntary labour codes and producing no products that are harmful to health or the environment. Most significantly, both households and corporate financial officers now have many alternatives to putting money in a bank.

Financial sector dynamism

A central characteristic of the financial sector in the developed countries in recent decades is its rapid pace of innovation. The financial markets, for example, now offer instruments covering the full spectrum of maturities, ranging from "commercial paper", which is a market-traded alternative to short-term bank loans for large corporations,[18] to bonds and equity shares. The markets have also developed instruments that combine features of different securities, such as "convertible bonds", which are bonds with equity warrants that give the bond-holder the right to exchange the bond for equity shares in the issuing firm during a pre-set time interval and at a pre-arranged swap ratio.

Financial instruments have also been developed that change the nature of the payment stream that a borrower has contracted. For example, if a borrower has issued a fixed-rate bond, it can arrange to swap its interest obligations with those of a borrower who issued a bond whose interest rate was tied to a fluctuating benchmark rate. Similarly, a foreign exchange swap can be arranged to change the currency of payment of debt servicing on a bond. These are examples of a large class of financial "derivatives", so-called because their valuation is derived from the prices of underlying securities.[19] Created by banks and other financial institutions as off-balance sheet fee-earning, low-cost and lightly regulated contracts, derivatives have been used for speculation and have thus become a focus of concern to those who ask whether financial systems are now routinely taking on excessive exposure to risk (see chap. IX).

Indeed, a distinction can be drawn between the above over-the-counter swaps and other derivative contracts that are traded by financial institutions and the standardized futures contracts that are listed on organized exchanges, such as "put" and "call" options to buy or sell equity shares at a future date at a pre-set price, or purchase or sale for future delivery of a commodity or foreign currency at a price agreed today. Whereas the volume and composition of the market for the former type are usually obscure, exchange-traded futures contracts are more transparent (each transaction is posted) and the exchanges are regulated.

[18] As banks typically guarantee payment in commercial paper issues, they indirectly participate in this non-bank market-financing instrument.

[19] The issuer of the derivative does not need to own the underlying security; it does not even have to exist (for example, a contract can be written on an index of stock market prices, which gives a return to buyers as if they bought all the stocks whose prices are in the index).

As derivatives and mortgage-backed securities illustrate, there are now multiple and intimate connections among the main components of the financial sector in a contemporary economy. The commercial banks, thrifts, pension and insurance funds, other non-bank financial institutions and the financial markets constitute an ever more closely integrated and still changing financial industry. This has made the financial system more competitive, as the market has become less segmented, although the plethora of options have reduced the capacity of policy to single out any one part of it for control.

In addition, with the lowering of international barriers to capital movements and the speeding up of communications across frontiers, the financial sectors of different nations are more and more closely linked together. As was seen in 1997-1998, crisis is now easily transmitted from continent to continent. Indeed, realization of the extent of this phenomenon has prompted the myriad proposals for reform of the international financial "architecture". It has also raised the importance of an integrated international approach to financial regulation and oversight (see chap. IX).

THE FINANCIAL SECTOR AND DEVELOPMENT

Countries differ greatly in the degree to which their financial sectors are active in each type of financial activity described above. Developing countries, in particular, generally lack well-developed financial markets and thus have tended to rely more heavily on the banking sector than do most developed countries (see, for example, figure IV.1).[20]

20 Figure IV.1 is meant to indicate broad differences between the two country groups shown, each of which has a large range of within-group differences. Moreover, if comparable information were available for a sample of low-income developing countries, it would show them to have even greater reliance on banks than that shown for the "emerging markets" category.

Figure IV.1.
STYLIZED FACTS ABOUT INSTITUTIONAL STRUCTURES
OF FINANCIAL SYSTEMS

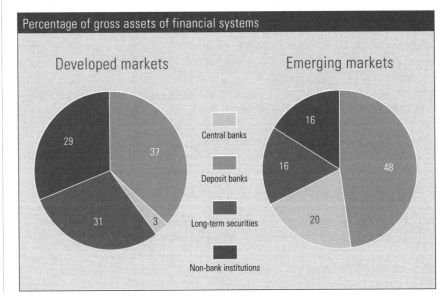

Source: Data of World Bank, *World Development Report 1989* (New York, Oxford University Press, 1989), table 2.4.

Note: Data based on averages of 8 developed and 13 emerging market economies in 1985.

One characteristic of the bank-centred systems is that the banks have a greater role than in more market-centred systems in collecting and assessing information about the corporate sector. In economies with more developed capital markets, there are market as well as governmental pressures to provide reliable and timely corporate information, including financial reporting requirements for listing on a stock exchange. There are independent bond-rating agencies whose classification of individual bond issues is required for purchase by various regulated investors (such as pension funds or insurance companies). There is also a host of interested business analysts: "sell-side" research which provides coherent investor information and "buy-side" analysts who ferret out investment opportunities. Little of this exists in a bank-dominated system, where the pricing of loans offered to a client firm, for example, depends very much on the bank's internal assessment of its client.

Nevertheless, over the past decade financial asset managers in developed countries have evinced greater interest in emerging market securities. This has boosted interest in developing and transition economies in welcoming inflows of such funds through the development and liberalization of their local securities markets. Indeed, this is one of the forces pulling these countries towards the complex financial structure described above. Yet, this has also raised the question whether portfolio investment by foreigners in emerging markets is a source of higher financial volatility (see box IX.1).

Meanwhile, small—and especially poor—borrowers have had and continue to have the fewest options for obtaining financial resources. Women—who have less effective claims than men to property that can be pledged as collateral—are distinctly disadvantaged in terms of access to credit.[21] Commercial banks have generally avoided serving the poor or women, and official institutions that lend to rural areas or for enterprise development have had a mixed history of successes and failures. Credit for the poor has been very much in the province of informal finance, although new types of institutions, in particular "microfinance" organizations, are increasingly playing a role in directing finance to the poor and particularly to women. Microfinance is a promising innovation which has become the focus of considerable policy attention in the development community (see chap. VII).

Allocating funds to private investment

Users of other people's funds can have a wide range of motivations, but of special interest in this *Survey* are funds for investment. Bringing savings decisions into equality with investment decisions is accomplished by a range of endogenous economic processes. Total saving in an economy very much depends on developments in income and employment and changes in the balance sheets of households, government and businesses. Investment depends on all the factors that influence profit expectations. The availability and cost of finance can be important in this regard, although a large part of investment by firms and households is financed out of internal savings (retained earnings in the case of firms) and thus does not pass through the financial system.

As economies develop, however, there is an increasing use of financial resources external to the firm or household. Indeed, this is reflected in the tendency of the financial sector to encompass a larger share of GDP in higher-

[21] Nevertheless, women in many developing countries contribute to household and small-enterprise debt servicing through their entry into the labour force, and they serve as a shock absorber in terms of the extra hours of work they perform during a time of financial crisis (María Floro, "Does gender matter in finance? Some lessons from the financial crisis", joint seminar of the Division for the Advancement of Women and Development Policy Analysis Division, Department of Economic and Social Affairs, United Nations, New York, 9 June 1999).

22 The data in the figure give only an approximate indication of the differences in value added in the financial sectors of different countries. National accounts data overstate the value added in the financial sector itself, as all of the interest spread between lending and deposit rates of banks is treated as value added, when in fact some of it should be counted as primary income. This is a matter that the 1993 revision of the System of National Accounts seeks to correct (see Robin Lynch, "What is FISIM?", *SNA News and Notes*, an information service of the Inter-Secretariat Working Group on National Accounts, issue 8, November 1998, pp. 2-4).

23 Data of the Reserve Bank of India, as presented and compared with other indicators in R. Nagaraj, "India's capital market growth: trends, explanations and evidence", *Economic and Political Weekly*, vol. 31, Special Number (September 1996), p. 2,555.

24 Ibid., p. 2,558.

income than in lower-income countries (although there is considerable variability in the relationship; see figure IV.2).[22] The financial sector thus provides increasing financing opportunities as economies grow, and thereby gains in importance in determining the composition of investment.

India provides a case in point. In the 1950s, gross domestic saving in India was about 10 per cent of GDP. Since the late 1970s, the saving rate has been about 20 per cent of GDP. Moreover, from the latter half of the 1970s to the latter 1980s, the share of domestic savings held in financial form rose from about one third to about one half, thus increasing the portion of savings intermediated into private investment by the financial sector. Reflecting this change, Indian corporations have reduced their reliance on internal financing from over 60 per cent of gross investment in the 1960s and 1970s, to about 50 per cent in the 1980s and early 1990s.[23] This reduction came despite the fact that a decrease in the gross profit tax from 40 per cent in the mid-1970s to about 15 per cent at the end of the 1980s, had significantly reduced the disincentive to declare and retain profits for investment.[24]

These data hint at the large changes in India in the savings-investment relationship as the financial sector developed and ideas evolved about development policy. In the early years of independence, savings were largely mobilized by the Government and allocated through official channels. In a second stage of financial development, the Government transferred resources to term-lending institutions that developed the capacity for project appraisal in their disbursement of official funds. The third major step has been the development of the

Figure IV.2.
RELATIVE SIZE OF FINANCIAL SECTORS

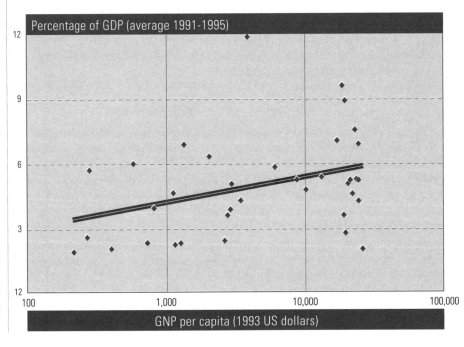

Source: UN/DESA, based on data of Statistics Division and *World Bank Atlas, 1996* (for GNP per capita).

Note: Average of data shares are for years available in 1991-1995 (data for value added in finance plus insurance sectors of 36 economies; GDP measured before deduction of imputed bank service charges).

capital market, including a burgeoning securities market, accompanied by tax reductions and overall loosening of controls on the corporate sector.

With investment in India and the developing and transition economies in general now more the result of private decisions and more reliant on financial sector operation, policy makers are paying increasing attention to improving the functioning of the financial sector. The goal is not only to stabilize the financial system, but also to raise the efficiency and equity of access to financial resources. In other words, well-functioning private financial systems embody important roles for government.

The role of government: strengthening the financial sector

Throughout history, banks have been prone to take excessive risks with depositors' funds, leading to individual bank failures that spread into general and costly banking crises. The gravest fear of monetary authorities begins when depositors in a bank come to believe that their bank has become weak and run to withdraw their funds, leaving the bank short of cash and unable to meet withdrawal demands. If this, in turn, raises fears among the depositors in other banks that they, too, may be unable to withdraw their funds, it can provoke a widespread loss of confidence, a generalized bank run, a severe contraction of liquidity and an economic recession.

Governments thus place a high priority on maintaining public confidence in the currency and in the banks. The first line of defence is to require prudent management of banks, such as through maintaining appropriate liquid reserves and eschewing excessively risky lending operations. It is typically recommended that banks be closely regulated by a public authority and frequently inspected by auditors from the authority. In addition to the regulatory function, Governments—or more precisely, central banks—often promote confidence in the banks by making it known that they stand ready to provide however much emergency credit is required by the banks to assure the liquidity of deposits in the event of a panic; that is to say, the central banks serve as "lenders of last resort", a role they can perform because of their role in creating and controlling the domestic money supply. A related option is arranging for most deposits in banks to be insured against loss.

Sometimes, emergency credit infusions by the central bank can prevent illiquid banks from entering bankruptcy. When bankruptcies of banks nevertheless occur, Governments often seek to merge the failed bank with a healthy bank or otherwise smooth the exit of the bank from the market. When, as has happened on numerous occasions in economies at all levels of development, many banks become insolvent simultaneously,[25] the Government usually has to develop an emergency rescue programme. Sometimes the Government nationalizes the commercial banks, at least temporarily. Typically, it will force consolidations and reorganizations and help to recapitalize the banks that are still left standing.

Aside from concerns about preventing systemic breakdown, financial markets and institutions remain subject to regulation in an otherwise liberalizing world environment because buyers and sellers need protection from unscrupulous operators. The buyer of a corporate security has to rely on the truthfulness of the information about the company reported in the prospectus about the security. There are financial incentives to misrepresent the corporation's per-

[25] Solid banks might become insolvent if a large number of their loans suddenly became non-performing owing, say, to a surprise terms-of-trade shock that was not expected to be reversed or if, in the midst of a panic, their marketable assets suddenly dropped in price precipitously; more frequently, banks slip into insolvency over time, as lending decisions are increasingly based on unrealistic assumptions such as unsustainable real estate prices, exchange rates and so forth.

formance and prospects, and history is replete with cases where this has happened. Thus, regulations to ensure transparency of information and accounting according to established standards are highly valued.

In some cases, individual financial markets establish their own regulatory authority and in other cases the task is performed by a government agency, but all such bodies act to maintain public confidence in the financial markets. They are concerned, for example, that prices not be manipulated by market traders. They can also establish automatic "circuit-breakers" to halt trading in securities when prices plunge by more than a pre-set amount, in order to let a panic pass before trading resumes.

A major question is what direction government oversight and guidance should take in the future. Liberalization may have been a juggernaut in the 1980s and 1990s, but the challenges as well as opportunities that it created now seem to have established more room for a plurality of views. To take one example, developing countries have been encouraged in the past to allow their banks to offer a full range of financial services, that is to say, to make those banks "universal banks".[26] Such banks are common in Europe, but in the United States, commercial banks are prohibited from directly engaging in the activities of investment banks and brokerage houses.[27] These are considered higher-risk activities and the concern is to not indirectly extend lender-of-last-resort protection to such activities, which do not warrant it. Indeed, there is an argument that commercial banks should be prohibited from undertaking many of their activities, so as not to burden the lender of last resort with excessive risk. The range of banking models being advocated today thus extends from "narrow" to "universal" banking.

Another area of concern is the increasing difficulty in managing the net risk exposure of today's complex financial institutions. In fact, one of the questions to emerge from the recent international financial and currency turmoil is whether risk management in banks and regulatory oversight of risk management are sufficiently robust. In the face of the burgeoning markets in derivative instruments and the booming bank lending to financial sector firms that take highly leveraged positions in financial markets, it is not clear that banks—even the most sophisticated—have adequately managed their overall risk.

This is important because the strategy being pursued in recent efforts to strengthen financial regulation of internationally active banks is, in essence, to make all banks follow industry best practices as defined by these banks. The committee at the Bank for International Settlements in Basel that deals with regulatory issues established standards a decade ago that call for banks to have minimum amounts of capital (equity) based on a few broad classifications of their loans and investments. A more recent approach of the committee has been to set guidelines for capital requirements according to overall measures of the "value at risk" of the bank, as determined by complicated computer models. However, these models were precisely the tools that failed to stop the international banks in the years leading up to the 1997-1998 crisis when their lending became excessively risky.

In this light, attention has focused lately on strengthening international standards for capital requirements of banks.[28] This is an area of great importance to global financial stability and to the developing and transition economies, which are increasing their integration into the global system and, being weaker economies, are especially vulnerable to its shocks.

[26] The case for universal banks has been argued back and forth since at least the end of the 1970s (see Maxwell Fry, *Money, Interest and Banking in Economic Development*, 2nd ed. (Baltimore, Maryland, Johns Hopkins University Press, 1996), pp. 336-337). For an advocacy view, see World Bank, *World Development Report, 1989* (New York, Oxford University Press, 1989), box 3.6.

[27] This notwithstanding, there has been a perennial battle in the United States Congress over dismantling this restriction, even though it has already been considerably eroded through the device of establishing holding companies to own both commercial banks and investment companies.

[28] See chap. IX on these and other regulatory reforms.

The role of government: policy intervention

A key goal of the financial institutions that build and hold portfolios of financial placements is to maximize profits, while protecting the value of the funds they have accumulated. They thus hold investments that reward risk. There are, however, investments that warrant financing for social or development reasons, but that market-oriented institutions are unwilling to finance. In many countries, Governments have thus sought to supplement available private financial intermediation by various interventions, including establishing (or supporting privately owned) financial institutions that are mandated to take the additional risks that the private sector eschews. Development banks, as noted earlier, are the most important among such financial institutions, and are still in use in developed as well as in developing countries.

Development banks have had a chequered history in developing countries, although in the countries in which they have functioned efficiently they have made major contributions to development. With government financial backing, these institutions provide subsidized credit (offering it for a longer term or at lower interest rates) to a wider clientele and for a broader range of uses than do commercial entities. While resources for the development banks may come from government budgets or loans from multilateral development banks, they may also tap the domestic and international financial system, for example, by issuing government-guaranteed bonds.

Governments also seek to fill financing gaps by influencing where private financial resources flow. Such interventions include tax incentives (such as reduced taxation of interest on specified classes of bonds) and guarantees (for example, to encourage bank lending to small enterprises). In addition, Governments have established lending guidelines for banks in order to direct credit into particular industries or geographical regions.[29]

Moreover, recalling the inescapable role of judgement in the decisions of loan officers in banks, it has been common for discrimination by gender, race or ethnic group to enter into lending decisions in gross or subtle ways. Loan officers are likely to reflect the social mores around them and reproduce the economic effects of discrimination through the biases they perpetuate in respect of access to financial resources. Policy has to break that link, both in government rule-setting and in management leadership.

Governments in an increasing number of countries and their international partners also foster the establishment and growth of new private sector activities to fill gaps in available financial services. One of those gaps entails the need for sufficient risk capital to exploit market opportunities. A once rare, but now increasingly familiar example of such activities is the nurturing of the development of a venture capital industry (see chap. VIII).

In most developing countries, Governments—aided by donors and other public agencies—also play an important role in the creation and support of financial institutions that serve lower-income people. In many countries, financial services for lower-income populations have been supplied mainly by the informal sector, with some role for non-governmental organizations and public sector institutions, such as rural development agencies and post offices. In a number of countries, however, postal-based services have been privatized or closed, but there has been a revival of interest recently in strengthening them and extending their services (see box IV.1).

[29] For an assessment of directed credit programmes in developed and developing countries, see *World Economic and Social Survey, 1996* (United Nations publication, Sales No. E.96.II.C.1 and corrigendum), chap. V, subsect. entitled "The role of government in credit markets", and box V.1.

Box IV.1.

POSTAL SAVINGS AND THE FINANCIAL SERVICES GAP

Private financial institutions tend to leave some segments of the population under-served, in particular women, rural residents and lower-income people in general, as noted in the present chapter and as discussed in more detail in chapter VII. Official financial institutions and other not-for-profit entities may provide alternative services. In some cases, they do function quite well, but in other cases they do not, although this is not inevitable.

One institution that has had a mandate in many countries to provide financial services to all population groups, and hence to those not well served by the private sector, is the postal savings bank (sometimes a free-standing savings bank operates, *inter alia*, through postal branches). The idea behind this institution is simple: given the extensive network of postal facilities in most countries, including in relatively isolated areas, and the possibility of containing costs through sharing of facilities and staff, it should be possible to make some financial services available to all the people in a country at an acceptable cost through the post office. Indeed, people can usually open and maintain postal savings accounts with very small balances.

Postal savings banks became almost ubiquitous in many developed and developing economies more than a century ago. They served an explicit policy goal of encouraging thrift, while providing financial services and mobilizing substantial indigenous resources. The first system was introduced in the United Kingdom of Great Britain and Northern Ireland in 1861, followed by systems in other European countries. The Japanese system was introduced in 1874; and after Japan's leaders observed the foreign indebtedness of the Ottoman and Chinese empires, they decided to utilize accumulating postal savings funds for development financing.

In recent decades, in the context of liberalization and the withdrawal of the State from numerous economic activities, a number of postal savings systems were privatized or closed. Others have been neither efficient nor effective. Still others, however, have been quite successful, most notably the Postal Savings Bureau of Japan. Indeed, there are a dozen countries in which there is at least one postal savings account per household (see table).[a] Half of the 20 countries with the highest density of postal savings accounts are developed countries.

According to the Universal Postal Union (UPU), there are 45 postal savings banks in the developing and transition countries, along with 28 "giro" payments systems which provide a safe means to make financial transfers and one that is much less expensive than those available from commercial banks (which are themselves less widely available than post offices).[b] In many instances, however, the usage of the postal system for financial services lags far behind the more successful cases shown in the table. In some countries, there is not even 1 account per 100 nor even per 1,000 households.

This notwithstanding, in recent years there has been a revival of interest in policy circles in a number of countries in the contribution that postal savings might make to filling a gap in the availability of financial services. Indeed, both the World Bank and the Japanese Postal Savings Bureau provide assistance in improving postal systems. Moreover, the United Nations Development Programme (UNDP) has been exploring the concept of promoting small-scale savings through postal systems in arrangements that could be linked to credit extended through microfinance institutions.[c]

[a] The unusually high number of accounts per household in Japan is a legacy of the time when there was a tax benefit for balances up to a certain amount held in each postal savings account.

[b] Many of these countries have linked their giro systems, forming an international network mainly among countries in Europe, West Africa, North Africa and the Middle East. This is particularly valuable to developing-country nationals working overseas who can make inexpensive, safe and easy remittances to families in their home countries.

[c] See UNDP, Special Unit for Microfinance, "Postal savings banks and their comparative advantage for developing savings mobilization strategies for the poor", presentation to the Forum on the Introduction of Postal Savings, Postal Savings Bureau, Tokyo, 18 and 19 March 1999.

Box IV.1 (continued)

Furthermore, the World Savings Banks Institute, 36 of whose members are postal savings banks, has recently sought to bolster these institutions. Thus, the Institute formed the Postal Savings Banks Forum in 1996 as a mechanism for annual exchanges of views among top management of these banks and with outside entities on best practices and opportunities for cooperation. This kind of networking can be very important in raising the awareness of postal savings officials of the possibilities for strengthening their programmes and serving their target populations more effectively. It also provides useful information which postal savings officials can bring home to use in their efforts to reform their institutions and win greater political support for their activities.

The success of a postal savings programme depends, after all, on convincing the governmental authorities that the institution can make an important and unique contribution. In fact, postal savings banks can be not only a tool of an equitable financial policy, but also an effective part of development financing.

In other words, one can conceive of ways and means to intermediate accumulated postal savings into investments in development ranging from infrastructure projects to policy-based credit institutions serving the poor, such as microfinance institutions. The resources mobilized by postal savings could be channelled to industrial development banks, agricultural and rural development banks, facilities to promote development of specific regions of a country, or even venture capital funds.

Individual accounts in postal savings banks are typically small; but efficiently collected by a widespread system, they can add up to considerable sums. If the resources are appropriately deployed and their use effectively monitored, a new constituency can be expected to take an interest in the effective operation of these institutions. Furthermore, synergy can be built with the collection of savings, through, for example, marketing campaigns (along such lines as "Safeguard your savings and build the country through postal accounts"). This can produce—and has produced—significant additions to development finance.[d]

d   For additional information, see Mark J. Scher, "Postal savings for development", DESA Discussion Paper, forthcoming.

NUMBER OF POSTAL SAVINGS ACCOUNTS PER HOUSEHOLD

Twenty largest countries	
Japan	13.9
Hungary	3.4
Norway	2.6
Samoa	2.5
Ireland	1.9
France	1.5
Republic of Korea	1.3
Finland	1.2
United Kingdom	1.0
Tunisia	0.9
Mauritius	0.9
India	0.8
Gabon	0.8
Algeria	0.8
Zimbabwe	0.7
Italy	0.7
Trinidad and Tobago	0.6
Austria	0.6
Germany	0.6
Bahamas	0.5

Source: UN/DESA, based on data of the Universal Postal Union and the Population Division of the Department of Economic and Social Affairs of the United Nations Secretariat (savings account data pertain to most recent year available, which was 1996 or 1997, except for Sweden, for which the year was 1994).

Postal savings operate on the collection side of financial intermediation. The poor have also not been well served on the lending side of the ledger. The cost of lending to the poor and to women is relatively high, owing to the small size of the loans and the usual unavailability of collateral. Recent innovations, in particular the growth of microfinance institutions, have made lending to them more cost-effective, but public support is required as a catalyst, to cover set-up costs, give technical assistance and establish a legal and regulatory framework (see chap. VII).

Once these institutions are running, policy makers have to confront another dilemma: if the microfinance institutions are asked to become self-sustaining, they are likely to focus on serving the less poor of the poor. If so, who services the poorest of the poor? The poorest also have a need for financial services, encompassing, for example, deposit of very modest savings and access to emergency loans. Today, this is mainly the province of informal finance. Formal institutions, such as postal savings facilities, may help at the margin, but a development strategy for the poorest of the poor requires a broader and bolder approach.

V THE FUNCTIONING OF BANKS

Since 1980, roughly two thirds of the member countries of the United Nations experienced significant banking sector problems, notably more than in the 1970s and many more than in "the more tranquil period" of the 1950s and 1960s.[1] The recent turbulence has been especially great in the developing world and is thought to be related to advances in technology and liberalization of restrictions on financial institutions. In exchange for the turbulence, countries are presumed to have more effective banking systems.

The present chapter deals with various aspects of how banks actually function in their new and changing environment and the implications for policy. The analysis is first directed at recent experiences in developed countries, where the changes and challenges may point out the path for the development of the banking sector globally, but this chapter examines as well selected issues in banking in developing countries and in the economies in transition, where commercial banking as such did not exist until recently.

THE NATURE OF BANKING IN DEVELOPED ECONOMIES

Banking is an unusual industry, first because of its role in operating a country's monetary system, but also because of how it handles the "asymmetric information" problem noted in chapter IV. That is to say, when a bank lends money, it has to monitor the borrower to ensure repayment, since it cannot know with certainty what the borrower will do with the funds.[2]

In a regular business transaction, both parties can walk away after completing an exchange and need have no further contact. In practice, suppliers and purchasers usually seek to develop continuing relationships in most business-to-business and business-to-household transactions. Like his or her industrial or commercial counterpart, the banker may see each transaction as part of a series with the customer. Yet in fact, loan contracts have traditionally entailed a continuing relationship with the borrower because the bank requires that the money that it loans be returned. The bank has to make an assessment of the borrower's "three C's"—capital, character and capacity—and come to a judgement that the borrower will repay. The purported ability of banks to carry out the required monitoring function is—along with operating the payments system—at the heart of why banks are considered to be a special part of the financial sector. Yet, this is changing.

[1] See Morris Goldstein and Philip Turner, *Banking Crises in Emerging Economies: Origins and Policy Options*, Bank for International Settlements (BIS), Monetary and Economic Department, BIS Economic Papers, No. 46 (October 1996), p. 5 and references cited therein.

[2] This uncertainty characterizes leasing arrangements in general, not just the leasing of money. In the event of non-payment in equipment leasing, however, the lessor repossesses the leased goods, whereas the banker receives the collateral that was pledged by the borrower or whatever assets of the firm may be collected in a bankruptcy proceeding.

The matter of credit assessment

In the light of the asymmetric information problem, the first question for the lending banker is how to choose the applicants to which to lend. Banking analysts have conceptualized the solutions to the problem into two broad models that may be called "arm's-length credit assessment" and "relationship banking".[3]

The first model posits a bank-loan officer who examines a formal credit application in which the prospective borrowing firm gives background information on its creditworthiness, its plans for using the funds, its prospective collateral for the loan and so on. There is no presumption in the model that the loan officer personally knows the representative of the applicant firm. The assessment is to be made against formal and informal benchmarks, applying standardized formulas (for example, involving calculations of the prospective rate of return on a project). The job of the banker is to decide whether or not to make the loan and to then monitor the timely payment of interest and principal, as well as the overall economic condition of the borrower (which gives information on future repayment capacity).

The second model presumes a continuing relationship between the borrowing firm and its bank. Here, the bank official knows the client, is likely to have made loans to the firm in the past, and can form a judgement about the business acumen of management and its capacity to repay. According to this model, the assessment of the projected use of a particular loan may be based on relatively intimate knowledge of the operations of the borrower. In addition, in making the loan, the borrower may have expectations that the bank would extend additional credit in case of need, rather than foreclose for non-payment. The banker might demand closer monitoring of the firm as a price of attempting to rescue it, but this would be part of the relationship. Indeed, one strength in the relationship model is alleged to be its capacity for monitoring client firms. Moreover, the information that the banking relationship produces over time about the client is privately held by the bank. It not only informally ties the client firm to its bank, but also ties the bank to its client.

In practice, lending decisions of banks embody aspects of both models. Even though loan officers may formally analyse loan requests, the better they know the operations of the applicant, the greater their ability to make a more informed judgement. This knowledge may arise from having provided other banking services to the applicant (chequing accounts, short-term credit and earlier loans). Indeed, there is evidence, for example, from the United States of America, that the longer a bank has had a relationship with a small firm, the more funds the bank is likely to lend to the firm.[4]

Although each model solves the asymmetric information problem, at least in principle, each also lends itself to certain socially and economically undesirable banking practices. In the arm's-length model, rules of thumb for lending decisions—if not formal decision rules—are seen to be rational techniques of assistance in making decisions in an inescapably uncertain environment. But sometimes these rules fall back on gender, racial or ethnic stereotyping.[5] These latter decision rules substitute prejudice for credit evaluation, are unjust, and are economically inefficient in that promising projects will go unfunded.

"Crony capitalism" is today's popular name for the most common abuse of the relationship banking model. The idea here is that the human relationships

[3] Some authors distinguish between the Anglo-American style of banks which is said to follow the arm's-length model in a market-dominant system and the style of Japanese and German banks following the relationship model in a bank-dominant system. However, while national differences in banking systems exist, they can be overdrawn, as is recognized in the saying in the American banking industry that "all banking is relationship banking" (For a critical assessment of the distinction between banking types in the mid-1990s, see Bert Scholtens, "Bank- and market-oriented financial systems: fact or fiction?", *Banca Nazionale del Lavoro Quarterly Review*, vol. L, No. 202 (September 1997), pp. 301-323).

[4] See Mitchell Petersen and Raghuram G. Rajan, "The benefit of lending relationships: evidence from small business loans", *Journal of Finance*, vol. 49 (1994), pp. 3-37.

[5] An example of such a decision rule in the United States of America was the practice of "red-lining" neighbourhoods in which loan officers were not to extend housing loans. Outright discrimination in credit by race, sex or national origin was made illegal in the United States, although more subtle forms of discrimination in credit remained. That, in turn, spawned political efforts to counter the discrimination, most notably in the movement for adoption and then strengthening of the Community Reinvestment Act (see James T. Campen, "Neighbourhoods, banks and capital flows: the transformation of the U.S. financial system and the community reinvestment movement", *Review of Radical Political Economics*, vol. 30, No. 4 (fall 1998), pp. 29-59).

into which the banker enters with the client can evolve into personal obligations that cloud instead of clarify the lending decision process. Thus, the relationship banker may make loans to "friends" that would not pass muster under an arm's-length assessment. Similarly, bankers may feel obligated or find it opportune to make loans to enterprises that are affiliated with politically important figures. As in the case of the stereotyping rules of thumb, these are unjust and inefficient practices.

Strength into weakness: banking in Japan

The banking system in Japan has been characterized as an extreme form of relationship banking and one reason for Japan's successful economic development. However, by the mid-1990s, the purported strengths of that system looked more like sources of weakness that were so deep that the continued viability of the system was no longer assured. The extent of the erosion of public confidence in the banks could be seen from the shifting of household deposits out of banks and into the already large Postal Savings Bureau (*Yubin Chokin*, popularly called "*Yucho*"), which turned it into the largest financial institution in the world.

To understand the crisis in the Japanese banking system, it is necessary to see the system in the context of the corporate groups that emerged after the Second World War. When the war ended, the large *zaibatsu* holding companies were disbanded. Each one had held shares in and controlled a group of firms, many of which held controlling interests in other firms. For example, the Mitsui *zaibatsu* controlled 40 companies in industry, agriculture and the service sector, including banking, life insurance and real estate; some of these firms, in turn, controlled other firms (for example, Mitsui Steamship held shares in nine other companies).[6] Ownership was often in the form of a minority stake and there were numerous instances of one subsidiary's owning shares in another. The structure that emerged after the war in essence replaced the vertical link to the holding company with horizontal links among the top-level firms, forming a corporate grouping called *kigyo shudan* (see figure V.1). The second-tier vertical links (called *keiretsu*, a term often misapplied to the horizontal group structure) remained. The group's "main" bank (sometimes along with a trading company) would be in the centre of the *kigyo shudan*.[7]

While the group's trading company supported project planning, development and marketing, which might be undertaken as a joint venture with other group members, the main bank supplied financial expertise and short-term and long-term finance. It organized lending consortia to finance investment of client firms in good times and coordinated rescheduling of loans of clients in bad times.[8] It may appear that this structure re-created the *zaibatsu*, but in fact the *kigyo shudan* companies acted with more independence and traded far less with each other than under the *zaibatsu*. This became especially important in the light of changes in the Japanese financial system in the 1980s and 1990s.

As the most pressing problem of Japanese banks today is the crushing amount of bad debt that has accumulated on their books, it may be asked if the monitoring function that banks must perform had broken down. It was expected that owing to the cross-shareholding built into the *kigyo shudan* and *keiretsu* structure, the main bank would have access to inside information about its clients, thereby reducing its asymmetric information problem. This information

[6] For a complete listing of the Mitsui interests as of 31 January 1946, see Mark J. Scher, *Japanese Interfirm Networks and Their Main Banks* (London and New York, Macmillan Press and St. Martin's Press, 1997), pp. 140-141.

[7] Not all the post-war groups were formed out of the former *zaibatsu*, but they all had main banks.

[8] The group might also have a trust bank which would supply long-term financing and an insurance company which might also supply financing, as well as underwrite property and casualty insurance for a project (see Scher, op. cit.).

Figure V.1.
RELATIONSHIPS WITHIN A CORPORATE GROUP IN JAPAN

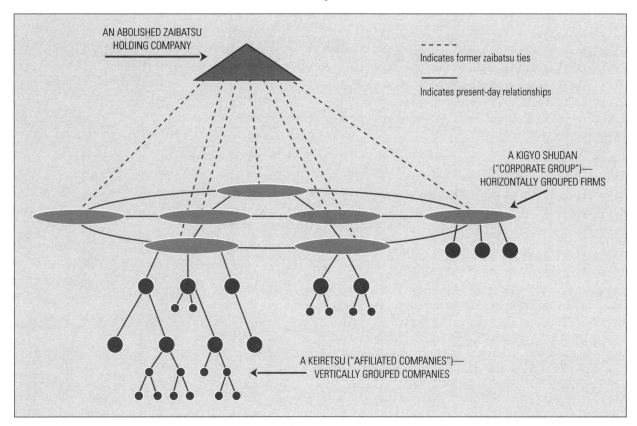

Source: Mark J. Scher, *Japanese Interfirm Networks and Their Main Banks* (London, Macmillan Press and New York, St. Martin's Press, 1997), p. 37. Used by permission.

9 See Iwao Nakatani, "The economic role of financial corporate grouping", in *The Economic
Analysis of the Japanese Firm*, Masahiko Aoki,
ed. (Amsterdam, Elsevier Publishing, 1984), pp.
227-258; and Paul Sheard, "The main bank system
and corporate monitoring and control in Japan",
Journal of Economic Behaviour, vol. 11 (1989), pp.
399-422.

10 The following draws heavily on Scher, op. cit.;
and Mark J. Scher, "Bank-firm cross-shareholding
in Japan: what is it, why it matters, is it winding
down?", DESA Discussion Paper, forthcoming.

was thought to be indirectly shared with other banks; that is to say, as large firms regularly drew credit from outside their group as well as from inside, there was said to be an implicit contract among main banks by which continued support of a client firm by its main bank was a signal to all the banks of its confidence in the creditworthiness of their mutual client firm.[9]

Whether or not this is how the system once worked, it was not operating this way by the early 1990s.[10] Domestic and international policy changes in a technologically dynamic global industry altered the nature of competition in the domestic banking market. Liberalization of the domestic regulatory regime led to reduced spreads between deposit and loan interest rates, adversely impacting profits. The result was increased competition among banks, which focused them on capturing more of the financial business of the large corporations. Each major firm had relations with a hierarchy of banks, their main bank being at the top. The main banks thus found themselves facing increasing competition from the other banks in the hierarchy or from outsiders which were only too eager to gain a foothold in the banking business of the client firm. In addition, with deregulation, large firms had more access to new forms of non-bank finance, in particular market finance, such as commercial paper.

The heightened competition among banks led them to offer more and more credit to their client firms, but not in order to raise lending volume and interest income. Rather, banks used loans—even if the low spreads made them loss leaders—to promote other sources of income for the banks. If one bank could displace another and become the main bank of a client, it would win the right to service the main depository accounts of the firm and hold a large number of employee accounts.[11] It would also hold the largest non-interest bearing compensating balances and more low-interest time deposits, and earn a disproportionate share of the client's commission and fee-based business (such as foreign exchange transactions or letters of credit).

In this situation, not only did large-scale potential borrowers have to worry less about convincing their creditors of the soundness of their proposed loan, but visits to a client firm by a bank's monitoring team took on a different orientation than that of traditional monitoring. The team's main purpose was to obtain information about the firm's future plans in order to promote sales of the bank's services. Indeed, given the alternative sources of credit, the monitoring team would in any case have little leverage over the client.

Thus, when the Japanese "bubble economy" burst as the 1990s began, banks found themselves holding assets of rapidly deteriorating quality, particularly on real estate-related lending. Bank management strongly desired to compensate for these losses with earnings elsewhere, as in East and South-East Asia, where they helped to create the asset inflation bubble whose bursting triggered the Asian financial crisis.

There is still, however, the puzzle why the banks continued to extend loans in Japan to what turned out to be increasingly troubled clients. A first reason seems to be that the banks did not obtain significant inside information about their client firms through their cross-shareholding. Management of the client firms appear to have regarded their main banks as rather low in the ranking of stakeholders that were entitled to monitor their activities.[12] Also, the banks themselves viewed the shares they held in a client not so much as an information channel but rather as a way to maintain "relational access" to the firm as a client. Cross-shareholding was viewed not as a mechanism for monitoring the borrower, but as another instance of essentially the same relational cross-shareholding that existed between firms and their main suppliers and corporate customers across many economic sectors. In short, the banks appear not to have had any special insight into their major borrowers' operations.

A second reason for continued lending to weak clients may have lain in what was perceived to be the main source of profits to the main bank, namely, selling financial services to the client. Moreover, as many banks were simultaneously lending to the client, any negative signal sent by main-bank expressions of concern about the client might discourage the other creditor banks. Were they to withdraw, the pressure would be great on the main bank to replace the withdrawing banks and increase its own exposure, thereby adversely changing the risk/reward mix for the main bank.[13]

A third reason for poor-quality lending and monitoring by the Japanese banks, at least at first, may have been the psychology of the bubble economy: having grown accustomed to rapid economic growth, few people expected conditions to change. The possibility of economic recession was seen to threaten only a temporary pause in the strong economic expansion. Bank management may thus have underappreciated the risk it was taking on.

A fourth reason is that even if bank management understood the risk, they might well have discounted it on the expectation that the Japanese Ministry of Finance would bail out any large troubled banks. This is an instance of the "moral hazard" problem of taking on excessive risk in the expectation that a "lender of last resort" will render assistance if needed (see box V.1). In fact,

[11] The firm would request its employees to open accounts at the chosen bank so as to facilitate direct deposit of their salary. The bank would then have a near-captive market to which to sell other banking services.

[12] See Mark J. Scher, *Japanese Interfirm Networks...*, pp. 126-128.

[13] By the same token, the client firm might have been willing to take larger risks than otherwise because of the expectation that, in the event of need, its main bank would extend new loans rather than see the firm collapse, this being an intra-corporate group version of the moral hazard problem.

Box V.1.

BANK SAFETY TOOL KIT AND MORAL HAZARD

In recognition of the special role that banks play in market economies, Governments generally accord banks a "safety net" that goes beyond the protection of other parts of the financial system or of other actors in the economy. However, the safety net entails a "moral hazard"; that is to say, it invites excessively risky bank behaviour because bank management is less afraid than it would otherwise be of the possibilities of failure. Yet, this does not mean that the safety net was a mistake: even if taking away the safety net were to eliminate the moral hazard, it would only return the economy to the earlier state of excessive vulnerability. The solution lies in identifying the proper tools for creating a safety net and how to best combine them with appropriate regulatory principles so as to minimize moral hazard.

The basic aim of a bank safety net is to prevent or quell a generalized run on the banks which might force strong banks as well as weak ones to close, contract the supply of money and credit and cause an economic recession. But runs are an instance of "herd" behaviour in economics and one reason why a herd instinct might be found among depositors and might spread contagion from weak banks to strong ones is that the public—above all small depositors—cannot easily assess the riskiness of the bank's balance sheet. This uncertainty leaves banks open to panic. In the midst of a panic, moreover, an otherwise solvent bank might not be able to raise sufficient cash from selling assets at "fire sale" prices to meet its depositors' demands.

More fundamentally, however, the possibility of a bank run is created by two key features of banking systems: intermediation and leverage. Intermediation is the operation whereby banks collect deposits and lend them out. While the deposits are liquid, many of the loans (or securities that banks might purchase) are not. As noted in chapter IV, this is usually safe, that is to say, there is a small chance (the liquidity risk) that it is not safe.

In addition, the banking system as a whole is typically highly leveraged. As depositors in a bank roughly maintain the size of their deposit balances, the bank can use a large proportion of the deposited funds to make loans (or purchase securities), retaining only a small proportion of the deposits in the form of liquid assets to meet the usual daily demand for cash. As this applies to all banks in the system, total loans (and securities held by banks) are a substantial multiple of the cash reserves.

Such a "fractional reserve" banking system may be seen as a wonderfully efficient financial engine. But it is equally efficient at multiplying the credit contraction consequences of a sudden withdrawal of cash from the banks. That is to say, banks' liquidity risks are magnified by their leverage and vice versa. Therefore, banks need a safety net under them to protect the economy from the *systemic* risk that a bank run might pose for the economy at large: should a bank default on its obligations to its depositors, the resultant contagion might lead to a collapse of the banking and payment system and take the rest of the economy with it. This is not merely theory, as it used to happen periodically before there were any safety nets.

Box V.1 (continued)

Tools for making a safety net

The classic bank safety net is the "lender of last resort", as formulated by Walter Bagehot in his book *Lombard Street* (1873). The policy is meant to be preventive and curative. The central bank announces well before a panic starts that, should a banking panic begin, it would be willing to make very large loans to banks against "good" collateral (valued at pre-panic prices) but at a "penalty" rate of interest (to discourage abuse of the credit line). The announcement is aimed at bolstering the confidence of depositors, but the central bank also provides the emergency liquidity in case an actual bank run begins. It appears that when this concept was consistently applied (albeit generally using market interest rates) in the late nineteenth century and after, as in England, France, Germany, Sweden and Canada, it worked successfully.[a]

Bagehot's lender-of-last-resort system is not, however, uniformly in use today. For example, during the financial scare in the United States of America in the autumn of 1998, the Federal Reserve System took two types of action, neither of which was the classical lender of last resort.

That is to say, concerned that liquidity was disappearing from the United States economy owing to financial market reaction to the Russian devaluation and suspension of debt servicing, the "Fed" engaged in open-market operations (it bought government bonds on the open market) and thereby pushed additional cash into the banking system. In this way, the Fed very quickly supplied liquidity to the banking sector, but without the "frown costs" that normally accompany the classical mechanism of emergency lending through the "discount window" and, moreover, not at a penalty rate. On the other hand, one could also argue that the open-market operation was less vulnerable to moral hazard, as individual banks could not be sure how much liquidity would come to them in any episode.

Second, the Federal Reserve Bank of New York sought to resolve the looming liquidity crisis at Long Term Capital Management (LTCM), a hedge fund that had borrowed and lost large sums from several major banks. If each of LTCM's creditors had tried individually to recover as much as possible of its loans, the firm would certainly have failed, there would have been a major disruption in the financial markets in which LTCM operated and most of the banks would have faced grave losses, not only from their loans to LTCM, but also from their exposures to the same markets as those to which LTCM had been exposed. Under these circumstances, the New York Fed coordinated a major infusion of private bank credit (and losses were imposed on the shareholders of LTCM) and the firm began to unwind its complicated and highly leveraged financial positions. In other words, the New York Fed managed the situation through action directly involving the crisis institution.

By mid-1999, it appeared that LTCM would survive and that the creditors would ultimately receive their funds back. Although creditors might conclude that they would be protected from default on loans to hedge funds (a moral hazard result), they also have to face the likelihood that stricter regulations will be imposed, as was being discussed in the summer of 1999 by the authorities of the United States and other major countries.

[a] For a review of the arguments and the historical experience, see Michael Bordo, "The lender of last resort: some historical insights", National Bureau of Economic Research, Working Paper, No. 3011 (June 1989).

Box V.1 (continued)

There is a third tool for creating the modern safety net in addition to the lender of last resort and crisis management. This is a scheme of deposit insurance which protects at least small deposits from losses if a bank fails. Whether for household or small or medium-sized business, such risk reduction is a socially and economically valuable service, addressing what had been felt to be a serious problem when—in the United States in the midst of the Great Depression—deposit insurance was first introduced. Deposit insurance is possibly open, however, to moral hazard, as banks know that at least their insured obligations would be covered by the insurance in the event of bankruptcy.[b]

Moreover, an additional practice which also has a moral hazard dimension gradually found its way into the safety tool kit. This arose from the doctrine that some banks were "too big to fail": a Government might bail out even an insolvent bank if not doing so would have adverse systemic effects.[c] Such assistance could take the form of more- than-usual access to credit from the central bank and "regulatory forbearance", wherein regulators would make exceptions to otherwise prohibited practices of a bank.

However, while central bank lending according to the "too big to fail" doctrine clearly violates Bagehot's admonition about lending against "bad" collateral, the fact that the intention of the practice is to protect the banking system from systemic risk only brings us back to the issue of the relative costs (in terms of increased moral hazard) and benefits (in terms of protection from systemic risk) of a bank safety net. Moreover, we should not confuse the dangers of moral hazard with the dangers of lax financial regulation.

Dealing with perverse incentives

It has been argued that, taken together, these and similar banking oversight policies created the "perverse incentives" that led banks to slip into the spate of crises in the 1980s and 1990s in developed and developing countries.[d] In fact, both greater instability in the global economy and the competitive winds of liberalization made banking a more volatile and risky business. This notwithstanding, "perverse incentives" may have exacerbated banking problems and thus efforts aimed at a reduction of moral hazard became a major focus of regulatory and safety net reform in the 1990s.[e]

With the benefit of hindsight, it can be noted that moral hazard in banking is sometimes increased as an inadvertent side effect of policies taken for reasons unrelated to prudential concerns. The Republic of Korea, for instance, raised the moral hazard in banking through liberalization. Banking in the Republic of Korea had been an intimate part of an industrial policy system that was dismantled in the 1990s. The banks were then expected to change their mode of operation to that found in a more decentralized and competitive market, while under "a legacy of poor management and credit analysis skills, as well as large exposures to the highly leveraged *chaebols* (conglomerates)".[f] The banks also remained under official pressure to extend loans and they helped finance the global expansion of the *chaebols*, in part with short-term foreign funds that the banks were able to access following liberalization.

After the Republic of Korea's financial and economic collapse at the end of 1997, the shortcomings became easy to see. Official regulation had been weak,

[b] In the United States, bank capital ratios—the amount of bank equity divided by the value of loans outstanding—halved in the decade following the introduction of federal deposit insurance, which can be taken as evidence of moral hazard (see Kevin Dowd, "The case for financial laissez-faire", *The Economic Journal*, vol. 106 (May 1996), pp. 683-684). On the other hand, it can be said that deposit insurance collectivized risk and made it less necessary for each bank to sequester large sums in reserves, and that this raised the efficiency of the banking system.

[c] This policy came into use in the United States after Penn Square Bank was allowed to fail in 1982, but Continental Illinois was rescued through a recapitalization in 1984.

[d] This is argued, for example, by Charles W. Calomiris, *The Postmodern Bank Safety Net: Lessons from Developed and Developing Countries* (Washington, D.C., American Enterprise Institute for Public Policy Research, 1997).

[e] This was the thrust, for example, of the 1991 revision of the deposit insurance scheme in the United States; that reform in part adopted the proposals of George J. Benston and George G. Kaufman, who had also argued that the only reason to have prudential regulation of the banking sector was to offset the moral hazard created by deposit insurance, which it was socially and politically necessary to have (see "The appropriate role of bank regulation", *The Economic Journal*, vol. 106 (May 1996), pp. 688-697).

[f] International Monetary Fund, *International Capital Markets: Developments, Prospects and Key Policy Issues* (Washington, D.C., September 1998), p. 154.

Box V.1 (continued)

with "regulatory forbearance" granted in one area after another. To meet competition from less-regulated non-bank financial institutions, banks were allowed to offer trust accounts that were kept off their balance sheets—and thus were not subject to standard capital backing rules—although they increased bank riskiness. In addition, loan-loss reserves, which had been 100 per cent of doubtful loans at the start of 1996, were lowered to 75 per cent and provisions for losses from revaluation of securities holdings were dropped from 50 per cent of exposure to 30 per cent.

One lesson for the future is the importance of strengthening regulatory rules.[g] In addition, new policy directions of the Republic of Korea included closure of some of the banks, reorganization and recapitalization of others and invigoration of official oversight capacity, beginning with the establishment of a new Financial Supervisory Commission.[h]

Globally, the new intellectual ferment over regulatory reform is producing some interesting proposals, although certain of them require a level of financial sector sophistication that seems to limit their applicability. One, for example, would require banks to issue subordinated debt instruments (such as uninsured certificates of deposit) and to require that the yield on them be less than, say, half of a percentage point above a risk-free debt instrument, such as a treasury bill. The instruments would have to be rolled over regularly and the bank would have to maintain a pre-set ratio of these instruments to total loans outstanding. If the market assessed the bank as becoming too risky, not all the subordinated debt would be rolled over and the bank would have to contract its loans and/or change its behaviour so as to regain market confidence.[i] The proposal depends, however, on there being an adequate supply of experienced securities analysts who would presumably be in a better position to judge the riskiness of bank balance sheets than are small depositors.

Other proposals seek to counter moral hazard by altering the risk/return calculus facing bank management. One proposal is to introduce uncertainty into whether or not a failed bank will actually be rescued. More direct is the proposal to raise the cost of bank insolvency by making it clear that "members of management will always lose their jobs and that shareholders (in the bank) will always lose their capital in the event of a failure".[j] Such threats would have to be credible, and this is not a trivial requirement. Even under existing practices, regulators are often under very considerable political pressure from the banks that they regulate, whose management is often very influential (again, this is an issue of poor regulation and not of moral hazard).

Such difficulties notwithstanding, reform of banking regulation and safety nets have become a high global—as well as national—priority, and there has been a flurry of international activity in trying to reach agreed directions for policy reform. One focus is to make stronger prudential regulation a quid pro quo for safety net protection at the national level and to establish minimum regulatory standards across countries. There are also important questions for policy makers, however, in respect of removing excess volatility from the economic and financial environment in which banks function, that involve policies beyond those narrowly focused on banks per se (see chap. IX).

[g] There is a general point here: analysts should not misperceive regulatory shortcomings as an excessively generous safety net; they are different (see Ha-Joon Chang, "The hazard of moral hazard: untangling the Asian crisis", *World Development*, forthcoming).

[h] For a more detailed discussion, see Soo-Won Lee and Ann Orr, "The financial restructuring and reform programme in the Republic of Korea: progress and constraints", in *Global Financial Turmoil and Reform: A United Nations Perspective*, Barry Herman, ed. (Tokyo, United Nations University Press, 1999), pp. 93-108.

[i] See Calomiris, op. cit., pp. 24-29.

[j] Andrew Crockett, *The Theory and Practice of Financial Stability, Essays in International Finance, No. 203* (Princeton, New Jersey, International Finance Section, Department of Economics, Princeton University, April 1997), pp. 25-26.

after some delay and with increasing appreciation of the severity the situation, the Government adopted a massive restructuring and bailout plan in October 1998. It is hoped that this will result in a considerable consolidation of banks and changes in management.

One consequence of this sequence of developments is that in Japan, as elsewhere in the world economy, the prospect is now for an increasing share of credit to be provided through financial market instruments and a decline in the share of bank credit. Indeed, there was a flurry of mergers in early 1999 among Japanese trust banks, which are institutional investors that intermediate funds through the capital markets (for example, pension fund management). It remains to be seen, however, how the small and medium-sized enterprises in Japan will fare in this new financial environment. They were hit especially hard by the contraction of bank lending that accompanied the final burgeoning of the financial crisis and they have fewer of the financial market options available to the larger firms with respect to raising funds.

Is there a future for commercial banking?

The changes in Japan that led up to its banking crisis had their roots in developments in banking and finance that had begun some three decades before in the United States. By the 1970s, the depth of the changes that had begun there were beginning to be perceived. A prominent book on the United States banking industry that appeared at that time began with a chapter entitled "The revolution" and ended with one entitled "Living on the edge of an abyss".[14] The author worried about the increasing fragility of the financial system that the revolution was creating. The United States subsequently went through a number of banking scares—most notably the 1980s debt crisis of developing countries which threatened the viability of several New York money-centre banks— and an actual crisis in the savings and loan industry, but in the 1990s banking scholars published articles with titles such as "Are banks dead?"[15] Does this presage what is to be the future of banking in the United States or in the world at large?

One important part of the initial change in the United States, as in Japan decades later, was a diminution in the relational aspects of bank lending. That is to say, banks in the United States became more and more transaction-oriented. Many banks stopped seeing the extension and monitoring of loans as their main function. However, while Japanese banks made and held loans in order to gain other business of their clients, the strategy of banks in the United States emphasized making a loan and then selling it to someone else. Today, banks in the United States not only off-load mortgages that are then bundled together into mortgage-backed securities, as discussed in chapter IV, but also sell almost any type of loan, including credit-card debt, automobile and consumer finance loans and corporate debt.[16]

In addition, while various types of loans are bundled together and sold for securitization, individual loans may also be sold to other banks or investors who wish to hold assets with the particular characteristics of the loan.[17] Indeed, in the 1980s, commercial banks from the United States—joined by banks from other developed countries—even sold non-performing credit obligations of the Governments of developing and transition economies that were in debt crisis,

[14] See Martin Mayer, *The Bankers* (New York, Weybright and Talley, 1974).

[15] J. H. Boyd and M. Gertler, "Are banks dead? Or, are the reports greatly exaggerated?", in Federal Reserve Bank of Chicago, *The Declining Role of Banking, Proceedings of the 30th Annual Conference on Bank Structure and Competition* (Chicago, 1994), pp. 85-117.

[16] See Frederic S. Mishkin and Philip E. Strahan, "What will technology do to financial structure?", National Bureau of Economic Research, Working Paper No. 6892 (January 1999).

[17] Alternatively, derivative contracts may be written on loans which have virtually the same effect as actually selling them (see chap. IX).

creating an actively traded secondary market in "emerging economy" distressed debt.[18]

When loans are sold by banks, it relieves loan officers of further responsibility to monitor the loans. The credit decision facing the loan officer changes from one of entering into a contract that will last as long as the loan is outstanding to one of entering into a contract that will look attractive enough to a potential purchaser of the contract. The purchaser of the loan—for example, a mortgage company in a housing case—will take over responsibility for the monitoring. Indeed, what the originating bank sells is a bundle of mortgages which the buyer understands contains a variety of different credit risks. In this context, the relationship between the borrower and the ultimate lender inevitably becomes less personal.

Moreover, as the financial industry became more complex and competitive, with more financial market alternatives to bank loans and with more banks able to contest other banks' individual markets, banks had to confront the fact that their largest customers had ever more alternative ways to obtain credit. These customers thus became less-and-less tied to individual banks. As a result, banks lost a considerable amount of their traditional business, although they compensated with new, fee-earning "off balance-sheet" activity.[19]

In other words, banks in the United States have increasingly sought to sell a full range of financial services to their corporate and household customers. Like their non-bank financial services counterparts, banks have sought to boost income from fee-earning activity and sales of ancillary services. However, they still provide the overwhelming bulk of short-term credit and demand deposits, although these are no longer a dynamic part of banking, owing, *inter alia*, to spreading electronic means of payment.[20]

Another aspect of the changing banking industry in the United States is the fall in the number of banks by almost 30 per cent during the 1990s and the rise in the share of banking assets held by the eight largest banking organizations from 22 to 36 per cent of the total, significantly larger changes than in other parts of the financial sector (other than savings, owing to the crisis therein).[21] The decline in the number of banks came about mainly through mergers, as the number of newly created banks in this period exceeded the number of bank failures. Certain mergers, particularly in 1998, were among very large banks, and in one case involved a bank with a major insurance company.

It does not appear, however, that this merger wave has reduced competition at the local level—the total number of bank offices rose. Moreover, there is little evidence of a diminution of services to small customers. While the large banking organizations lend less than before to small businesses, it appears that new banks enter and serve this market (although the evidence is limited).[22] Moreover, the market for lending to small firms has recently seen new competition from non-bank financial services companies that have begun to offer loans as part of efforts to cement their relations with the firms to which they sell their main services.[23] In this regard, non-bank companies in the United States are reproducing on a small scale an approach—of loan-as-marketing-device—that resembles what the large commercial banks of Japan employed earlier this decade.

This seems to indicate both that there may still be a niche for small banks in the world of mega-banks, and that small firms will be less dependent on

[18] For a brief history of that market, see *World Economic and Social Survey, 1995* (United Nations publication, Sales No. E.95.II.C.1), chap. XII.

[19] See Allen N. Berger, Anil K. Kashyap and Joseph M. Scalise, "The transformation of the U.S. banking industry: what a long, strange trip it's been", *Brookings Papers on Economic Activity*, 1995, No. 2, pp. 55-218.

[20] See Mishkin and Strahan, loc. cit.

[21] Data pertain to the period 1988-1997 (see Allen Berger, Rebecca Demsetz and Philip Strahan, "The consolidation of the financial services industry: causes, consequences, and implications for the future", *Federal Reserve Bank of New York Staff Reports*, No. 55 (December 1998), p. 3 and table 1).

[22] Ibid., pp. 28-34 and 43.

[23] See Joseph Kahn, "Banking on the unbanks", *The New York Times*, 4 February 1999.

these or other banks than was the case in the past. Banks will have to compete on the basis of a range of services offered even to small firms, not just access to credit.

In addition, there still seem to be some things that banks can do that the market will not do, things that grow out of the unique ability of a bank to form an ongoing relationship with a client on the basis of which the bank may lend in unusual circumstances. Historically, it has been the role of banks to fund "complex positions", the major difference today being that the range of credits that cannot be securitized or sold has narrowed considerably. But that role has not disappeared. In particular, it is expected that banks, especially large banks, will continue to innovate in the design of lending vehicles for corporate customers, supplying non-standard financial products that customers would utilize in conjunction with "informal contracts", wherein the bank implicitly agrees to provide further financial flows so as to unwind any unexpected negative outcomes from the innovative programmes.[24]

The conclusion here is thus that there is still a role in the United States—and even more of a role in the rest of the world—for commercial banks, which can be expected to supply a diverse mixture of financial services, along with traditional loans. However, it also follows that as banks, even small banks, increasingly offer non-traditional services, the burden grows on the supervisory authorities to ensure their prudential operation. It is also important that policy makers monitor the state of competition in the banking sector to ensure that the market for banking services is contestable and fair—that they determine, for example, if it is warranted that newcomers or alternative services should be encouraged to replace banks that merge and then withdraw from serving individual communities.

POLICY ISSUES FOR THE BANKING SECTOR IN DEVELOPING COUNTRIES

The picture of banking in the developed countries presented above is one of a very dynamic and innovative industry, albeit an industry vulnerable to crisis. It requires strong prudential oversight, as well as monitoring, with a view to promoting effective competition and equitable (non-discriminatory) provision of banking services. This applies equally to banking in the developing economies, especially as globalization brings competition from the international banking industry to their doorstep. There are additional policy considerations, however, that are particularly salient for developing countries.

Policy on liberalization

"Ever since the Third World debt crisis broke in August, 1982, debtor countries have been called on to 'adjust' as their contribution to resolving the debt problem."[25] This is how the book began that tried to define the basic propositions that make up what has come to be called the "Washington consensus" on appropriate domestic economic policy "adjustments".[26] Although the focus at the time was on Latin America, the Washington, D.C.-based institutions have offered basically the same prescription to all developing countries, with little change for at least two decades (albeit with new prescriptions added, such as those concerning transparency, as discussed below). Three sections of the

[24] See Raghuram G. Rajan, "Do we still need commercial banks?", *NBER Reporter* (National Bureau of Economic Research), fall 1998, pp. 14-18.

[25] John Williamson, "Introduction", in *Latin American Adjustment: How Much Has Happened?* (Washington, D.C., Institute for International Economics, April 1990), p. 1.

[26] The term "consensus" was meant in the sense of intellectual agreement among the economists who are active in policy advice and policy-making as they related to the Bretton Woods institutions and the Inter-American Development Bank a decade ago. However, since the principles in the Washington consensus were (and are) regularly found in the adjustment programmes that have been financially supported by the multilateral institutions and in communiqués of the policy-making bodies in Washington, D.C., one can understand them as reflecting a more-or-less formal consensus, at least among most of the world's finance ministries.

Washington consensus pertain to the banking sector: one on interest rates, another on privatization and a third on foreign direct investment (FDI).

The advice on interest rates was to remove policy controls and let the "market" determine their level. The concern was that interest rates were kept artificially low in developing countries—even negative in real terms in some countries in some periods—and that the economy was underutilizing and misallocating money and credit as a result. Developed countries also used controls on interest rates but these had been largely lifted by the end of the 1980s and the developing countries were being urged to do the same.

The advice on privatization was simple: do it. There was considerable criticism of the operation of State enterprises in developing countries and many banks were State-owned. They were seen to be inefficient, and overstaffed; they unnecessarily absorbed subsidies; and they were subject to political influence in allocating credit. Banks (and other firms) in which management sought to maximize profits—or more precisely, shareholder value—would not be subject to these failings, in the view of the Washington consensus.

The advice on FDI was also simple: remove restrictions. The focus here was not mainly on attracting foreign financial flows—indeed, the original Washington consensus had not included the liberalization of external capital flows, which was introduced only in the 1990s[27]—but rather on how foreign entry would add competition to local markets, bring technology (and some funds) and facilitate integration into the international economy (in the case of banking, this pertained mainly to facilitating access to financial instruments and services that were available overseas).

While each of the aforementioned parts of the Washington consensus has been more or less embraced by the developing countries, in the end there is less consensus about some parts than others. In the case of ceilings on interest rates, the argument for their removal is now widely considered to have been flawed, although there is no broad interest in reasserting the controls.

The argument on interest rates was somewhat confounded by a mixing of macroeconomic and structural concerns, but the central focus was on monetary stabilization. Indeed, inflation rates have fallen across the developing world and have averaged about 11 per cent a year since 1997, in contrast to triple-digit figures earlier (see table A.10). In addition, a large number of countries have removed interest-rate ceilings on loans and deposits, in particular in the period 1986-1992, a period that one author described as "the golden age of interest rate reform".[28]

The results of the interest-rate liberalization, however, were not always what had been expected. In some countries, real interest rates not only became positive, as desired, but rose to destructively high levels during the anti-inflation struggles and again in conjunction with the events surrounding the financial and currency crises in several emerging market economies, particularly in Asia and Latin America. In Africa, on the other hand, real interest rates in some countries did not even become positive following liberalization, while the spread between lending and deposit rates grew, owing to the monopoly power of the decontrolled banks.[29] Apparently—and a reminder of the continuing relevance of the "general theory of the second best"[30]—the efficacy of interest-rate liberalization is contingent on other policies' being also adopted.

Concerns about interest-rate liberalization, however, ran deeper, even at the level of economic theory. There has been an increasing questioning of the con-

[27] See Barry Herman and Barbara Stallings, "International finance and the developing countries: liberalization, crisis and the reform agenda," in *Global Financial Turmoil and Reform: A United Nations Perspective*, Barry Herman, ed. (Tokyo, United Nations University Press, 1999), pp. 13-17.

[28] Adam Bennett, "Behaviour of nominal and real interest rates", in *IMF Conditionality: Experience Under Stand-By and Extended Arrangements*, Part II (Background Papers), International Monetary Fund, Occasional Paper, No. 129 (Washington, D.C., September 1995), p. 37.

[29] Henk-Jan Brinkman, "Financial reforms in Africa and the lessons from Asia", in *Global Financial Turmoil and Reform...*, p. 223.

[30] R. G. Lipsey and Kelvin Lancaster, "The general theory of second best", *Review of Economic Studies*, vol. XXIV (1956-1957), pp. 11-32.

tribution that can reasonably be expected from interest-rate liberalization in raising economic efficiency and growth, which are especially important in developing economies. The kernel of the argument is that banking markets are not efficient in the theoretical sense because banking markets do not "clear". That is to say, because of the asymmetric information problem, which, as noted in chapter IV, is inherent in banking, there is an "adverse selection" problem that confronts banks. Their "rational" response is to hold interest rates below the maximum that would equalize supply and demand. Instead, banks ration the credit among prospective borrowers.[31] This is important because the original critique of interest-rate ceilings was that they created a credit rationing problem: the ceiling prevented the price of credit from rising until demand for credit equalled supply. It is now believed that credit will be rationed even without the ceiling's being set by policy.

The most important conclusion from this controversy is that there should be no presumption that private commercial banks, left to themselves, produce an allocation of credit that can be called "optimal" in any developmental sense. Governments may still find it useful to privatize their State-run banks and to withdraw from direct intervention in banking markets; but they should not presume that a totally passive policy on banking—or a policy limited to prudential concerns—would be sufficiently "pro-development".

On the other hand, it does not follow either that Governments will necessarily do a better job than private banks of allocating credit. In a great many cases, government direction of credit allocation was far from effective and in some cases hardly in the public interest. Nevertheless, a recent assessment of programmes in which Governments intruded into lending decisions of banks—in particular in "directed credit programmes"—is that "those programmes can indeed achieve their intended goals, at least for a certain time and under certain conditions. When they work well, they seem to be part of an array of tools that a government employs, as other factors are required in combination with direction of credit for such mechanisms to be successful".[32]

These complementary factors were not consistent with the main thrust of national and international policy and financial sector development in developing countries at the end of the twentieth century, namely, fostering a highly liberalized domestic financial environment and deepening integration into the international banking and financial universe. At least, it seems unlikely that finance ministries and central banks in developing countries—not to mention the commercial banking sector that has had to learn how to operate in the new global financial environment, sometimes at great cost—would countenance any time soon a reversal of the liberalization strategies of the past decade. Some new policy instruments may thus need to be developed for this new environment.

Policy on information and competition

One question that policy makers concerned with the functioning of the liberalized banking sector have to confront is how to ensure effective competition in the domestic market for loans. Large and well-established firms are likely to have an advantage over new or small firms in this regard, as they will be known to a larger circle of potential creditors and thus can negotiate better lending terms. In small countries with a limited number of large businesses and bank-

[31] The argument is, roughly, as follows: assume a bank manager can raise interest rates and that two entrepreneurs have projects with the same expected return, but different risks of failure. The banker would fund both projects at both low and high interest rates, but the entrepreneur with the low-risk project would withdraw it as being no longer viable at the high rate. The entrepreneur with the second project, however, might still go ahead. This is because the two projects were assumed to have the same expected return, which means that if the project succeeds, the pay-off is higher in the second project (while the probability of seeing that pay-off is smaller). The second entrepreneur understands that, if the project fails, he does not have to fully repay the loan. In effect, the bank shares the down-side risk with the entrepreneur, but not the profits if the project succeeds. Therefore, at the high interest rate the banker would have only high-risk projects to choose from, and this is the "adverse selection" result (the classic proof is Joseph E. Stiglitz and Andrew Weiss, "Credit rationing in markets with imperfect information", *American Economic Review*, vol. 71, No. 3 (June 1981), pp. 393-410).

[32] *World Economic and Social Survey, 1996* (United Nations publication, Sales No. E.96.II.C.1 and corrigendum), chap. V, last paragraph.

ing groups, this can be a major factor in the allocation of credit (without warranting the appellation of crony capitalism).

The "reputational capital" of well-known firms can be important, but it is especially significant when standards of accounting and reporting are low and information supplied by firms is not trustworthy. It has been argued that firms that gain reputational capital will have a financial incentive to maintain this through responsible behaviour, such as eschewing excessive risk.[33] This may well be the case, but from a policy perspective the most important task seems to be to create conditions in which creditors will be less dependent on reputational indications of creditworthiness and thus more open to newcomers.

In other words, the economic services of the financial sector can be enhanced to the degree that the information needed to make a loan decision about a prospective borrower can be standardized and depersonalized. Important ways include establishing and enforcing codes of business transparency, especially as regards adoption of agreed standards of accounting and reporting. These standards can always be evaded and so there also needs to be a culture of abiding by the standards. In countries where this does not already exist, the process of building such standards can take considerable time. By the same token, zero tolerance in credit allocation for discrimination by gender, race or ethnicity is required—as well as non-interference by government in the lending decisions of banks—so as to create and then bolster a culture of equality of treatment.

Expectations for improved information and transparency should, however, not be exaggerated. The experience of foreign direct investors, for example, is that in some countries in which they operate, information is available and reliable, if expensive to obtain. But its interpretation also requires local knowledge. In other countries, information is deemed poor and unreliable, and interpretation requires access to informal networks. A single piece of information, moreover, may mean different things in different national circumstances. There is, in other words, a contextual complexity that is often not transparent, especially to the foreign investor.[34]

Thus, while adoption of internationally agreed codes on transparency, reliability and timeliness of information needs to be encouraged, they will not per se draw aside the cultural curtain and homogenize business practices on the norms of any one country or group of countries (indeed, there are important differences in business culture among the countries of the Group of Seven). Adoption of international standards will not eliminate all distinct cultural norms ... and it would be presumptuous to say that they should.

Policy on foreign entry

There has been a range of attitudes towards the participation of foreign banks in domestic economies and a range of practices. In the mid-1990s in the developed countries, for example, foreign banks accounted for less than 2 per cent of total bank assets in Japan, and for less than 4 per cent in Germany, but for 22 per cent in the United States. The range in developing countries has been similar: from zero in Israel and 1 per cent in Mexico and Venezuela, through 3-5 per cent in Colombia, Indonesia, the Republic of Korea, South Africa, and Taiwan Province of China, and 7-9 per cent in Brazil, India and Thailand, 16 per cent in Malaysia, but to over 21 per cent in Argentina and Chile.[35]

[33] See Thomas Hellmann and Kevin Murdock, "Financial sector development policy: the importance of reputational capital and governance", in *Development Strategy and Management of the Market Economy*, vol. II, István Székely and Richard Sabot, eds. (Oxford, Clarendon Press on behalf of the United Nations, 1997), pp. 269-323.

[34] See Ray Loveridge, "Crisis and reform in South-East Asia: institutional issues and multinational enterprise", DESA Discussion Paper, forthcoming.

[35] See Morris Goldstein and Philip Turner, op. cit., p. 35.

It appears from the above that Governments find very different mixtures of foreign bank participation in their domestic banking markets to be desirable. Developments in East Asia since the financial crisis began there and in Latin America since mid-decade suggest that policy is shifting towards a greater role for foreign investment in banking. How a Government undertakes to welcome such a larger foreign presence, however, appears to be an important determinant of how successful it will be.[36]

Multinational banks (MNBs) traditionally serve market segments in which their multinational presence gives them a clear competitive advantage. One of the main reasons that MNBs seek to enter a new economy is to provide services to transnational corporations that are already their customers in other parts of the world. Further, MNBs provide services that other banks either are less familiar with or cannot provide. Such services include loans in foreign currency, acceptances and guarantees related to international trade, internationally syndicated loans and derivative products. Owing to the nature of these services, large domestic corporations become MNB clients, whereas smaller enterprises are less likely to require these services. Finally, MNBs offer their services to high net worth individuals to attract new deposits and to provide consumer finance. Such retail banking services include brokerage services, savings products, mortgages, credit cards and consumer loans.[37]

In most cases, MNBs have not expanded their activities beyond these market segments, although this seems to be changing. In particular, as home banking markets became saturated and profit opportunities seemed still large in emerging economies, some MNBs began to expand into foreign markets to service medium-sized enterprises and middle-income households. This has been the case recently, for instance, in Latin America, where entry of international banks into domestic banking poses competitive challenges for the local banks (see box V.2).

Both the traditional type of MNB entry into a market and the newer, direct competition entry are expected to improve competitive conditions in the local sector and the robustness of the banks. That is to say, policy makers usually seek to attract the foreign entry in order to bring foreign expertise and capital into local banking, while strengthening market discipline. It is possible, however, that foreign entry—particularly, the traditional type—may weaken the domestic banking sector and push it either to raise the risk and lower the quality of its lending portfolio or to curtail its lending, possibly leaving small and medium-sized enterprises with less access to credit than before.

The steps by which such unintended results may arise begin with liberalization policies, wherein domestic banks find themselves newcomers to an unregulated market environment, one into which powerful new banks suddenly enter. The local banks need new capital to compete with the MNBs, but the presence of MNBs limits the options for raising capital through retained profits. This is because more competition lowers the margin of interest rates charged on loans over interest rates paid on deposits and thus it lowers domestic bank profits and retained earnings.[38] Retained earnings are the main source of new capital, as official capital injections are generally eschewed and arranging new equity issues may be difficult.

The problem for the domestic banks is that not only will overall earnings on loans be lower, but some of their former low-risk credits will be siphoned off

[36] The present section draws heavily upon Christopher Weller, "The determinants and effects of multinational banks in developing and transition economies", DESA Discussion Paper, forthcoming.

[37] See Lawrence J. Brainard, "Capital markets in Korea and Taiwan: emerging opportunities for foreign banks", *Journal of Asian Economies*, vol. 1, No. 1 (1990), pp. 172-177; and Yoon-Dae Euh and James C. Baker, *The Korean Banking System and Foreign Influence* (New York, Routledge, 1990).

[38] These are the results, for example, of Stijn Claessens, Asli Demirgüç-Kunt and Harry Huizinga, "How Does Foreign Entry Affect the Domestic Banking Market?", *World Bank Policy Research Working Paper*, No. 1918 (1998).

Box V.2.

A NEW ROLE FOR FOREIGN BANKS IN LATIN AMERICA

There is a long history of foreign banking in Latin America; but there is also a new interest on the part of foreign banks in coming to the region. It appears that they will participate in the domestic market in a different way than their predecessors and are likely to have different effects.

The surge in foreign entry

While a number of foreign banks have long had branch networks in Latin America, there has been a strong new inflow of foreign direct investment (FDI) in Latin American banking since around 1995. Two Spanish banks (Banco Bilbao Vizcaya (BBV) and Banco Santander Central Hispano) were the first to aggressively enter these markets, aided by the competitive advantage of their cultural affinities. But they were closely followed by Canadian banks (Bank of Nova Scotia and Bank of Montreal), the Italian Sudameris, the Dutch ABN Amro and HSBC, the London-based parent of Hong Kong and Shanghai Banking Corporation. In addition, some Latin American banking groups (especially from Chile) are also building regional networks.

As of early 1999, several foreign banks that are relatively new in Latin America had established sizeable operations in a number of countries and were outpacing other long-established financial institutions. For instance, BBV now has holdings in Argentina, Bolivia, Brazil, Chile, Colombia, Mexico, Panama, Peru, Uruguay and Venezuela. On average, it controls 65 per cent of the institutions in which it has invested in the region. It employed more than 38,000 people in more than 1,600 branches as of October 1998. This presence contrasts dramatically with that of Citibank, which has been in the region more than 80 years, but at the end of 1998 had less than 12,000 bank employees and close to 200 branches.[a]

The recent surge of foreign banks has no precedent in Latin America, although the size of the foreign presence varies sharply from country to country.[b] As of September 1998, Peru had the highest foreign penetration among the major Latin American countries. Foreign banks there were estimated to control 61 per cent of total loans in the system. Foreign financial institutions had expanded substantially in Peru during 1997, as in Argentina, and that growth accelerated during 1998. Mexico, on the other hand, had a relatively low foreign presence, owing to regulations that limited foreign ownership of the three largest domestic banks, which accounted for about one third of the financial system's loans (these restrictions were removed at the end of 1998).

This trend is likely to continue. Even during the last half of 1998, when the economic environment in the region became increasingly difficult because of the international financial turmoil swirling especially around Brazil, foreign banks still made acquisitions, albeit fewer ones. Some foreign banks saw that episode as, in other words, an opportunity to expand by taking advantage of the very low stock market valuation of financial firms in Latin America at the time. Indeed, foreign banks have diversified from standard banking operations into private pension funds and the insurance sector.

The attraction to international banks

The new entrants into Latin American banking were encouraged by the turn to privatization and liberalization policies, the resolution of the foreign debt crises of the region and improved economic growth prospects. Also, with the end of high inflation and the maintenance of macroeconomic stability, the demand for financial

[a]   Andrew B. Collins and Thomas H. Hanley, "Citigroup's Latin American Banking Operations", Warburg Dillon Read, New York, March 1999.

[b]   Salomon Smith Barney, "Foreign financial institutions in Latin America", New York, September 1998; and "Update on foreign financial institutions in Latin America", New York, March 1999.

Box V.2 (continued)

c   Mauro F. Guillén and Adrian E. Tschoegl, "The Spanish banks in Latin America: a breakthrough in foreign retail banking", The Wharton School, University of Pennsylvania, mimeograph, January 1999.

services in Latin America is spreading. The foreign banks have thus chosen to compete for the middle-income customers and are investing for the long term, so as to be able to profit from the expected growth in banking in the region. Their quickest way into the market has been to acquire a large domestic bank, immediately giving a significant market share. They have also sought to create extensive branch networks through which to introduce new products. In the case of the Spanish banks, interviews suggest that they seek management control because they believe they can raise efficiency, introduce skills and experience and improve cash flow.[c]

The strategy of the new entrants differs from that of the long-established foreign-owned banks, which largely confined themselves to the "top" of the market, servicing multinational companies, local blue-chip firms and rich individuals. Now, however, the long-established foreign banks have begun to respond to the new competition by moving "down-market" in order to target middle-class retail consumers and medium-sized businesses. The goal is to be able to offer each customer a wide variety of financial services.

The attraction to local banks and policy makers

In some Latin American countries, such as Mexico, large domestic banking institutions have been actively seeking financial support from big foreign entities in order to be better able to compete. It is expected that most of the small and medium-sized banks will not be able to adapt to the new situation and will become "acquisition opportunities" for the foreign banks. Both of these developments illustrate a point made in this chapter about the impact of foreign entry on the capital needs of local banks. Indeed, financial authorities in Latin America have promoted the entry of foreign banks to strengthen the capital bases of ailing domestic banks through merger and acquisition and to increase competition and overall performance of the domestic banking system.

Also, foreign bank entry is seen to decrease the riskiness of the local financial sector. Local banks that are affiliated with a foreign institution are perceived to be less vulnerable during a domestic liquidity crisis, as they can generally call on support from their overseas parents. Moreover, the growing presence of foreign or foreign-controlled banks may increase the confidence of the Latin American public in the use of financial institutions and limit the number of occasions of panic withdrawals of deposits. Foreign banks are usually associated in the public mind with sound management and performance and are normally ranked high in terms of service and, consequently, the public perceives them as less risky than domestic institutions. This is important in Latin America, as many segments of the population still lack confidence in the financial system, owing to the high personal losses of small-scale depositors and investors resulting from the many banking crises of the past.

Moreover, foreign banks seem to have put pressures on domestic banks in the region to modernize, to reduce inefficiencies and to adopt new technology so as to be able to offer new products. Besides, as a result of increased banking competition, the net interest margin (the difference between what banks pay for deposits and what they charge for loans) has been falling in many Latin American countries.

However, although interest rates for domestic credit may have declined, this has mostly benefited the large firms, which are perceived as lower-risk clients. The challenge is to lower the cost and spread financial intermediation activity in Latin America to the economic agents that are now excluded from these services, extending both credits for small and medium-sized local enterprises and mortgages for households.

by the new MNB entrants. Credit to transnational corporations or to large, internationally-oriented domestic corporations is generally counted among lower-risk lending and these are precisely the customers that the MNBs have a competitive advantage in serving (capturing these clients is called "cherry-picking" in the financial community). Moreover, liberalization would likely raise the overall real interest rate initially, which would in any case discourage the low-risk, low-return borrowers and skew loan demand towards the higher-risk borrowers.

To maintain their level of lending, then, domestic banks would have to take on more of the higher-risk clients. If their capital backing were adequate to the task, this rise in the overall riskiness of their loan portfolios would not be a concern; however, the premise is that they are unable to add to their capital. Moreover, competition would in any case reduce the profitability of the domestic banks and thus the value of their equity. For a bank that begins the process inadequately capitalized, the ratio of loans to capital might fall perilously low. Such banks would have little to lose from adding higher-risk loans and raising the overall riskiness of the domestic banking system.

Banks that start off the liberalization process with stronger capital backing might respond with more caution to the loss of low-risk business. Evidence from some liberalizing emerging economies facing new MNB competition is, in fact, that domestic banks are more likely to curtail their lending.[39] This means that not only do they lose large clients to the MNBs, but they choose to serve fewer of their smaller clients than before. The problem is that, while they might have had a prudent level of capital for the amount and composition of lending undertaken in the pre-deregulation environment, that capital is sufficient to back only a smaller level of loans in the more competitive environment once the best credits are no longer available.

The policy question thus comes down to how best to prepare domestic banks for the impact of deregulation and foreign entry and how to assure continued availability of banking services to domestic banking clients. Regarding the latter, domestic banks in many cases served smaller, less profitable clients as a required part of a business that included substantial earnings on big clients.[40] After liberalization, there may well be fewer banks left operating and one has to ask whether the smaller clients will still be served by the remaining banks and, if not, what alternative sources will be supplied?

One aspect of preparing domestic banks for liberalization is prompting or helping them raise capital sufficient to withstand the shock of opening the market to new competition. By the same token, policy needs to ensure that domestic banks can access capital adequately after deregulation and foreign entry, so as to be able to appropriately respond to the competitive challenge of the foreign banks. Neither the ability of domestic banks to compete nor their ability to raise capital is assured. In this light, one option has been formation of "strategic alliances" (a limited form of corporate partnership) or joint ventures between domestic and foreign banks. Another is to anticipate that domestic banks will increasingly become takeover targets for aggressive foreign banks, as appears to have been happening in Latin America, as noted in box V.2. There is no single correct answer to the question how to proceed, but it is imperative that the question be asked.

[39] Case studies of Hungary, Poland and the Republic of Korea, as well as cross-sectional econometric exercises, point in this direction (see Weller, loc. cit.).

[40] That is to say, before deregulation, serving small clients (or serving rural areas) might have been implicitly subsidized by earnings on the big customers who will now switch to the MNBs. In some cases, there may have been explicit subsidies (or a State-owned bank might have used now-disappearing profits from its big customers to cover losses on its small customers).

BANKING IN ECONOMIC TRANSITION

41 The literature on banking reform and development in the transition economies burgeoned with the onset of the transition process in Central and Eastern Europe a decade ago. Two recent major overviews are Economic Commission for Europe, *Economic Survey of Europe, 1998, No. 2* (United Nations publication, Sales No. E.98.II.E.18), Part two; and European Bank for Reconstruction and Development (EBRD), *Transition Report, 1998: Financial Sector in Transition* (London, October 1998).

42 For a review beginning with the 1950s in Central and Eastern Europe, see *World Economic Survey, 1988* (United Nations publication, Sales No. E.88.II.C.1), chap. VI.

Although the formerly centrally planned economies had institutions that were called banks, there were no commercial banks in the sense, used here, of independent institutions that receive deposits and loan out the proceeds for short- and medium-term use, mainly by the business sector. Banking "reform" in the economies in transition was thus a project for building banks, almost *ab ovo*, out of institutions that had been very little like banks.[41]

The central planning authorities had mobilized the great bulk of investable resources, mainly from the enterprise sector, and allocated them to investment programmes that were decided upon centrally. The banking system was little more than a large accounting and payment service that passively carried out the central directives. It advanced working capital to enterprises and returned profits to the central accounts, where they offset losses of other enterprises and were used for new investment.

The economic and social transition that the planned economies embarked upon thus entailed a complete switch of methods of economic organization and development. This is not to say, however, that the system of central planning had functioned smoothly or without criticism before being jettisoned. Indeed, through much of the post-war era, reform of the planning mechanism was debated and various reforms were adopted by the centrally planned economies.[42] However, the repeatedly unsuccessful efforts to reform the planning system compromised its legitimacy without changing its essence until the political and economic eruptions in Europe and the former Union of Soviet Socialist Republics in the 1990s. Meanwhile, deep economic reforms began in China at the end of the 1970s and released the economic forces that have raised average incomes so dramatically in that country over the past two decades.

Whether undertaken gradually or suddenly, or in a context of economic growth or contraction, certain tasks have been essential to the introduction of commercial banking in transition economies. They involve institutional development (such as setting up new banks and supervisory and regulatory agencies) and human development (such as upgrading and developing the skills needed for conducting market-based banking business). They also involve questions of refining institutional structures, alleviating inherited burdens and increasing the autonomy of the new commercial banking institutions.

Reforming institutional structures

The first step in financial reform was typically to break apart the "monobank" system of central planning into a "two-tier" financial system that comprised a central bank and a group of commercial banks. The central bank was then to serve as the monetary authority and provide services to and oversee the commercial banks. They, in turn, were to become profit-seeking institutions that made loans, especially to companies—and these based on assessments of the firms and their projects—and charged them a realistic rate of interest that had to be paid. In all the countries, the introduction of such institutions was a major step, requiring new management goals and operating procedures not only in the new banks themselves, but throughout a new and evolving enterprise sector itself.

The formal establishment of the two-tier banking system took place relatively early in the overall reform process in most countries. China was the first case. The People's Bank of China transformed itself into a central bank and transferred its deposit-taking and lending functions to the newly established Industrial and Commercial Bank of China on 1 January 1984, as sanctioned by a September 1983 State Council decision. Hungary established a two-tier banking system in 1987 and also introduced a relatively liberal policy to license new entrants to the banking sector, although it protected the banks from foreign competition.

In the Soviet Union, liberalization of banking started in 1987, ahead of most other economic sectors. As a result, after the dissolution of the Soviet Union, all of its successor States boasted a large number of banks. For instance, the Russian Federation already had 1,360 commercial banks at the outset of the transition in early 1992.[43] The rapid expansion in the number of banks continued during the first years of transition in virtually all countries of the Commonwealth of Independent States (CIS).

Viet Nam followed, as the State Bank of Viet Nam started to withdraw from commercial banking activities in 1988. However, it only stopped direct lending to the productive sectors and direct financing of the state budget in 1992, thus gradually evolving into an institution primarily discharging central banking functions. Poland followed the Hungarian banking example in 1989 and the other countries in the region adopted similar structures thereafter in the context of the political and economic upheavals of the 1990s. Mongolia adopted its two-tier system in 1991, carving five commercial banks from the original monobank, and creating nine new ones (although they were small).

Of course, it is a simplification to focus only on the conversion of the single State bank into a central and commercial banking system. Other, more specialized financial institutions also existed under central planning and new ones were added under the reforms. For example, China's pre-reform banking system consisted of the People's Bank of China, the main bank that conducted both central and commercial banking activities, the Bank of China (the part of the People's Bank in charge of foreign exchange and international payment transactions), the Construction Bank (a subsidiary of the Ministry of Finance, disbursing investment funds for construction projects under the State economic plan and financed by the central budget) and a network of rural credit cooperatives. In 1979, the Agricultural Bank of China was established and the Bank of China officially separated from the People's Bank, while also widening its business scope to include issuing bonds on the international capital market in support of China's "open-door" policy. The Construction Bank also gained independence from the Ministry of Finance in 1979, and was authorized to take deposits and make loans to finance investment projects outside the State budget in 1980. The China Investment Bank was created in 1981 to handle project finance funded by international financial organizations such as the World Bank and the Asian Development Bank. As already noted, when the People's Bank became the central bank in 1984, the Industrial and Commercial Bank of China was created to take over the commercial banking activities of the People's Bank. Beginning in the mid-1980s, the Government of China instituted regulations to allow the establishment of joint-stock banks and non-bank financial institutions such as urban credit cooperatives, trust and investment companies, and finance companies affiliated with State-owned conglomerates.

[43] Organisation for Economic Cooperation and Development, *OECD Economic Surveys: Russian Federation, 1997* (Paris, 1997), p. 79.

In other words, over time the institutional structure filled out. China has been quite cautious, however, in respect of the number of banks that it has allowed to open. Foreign banks, with better technology and more expertise in commercial banking than China's relatively new banks, have been especially restricted. Representative offices of foreign banks are limited to foreign currency transactions, except that local currency business is allowed in the economic development zone of Pudong in Shanghai, albeit only in transactions involving foreign companies that invested locally.

In any event, a large number of banking institutions operating in a transition economy does not necessarily indicate a high degree of competition in financial activity. One can compare China, for example, where in 1995 four State-owned commercial banks accounted for over 60 per cent of total financial assets, with Viet Nam, which has a far greater number of non-State banking institutions. There, however, the four State-owned commercial banks accounted for about 75 per cent of banking system assets.[44]

The growth in the number of banks also does not necessarily indicate a healthy situation. Kazakhstan's experience, which is typical for countries in CIS, can illustrate this point. At the time of independence in 1992, the banking system consisted of the National Bank of Kazakhstan (NBK), which had been a branch of the Soviet *Gosbank*, and the five specialized banks—the Savings Bank (renamed People's Bank, following independence), the Bank for Foreign Trade (*Vneshekonombank*), the Agricultural Bank (*Agroprombank*), the Industry and Construction Bank (*Promstroibank*) and the Social Investment Bank (*Zhilsotsbank*). In addition, enterprises had established 72 commercial banks. There then followed a period of rapid expansion of the banking system. Immediately, four of the five specialized banks (all except People's Bank) were re-established as joint-stock companies and 112 new commercial banks were licensed, increasing the number of financial institutions to 184 by end-1993, including 177 private banks.

Most of the 177 banks established by State enterprises did not play a significant role in mobilizing domestic deposits, but merely channelled NBK credits to the parent enterprises. A large portion of their total credits reflected insider lending to shareholders. Moreover, accelerating inflation and falling real output led to severe financial disintermediation, as the private sector shifted its money holdings from rubles into foreign currency held outside the banking system. The deposit base fell from 96 per cent of gross domestic product (GDP) at end-1991 to only 20 per cent at the end of 1993.

This reflected in part the low level of confidence that people had in the viability of the banks. Commercial banks, on the other hand, had little incentive to attract private deposits for lending to firms that they considered to be of uncertain creditworthiness, owing, *inter alia*, to the weak accounting practices and poor state of financial information. Rather, banks had an incentive to concentrate their portfolios in relatively risk-free assets such as treasury bills and short-term trade financing; however, as the scope for increasing their holdings of such assets was limited, there was little incentive to try to increase their deposits.

In short, the rapid growth of the banking system in 1992 and 1993 did not increase financial intermediation in Kazakhstan.[45] It was also soon clear that the newly born banking system needed to be streamlined. Indeed, NBK at first allowed banks to operate that did not comply with prudential regulations. This

[44] At the end of 1996, in addition to the four State-owned commercial banks, there were 52 joint-stock banks (some with State-owned commercial banks as shareholders), 23 foreign bank branches, 4 joint venture banks, 62 foreign bank representative offices and 68 credit cooperatives in Viet Nam (World Bank, "Viet Nam: deepening reform for growth, an economic report", Report No. 17031-VN, 31 October 1997).

[45] This was quite unusual and contrary to expectations. However, Kazakhstan was not the only exception, as Belarus, the Russian Federation and Ukraine have also experienced a decline in the scale of banking activity since the start of the transition (see EBRD, *Transition Report, 1998...*, p. 118).

changed after 1995, especially once NBK began to impose more effective regulatory requirements. By 1997, the number of banks had fallen to 83.

Finally, it may be noted that the ownership structure of banks has not thus far figured in the discussion. Most of the banks began life in the transition period as State enterprises, although in several countries a number of new private banks arose. Two factors, however, seem more important than ownership structure in assessing bank performance. One is the structure of incentives given to management by the oversight regime. Indeed, the very low quality of regulations and supervision in the early years of transition in some countries may even have acted as an invitation to corruption. The second factor is the capacity of banks to become learning institutions, in particular as they had not heretofore engaged in the basic functions that banks perform in market economies—neither as traditional banks nor as the contemporary multi-service banks discussed earlier in this chapter. To hasten their internal reform, some banks have formed "strategic alliances" or "twinning" arrangements with foreign banks or became joint ventures. In other cases, banks remained wholly domestic institutions and policy focused on consolidating the number of banks through merger in order to create more viable institutions. As in the case of the developing countries discussed above, there are benefits and costs to foreign involvement, and easy and more difficult mixing of foreign and domestic business cultures, and thus no hard-and-fast conclusion may be drawn about the role of such involvement.

The burden inherited by the new banks

Each commercial bank that was carved out of a monobank inherited the loan portfolio and deposit base—indeed, the clients—that it had as a branch of the monobank. These banks thus remained under pressure to continue operating as before. Also, since this was a wholesale transfer operation based mainly on bureaucratic and political considerations, the composition of the asset portfolios of the newly created banks was usually very far from what might have been selected on business principles. In particular, whereas it is prudent for banks to have highly diversified loan portfolios, the portfolios of these banks were excessively concentrated either in individual industries or geographical regions, or in both.

One particular problem was the large and growing stock of non-performing loans on the books of the new banks. These loans had arisen under the planning system when the cash flow of the State enterprises had not met their payment needs. The State bank would automatically renew maturing credits and almost routinely capitalize interest obligations when the firms had difficulty making the payments. Had this taken place in a market economy, considerations of the bank's own profitability and regulatory restraints would have limited the degree to which it could be done. However, there were no effective limits in the transition economies; the opposite was more the case, as there was political pressure to extend the practice. The result was the rapid build-up of the stock of "bad loans", which quickly created solvency difficulties for the banks.

There have been three main approaches to treating the problem (perhaps four, if inflating away the debt is included). Poland followed a so-called decentralized approach to resolution of the debt burden. It put the banks in charge of loan recovery from their clients, while providing assistance. Within a year of the adoption of the March 1993 law on financial restructuring of enterprises and banks, the debt of about 800 enterprises accounting for most of the bad loans had been restructured through negotiated settlements with the banks, including debt-equity swaps and liquidation. Non-performing loans went from 60 per cent of total bank loans in 1991-1992 to 8 per cent of the loan portfolio of banks by 1995, while the average capital adequacy ratio reached 27 per cent, well above international standards. Behind these statistics, however, a number of weak banks held equity in weak firms to which they made weak loans, and enterprise restructuring was delayed.[46]

The Czech Republic (then part of Czechoslovakia) followed a centralized approach. In March 1991, the Government established the *Konsolidachni Banka* as a "loan hospital" to work out the non-performing loans of major banks. The banks swapped their non-performing loans for government bonds at a discount, and it was left to the loan hospital to arrange a work-out with the firms.

One may see that this approach made it quite easy for the banks to clean their books of bad debt, thereby creating a moral hazard problem. Indeed, a similar rescue was required again in 1993. The centralized asset recovery approach is useful when the scale of the problem is overwhelming for the banks and the skills are thin. It allows them to immediately concentrate on developing normal banking business. However, such rescue programmes have to be designed so as to discourage bank management from assuming that they will be relieved of the responsibility for future bad debt. Also, this can be a costly approach and can threaten the macroeconomic situation. In the Czech case, the financial cost of the two rescues reached $10 billion, or 15-20 per cent of GDP in those years.[47]

A third approach is explicitly aimed to buy time: policy makes it possible for banks to carry large amounts of bad debt on their books and not fail. This has been the case, for example, in China. The initial stock of bad loans had resulted from lending to State-owned enterprises (SOEs) before economic reforms were put in the agenda. However, government direction of credit allocation continued during the reform period (through the national credit plan before 1997), which led to the ballooning of this debt. Indeed, the difficult situation of the State enterprises continues.

Given that State-owned commercial banks in China are still burdened by problem loans to SOEs and that their primary borrowers remain SOEs, the entry of new banks with a clean slate and no obligation to support inefficient SOEs would have put the existing banks at a competitive disadvantage. Even new State-owned banks without the burden of inherited non-performing loans were more competitive than existing ones.[48] These new banks might have tried to use their operating profits to offer higher deposit rates in order to attract deposits for expansion, except that they could not: interest rates were controlled. In short, banking market regulations prevent State banks from collapsing under the weight of their bad loans, at least for the time being.

In the Russian Federation, some mixture of the second and the third approaches has been pursued. After the August 1998 crisis caused the collapse of financial intermediation in the economy, the state Agency for the Restructuring of Credit Organizations was set up to acquire controlling stakes in troubled banks, manage bad assets and initiate bank liquidations. However,

[46] See Cheryl Gray and Arnold Holle, "Bank-led restructuring in Poland: the conciliation process in action", *Economics of Transition*, vol. 4, No. 2 (1996), pp. 349-370.

[47] This was not the largest bank rescue. At the time of Bulgaria's banking crisis, 70 per cent of bank loans were "qualified" and the recapitalization cost 35 per cent of GDP, illustrating how "lethal" the mixture was of severe macroeconomic instability and structural distortions in banking (see John Bonin and Paul Wachtel, "Financial sector development in transition economies: a retrospective on the first ten years", prepared for the Fifth Dubrovnik Conference on Transition Economies, Dubrovnik, Croatia, 23-25 June 1999).

[48] For example, the Bank of Communication, established in 1987, has bucked the trend of declining capital-to-loan ratio and low profitability among large Chinese State banks.

it lacks the necessary financial resources and skills, and has limited legal powers, and its activities thus far have not been significant. Meanwhile, the bulk of household deposits at the commercial banks were transferred to the State-owned *Sberbank* (savings bank), although there was no sign as of early 1999 that the commercial banks were compensating *Sberbank* for assuming their deposit liabilities. On its part, the Central Bank has provided "stabilization credits" to the largest commercial banks with little control over the use of the funds and no clear definition of the basis on which the selection of banks was made. At the same time, the Central Bank has been slow to take administrative control of insolvent banks and to withdraw bank licences. As a result, the process of commercial bank decay continues, with many banks said to have engaged in asset-stripping.[49]

Policy environment and operational autonomy

Aside from their inherited burdens, many of the new commercial banks in transition economies were constrained by policy guidelines and, in particular, by government expectations that they would lend to SOEs that were probably insolvent, as noted above. Thus, not only did these new banks need to overcome their inexperience in acting as independent financial intermediaries, but they also needed to expand the realm in which they were free to make autonomous lending decisions.

Indeed, banks in Belarus, the Russian Federation and Ukraine are operating under firm State guidance, both formal and informal, despite having been privatized.[50] Their major functions are tax enforcement, managing and channelling State funds, and financing State debts: largely what their functions were in Soviet times.

In China, commercial banks were required to support politically important enterprises or economic endeavours through what was called "policy lending". It was realized, however, that the practice was impeding the "commercialization" of the banks. Thus, the Government established three "policy banks"— the State Development Bank, the Import-Export Bank and the Agricultural Development Bank—to relieve the commercial banks of their bad debt and of the need to make further policy loans.[51]

Policy lending thus began to decline in 1997, although as of 1998 most of the outstanding loans on the books of the commercial banks had not been transferred. Then, in February 1999, the Government announced a plan to reorganize the four large State-owned commercial banks, splitting off their trust and investment subsidiaries and organizing them into "asset management companies". These were meant to take over the bank loans of SOEs that had been overdue by two or more years.[52]

Vietnamese banks were also required to lend to troubled SOEs. Such lending accounted for 90 per cent of total bank lending in Viet Nam in 1990. It was reduced to 55 per cent by late 1996, but this still left the financial health of the banking system closely tied to that of the State enterprises. Moreover, having allowed a large number of new banks to be established, some of which were quite weak, Viet Nam faced a nascent banking crisis by 1998. In autumn 1998, the central bank was forced to close some of the weakest banks and placed 10

[49] EBRD, *Transition Report Update, 1999* (London, April 1999), p. 43.

[50] In Ukraine, of the five large banks, which together account for about 60 per cent of all bank assets, two are State-owned and the senior management of the other three banks remain closely associated with the Government. Those banks have been most often targeted for government-directed lending operations. In Belarus, the four former "specialized banks" account for more than 80 per cent of all deposits and loans. One of them is 100 per cent State-owned, while the shares of the State and State-related entities in the statutory capital of the other three vary from 39 to 53 per cent. And in the Russian Federation, although formally more independent, private commercial banks are largely functioning as an extension of the State and local administrations (on the role of the State in the development of Russian commercial banks, see, for instance, William Thompson, "Old habits die hard: fiscal imperatives, state regulation and the role of Russia's banks", *Europe-Asia Studies*, vol. 49, No. 7 (1997), pp. 1,159-1,185).

[51] The State Development Bank, the largest of the three, was to finance long-term infrastructure investment and support strategic or "pillar" industries. The Agricultural Development Bank would provide short-term loans to State agencies for agricultural procurement and it would fund projects for assisting the rural poor and for agricultural development in general. The Import-Export Bank's primary responsibility would be in external trade promotion. As envisaged, however, the policy banks were unlikely to be sustainable and would require repeated State injections of new resources. This has happened, both in the form of central bank loans and in mandatory purchase of their bonds by other financial institutions, which was meeting resistance (Ping Xie, "A theoretical analysis of difficult problems in the next stage of our country's financial system reform" (in Chinese), in *Guoji Jingrong Yanjiu* (International Finance Research), 5-11 May 1997).

[52] In addition, the securities business of these subsidiaries was to be merged into a new entity under the State Development Bank.

commercial banks under special supervision, while strengthening prudential requirements.

In a market economy, banks can decline to lend to some firms and charge higher interest rates on loans to others that they deem to be high-risk borrowers. This was not the case in Viet Nam. Interest rates were liberalized, but only partially. Controls were lifted on deposit rates to allow banks to compete for depositors, but interest-rate ceilings were maintained on loan rates, squeezing earnings.[53] Thus, banking policy had in a sense exacerbated what would have in any event been a difficult situation.

An important source of the banking problem in Viet Nam and China, as elsewhere, was outside the banks. That is to say, until the financial performance of the main clients of the banks improved, the banks would be hard-pressed to become more robust institutions.[54] Of importance in this regard is not only managerial capacity and management incentives to increase enterprise profits, but also the overall environment for business. The CIS countries may be an extreme case in point: in those countries, the main competitors of the banks were not other banks, but firms through their ability to increase their arrears to suppliers, tax collectors or workers. These arrears were expected to be forgiven at a later time, or at worst repaid without any interest charges. Loans from commercial banks could hardly compete in this situation.

While policy environments such as have been discussed in this section were initially pervasive, in some countries they were changed relatively quickly in the transition period. In Estonia, for example, an externally initiated financial crisis severely disrupted the financial sector and a widespread appreciation of vulnerability gave credence to the argument of the authorities that there was no alternative to strong reform measures (which also would mark a sharp break with the past).

In other words, the Estonian banks, which could be characterized at the start by weak and sometimes corrupt management and an ineffective regulatory regime, had to absorb two shocks in 1992: the freezing of the assets of non-Russian banks held in Moscow at *Sberbank* and *Vneshekonombank*, and the commitment to establish a currency board for foreign exchange management, which removed the possibility of easy credit infusions from the Bank of Estonia (BOE).[55] Any assistance would have had to come from the government budget and the Prime Minister said that there was no room in the 1993 budget for a bank bailout. The BOE thus closed or merged local banks, reducing their total number from 43 to 23 by mid-1993, removing management and imposing significant losses on shareholders and depositors (significantly, there were relatively few small depositors in these banks, as the crisis came early in transition and most household deposits were in the Savings Bank). In addition, the tough approach taken to the banks was mirrored in the approach taken in the business sector, where many State enterprises were placed into bankruptcy (and State banks were given no priority over other creditors in recovering funds). Indeed, the "hard-budget constraint" in the enterprise sector, combined with the knowledge that bank bailouts would not be forthcoming, led to much more cautious bank lending.

This approach was not without broader consequence, as the Estonian economy collapsed (output plummeted 22 per cent in 1992 and another 8 per cent in 1993). Economic recovery began, however, in 1995 and in a stronger insti-

[53] There was an international dimension to the difficulties in Viet Nam: as foreign interest rates had been below domestic ones and with the exchange rate fixed, there was a considerable incentive for foreign bank borrowing for onlending to domestic firms, especially SOEs. In the aftermath of the Asian crisis, however, the Vietnamese dong was devalued. As local borrowers had generally not been hedged, there were a number of defaults and payment delays in 1997.

[54] The need to focus the attention of policy makers on managerial incentives and performance in transition economy enterprises was already being discussed at mid-decade (see, for example, *World Economic and Social Survey, 1995...*, chap. VI).

[55] The currency board arrangement allowed for Bank of Estonia (BOE) credit in a banking crisis, but the central bank considered that unrealistic in this case, given the size of the banking problem and thus the inflationary consequences and undermining of the currency board that a BOE bailout would entail (the inflation rate was over 1,000 per cent in 1992, but 90 per cent in 1993).

tutional environment and with a deepening financial system. Other transition economies have seen equivalent—indeed, deeper—economic declines without the same degree of institutional reform, albeit in political environments that precluded consensus over policy directions and how the burden of adjustment would be shared. In yet other countries, reform of the policy environment has been spread out over many years, with new departures sometimes first introduced as experiments and then adopted more broadly, and without the punishing decline in living standards that the people of some countries have had to bear. Clearly, the political economy of reform does not lend itself to simple formulas, but without reform the development of the banking sector in transition economies will be severely constrained.

BANKING IN FINANCE AND DEVELOPMENT

If there is a common subtext in the review of banking in developed, developing and transition economies undertaken in this chapter, it is that even with government increasingly withdrawing from traditional roles in the banking sector, government retains an essential role. That role is more systemic than operational, a role more of oversight than of intervention, and more in the style of creating incentives for markets to produce socially desired ends than of erecting administrative barriers that markets seek to overcome.

In addition, the analysis of banks in this chapter has been from the viewpoint that banks need to be seen as complex institutions whose decision-making processes are to be explicitly taken into account in the analysis. Indeed "banks allocate funds, forming judgements of the likelihood of success of the project, not unlike a process that might occur within a government bureaucracy evaluating proposals."[56] There are, of course, important differences: first, banks pay for poor decisions through bankruptcy (assuming, one could add, the bank is not "too big to fail"), while governments do not; and second, banks look only at private returns in making decisions while Governments look at social and developmental dimensions, which may differ from such returns.

Government organizations can and have acted in a commercial and entrepreneurial way in various countries, but even if Governments wish to withdraw from such activities, the public purpose is best served when Governments undertake an active policy of financial sector monitoring and development. It may be important to know, for example, whether various population groups can access financial services through the banking sector or if not from that sector then through other financial institutions or markets, or whether innovative entrepreneurs can raise financial resources, and whether resources are impeded from being allocated to one economic sector or another (and if so whether it is economically warranted), and so on. The starting point in the current economic and political reality is that the banking sector is being increasingly liberalized and privatized and the challenge for policy is to oversee the banking sector in such a way as to strengthen it while also ensuring that it serves societal goals.

56 Joseph E. Stiglitz, "The role of government in the economies of developing countries", in Edmond Malinvaud and others, *Development Strategy and Management of the Market Economy*, vol. I (Oxford, Clarendon Press, 1997), pp. 90-91.

VI CAPITAL MARKETS IN DEVELOPING AND TRANSITION ECONOMIES

The trading of financial securities on exchanges began hundreds of years ago, but it has had varying degrees of importance in the financial systems and economic growth of the developed economies. As part of the global expansion and innovation in securities markets in the 1990s which were noted in chapter IV, securities markets have expanded very rapidly in some developing and transition economies, although often from very small bases. Having domestic capital markets—especially a stock exchange—has even taken on a symbolic value and has become an emblem of modern capitalism in certain economies. Experiences in capital-market development have been diverse, as they have occurred against very different economic backgrounds. The present chapter thus examines a range of experiences in the growth of capital markets in developing and transition economies, and seeks pointers towards a policy on capital-market development.[1]

CAPITAL-MARKET TRENDS IN DEVELOPING AND TRANSITION ECONOMIES

Domestic equity markets

Equity markets in emerging developing and transition economies grew rapidly in the 1990s. Their market capitalization—the market value of the shares of all companies listed on the exchanges—increased more than threefold between 1990 and 1996, the peak year. This reflected strong expansion in Asia and Latin America, as well as in Africa and the economies in transition. Price increases were substantial—although the index in United States dollar terms peaked in 1993 (see figure VI.1). The number of listed companies also grew rapidly, fed by privatization of State enterprises and the decisions of privately held companies to issue shares to the public. As a result, the share of these markets in the capitalization of world stock markets increased from about 7 per cent in 1990 to almost 12 per cent in 1996. With the several financial crises since 1997, this share dropped to under 10 per cent in 1997, the last year for which comprehensive data were available at the time of writing.

The development of several markets in Eastern and Southern Asia began to take off in the 1980s and their expansion continued at a rapid pace in the 1990s, at least until 1996. Indeed, the data shown in table VI.1 for 1997 are after a fall of more than half from 1996 in overall market capitalization in that region. The acceleration in stock market growth in the 1990s was most pronounced in Latin America, where capitalization of the major markets increased almost eightfold in the 1990-1997 period (see table VI.2). Selected markets in Africa grew sig-

[1] Capital markets especially in developed economies are also sources of short-term funds (for example, commercial paper and treasury bills). The present chapter focuses, however, on markets for long-term financial instruments, principally corporate stocks and government and corporate bonds.

Figure VI.1.
EMERGING STOCK MARKET CAPITALIZATION
AND PRICE INDEX, 1991-1997

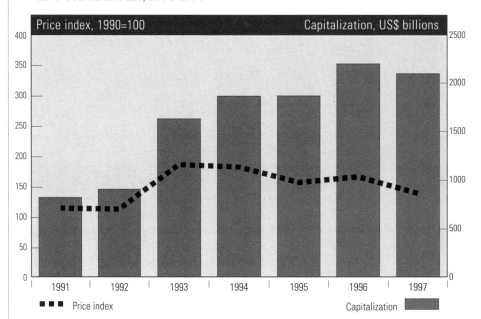

Source: International Finance Corporation, *Emerging Stock Markets Factbook 1998* (Washington, D.C., 1998).

Note: Capitalization and price index are for dollar values, converted from local currencies at market exchange rates, of all markets in the International Finance Corporation composite index.

nificantly but, with the exception of northern African countries and South Africa, this was from a very small base (see table VI.3). The history of such markets in the transition economies is the shortest overall, but quite dynamic (see table VI.4).

While the total market value of the companies listed on a stock exchange says something about the role of publicly held companies in the corporate life of individual countries, it would be a misleading indicator of how much finance is raised through new equity capital. Compared with market value, the latter has been quite modest, although it has represented a significant share of fixed investment in some developing countries, as discussed below. According to one estimate, the total value of new share issuance in the major East Asian markets from 1990 to 1996 ranged from 3 per cent of market capitalization in the Republic of Korea and Malaysia to 4 per cent in Thailand and 7 per cent in Indonesia. The average ratio for a sample of Latin American countries (Argentina, Brazil, Chile, Mexico and Venezuela) was even lower, about 1.5 per cent.[2]

There is also a wide variation among the regions in the liquidity of stock markets. An indicator of liquidity is the turnover ratio, which is the ratio of traded value in a period to market capitalization. By 1996, the turnover ratios in Asian markets were generally 30 per cent or higher, having increased significantly from the 1980s. Turnover in Latin American countries was lower, with the exceptions of Argentina, Brazil and Mexico. African markets, with the exception of South Africa and some of the northern African countries, showed much less trading activity, with turnover ratios rarely exceeding 10 per cent. Turnover in the transition economy markets has been relatively high.

[2] Based on data from the International Finance Corporation's Emerging Market Data Base (see C. R. Harvey and A. H. Roper, "The Asian bet", paper presented at the World Bank Group-Brookings Institution Conference, "Preventing Crises in Emerging Markets", 26 and 27 March 1999, Palisades, New York).

Table VI.1.
EQUITY MARKETS IN SELECTED EAST AND SOUTH ASIAN COUNTRIES, 1985-1997

| | Market capitalization[a] | | | | | | Number of companies listed | | | Traded value[b] (Millions of dollars) | | | Turnover ratio[c] (Percentage) | | |
| | 1985 | | 1990 | | 1997 | | | | | | | | | | |
	M$	%GDP	M$	%GDP	M$	%GDP	1985	1990	1997	1985	1990	1997	1985	1990	1997
India	14364	6.8	38567	12.6	128466	33.8	4344	6200	5843	4959	21918	53954	34.5	56.8	42.0
Indonesia	117	0.1	8081	7.1	29105	13.5	24	125	282	3	3992	41650	2.6	49.4	143.1
Korea, Republic of	7381	7.8	110594	43.6	41881	9.5	342	669	776	4162	75949	170237	56.4	68.7	406.5
Malaysia	16299	52.0	48611	113.6	93608	95.6	222	282	708	2335	10871	147036	14.4	22.4	157.1
Philippines	669	2.2	5927	13.4	31361	38.1	138	153	221	111	1216	19783	16.6	20.5	63.1
Thailand	1856	4.8	23896	28.0	23538	15.3	100	214	431	568	22894	23119	30.6	95.8	98.2
Total	40616	8.2	235676	27.8	347959	25.4	5170	7643	8261	12138	136840	455779	29.9	58.1	131.0
China	-	-	2028[d]	0.5[d]	206366	22.5	-	14[d]	764	-	820[d]	369574	-	40.4[d]	179.1

Sources: International Finance Corporation, *Emerging Stock Markets Factbook 1998* (Washington, D.C., 1998); International Monetary Fund, *International Financial Statistics,* various issues.

Note: M$: Millions of dollars; %GDP: Percentage of GDP.

[a] Year-end total market values of listed domestic companies.
[b] Annual total traded value.
[c] Ratio of total value traded to year-end market capitalization.
[d] Data for 1991.

Table VI.2.
EQUITY MARKETS IN SELECTED LATIN AMERICAN COUNTRIES, 1985-1997

| | Market capitalization[a] | | | | | | Number of companies listed | | | Traded value[b] (Millions of dollars) | | | Turnover ratio[c] (Percentage) | | |
| | 1985 | | 1990 | | 1997 | | | | | | | | | | |
	M$	%GDP	M$	%GDP	M$	%GDP	1985	1990	1997	1985	1990	1997	1985	1990	1997
Argentina	2037	2.3	3268	2.3	59252	18.3	227	179	136	631	852	25702	31.0	26.1	43.4
Brazil	42768	30.9	16354	3.7	255478	31.8	541	581	536	21484	5598	203260	50.2	34.2	79.6
Chile	2012	12.2	13645	45.0	72046	93.4	228	215	295	57	783	7445	2.8	5.7	10.3
Colombia	416	1.2	1416	3.5	19529	20.5	102	80	189	30	71	1894	7.2	5.0	9.7
Mexico	3815	2.1	32725	12.5	156595	38.9	157	199	198	2360	12212	52646	61.9	37.3	33.6
Peru	760	4.4	812	2.4	17586	27.0	159	294	248	38	99	4033	5.0	12.2	22.9
Venezuela	1128	1.9	8361	17.2	14581	16.7	108	76	91	31	2232	3858	2.7	26.7	26.5
Total	52936	9.8	76581	7.7	595067	32.1	1522	1624	1693	24631	21847	298838	46.5	28.5	50.1

Sources: International Finance Corporation, *Emerging Stock Markets Factbook 1998* (Washington, D.C., 1998); International Monetary Fund, *International Financial Statistics,* various issues.

Note: M$: Millions of dollars; %GDP: Percentage of GDP.

[a] Year-end total market values of listed domestic companies.
[b] Annual total traded value.
[c] Ratio of total value traded to year-end market capitalization.

Table VI.3.
EQUITY MARKETS IN SELECTED AFRICAN COUNTRIES, 1990-1997

	Market capitalization[a]				Number of companies listed		Traded value[b] (Millions of dollars)		Turnover ratio[c] (Percentage)	
	1990		1997							
	M$	%GDP	M$	%GDP	1990	1997	1990	1997	1990	1997
Northern Africa										
Egypt	1765	6.0	20830	27.5	573	650	126	5859	7.1	28.1
Morocco	966	4.0	12177	36.3	71	49	62	1048	6.4	8.6
Tunisia	533	4.6	2312	12.2	13	34	19	285	3.6	12.3
Subtotal	3264	4.9	35319	27.6	657	733	207	7192	6.3	20.4
Sub-Saharan Africa (excluding South Africa)										
Botswana	-	-	613	12.4	-	12	-	74	-	12.1
Côte d'Ivoire	549	5.7	1228	11.9	23	35	18	24	3.3	2.0
Ghana	-	-	1130	16.4	-	21	-	47	-	4.2
Kenya	453	6.4	1811	17.7	54	58	10	104	2.2	5.7
Mauritius	268	10.7	1663	39.8	13	40	6	137	2.2	8.2
Namibia	-	-	689	21.8	-	13	-	24	-	3.5
Nigeria	1372	5.2	3646	2.6	131	182	11	132	0.8	3.6
Swaziland	17	2.1	129	9.8	1	4	0	378	0.0	293.0
Zambia	-	-	705	18.1	-	6	-	9	-	1.3
Zimbabwe	2395	40.5	1969	24.9	57	64	51	532	2.1	27.0
Subtotal	5054	22.4	13583	16.7	279	435	96	1461	1.9	10.8
South Africa	137540	137.6	232069	179.8	732	642	8158	44893	5.9	19.3
Total	145858	66.6	280971	63.0	1668	1810	8461	53546	5.8	19.1

Sources: International Finance Corporation, *Emerging Stock Markets Factbook 1998* (Washington, D.C., 1998); International Monetary Fund, *International Financial Statistics*, various issues.

Note: M$: Millions of dollars; %GDP: Percentage of GDP.

[a] Year-end total market values of listed domestic companies.
[b] Annual total traded value.
[c] Ratio of total value traded to year-end market capitalization.

In many of the emerging economies, a large number of the listed companies are infrequently traded. In addition, in many countries, only a small proportion, often less than half, of the total shares of a listed company are traded, owing to the high concentration of "insider" shareholders who do not trade their shares. Examples of this are the large holdings by founding families of conglomerates and government holdings of partially privatized companies.

Moreover, despite the growth of market capitalization and the number of listed companies, a small number of companies usually account for a dispro-portionate share of the market (see table VI.5). Asian markets are generally the least concentrated, with the share of the 10 largest stocks accounting for about 25 to 50 per cent of total market capitalization. They are also least concentrat-ed in terms of total value traded. In Latin America, the share of the 10 largest

Table VI.4.
EQUITY MARKETS IN SELECTED ECONOMIES IN TRANSITION, 1991-1997

	Market capitalization[a]				Number of companies listed		Traded value[b] (Millions of dollars)		Turnover ratio[c] (Percentage)	
	1991		1997		1991	1997	1991	1997	1991	1997
	M$	%GDP	M$	%GDP						
Czech Republic	5938[d]	16.5	12786	24.6	1024[d]	276	1328[d]	7055	22.4[d]	55.2
Hungary	505	1.5	14975	33.3	21	49	117	7684	23.2	51.3
Poland	144	0.2	12135	8.9	9	143	28	7977	19.4	65.7
Russian Federation	244	0.05	128207	27.8	13	208	..	16362	..	19.4
Slovakia	1093[d]	7.9[d]	1826	9.3	18[d]	872	120[d]	2165	11.0[d]	118.6

Sources: International Finance Corporation, *Emerging Stock Markets Factbook 1998* (Washington, D.C., 1998); International Monetary Fund, *International Financial Statistics*, various issues.

Note: M$: Millions of dollars; %GDP: Percentage of GDP.

[a]   Year-end total market values of listed domestic companies.
[b]   Annual total traded value.
[c]   Ratio of total value traded to year-end market capitalization.
[d]   1994 data.

stocks in market capitalization is somewhat higher and concentration in turnover is even higher. This reflects the slow growth in the number of listed companies in most countries and the importance of new issues by a small number of large, well-known, often privatized State enterprises, including oil companies, mining companies, utilities, major State banks and telecommunications giants. The increase in market capitalization in most African countries is also associated with the increased value of the shares of a limited number of well-known companies in the natural resources, finance and infrastructure sectors. The corresponding ratios for the transition economies reflect the different privatization policies followed in those countries, as discussed below.

Domestic bond markets

The market value of bonds listed on domestic markets in the developing economies is substantially smaller than that of equities, even in the largest markets. The value of domestic bonds outstanding in Asian, Latin American and the transition economies, is about 20 per cent of gross domestic product (GDP) and in Africa about 30 per cent of GDP (see table VI.6). In Africa, domestic bonds are largely accounted for by South Africa and some northern African countries.

In general, government bonds dominate the market, although corporate bonds have come to represent a sizeable share of the total in a number of countries. As bonds are mainly purchased and held, liquidity in the secondary market for bonds is highly limited.

Most bond markets in Eastern and Southern Asia began to grow significantly in the 1990s as a number of Governments began to actively encourage their development. During the period 1989-1994, the aggregate East Asian bond market grew by almost 10 per cent annually, but from a very small base.[3] Despite these attempts to expand the bond markets, they are not extensively

[3]   See World Bank, *The Emerging Asian Bond Market* (Washington, D.C., 1995).

Table VI.5.
CONCENTRATION IN MARKET CAPITALIZATION AND TOTAL VALUE
TRADED IN EMERGING EQUITY MARKETS

	Percentage of 10 largest stocks in total market capitalization		Percentage of 10 largest stocks in total value traded	
	1990	1997	1990	1997
Latin America				
Argentina	60.2	51.9	73.7	85.4
Brazil	22.4	42.4	34.4	63.7
Chile	48.8	42.2	56.7	58.3
Colombia	76.9	49.8	38.5	67.8
Mexico	35.5	35.5	25.7	45.6
Peru	..	51.1	..	56.4
Venezuela	60.9	61.5	86.6	65.8
East and South Asia				
India	23.5	24.8	30.6	81.1
Indonesia	51.0	47.6	41.1	32.1
Korea, Republic of	30.9	38.8	25.6	12.5
Malaysia	28.0	36.4	19.2	15.5
Philippines	56.3	48.1	56.0	35.2
Thailand	35.7	47.6	20.4	36.0
China	-	..	-	13.8
Africa				
Egypt	..	29.8	..	36.4
Morocco	..	65.2	..	73.4
Nigeria	53.1	45.8	60.7	57.2
South Africa	..	26.1	..	27.6
Zimbabwe	48.3	67.4	33.5	42.9
Economies in transition				
Czech Republic	-	58.4	-	4.0
Hungary	-	85.2	-	73.0
Poland	-	40.0	-	23.5
Slovakia	-	76.8	-	1.7
Russian Federation	-	58.5	-	71.9

Source: International Finance Corporation, *Emerging Stock Markets Factbook 1998* (Washington, D.C., 1998).

used by corporations. The vast majority of the bonds are issued by Governments and State-owned enterprises.

The development of most Latin American bond markets also accelerated in the 1990s with the end of the foreign debt crisis, but they are still small relative to equity markets. Within Latin America, Brazil, Mexico, Argentina and Chile have developed the largest bond markets. As in Asia, bond issuance in most of these markets is dominated by government except for Chile, which has the most well-developed corporate bond market in the region, and Mexico, where corporate issues represent nearly half of total bonds outstanding.

Table VI.6.
VALUE OF BONDS OUTSTANDING IN DEVELOPING COUNTRIES AND ECONOMIES IN TRANSITION[a]

Millions of dollars	Domestic			External	Percentage of GDP	
		of which:			Total	Domestic
	Total	Sovereign	Corporate	(total)	bonds	bonds
East and South Asia (excluding China)	173 699	104 496	20 600	39 904	22.0	17.8
Latin America and the Caribbean	309 280	275 492	33 788	256 284	35.3	19.2
Africa	103 636	86 006	17 630	26 371	35.7	28.4
Northern Africa	25 400	25 250	150	10 383	78.5	49.7
Sub-Saharan Africa	78 236	60 756	17 480	15 988	44.7	37.1
Economies in transition	200 681	197 791	2 890	58 529	27.1	20.9
Selected countries						
Brazil	186 823	185 972	851	80 933	39.2	27.3
South Africa	77 600	60 340	17 260	3 602	53.8	51.4
India	73 530	36 708	..	4 382	21.3	20.1
Russian Federation	60 711	60 691	20	37 365	19.9	12.3
China	45 400	41 400	..	11 901	6.7	5.3
Malaysia	41 600	29 100	..	6 227	50.6	44.0
Poland	41 080	41 020	60	6 673	35.5	30.5
Mexico	38 304	21 258	17 046	59 620	15.7	14.2
Turkey	23 214	22 604	610	13 438	17.2	10.9
Chile	31 042	19 849	11 193	7 142	57.1	46.4

Sources: World Bank, *Global Development Finance*, 1998 (Washington, D.C., 1998), table IA.1; and World Bank data.

[a]   Data representing either 1995 or 1996.

While equity markets have begun growing in many countries in Africa, bond markets are still in the incipient stage in most countries, except South Africa. A survey of 40 African countries found that about half of them have neither primary nor secondary markets for long-term bonds. Secondary markets exist only in seven countries and trade mainly government bonds. Only markets for large issues such as South Africa are liquid.[4]

The South African bond market is the largest and the only well-established market in Africa. Government debt accounts for about 75 per cent of the total value outstanding, the rest being State-controlled utilities and a few corporate bonds. Non-resident investment into the domestic bond market has been substantial since the early 1990s, attracted by the ending of the anti-apartheid sanctions, the abolition of the dual currency system, and increased transparency and liquidity in the market. A central depository and an electronic clearing house have been operational since 1995, and by 1997, bond settlement procedures had met international standards.

In the transition economies, bond markets are almost exclusively for sovereign issues. There have been a few private corporate issues, particularly private

[4]   See M. Ncube, "Financial markets and monetary policy in African countries", The African Economic Research Consortium (AERC) Collaborative Research Project Report, 1997.

placements, but overall domestic bond markets have not been a major source of enterprise financing.

International flows into emerging markets

As part of their financial liberalization drive, many developing and transition economies relaxed restrictions on foreign purchases of the securities traded on their domestic markets in the late 1980s and early 1990s. At the same time, with the resolution of the Latin American external debt crisis, Latin American government and private borrowers joined increasing numbers of borrowers from other regions in floating international bond issues. International equity issues also burgeoned. The net result, as may be seen in table VI.7, was a substantial increase in foreign financial inflows into the stocks and bonds of these countries. While there were large inflows into the domestic securities markets of several countries, there was also a burgeoning of international issues of equities and bonds (see tables VI.8 and VI.9).

International equity issues take place mainly in a special financial instrument. Companies from developing and transition economies generally do not meet fully the accounting and reporting standards required for listing on the exchange of a major developed economy, although this is improving. A mech-

Table VI.7.
NET FOREIGN FLOWS INTO PORTFOLIO EQUITY AND
BONDS OF DEVELOPING COUNTRIES,[a] 1990-1997

Billions of dollars								
	1990	1991	1992	1993	1994	1995	1996	1997
Portfolio equity flows								
All developing countries	2.6	6.8	13.5	50.4	34.0	34.0	41.6	26.0
of which:								
Latin America	0.9	5.7	8.0	27.2	13.2	7.6	13.9	9.9
East and South Asia	1.7	1.1	5.5	22.7	18.8	20.6	23.3	11.7
Africa	0.0	0.0	0.0	0.0	0.9	5.0	3.5	3.6
Bonds								
All developing countries	0.0	9.2	9.9	32.8	34.2	25.2	52.7	35.9
of which:								
Latin America	0.1	4.1	4.7	20.9	14.3	11.8	29.8	12.8
East and South Asia	-0.6	4.6	2.6	9.0	18.0	11.2	19.9	18.4
Africa	-0.1	0.0	-0.2	-0.7	1.0	1.2	1.0	1.8

Sources: UN/DESA, based on World Bank, *Global Development Finance 1999* (CD-ROM) (Washington, D.C., 1999).

[a] Including purchases on domestic and international markets.

anism was thus developed that indirectly allowed such companies to tap the equity market, first in the United States of America (the American Depositary Receipt, or ADR) and then in Europe (the Global Depositary Receipt, or GDR). An ADR, for example, is a negotiable certificate issued by a bank in the United States that represents a certain number of a company's shares that are held by the bank as depositary. New depositary receipts can be issued either from existing company shares or by creating new shares.

Companies listing depositary receipts on a foreign stock exchange have to meet certain regulatory requirements determined by the supervisory authority of the exchange.[5] This not only permits trading in the deep markets of developed countries, but also boosts investor confidence. Transaction costs are lower than in the home market owing to the more efficient settlement and custody of shares in the developed-country stock markets. Finally, for the dollar-based investor, currency exchange costs are eliminated, as the depositary receipts trade in the currency of the host stock market.

Issues of depositary receipts by emerging market companies grew from an average of about $5 billion annually from 1989 to 1995 to $7.7 billion in 1997.[6] Latin American companies have been the most active issuers, particularly those of Argentina, Brazil, Chile and Mexico.[7] Issuers are attracted because this form of equity instrument overcomes the low liquidity and partial restrictions on foreign investment in domestic equity markets. Chile's 25 ADRs, for example, have an average daily traded value that is more than four times that of the entire Santiago stock exchange, where some 300 companies are listed. Similarly, traded value in some Argentine ADRs is several times greater than that of domestically listed shares of the same company.[8] In Asian countries, in contrast, the value of international equity issues was only 15 per cent of the value of issues in domestic markets.

International bond issues by developing economies grew rapidly in the 1990s. At mid-decade, the total outstanding value of these bonds was largest by far in Latin America, equivalent to about 16 per cent of GDP and almost as large as the value of domestic bonds (see table VI.6). Although sovereign bond issues predominate, averaging about 70 per cent of total issues, corporate issues have grown enormously, particularly those of Latin American countries.

[5] For example, the United States Securities and Exchange Commission (SEC) established different registration and reporting requirements for different types of ADR facilities. The most common among publicly traded ADR issues are sponsored ADRs, classified into three levels, according to different regulatory requirements. Level I ADRs, traded over the counter only, are the simplest and the fastest growing segment among the ADR programmes and do not require full compliance with generally accepted accounting principles (GAAP) or SEC rules; Level II and III ADRs are listed on a United States exchange, with Level III ADRs differing from Level II ADRs in two respects: Level III ADRs are derived from the additional issue of domestic shares and are sold to raise capital and they need to adhere to more stringent GAAP and SEC reporting requirements. In addition to using the three levels of sponsored ADR programmes, companies can raise capital through a private placement of sponsored ADRs with large institutional investors, without the need for SEC registration.

[6] See World Bank, *Private Capital Flows to Developing Countries: The Road to Financial Integration* (Washington, D.C., 1997), p. 308; and data received from International Finance Corporation.

[7] See Harvey and Roper, loc. cit., p. 13.

[8] See World Bank, *Private Capital Flows to Developing Countries ...*, pp. 306-307.

Table VI.8.
INTERNATIONAL EQUITY ISSUES OF EMERGING ECONOMIES, 1990-1998

Millions of dollars									
	1990	1991	1992	1993	1994	1995	1996	1997	1998
Total equity issues	1166	5574	7247	11915	18038	11193	16414	24802	8486
Asia	900	952	2914	5156	12130	8864	9789	13240	4398
Africa	0	143	154	215	574	542	781	1118	1435
Latin America	98	3891	3876	6022	4604	962	3661	5102	164
Europe	97	81	21	186	641	570	1289	2945	2489

Sources: IMF, *International Capital Markets: Developments, Prospects, and Key Policy Issues* (Washington, D.C., IMF, September 1998); and data received from IMF.

Table VI.9.
INTERNATIONAL BOND ISSUES OF EMERGING ECONOMIES, 1990-1998

Millions of dollars									
	1990	1991	1992	1993	1994	1995	1996	1997	1998
Total bond issues	7789	13946	24394	62671	56540	57619	101926	128142	75517
Asia	2604	4072	5908	21998	29897	25307	43144	45532	11484
Africa	0	311	724	170	2116	1947	1648	9358	1381
Latin America	2850	7085	12933	28794	17990	23071	47157	54365	38338
Europe	2335	2077	4829	9658	3543	6583	7408	16217	24314

Sources: IMF, *International Capital Markets: Developments, Prospects, and Key Policy Issues* (Washington, D.C., IMF, September 1998); and data received from IMF.

The level of participation of these countries in the international bond market has fluctuated with their access to international finance in general. International bond issues surged with the return of Latin American countries to the international debt market in the early 1990s. They continued to grow until the Mexican crisis (see table VI.9). Issues then recovered strongly in 1996 and, in spite of the Asian crisis, continued to increase in 1997 along with substantial narrowing of interest rate spreads of these bonds over a riskless benchmark, a United States Treasury bond of equivalent maturity. In 1997, investors shifted their investments from Asian to Latin American debt, but by 1998 the full brunt of the Asian and Russian crises was felt and bond issues fell sharply from 1997 levels.

CAPITAL-MARKET DEVELOPMENT IN DEVELOPING COUNTRIES

The rapid growth of financial markets in developing countries noted above was primarily the result of a shift towards an increased market orientation in economic development policy. As part of that shift, Governments sought to promote the domestic market for finance, both equities and bonds.

Factors pushing capital-market growth

Equity market development was given a major boost by the privatization of State enterprises, which has been an important component in structural adjustment policies, especially in Latin America. Privatization of State enterprises— and in some countries a desire of the owners of closely held companies to cash in some of their capital gains by a public offering—has provided a supply of new shares to the market. On the demand side, the development of contributory pension funds in a growing number of countries, particularly in Latin America and Asia, has channelled contractual household savings to institutional investors who place the funds in the securities market. However, the generally small size of these funds and restrictions on their asset allocations in many countries have limited their role in boosting liquidity in equity and bond markets, as discussed below.

Governments have taken various specific measures to promote the development of equity markets. These include public education programmes on securities ownership and government requirements that companies distribute share offerings to their employees. Tax incentives were also given in some cases to both issuers and investors. A number of Asian and Latin American countries modernized the infrastructure for trading, clearing and settlement and custody of equities. This improves the speed and lowers the transaction cost of the equity market. The cost and requirements for listing a company on an exchange have also been reduced and streamlined over time. Intensive efforts have been made to strengthen the regulatory and supervisory system of capital markets. These efforts have helped to build investor confidence in the markets, although much remains to be done.

With the enormous infrastructure needs that emerged in the 1990s, Asian Governments have also actively promoted domestic bond markets. In some cases, this included issuing government debt instruments, since the extended period of fiscal balance or surplus in a number of countries in East Asia meant that there was only a small government bond market. This in turn hindered the development of a corporate bond market insofar as the yield (and thus the price) of a corporate bond is usually determined as a risk premium to be added to the interest rate on a comparable "risk-free" government bond. With a limited number of government securities to serve as benchmarks, there would be more uncertainty about whether the market pricing of a specific corporate bond was appropriate. As a result, a number of economies in the region, such as Hong Kong Special Administrative Region (SAR), Malaysia and Thailand, issued government bonds to serve as benchmarks that would facilitate development of the market.

In Latin American countries, the growing number of privatized companies and the generally low leverage of corporations (with the exception of those in Chile) have prompted recent development of the bond markets. Furthermore, the sharp decline in inflation in the region in the 1990s has also improved conditions for bond market development. In Argentina, small and medium-sized companies have recently started to participate in the bond market, encouraged by tax incentives, declining trading costs and the easing of rating requirements for such companies.

Foreign financial inflows have also spurred growth of equity markets in developing countries, particularly in Asia and Latin America in the 1990s. The surge in foreign inflows was prompted by improvements in economic and institutional conditions and changes in the international financial environment, as well as advances in information technology. The end of the debt crisis, the intensive market-oriented reforms in several countries in Latin America and macroeconomic stabilization fostered a favourable environment for corporate growth and profits. In Asia, trade dynamism fuelled strong growth and thus profits in the first half of the decade. As a result, rising returns to equities, reinforced by reduction in restrictions on foreign ownership of equities in a growing number of economies and varying degrees of liberalization of the capital account for external transactions, attracted large flows of foreign funds. Meanwhile, low interest rates and slow economic growth in the developed countries reinforced the attractiveness of investments in developing-country markets.

Factors impeding capital-market growth

The institutional factors making for strong growth of securities markets in some developing countries were absent in other countries whose markets have not taken off. Inefficient infrastructure for clearance and settlement procedures, for example, delays transactions and raises the risk that settlement will not be correct. This and generally weak regulatory and supervisory systems and inadequate protection of the interests of minority shareholders—the safeguards usually sought by portfolio investors—have also undermined investor confidence.

Compounding the problem is the dearth of companies for listing, especially in low-income countries. The high cost of issuing public shares deters small companies everywhere from "going public". In addition, the dilution of insider control of the corporation and disclosure requirements may also be disincentives for public share issues. At the same time, financial and technical weaknesses of investment banks limit their capacity to perform underwriting functions and contribute to illiquidity in the market.

A further limitation in the case of bond markets is the weakness of credit rating agencies. Bond ratings are important in helping investors estimate the risk premiums to be demanded as compensation for taking on the risk of default on debt payments. Also, some institutional investors are restricted to purchases of bonds with certain minimum ratings. In developing countries, most independent rating agencies are still struggling to fully establish themselves. The problem for these agencies is that, owing primarily to a lack of market confidence, the demand for their services is not yet large. In Asian countries, moreover, it has been argued that political interference in their functioning has constrained their development and independence.[9]

The legal and regulatory framework has also constrained the growth of bond markets in many countries. Generally weak disclosure, financial reporting and accounting practices in developing countries reduce the confidence of potential bond buyers even more than that of potential stock purchasers who accept that their investment involves high risk. Bonds are less in the nature of a speculative purchase, although high-risk ("junk") bonds have a more speculative following.

Pension funds and capital markets

Contractual savings—mainly pension funds and insurance plans—have been important vehicles for channelling domestic savings into capital markets in many developed countries. The recent development of these non-bank savings institutions, in particular pension funds, in a number of developing countries can also foster development of the securities markets in these countries.

On the other hand, the buy-and-hold investment strategy of pension funds limits their impact on equity and bond market liquidity. Also, regulations aimed at curbing the riskiness of their portfolios restrict the share of pension fund assets invested in equities. Moreover, most of these pension funds are small and do not yet generate substantial demand for private market instruments, investing their assets primarily in government bonds. However, as they grow, they can be expected to invest larger amounts and engage in more active trading in the markets.[10]

[9] See P. Basu, "Financial reform in Asia: an overview", in *Creating Resilient Financial Reforms in Asia: Challenges and Policy Options*, P. Basu, ed. (Hong Kong, Oxford University Press, 1997).

[10] See H. Reisen, "Liberalizing foreign investments by pension funds: positive and normative aspects", *World Development*, vol. 25, No. 7 (1997), pp. 1,173-1,182; and D. Vittas, "Institutional Investors and Securities Markets: Which Comes First?", World Bank Policy Research Working Paper, No. 2032, December 1998.

Developments are perhaps most advanced, in this regard, in Latin America, where pension fund reform began mostly in the early 1990s (except in Chile where it was initiated in 1981). Growth of assets has been substantial but the average size of pension fund assets is still below 10 per cent of GDP, with the exception of Chile where it has reached 40 per cent of GDP. This compares with a size of pension fund assets of over 50 per cent of GDP in many developed countries.

The common element of pension reform in Latin America is the shift from a public pay-as-you-go system to a privately managed and funded one wherein the amount of retirement income depends, *inter alia*, on the earnings of the payments into the fund. The first country implementing such a reform was Chile in 1981, where the new system is based on individual mandatory retirement accounts for each insured individual. A group of private pension fund management companies, the *Administradoras de Fondos de Pensiones* (AFPs), administer the funds under strict government regulations.[11] Portfolio composition, while tightly controlled, has evolved *pari passu* with the system.

The recent reforms adopted by several other countries of the region consist of multi-pillar systems, where the reduced pay-as-you-go system is kept as the first pillar. Another pillar is usually a voluntary or mandatory scheme to collect payments from employees and/or employers which are then privately or publicly managed.

Pension funds assets in Chile, where the experience is longest, increased from just over $200 million in 1981 to nearly $30 billion in 1997. A significant part of the resources have been invested in capital markets, thus becoming a source for their expansion.[12] The value of their equity and bond holdings rose from a negligible amount in the mid-1980s to $7 billion at the beginning of the 1990s and to $17 billion in 1997. This reflects both the growth in funds mobilized and the significant shift in asset allocation from bank deposits, bank bonds and mortgages to equities and, to a lesser extent, corporate bonds. The concurrent deepening of capital markets is evident from the growth of stock market capitalization, the number of listed companies and the growth of bond markets.[13]

The positive effect of pension funds in the development of Chilean financial markets was abetted by certain preliminary developments. First, reforms took place when there was already a relatively well-developed banking sector with a strong regulatory and supervisory system. During the five years preceding the pension reform, several other reform and liberalization measures were implemented, which increased new issues and made financial markets deeper and more liquid. Another factor is that the Chilean pension system reform was conducted simultaneously with an extensive privatization programme. These two processes acted in a mutually reinforcing way in developing the supply of blue-chip equities and debentures and the institutional demand for these instruments.[14] Moreover, macroeconomic stability and strengthened investor confidence, fostered by sustained and prudent macroeconomic policies and sustained growth of GDP, further boosted pension fund growth and financial market growth.

The private component of the Argentine pension scheme has attracted two thirds of all workers who participate in the new integrated system and thus total funds mobilized by the pension system are growing rapidly. Nevertheless, they

[11] AFPs are not allowed to conduct any business other than pension fund management. The companies are licensed, regulated and supervised by a specialized public agency, the AFP Superintendency.

[12] See Economic Commission for Latin America and the Caribbean (ECLAC), "Pension funds, the financing of transition costs and financial market development: lessons from the Chilean privatization reform" (LC/R.1822), 26 June 1998.

[13] See P. Boeker, "Developing strong capital markets", in *Pathways to growth: comparing East Asia and Latin America*", N. Birdsall and F. Jaspersen, eds. (Washington, D.C., Inter-American Development Bank, 1997), pp. 192-225; and R. Holzmann, "Pension reform, financial market development and economic growth: preliminary evidence from Chile", International Monetary Fund Working Paper, No. 96/94 (August), 1996.

[14] Boeker, loc. cit.

are currently still under 3 per cent of GDP. Moreover, the investment strategies of the country's pension funds have been quite conservative: in 1997, 64 per cent of their assets were held in government securities and term deposits. As a result, the impact on capital markets has not been large.

Assets of pension funds in Colombia and Peru are also small. In Colombia, the diversification of the pension fund portfolio has been slow as a consequence of the attraction of high yields on Government bonds and the underdeveloped state of the stock market, even though investment in equities was permitted from the beginning of reform. Peru's financial markets were thin and underdeveloped at the beginning of the reform. In recent years, a more stable macroeconomic environment, together with new capital market legislation and the privatization of public enterprises, contributed to the expansion of Peruvian capital markets. Equity market capitalization reached 27 per cent of GDP in 1997 (see table VI.2). As pension funds are still small in both countries, their evolution was probably just one of several factors contributing to capital-market development.

Besides performing their role as buyer of securities, pension funds and other institutional investors can strengthen the markets in various ways. One is through their development of a greater capacity for evaluation of financial information and risk assessment and their ability as a large player in the market to effectively demand that such information be reliable. Another emerges if they push for improved market infrastructure which can reduce transaction costs and payment risks. Yet another, as the Chilean experience shows, is through development of new financial instruments and institutions, used mainly by institutional investors, such as rating agencies, which enhance the sophistication and functioning of capital markets and promote the availability of information.

Privatization and capital markets

A Government that intends to privatize a State enterprise has several options, some of which facilitate the development of the domestic equity market. One such method is a public offering on the stock market of some or all of the equity in the enterprise. Another method, used extensively in transition economies (see below), but rarely in developing countries, is to issue vouchers, to selected groups of people (for example, employees) or the general public, which could be exchanged for shares in a newly privatized company.[15]

The main alternative is sale of some or all of a State enterprise to a "strategic investor", either a domestic or a foreign firm or group which directly takes over its operation. The main advantage is that the strategic investor can transfer technology and management skills, along with a commitment to bring additional financial resources to the acquired enterprises (it can be made part of the sales agreement). However, though price-setting of the companies to be divested is normally carried out through a competitive bidding process, the Government needs to have the capacity to make a proper valuation of the assets that it intends to sell.

Compared with a private sale, public offerings of shares to the public entail a higher cost in respect of preparing the offering, resulting from prospectus preparation, underwriting and marketing, which are justified only by large

[15] Bolivia, where the domestic market was not in a position to absorb large shares of privatized companies, adopted a variation of the voucher scheme, in which half of the shares were sold to a controlling group and the other half assigned to the adult population. Democratization of ownership was an important goal in this case.

transactions. However, issuing shares of privatized companies on a local stock exchange provides access to domestic investors and may be seen as preferable to direct sale to foreign interests in some cases.

While privatization through public offering is a way to transfer State assets to the public, increasing the supply of blue chip securities also contributes to development of the domestic stock market (although some public offerings have also been placed in international equity markets).

Among developing countries, privatization revenues have been highest in Latin America, totalling an estimated $83 billion between 1990 and 1996. Direct sales, such as public auctions and tender offers, accounted for 60 per cent of all privatization revenues and about 80 per cent of all privatization transactions.[16] These sales were an important factor in the large flow of foreign direct investment particularly in Argentina, Brazil, Mexico and Colombia. Public offerings in the stock market, however, accounted for another third of total revenues and some 10 per cent of all transactions. Given the relatively small base, this became reflected in the extraordinary increase in market capitalization in several Latin American equity markets in the 1990s noted earlier (see table VI.2). Privatized companies represent today a substantial part of stock market capitalization in several countries (over 50 per cent in Argentina and Peru and 28 and 19 per cent, respectively, in Chile and Mexico).[17]

The divestiture of State telecommunication companies, very large firms, some of whose stock had already been actively traded, was implemented largely through full or partial public offerings in Argentina, Brazil, Mexico and Peru. In Argentina, many of the largest divestitures followed a scheme in which a controlling share was first offered through public bidding. The Government retained another portion, which was offered on the stock exchange at a later stage. Finally, a portion (usually about 10 per cent) was made available to the company's employees. In Brazil, a minority of the shares of the telecommunication company were listed for purchase on the stock exchange in 1995. The remaining government holdings were subsequently sold to large corporate interests in 1998.

In Chile, privatization took place in two stages. In the first stage, in the 1970s, as the stock market was not adequately developed, the Government sold controlling stakes of enterprises in auctions. This concentrated ownership in a few conglomerates. In contrast, in the 1980s, public offers in the stock market, in combination with other methods, were most common. In this second phase, the timely combination of the privatization process with the establishment of pension funds that needed to invest in equity shares created, as noted above, a mutually reinforcing process and resulted in increased domestic ownership of privatized shares.

Since the early 1990s, there has been an intensification of privatization in Africa. Between 1991 and 1996, Egypt, for example, partially divested several State enterprises, with public offerings accounting for about 40 per cent of the privatization revenues.[18] In many cases, public offerings were oversubscribed by both local and foreign investors, reflecting the progress of overall economic reform as well as equity market reforms.

In the initial stage of privatization in Egypt, divestiture was effected mainly by offering share subscriptions to employees. In the next stage, privatization by public offerings was introduced. This was followed by new capital-market

[16] Inter-American Development Bank, *Economic and Social Progress in Latin America* (Washington, D.C., 1996), p. 180.

[17] See P. Kuczynski, "Privatization and the private sector", *World Development*, vol. 27, No. 1 (1999), pp. 215-224.

[18] See World Bank and Flemings, *Privatization and emerging equity markets* (Washington, D.C., World Bank, 1998).

reform measures which included the removal of the capital gains tax from most stocks and bonds, strengthened requirements for financial disclosure for listed corporations, the allowance of full access to the market for foreign investors, the elimination of interest ceilings on corporate bonds, and the establishment of a regulatory authority for supervising the securities industry. The reform was accelerated in the later stage by reducing the cost of listing on the stock exchange and the establishment of a new clearing and settlement company.

In Morocco, the first public offerings of privatized companies were in 1993, and in 1995 one of the largest banks in Morocco (Banque marocaine du commerce extérieur) was privatized through a public offering. Between 1993 and 1996, about a quarter of the 45 State enterprises, including hotels, banks and investment companies, were wholly or partially privatized using a combination of public offerings and direct sales. Some of the most popular offerings were oversubscribed more than six times. Offerings were targeted to the general public by setting a ceiling on shares per applicant to avoid the accumulation of large holdings by individual or institutional investors.

Privatization law and special-purpose institutions were created as a framework for privatization. At the same time, a number of reforms have supported the privatization process: introduction of new regulations on disclosure requirements and new accounting standards, new legislation such as laws governing mutual funds, and allowing unrestricted repatriation of capital gains and dividends by foreign investors.

In sub-Saharan Africa, some large privatizations have also been effected through public offerings on the local stock markets. In Côte d'Ivoire, a major power company was listed on the domestic stock exchange, with 49 per cent of shares sold to small investors. In Ghana and Kenya, shares of major public companies, the Ashanti Goldfields and Kenya Airways, were floated on the local stock exchanges. Both issues had the effect of greatly deepening the equity market: market capitalization of the Ghana Stock Exchange increased from $118 million in 1993 to almost $2 billion in 1994. About a quarter of Ghana's privatizations between 1991 and 1995 was effected through public offerings, including listing of shares in Ashanti Goldfields on the London Stock Exchange. In Zambia, a stock exchange opened in February 1995 and six privatized companies were listed by the end of 1997. One of the most important was the Zambia Consolidated Copper Mines.[19]

This variety of experience points to a number of conclusions. First, well-functioning financial systems broaden the set of privatization options. Second, as companies being privatized need capital infusions, not just ownership transfer, success depends on being able to bring adequate sources of funds into the market (for example, from pensions or foreign investors). Third, the methods of implementing privatization appear to have made some direct contribution to the growth of capital markets.[20]

Who raises which funds in the capital markets?

While most of the activity in securities markets is the trading of already issued stocks and bonds, a key developmental question is whether this liquidity function also facilitates the flow of long-term capital resources to companies. The experiences of developing countries have been mixed on whether the rapid development of stock markets has yielded such benefits.

[19] See C. Kenny and T. Moss, "Stock markets in Africa: emerging lions or white elephants?", *World Development*, vol. 26, No. 5 (1998), pp. 829-843.

[20] See A. Demirgüç-Kunt and R. Levine, "The financial system and public enterprise reform", *Financial Development and Economic Growth: Theory and Experiences from Developing Countries* (London and New York, Routledge, 1996).

In Asia, the data suggest a positive effect. The growth of new issues has been substantial and equity financing has constituted a significant share of investment finance in some countries. In 1994-1996, new issues in Indonesia, the Republic of Korea, Malaysia, the Philippines and Thailand ranged from 7 to 20 per cent of domestic private investment.[21] The increase in the number of listed companies in equity markets in many Asian economies and in a number of Latin American and African economies, as noted earlier, also suggests that such companies will (if they do not already) have growing access to equity finance in the future.

However, the improved access has benefited mainly the largest companies. Smaller firms are usually deterred by the high cost of listing shares on the stock exchange and their generally low recognition level—low "reputational capital"—in local markets. A study of the largest publicly listed companies in a sample of developing countries showed that those companies relied quite heavily on equity finance in the 1980s: in 5 of the 10 sample countries, more than 40 per cent of the growth in assets of these firms was financed by new share issues.[22] However, when the scope of analysis is widened to the whole corporate sector, the results change; for example, analyses of the sources of finance in India and the Republic of Korea found that, for the corporate sector as a whole, while equity finance is growing, it still represents a small share of financing, even excluding retained earnings and counting only the funds external to the firm. In India, public issue of equity as a proportion of total financing external to the firm increased from about 4 per cent in the early 1980s to 12 per cent by the early 1990s. In addition, private placement of shares, which are shares that are not expected to trade subsequently on the stock market, was an important source of external financing. The share of longer-term borrowing remained stable at about 50 per cent, although the share of debentures (bonds) increased while that of bank loans declined.[23] In the Republic of Korea, the share of equity finance increased sharply in the 1980s but much less so in the 1990s and averaged about 15 per cent in the first half of this decade.[24] Bond financing followed a similar trend so that by 1995 bonds and equity accounted for about 30 per cent of external corporate financing.

In Latin America, bank credit remains the predominant source of corporate external financing. The new equity issues in the region in the 1990s have been primarily in privatized utility, telecommunications and transport companies. In sub-Saharan Africa, equity and bond financing is generally an insignificant source of investment funding. Most of the funds in stock markets have been raised by privatized financial companies, or mining or infrastructure concerns and stock markets are currently unlikely to finance investment in smaller-scale manufacturing companies.[25]

While the funding contribution has been positive but modest, it is increasingly appreciated, especially in the light of the Asian financial crisis, that more developed capital markets—corporate bond markets in particular—would have been beneficial in a number of ways. Bond markets would have provided an alternative source of corporate credit, reducing the concentration of risk of debt default in the banking system. Also, bonds are generally longer-term credit instruments, albeit available under stricter reporting requirements, than bank loans. In addition, by providing an attractive domestic security (before the Asian crisis dampened the prospects of the corporate sector), bonds would have

[21] See Asian Development Bank and World Bank, "Managing global finance integration in Asia: emerging lessons and prospective challenges—overview", Asian Development Bank and World Bank Senior Policy Seminar, Manila, 10-12 March 1998, p. 27.

[22] See A. Singh, "Corporate financial patterns in industrializing economies: a comparative international study", International Finance Corporation Technical Paper, No. 2, 1995.

[23] See R. Nagaraj, "India's capital market growth: trends, explanations and evidence", *Economic and Political Weekly*, vol. 31, Special Number (September 1996), pp. 2,553-2,562.

[24] See J. Oh, "Financial reforms, their effects and management issues: a Korean experience", paper prepared for the Conference on Improved Management of the Financial Sector, United Nations Economic and Social Commission for Asia and the Pacific (ESCAP), Bangkok, March 1998.

[25] See Kenny and Moss, loc. cit.

helped retain more of the region's large pool of savings for domestic uses and reduced the exposure of the currency market to turmoil when savings left the countries of the region for foreign placement and regional firms borrowed abroad. Finally, had there been more reliance on financial markets and thus exposure to sharper market analysis of the financial situation of corporations, the excessive leveraging might have been reduced. With a lower debt-equity ratio, companies encountering earnings setbacks can cut dividends while meeting smaller interest payments, which are contractual obligations.

Corporate governance and equity markets

It has long been understood that large corporations with considerable oligopoly power and diffuse ownership may be under less pressure than small, closely held and competitive companies to follow high-profit business strategies. In the former situations, management may pursue its own agenda. One question is the extent to which equity markets operate so as to return control and a high-profit orientation to the owners of publicly traded companies, that is to say, to the shareholders, when management does not act effectively as their agent.

There is, in general, a range of factors that affect the degree to which shareholders control management. These include ownership concentration, the extent and enforcement of legal protection of minority shareholders, the reliability and timeliness of company information in the public domain, the strength and enforcement of financial contracts, and the incentive for large shareholders to enforce discipline of managers. The conditions conducive to adequate monitoring of corporate performance by outsiders are generally not fulfilled in most developing countries or even in some developed countries.[26]

In East Asia, "insider" ownership concentration is high, as many founding families hold large shares of equity. The concentration is even higher as a result of cross-shareholding between conglomerates with ultimate control in the hands of the founding family. In this sense, management is the owner to a large degree and thus management probably does act effectively as the agent of the majority owners.

Outside owners can have a large majority of shares but still not exert control because of their wide dispersal. The growth of institutional investors in developing-country capital markets, however, offer a new opportunity for outside-owner control, as these investors tend to accumulate significant blocks of shares. Nevertheless, evidence on the effectiveness of large institutional investors in corporate governance even in industrialized countries has been inconclusive, although their increased activism in the 1990s has been notable.[27] In developing countries, the role of institutional investors in this regard is far less significant. Besides the fact that they are limited in size and number, until recently they have not invested heavily in stocks. The privatized pension funds in Chile, for example, were limited in their investment in equities until the early 1990s, although they have played a role in the development of the mortgage and corporate bond markets since the 1980s. The centralized provident funds, such as those in Malaysia, have held mainly government bonds or other low-risk instruments.[28]

The growing presence in developing countries of institutional investors from developed economies has yet to translate into a more active governance role.

[26] See A. Shleifer and R. Vishny, "A survey of corporate governance", *Journal of Finance*, No. 52 (1997), pp. 737-783.

[27] See C. Samuel, "Stock market and investment: the governance role of the market", World Bank Policy Research Working Paper, No. 1578, March 1996.

[28] See Vittas, loc. cit.

Besides being characterized by passive financial investment goals, they would be hindered from taking a more active governance role by the lack of familiarity with local legal conditions and practices.

Direct inputs into the governing of corporations aside, the main mechanism by which shareholders influence corporate management in developed economies is through collectively bidding up or reducing the prices of their company's shares. Moreover, to the extent that management is compensated with options to buy shares in the company at a pre-set price, management can be given a pecuniary interest in raising the stock price; and if management is perceived as weak and this is reflected in the share price, the company becomes more of a target for takeover through purchase of a large block of shares. Such mechanisms are only beginning to play a role in developing countries.

CAPITAL-MARKET DEVELOPMENT IN CHINA

The development of a market-based financial system in place of one that relied on administrative fiat under the previous centrally planned economic system is an integral part of the economic reform programme in China. As one part of this programme, the Government has implemented new policies and institutional changes since the 1980s that have focused on reform of the banking system (see chap. V) and, more recently, on developing capital markets. Policy development has reflected the gradualist approach in the strategy of overall economic transformation which has maintained the centrality of public ownership. Because of these historical factors, the experience of capital-market development in China differs significantly from that in other developing countries in Asia as well as from the experience of the economies in transition.

Domestic equity markets

China's capital markets have grown rapidly in the 1990s, primarily owing to the growth of equity markets. However, capital markets as a whole remain small relative to the banking sector which is the mainstay of the financial system. Equity share issues were authorized only in 1990 and two stock exchanges, one in Shanghai and the other in Shenzhen, were opened. A network of over 50 regional trading centres have since been established. The number of companies listed on the two stock exchanges increased from 14 in 1991 to 764 by the end of 1997 and market capitalization grew from $2 billion to over $206 billion (see table VI.1).

The growth of China's equity market accelerated after 1995 when the State Council approved the plan to revitalize State-owned enterprises (SOEs) through gradual "corporatization", that is to say, turning of SOEs into joint-stock companies. The number of listed companies jumped by 67 per cent in 1996 alone, to reach 540 by the end of the year, while market capitalization increased by 170 per cent.[29] During 1996, the value of new shares issued on the two exchanges totalled 34.5 billion yuan (about $4.2 billion),[30] about a quarter of market capitalization by year-end.

China has also made special provision for foreign participation in Chinese stock markets. Chinese listed companies can secure approval to issue a special class of shares, labelled B shares, which can be bought only by non-residents

[29] See International Finance Corporation, *Emerging Stock Markets Factbook 1998* (Washington, D.C., 1998), pp. 16 and 22.

[30] See N. Lardy, *China's Unfinished Economic Revolution* (Washington, D.C., Brookings Institution Press, 1998).

with United States dollars on the Shanghai Stock Exchange and with Hong Kong dollars on the Shenzhen Stock Exchange (A shares are issued in local currency to local investors). Although the two classes of shares bear the same legal rights except as regards who can own them, the fact that domestic investors pay a threefold premium for the A shares of a company that also issues B shares indicates a high degree of market segmentation. This may reflect a dearth of alternative financial assets for domestic residents.[31] Also, foreign investors may value holding equities of Chinese companies less than do domestic investors, as they are less familiar with the environment and less trustful of company information disclosure.[32]

As the equity market is regarded as an experiment in resource mobilization, not a means of privatization of ownership, the Government retains controlling shares in the SOEs now listed on the stock exchanges.[33] Shares available to the general public for trading in the stock market are rather limited, compared with the capitalizations of listed companies. As savings of households have increased significantly during the reform period, along with the growth of personal income, the many investors (individuals as well as financial institutions) have been chasing a limited number of available shares, bidding up prices. Thus, during the period December 1992 to December 1997, the mean percentage change in the total return index of China's equity market was the highest among 10 South and East Asian emerging markets tracked by the International Finance Corporation (IFC).[34] Also, rising stock prices attract more individuals with hopes of making a quick profit in stocks. As a result, the turnover ratio is very high, almost 180 per cent in 1997. This contrasts with the behaviour in the Chinese bond market, where individual investors generally buy and hold.

Domestic bond markets

The value of bond issues in China has experienced phenomenal growth during the reform period, particularly in the 1990s. In the 1980s, government bonds were administratively allocated to State-owned banks, SOEs and government agencies; thus, a bond market did not really exist. In the 1990s, the administrative placement of government bonds was abolished. Bond issues grew rapidly and became a means to finance public investment projects, enterprise expansion and bank recapitalization, as well as the fiscal deficit. The rapid increase in fiscal deficits reflected the decline in central government revenues that accompanied fiscal decentralization and the purpose of financing the deficit with bonds was to avoid inflationary financing.[35] Today, government bonds that carry administratively determined coupon rates that are greater than the interest rate on savings deposits of comparable maturity are the mainstay of the Chinese bond market.

Enterprises may also issue bonds, although these make up a small share of the total value of bond issues, as the Government tightly controls the approval process for the issuance of enterprise bonds. This policy has hindered the development of the market for non-government bonds. Moreover, speculation and fraudulent activities in the bond market led to a government clampdown in 1996 which closed one large securities company and temporarily shut the secondary market for government bonds.

Households held about 75 per cent of the government bonds outstanding at the end of 1995.[36] Given the high rate of savings and the lack of alternative

[31] See J. Fernald and J. H. Rogers, "Puzzles in the Chinese stock market", Board of Governors of the Federal Reserve System, International Finance Discussion Paper, No. 619 (1998).

[32] See S. Chakravarty, A. Sarkar and L. Wu, "Information asymmetry, market segmentation and the pricing of cross-listed shares: theory and evidence from Chinese A and B shares", Federal Reserve Bank of New York, Research Paper, No. 9820 (1998).

[33] On average, about 75 per cent of a publicly listed State enterprise's outstanding shares are held by the State.

[34] See International Finance Corporation, *Emerging Stock Markets Factbook 1998* ..., p. 60.

[35] See *World Economic and Social Survey 1997* (United Nations publication, Sales No. E.97.II.C.1 and corrigenda), chap. VII.

[36] See Lardy, op. cit.

investment instruments, the safety of the higher return offered on government bonds compared with savings deposits makes them very attractive to individual investors. Moreover, institutional investors other than banks, such as pension funds, insurance companies and mutual funds, are still in their infancy as China experiments with pension reform and other components of a social safety net.

Access to international capital markets

In addition to development of its domestic capital market, China has sought to develop its access to international capital markets. Forty-one SOEs that are publicly traded in China have also been approved to issue H class shares which can be purchased and traded on the Hong Kong Stock Exchange. In addition to companies issuing H shares, there are also 47 so-called red-chip companies listed on the Hong Kong Stock Exchange. These are companies incorporated in Hong Kong Special Administrative Region (SAR) and traded on the Hong Kong Stock Exchange, but controlled by Chinese central or local governments. This has opened an avenue to Chinese companies for raising international funds while not having to meet the stringent regulatory and accounting standards of stock markets in New York or London.

Large Chinese corporations have also raised equity funds overseas through the issuance of ADRs. Between 1992 and 1997, 10 Chinese companies issued ADRs that were approved for public trading on the New York Stock Exchange, the largest number among Asian countries during this period. In addition, 28 firms issued ADRs for private placement by 1997.[37] In 1997 alone, Chinese companies issued $3.2 billion of ADRs, but the amount of issues in 1998 was only $0.4 billion, as the Asian financial crisis eroded investor confidence in emerging market stocks.

[37] See Harvey and Roper, loc. cit.

Chinese corporations have also been successful in raising debt capital in the Eurobond market. They issued $22.9 billion of bonds from 1990 to 1997[38]

[38] Ibid.

Functioning of capital markets

Capital markets in China are in an early stage of development, with limited scope and functions. The Government's primary motivation in developing the markets has been to mobilize financial resources and in this they have been successful. The bond market has become an important source of non-inflationary financing of government fiscal deficits. State enterprises also raise funds through the stock and bond markets, albeit in limited amounts (for example, about 1 per cent of total fixed investment in 1996).[39] Thus, capital markets have primarily channelled funds to the government sector.

[39] See State Statistical Bureau of China, *Statistical Yearbook of China, 1998.*

In China, approval for public listing of equity shares is subject to a system of regional quotas, in addition to certain financial and disclosure standards. Which companies succeed in raising finance through equity issues largely depends on bureaucratic decisions, rather than on transparent, well-defined standards of performance. The protection of shareholder rights is not yet clearly legislated. Moreover, disclosure of enterprise information is uneven, and the rules of corporate governance are not formalized. The lack of a legal framework regulating transfer of ownership, mergers and acquisitions, and bankruptcy proceedings further compromises the role of the equity market.[40]

[40] See X. Xu and Y. Wang, "Ownership structure, corporate governance, and corporate performance: the case of Chinese stock companies", World Bank Policy Research Working Paper, No. 1794 (Washington, D.C., 1997).

The Government is committed to furthering the development of a financial sector compatible with a market-oriented socialist economy. However, the equity market of China, which is similar to many other economies in this respect, was established before all the institutions and infrastructure for markets had been fully put in place. The Asian financial crisis highlighted the need to act with a new sense of urgency, as was reflected in the passage in December 1998 of the National Securities Law (to enter into force on 1 July 1999). Before adoption of this law, the country's security markets were governed by a combination of regulations, some of which, formulated at the central level, applied nationally while others applied only locally. Efforts are also being made to strengthen the enforcement of financial disclosure rules of listed companies. In an attempt to improve transparency, regulatory authorities have started to hold accountants and lawyers employed by listed companies responsible for the accuracy of disclosed information.

While various regulatory provisions will be consolidated under the new National Securities Law, the compartmentalization of regulatory authorities is also being addressed. For example, the licensing of securities dealers used to be under the purview of the central bank, while dealers' activities on the secondary market were regulated by the State Council Securities Committee; the approval for issuing different types of securities belonged among the responsibilities of different government departments. The new law transfers regulatory authority over all aspects of the securities market to the China Securities Regulatory Commission.

The passage of the new National Securities Law is therefore a very important step in the consolidation and strengthening of the regulatory framework. However, having improved regulations on the books for equity listings will not guarantee either transparency or compliance. Enforcement will remain key to improved capital-market regulation, which will require continuing efforts to strengthen institutional and human capacity.

CAPITAL-MARKET DEVELOPMENT IN THE ECONOMIES IN TRANSITION

Financial sector development has been one of the most important steps in the transformation of the economies in transition in Central and Eastern Europe and the former Soviet Union. In the earlier, centrally planned economic system of these countries, the mobilization and allocation of financial resources were largely conducted by administrative measures and there were few market-oriented financial institutions. Reform of the financial system has focused on the development of such institutions, with emphasis on the banking system (see chap. V). Capital markets, particularly equity markets, have emerged very quickly, driven by the rapid privatization of State-owned companies. For such developments, these countries have been unique, although these markets are still small and not very liquid.

Domestic equity markets

While equity markets operate in 11 transition economies, market capitalization is a small fraction of GDP in almost all of them. The Czech Republic has the highest capitalization ratio among the transition economies (it peaked at 33 per cent in 1996). The Russian stock market grew rapidly in 1996 and 1997, albeit from a small initial level. Total market capitalization doubled in 1996 and tripled in 1997, reflecting the soaring prices of shares, particularly of a number of large resource companies. In some other transition countries with "large" equity markets, the capitalization ratios are about 10 per cent of GDP (see table VI.4).

In several cases, market capitalization is dominated by just a handful of large companies (see table VI.5). Even in those countries with larger markets, the 10 largest stocks account for almost 60 to 85 per cent of total capitalization. Poland is an exception: the share was 55 per cent at the end of 1995 but has since become somewhat less concentrated. Four of the 10 largest companies on the Polish stock exchange at the end of 1995 were banks. Several banks had been privatized with initial public offerings on the Warsaw exchange, which attracted a great deal of investor interest.[41]

Foreign investment in equities in the transition economies was modest until 1995. Stocks in the transition economies surged in the following years as capital inflows pushed up prices until the Russian crisis. In Poland, the Czech Republic, the Russian Federation and particularly Hungary, foreign stock holdings account for substantial shares of the total. While improvement in regulatory institutions and increased listings attracted international investor interest, the soaring interest in investing in emerging markets in general was also an important factor.

The development of equity markets in the transition economies is related to the privatization process. Mass privatization placed ownership of shares in firms in the hands of large numbers of citizens very quickly. The stock markets were opened to provide some means of allocating and trading the ownership rights that came with privatization. Even in countries with more gradual privatization strategies, such as Hungary and Poland, the pace accelerated in the mid-1990s and generated an increase in the number of share listings.

There were suddenly enormous numbers of publicly listed companies, but there was little market activity in the vast majority of them. The existence of a public listing was no guarantee of liquidity, let alone transparency in corporate governance. This was especially marked in the Czech Republic, where many of these companies have since been de-listed. Whereas over 1,000 companies were listed on the Czech exchange in 1994, only 276 were listed in 1997, although market capitalization of these firms was almost $13 billion, compared with less than $6 billion in the earlier year (see table VI.4). This curious development was a direct consequence of the mass privatization programme that started in 1990. Most large enterprises were privatized in two waves of voucher privatization in 1992-1994. Ownership tended to be very diffuse except that large blocks of shares are owned by investment privatization funds (IPFs).[42]

Russian equities markets date back to the initial stages of transition, 1990-1991, when a number of Russian firms, mostly banks and trading companies, were established as joint-stock companies and began to sell shares to the public. The extensive mass privatization programme in 1992-1994 spurred the development of trading in equity and in privatization vouchers on the regional markets and through over-the-counter arrangements.

Widespread stock ownership emerged in many transition economies before there was an effective regulatory and supervisory framework or functioning

[41] J. Bonin and P. Wachtel, "Toward market-oriented banking in the economies in transition", in *Financial sector transformation: lessons for the economies in transition*, M. Blejer and M. Skreb, eds. (New York, New York, Cambridge University Press, 1999).

[42] The investment privatization funds (IPFs) in the Czech Republic collected vouchers from the public during the two waves of voucher privatization (1992-1994). One of the intentions underlying the establishment of IPFs was to create significant ownership influence over privatized firms which would be able to force restructuring. Many IPFs, including the strongest, were established and are controlled by banks.

market infrastructure. This undermined investor confidence and limited the depth and liquidity of these markets.

Throughout the transition countries, reform of the banking sector was the first element of financial sector reform, as bank reform was needed to assure operation of the payments system and to end "soft budget" constraints on enterprises, wherein banks would extend credit as needed to cover company operating losses. Reform of existing banking institutions thus preceded new institutional development in the equity markets. It was only as of 1994 in the Russian Federation and 1997 in the Czech Republic that regulatory institutions for equity markets were put in place. By 1995, development of the Russian equity market seemed very promising, as extensive reform of the trading system and regulatory structure promised to bring transparency of prices and to eliminate registration problems that had existed earlier. In the Czech Republic as well, regulatory reforms began to strengthen investor confidence. In Poland, more gradual privatization enabled market institutions to develop along with the increase in listings. Improvements in securities regulations in 1995 helped to bolster market growth.

Domestic bond markets

Despite their limitations, equity markets in the transition economies are more advanced than bond markets which, with the exception of markets for government bonds, are all very small. Few issues of private debt instruments have been sold locally in the transition economies and those that exist were usually private placements rather than public issues. Secondary markets for private debt are virtually non-existent. The domestic bond market in the Czech Republic is the biggest in the region, but by mid-1995 there were only eight so-called blue-chip corporate bond issues with a total of about $1.25 billion outstanding and there was little secondary market trading.

There have also been instances of debt financing by Hungarian companies, with issues in local currency purchased by foreign and domestic investors, although there is little evidence of a secondary market emerging for such issues either. In 1996, corporate bonds accounted for 0.1 per cent of trading on the Budapest Stock Exchange. The domestic corporate bond market in Poland is also very small. Some large companies have issued bonds internationally but there have been fewer than 10 domestic issues with maturities of more than one year. Nevertheless, with the economy growing rapidly, there are indications that the domestic bond market might begin to grow and expand to include issuances by smaller enterprises.

Private sector domestic debt instruments (other than the interbank market) are virtually non-existent in the Russian Federation. There have been a few issues of collateralized debt by companies but there are no domestic corporate bond issues.

Most of the factors that hindered the development of equity markets have also slowed the growth of private bond markets. In addition, the macroeconomic environment in some countries has not been sufficiently stable to encourage much long-term bond financing of firms. In some countries, the slow pace of banking sector reform inhibited the development of local bond markets: if bank financing is available without any serious judgements of credit quality, there is no reason to expect market-oriented domestic or international lending

channels to emerge. Capital-market development will get started only when traditional bank lending arrangements are replaced by market-oriented credit
standards. After that, investor reluctance might be overcome through experience. In this regard, the European Bank for Reconstruction and Development
(EBRD) is considering issuance of its own bonds in domestic currency on transition economy markets as a means of developing the local capital market. It
has made one local currency bond issue in Hungary.

Access to international capital markets

It is common for both Governments and the largest and most successful
enterprises in the transition economies to tap international capital markets
directly. There is a surprisingly large number of issues by the advanced transition countries and privately placed and publicly traded issues are common
and substantial.

Hungarian and Russian companies have been the most active issuers of
depositary receipts. Hungary was the first issuer and the Russian Federation
followed suit in 1995. There are now 12 Russian ADRs, including three with
listings on the New York Stock Exchange. In addition, at least six Russian
companies have depositary receipts issued in the Russian Federation (RDRs)
for trading in Europe. Russian depositary receipts in the amount of almost $1
billion have been issued, mostly in 1996, and little since then. Receipts for a
similar amount of shares of Hungarian companies have been issued. Also, at
least four big Czech companies are listed as having global depositary receipts
in London.

The issuance of depositary receipts by companies in transition economies
has advantages and disadvantages. On one hand, it is an indicator of the
attractiveness of these companies to foreign equity investors. Notably,
Russian companies were able to use depositary receipts to access international capital markets even though Russian corporate governance and disclosure standards lagged Western standards. On the other hand, increased use of
depositary receipts might inhibit the development of local equity markets. If
the largest and strongest companies floated share issues exclusively on international equity markets, then the local market would be restricted to small
and illiquid issues.

The Polish Government was not able to tap international bond markets
until 1994 when it restructured its pre-transition foreign debts. The Czech
Government has tapped foreign bond markets throughout the 1990s, in the
amount of about $350 million per year from 1990 to 1996.[43] Hungary is by far
the largest sovereign borrower in the region, having raised almost $4 billion
in 1993.

For several years the Russian Government was able to actively tap interna-
tional capital markets for substantial sums, beginning with the issuance of
Eurobonds in November 1996. Many local government authorities in the
Russian Federation have also issued their own bonds.

As firms commenced restructuring in the advanced transition economies,
bond issues in eurodollars began to appear. Among the first were issues in 1996
by a Polish and a Czech bank. Foreign capital market access by Czech firms
has outpaced domestic market development, where only a few bond issues have
been made. The foreign capital market has also been tapped indirectly by

43 D. Sobol, "Central and Eastern Europe: financial markets and private capital flows", paper pre-pared for Study Group on Private Capital Flows to Developing and Transitional Economies, Council on Foreign Relations, New York, 1997.

44 International Monetary Fund, *Country Study: Czech Republic* (1998/36) (Washington, D.C., 1998).

Czech companies. There is an offshore market for Eurokrona bonds which have been issued mostly by banks that onlend the funds to Czech entities.[44] By mid-1997, there were $4 billion in such liabilities (similar markets in Poland and Hungary had about $600 million and $400 million respectively).

The Russian Government's entry into the international market was followed quickly by private sector borrowing. The first Russian companies to directly access world debt markets were three Russian banks which sold three-year dollar bonds in 1997. The yields were very high but the deals were viewed as a way to gain international exposure for Russian institutions which obtained credit ratings and had their reputations enhanced by the deals. Over $3 billion was raised in international capital markets in 1997, but such borrowing ended in the summer of 1998.

Functioning of capital markets

The capital markets in the transition economies are not yet used intensively, largely because these markets arose from specific institutional features of the transition process rather than as institutional responses to a demand for the financial services that such markets perform. At the same time, the brief life of these markets has to be taken into account in the assessment of their performance.

Even in relatively large markets, weakness of the market infrastructure and regulatory institutions has prevented the market from pricing assets efficiently. For example, the stock market in the Czech Republic has been widely criticized for a lack of transparency in trading activity. The poor reputation of the Czech market stemmed from its being an "over-the-counter" market (rather than a formal market where all trades are posted) where the absence of any regulatory structure led to practices that would have been considered fraudulent in most places.[45]

45 Organisation for Economic Cooperation and Development (OECD), *Economic Surveys: Czech Republic 1998* (Paris, 1998).

Developments in the Russian Federation are illustrative. Once the privatization programme ended there in mid-1994, trading on the stock exchanges diminished, prices were often manipulated by insider trading of blocks of shares, and there was little confidence in reported stock prices. The lack of a reliable institutional structure for trading, clearing, settlement, registration or oversight of brokers and dealers made it problematical to register share purchases. In 1994-1995, most companies in the Russian Federation, including the large, internationally known natural resource companies, were trading at a fraction of book value. There are several explanations for this. It was feared first, that the firms might have hidden liabilities, such as social obligations to workers or unspecified taxes and regulations; second, that the assets of the firm could be looted by managers and others without any respect for the rights of shareholders; and third, that share sales would not be properly registered and shareholders would be unable to prove share ownership.

A regulatory agency—the Federal Commission on Securities and the Capital Market—was established in 1994 and assisted in the establishment of the Russian Trading System in mid-1995. It is a self-regulating national electronic market which links various markets and brokers and brought market infrastructure to a new level of development. The system has become the main price-setting mechanism and has added a great deal of transparency to the pricing of stocks in the Russian Federation. The World Bank reports that the system has been very successful in improving the stock trading environment in the Russian Federation.[46]

More generally, the incipient markets in some countries have provided a market orientation for some privatization activity, particularly in instances where market initial public offerings (IPOs) have priced and distributed large blocks of stock that were held by the State. A case in point is Poland, where a number of privatizations have taken place with IPOs that have used the Polish equity market to determine the value of the firm. The IPO privatizations have been made possible—and have raised more revenue than would otherwise have been possible—because of the improved liquidity of the Polish equity market. In addition, there have been a few successful equity offerings by new enterprises in Poland. In this sense, the markets are becoming a potentially important mechanism for spreading and transferring share ownership.

One particular concern in the transition from central planning to market institutions has been that of transferring the governance of enterprises from the State (sometimes together with workers' councils) to more centralized mechanisms. Up to now, the boards of directors, representing the interests of the shareholders, have operated with considerable autonomy, especially when management groups have a controlling interest in the firm. In fact, corporate boards are rarely responsive to signals from the market.[47]

A drawback of mass privatization was that it usually led to very diffuse ownership of shares which enabled the existing management to retain control of the enterprise. Entrenched management may be unwilling or unable to work in the best interests of the firm. If managers from the pre-transition era lack the pecuniary incentive to restructure the firm's activities, they may choose to not do so, and to retain their positions.

In the Czech Republic, for example, one of the intentions underlying the establishment of IPFs was to create significant outside ownership which would push the firms to restructure. However, the banks' large ownership interest in the IPFs meant that the IPFs would continue traditional business relationships between the banks and the enterprises rather than undertake any radical restructuring which would endanger their positions or their control of the firms.

In 1997, the Government of the Czech Republic and the financial community began to respond to this situation by taking steps to create a regulatory structure for the equity markets and to introduce some rules for corporate governance. Next, changes in banking law in 1998 limited the banks' ability to hold controlling interests in non-financial firms, and placed limits on shareholding by banks and on the activities of bank managers in other companies. The Government also approved legislation that limited the holdings by an IPF in any one company in order to clearly distinguish between investment funds and holding companies. The effect has been to put limits on the influence of bank-owned IPFs. This should promote enterprise-restructuring. On the other hand, the fact that these limits are also likely to prevent any large shareholder from emerging and seeking to exercise control over the firm may inhibit restructuring.

In the Russian Federation, the extensive control by Russian financial groups and interlocking ownership by these groups have inhibited the development of transparent financial markets. Many of the problems with Russian equity mar-

[46] G. Fine and E. Karlova, "Privatization and the new securities markets in the Czech Republic, Poland and Russia", in *Privatization and Emerging Equity Markets*, I. Lieberman and C. Kirkness, eds. (Washington, D.C., World Bank and Flemings, 1998), chap. 2.

[47] For a more detailed review of the governance issue in transition economy corporations, see *World Economic and Social Survey, 1995* (United Nations publication, Sales No. E.95.II.C.1), chap. VI.

48 See Organisation for Economic Cooperation and Development (OECD), *Economic Surveys: Russian Federation 1997* (Paris, 1997).

kets stem from the privatization procedures of the mid-1990s.[48] Privatization often solidified the power of managers by transferring controlling blocks of shares to employees who supported manager control. Insiders thus controlled almost three quarters of the privatized firms and in some cases outside ownership was less than 20 per cent. Expectations that the sale of residual State-owned shares and the development of markets for shares would transform corporate control turned out to be unrealistic. Ownership of the largest companies is much less concentrated than the average; but while insiders tend not to have a controlling interest, they are, along with the banking groups, able to maintain control of management.

Over time, increased market liquidity, it is hoped, will provide important mechanisms for disciplining management. The equity markets in most countries now facilitate ownership transfers. A related function of equity markets is to facilitate corporate changes through mergers and acquisitions. Thus far, there has been little use of the stock markets for such changes in corporate control through takeovers, buyouts or mergers, but they will develop in time.

CONCLUDING OBSERVATIONS: CAPITAL MARKETS AND BANKS

Capital-market development in many developing countries and in the economies in transition is a work in progress and any assessment of the performance of these markets has to take this into account.

The experiences of developing countries, while diverse, suggest that capital markets can and do channel financing to corporate investment. Stock markets have also facilitated the privatization of public ownership in many countries. However, most markets had been established before a strong banking sector was in place and other supporting structures of the market and regulatory and legal frameworks remained weak. This constrained the functioning of the markets and limited the benefits that they yielded with respect to the allocation of finance and improved corporate governance. Nevertheless, in countries where market development reached a certain level, the diversification of the financial system has been beneficial. Further development should focus on strengthening market infrastructure and regulatory and legal institutions.

At the same time, the development of capital markets should not detract from the priority of strengthening the banking system. In addition, inasmuch as a strong commercial banking system underpins the development of capital markets by providing liquidity for market transactions and an efficient payment system to support trading and settlement, the development of the banking sector and that of capital markets can be seen as complementary. Moreover, weak banking systems can amplify the spillover effect of stock market volatility on the real economy.

Besides the development of the banking sector, the growth of non-bank financial institutions such as pension funds is also an important complement to capital-market development. As they mature in size and investment expertise, such institutions channel savings into the capital markets, creating a demand for securities while contributing to innovations in financial instruments and improved information-generation and -dissemination.

The resources needed for the development of capital markets suggest that it may not be feasible for most small, low-income countries to develop sufficiently deep domestic markets. Initially, they may wish to establish regional capital markets collaboratively among countries with strong economic links. Capacity in developing the requisite infrastructure and regulatory institutions for capital markets can also be acquired through these efforts.

In economies undergoing transformation from central planning to a market-based economic system, newly established capital markets cannot thus far be said to have channelled significant finance to investment or to have improved the efficiency of resource allocation. Their primary function has been to give effect to the partial or wholesale privatization of State enterprises. The necessary institutions of capital markets have been slow to develop, although there has recently been significant progress in this area in some countries.

This wide range of experiences in financial sector development appears to underline the argument made elsewhere in the present *Survey* that the focus in the early stages of financial development should be on the strengthening of the banking sector. As the financial system develops, however, capital markets should be encouraged to play an increasing role in the mobilization and allocation of financial resources. There is no clear agreement on the speed at which they should develop, but they are a natural part of a full financial system in the contemporary world—indeed (as discussed in chap. IV), an increasingly important part.

VII   BRINGING FINANCIAL SERVICES TO THE POOR

Some groups of people have limited or no access to the kinds of formal commercial finance discussed in previous chapters. These people are generally poor and reside mostly in developing countries. Groups in other countries also have difficulties obtaining commercial finance, but those groups are relatively smaller in developed countries and in most economies in transition (although little is known about finance outside formal channels in the latter).

Poor people require credit for several reasons. Many are, or can become, entrepreneurs, as either farmers or traders or as producers of goods. For this they need credit to purchase inputs, such as seeds, to start a production cycle, or to invest and expand production. The poor sometimes seek credit also for consumption because some expenditures—for example, expenditures on health care, education, housing and life cycle events such as weddings and funerals—arise unexpectedly or are "lumpy". However, credit is not the only way to pay for expenditures that exceed current income. Savings and various insurance mechanisms can also fulfil the role of smoothing consumption and reducing risk. Moreover, access to a safe and liquid placement of their savings is an important financial service to offer the poor.

Several arrangements offer credit where formal financial institutions do not. Family, friends, moneylenders and other sources of "informal finance" have traditionally played an important role in all parts of the world but they have limitations which curtail their expansion. "Semi-formal institutions", such as microcredit facilities operated by non-governmental organizations, have expanded their role in recent years. They have been able to deliver financial services to the poor partly because they have imitated and adapted characteristics from the informal sector. Recently, even a few commercial banks have ventured into lending to the poor by adopting microfinance practices. The present chapter examines various arrangements for providing financial services to the poor. The question is whether these modalities adequately meet their needs.

WHY SOME GROUPS LACK ACCESS TO FORMAL COMMERCIAL FINANCE

In nearly every society, there are groups that are unable to access formal finance from financial institutions and markets. Sometimes this is the result of discrimination, but in most cases it reflects economic factors.

For several reasons, commercial banks, in particular, are hesitant to lend to certain groups. As discussed in earlier chapters, banks face an information asymmetry in that they do not have knowledge of the ability and willingness to repay. Banks, to ensure that loans will be repaid, take actions to reduce the likelihood of default. They do not lend to everybody and they are likely to exclude risky borrowers. Banks might lend less to farmers, for example, because their income fluctuates more than that of groups in other sectors and the risk to the bank is thus higher. Banks can also restrict loans to geographical areas, or bankers might lend only to their own kinship group because of better knowledge. Banks can also use the reputation of the borrower, which makes new loans dependent on past behaviour.[1] In addition, banks ask for collateral because collateral encourages the borrower not to default and reduces the cost of default to the lender. Moreover, safer borrowers are willing to put up more collateral. Although it is uncommon, some banks require that the output of some of their borrowers be sold to them, making repayment less uncertain.

Besides screening loan applicants, a lender needs to monitor the behaviour of the borrower after the loan is disbursed and to enforce regular repayments. This can be costly and is a particular disincentive to small-scale lending because it costs virtually as much to monitor small loans as large ones (if not more). Moreover, there are fewer companies that track credit histories in developing countries, and with poor communication and transportation infrastructure, especially in rural areas, transaction costs can be very high.

For example, a study of informal loans to farmers in Pakistan found that screening takes one day on average and costs 20 Pakistan rupees (PR 20) ($2.02) in transportation expenses, while the costs of pursuing delinquent loans, overhead and the opportunity cost of capital (including the loss from unrecoverable loans) amount to between 68 and 79 per cent of the loan.[2] Screening, monitoring and enforcement costs to service the same community can be expected to be even higher for a formal institution, as it has less knowledge about the local circumstances and is often further away, making transportation costs higher. In addition, delinquency rates are usually much higher for formal than for informal loans.

The high screening, monitoring and transaction costs per loan and the high share of rejected loan applications partly explain the low density of formal financial institutions in poor and rural areas.[3] Banks prefer urban areas because they generally have higher population density, higher income, a more diversified deposit base, better communication and transportation infrastructure and less seasonality in income and borrowing demands.

There are also disincentives from the demand side to borrowing by the poor. Demand by rural residents can be limited because obtaining a formal loan requires travel and waiting time, finding a lender, filling out forms, negotiating a loan (which might be difficult for the illiterate) and providing references and titles of assets for collateral. Moreover, in some countries, the borrower may have also to pay bribes and entertainment costs to secure a loan. In addition, the terms of loans that banks are willing to offer are usually inflexible and the approval process can be lengthy. All this discourages formal borrowing.

[1]   This explains why many borrowers do not switch easily to other lenders. This phenomenon is common in informal finance as well; for example, in six villages in Thailand, 80 per cent of borrowers borrow from only one (informal) source (see Ammar Siamwalla and others, "The Thai rural credit system: public subsidies, private information, and segmented markets", *The World Bank Economic Review*, vol. 4, No. 3 (September 1990), pp. 271-295). vol. 4, No. 3 (September 1990), pp. 271-295).

[2]   See Irfan Aleem, "Imperfect information, screening, and the costs of informal lending: a study of a rural credit market in Pakistan", *The World Bank Economic Review*, vol. 4, No. 3 (September 1990), pp. 329-349.

[3]   This is a general phenomenon which can be found in a low-income neighbourhood of a large city in a developed country as well as of a remote rural area of a low-income country.

Who is excluded from bank loans?

The screening devices used by lenders cause certain groups to have little or no access to loans from formal financial institutions. Nearly everyone without collateral will be excluded. The poor are almost by definition part of this group, as are micro-entrepreneurs, the landless and smallholder farmers who do not have a title to their land. Women, whose rights to own land or other property are often legally restricted, are also largely excluded.

There are a number of characteristics peculiar to the agricultural sector that discourage lending to farmers, such as geographical dispersion, high risk and lack of collateral. Risk is high as a result of the price volatility of crops and the possibility of adverse weather, often affecting many debtors simultaneously. In addition, the seasonal nature of agriculture leads to the concentration of loan applications and repayment during certain periods of the year, resulting in peak demands on lenders and an irregular cash flow.

Rural and urban micro- and small enterprises (MSEs) usually do not keep records that would be accepted by banks to assess creditworthiness. New entrepreneurs also have difficulties securing finance because they have not built up a reputation with a lender. In sum, the poor, smallholder farmers, the landless, many women, small traders, informal sector participants and owners of MSEs would probably have difficulty getting a formal loan because of the high screening, monitoring and enforcement costs.

This has economic and social consequences. First, the production of small-holder farms or micro-, small and medium-sized enterprises is curtailed. Many studies have shown that credit is one of the most important constraints on the adoption of new technology, such as high-yield seed varieties, as this step involves the use of more purchased inputs than is the case for traditional agriculture.[4] Other studies have emphasized the negative effect of a lack of credit on nutrition and education.[5] Likewise, small entrepreneurs often list the lack of access to finance as the first and most important constraint on expansion.[6] Indeed, micro-, small and medium-sized enterprises obtain most of their finance from personal savings or loans from family and friends.

INFORMAL INSTITUTIONS: PARTLY FILLING THE GAP

Several informal financial institutions have emerged over time to meet a part of the demand of poor people for financial services (see table VII.1). Most of them pre-date the creation of formal financial institutions and some, like rotating savings and credit associations (ROSCAs), even pre-date monetization. What informal loans have in common is that they are usually unsecured, small and short-term; they also have lower transaction (screening, monitoring and enforcement) costs and a lower risk of default than formal loans (see table VII.2).[7] Most of these institutions are part of the community they lend to and are therefore able to use their knowledge about borrowers to screen loan applicants. Peer pressure and social sanctions can be important in reducing the monitoring and enforcement costs. Lending is cheaper, as little or no office space or paperwork is involved and decentralized decision-making ensures a quick approval process.

4 See, for example, Gamini Herath and Sisira Jayasuriya, "Adoption of HYV technology in Asian countries: the role of credit revisited", *Asian Survey*, vol. 36, No. 12 (December 1996), pp. 1,184-1,200; and Paul Mosley, "Policy and capital market constraints to the African green revolution: a study of maize and sorghum yields in Kenya, Malawi and Zimbabwe, 1960-91", *UNICEF Innocenti Papers*, No. 38 (December 1993).

5 See, for example, Karnit Flug, Antonio Spilimbergo and Erik Wachtenheim, "Investment in education: do economic volatility and credit constraints matter?", *Journal of Development Economics*, vol. 55, No. 2 (April 1998), pp. 465-481; and Manfred Zeller and others, "Rural finance for food security for the poor: implications for research and policy", *Food Policy Review* (International Food Policy Research Institute (IFPRI), Washington, D.C.), No. 4 (1997), pp. 77-81.

6 See, for example, Gerard Caprio, Jr., and Asli Demirgüç-Kunt, "The role of long-term finance: theory and evidence", *The World Bank Research Observer*, vol. 13, No. 2 (August 1998), pp. 171-189; Donald C. Mead, "The contribution of small enterprises to employment growth in southern and eastern Africa", *World Development*, vol. 22, No. 12 (December 1994), pp. 1,881-1,894; and Christian Morrison, Henri-Bernard Solignac Lecomte and Xavier Oudin, *Micro-Enterprises and the Institutional Framework* (Paris, Organisation for Economic Cooperation and Development (OECD) Development Centre, 1994).

7 Yet, there are instances of informal financial institutions that have provided large loans to the corporate sector, such as the curb markets in the Republic of Korea and Taiwan Province of China and the chit funds in Thailand. However, these are the exceptions rather than the rule.

Costs in informal institutions can be lower than in formal institutions also because the former are often not regulated and have no reserve requirements. However, some of these informal institutions are not completely outside the formal legal and monetary systems. Some ROSCAs, like the chit funds in India, are now regulated. Some countries have legislation pertaining to the informal sector, including usury laws, restrictions on deposit-taking and requirements on lending to certain sectors.

Informal finance accounts for a large share of—and often dominates—finance in rural areas of Africa and Asia, but its share is less in Latin America. In Africa and Asia, this share is nearly always larger than one third and often reaches two thirds in rural areas.[8] The share generally declines with development, although it rarely vanishes. In some countries, such as India and the Republic of Korea, the informal sector was reduced by government action. In others, informal institutions have become formal or were absorbed by the formal sector. Yet, this process is not automatic and not monotonic.

Types of informal financial institutions

Several types of informal financial institutions can be found all over the world, although their relative sizes differ considerably across countries.

Little comprehensive information is available on loans from friends and family, although they appear to be quantitatively important in developing countries and also exist in developed and transition economies. Surveys in Madagascar and Pakistan show that they accounted for about a third of all informal credit in the early 1990s; this share was generally higher for poorer households, which generally relied more on informal credit.[9] Loans from friends and family are usually small, unsecured and very flexible with regard to the term, interest rates and repayment conditions. Interest rates are usually low or non-existent and repayment is often contingent on borrowers' and

[8]   For example, formal credit accounted for only 8 per cent of all rural credit in four villages in northern Nigeria in 1987-1988, for 44 per cent in six villages in Thailand in 1984-1985, for 39 per cent in India in 1981, and for 25 per cent among 60 farmers in the Chamber area of Pakistan in 1980-1981. See Karla Hoff and Joseph E. Stiglitz, "Introduction: imperfect information and rural credit markets—puzzles and policy perspectives", *The World Bank Economic Review*, vol. 4, No. 3 (September 1990), pp. 235-250.

[9]   See Manfred Zeller and others, "Rural finance for food security for the poor", *Food Policy Review* (IFPRI, Washington, D.C.), No. 4 (1997), p. 67.

Table VII.1.
INFORMAL FINANCIAL INSTITUTIONS

	Friends and family	ROSCA[a]	Moneylender	Pawnbroker	Tied credit
Loan size	Small	Small	Small	Small	Small
Loan term	Varies	Short-term	Short-term	Short-term	Varies
Terms	Very flexible	Flexible	Flexible	Flexible	Flexible
Interest rate	None or low	Medium	High	Less high	Low
Collateral	No	No; group peer pressure	Sometimes	Yes	Economic relation
Transaction costs	Low	Low	Medium	Low	Low
Deposits	No	Fixed amount	Usually not	Sometimes	Usually not
Source of funds	Own	Members	Own, some borrowed	Own, some borrowed	Own, some borrowed

Source: UN/DESA.

[a]   Rotating savings and credit association.

lenders' economic circumstances. Social sanctions and reciprocity are very important.

Some of these loans come from relatives or friends who have moved to urban areas or abroad. As reciprocity is important, it is not always clear to an outsider whether a transfer is a loan, a gift or a repayment of a loan. Migration is often financed by relatives, particularly when it involves international migration, the cost of which can be substantial. A financial transfer from abroad or from an urban area can be a repayment of the loan that financed the migration.[10] These transfers can be large and have a significant impact on household behaviour, alleviating a credit constraint, and allowing consumption smoothing, investment in human and physical capital, insurance and risk sharing.

ROSCAs are found all over the world, including in the developed countries. They are known under different names, for example, as *susu* in Ghana, *tontine*

[10] See, for example, Nadeem Ilahi and Saqib Jafarey, "Guestworker migration, remittances and the extended family: evidence from Pakistan", *Journal of Development Economics*, vol. 58, No. 2 (April 1999), pp. 485-512.

Table VII.2.
FINANCIAL INSTITUTIONS

	Formal	Semi-formal	Informal
Examples	Commercial bank	Microcredit non-governmental organization	ROSCA[a]
Characteristics	Regulated	Often not regulated	Not regulated
Loan size	Large	Very small – medium	Very small
Loan term	All terms	Medium- and short-term	Short-term
Terms	Rigid	Less rigid	Flexible
Interest rate	Low	Medium	Medium
Collateral	Usually	No; group peer pressure, character lending	No; group peer pressure
Transaction costs of small loan			
For lender	High	Medium	Low[b]
For borrower	High	Medium – high	Low[b]
Deposits	Yes	Sometimes; compulsory savings	Fixed amount
Main Clients	Corporations	Poor, women, MSEs[c] SMEs[d]	Poor, women, MSEs[c]
Use	Fixed investment, working capital	Consumption, working capital, fixed investment	Consumption, working capital, fixed investment
Financial intermediation	Large	Small, but growth potential	Small
Linkages[e]	Small	Small, but growth potential	Small, but growth potential

Source: UN/DESA.

[a] Rotating savings and credit association.
[b] For ROSCA, lender and borrower are the same.
[c] Micro- and small enterprises.
[d] Small and medium-sized enterprises.
[e] Referring, for example, to linkages between bank on the one hand and non-governmental organization or ROSCA on the other hand. Linkages between banks and money-lenders or traders who onlend are more common.

in the Niger and Senegal, *hui* in China, *kye* in the Republic of Korea, *tanda* in Mexico and *san* in the Dominican Republic. A ROSCA is a group, usually comprising 5 to 50 people, in which each individual periodically puts a certain small amount of money into a pot. The pot is then allocated to one member randomly, by bidding or through negotiation. The bid payments by those who received the pot in earlier rounds (net borrowers) can be viewed as interest payments to the net lenders who receive the pot in later rounds. Each member receives the pot only once and the process repeats itself during each period until all the members have won the pot.

Membership is usually restricted to people with a common interest or background, like an office or a village, and local knowledge is used to select the members. This gives the ROSCA the opportunity to use mutual trust and social sanctions to enforce contributions, even from someone who has already received the pot. The fact that ROSCAs select their own members and do not screen the loans reduces transaction costs. ROSCAs are common in developing countries, although comprehensive data on them are lacking. Some studies have found that half the adult urban residents in several African countries belong to a ROSCA.

Other group-based institutions, such as savings and credit associations (SCAs), self-help groups and mutual assistance groups, direct savings to community needs or specific activities. An SCA collects savings and pays depositors high real interest rates; in a manner similar to a credit union, the SCA lends proceeds to its members. The extent of financial intermediation is thus much larger than in other informal financial institutions. Yet, membership is usually restricted and loans are usually small and short-term.

Informal moneylending is one of the most ubiquitous forms of informal finance in the developing world. Moneylenders are often notorious because of the fact that they charge high interest rates (5 to 10 per cent per month), which are thought to be a product of their presumed monopoly. Yet, research has shown that high interest rates largely reflect high costs and risks, although moneylenders often have some market power based on their informational and enforcement advantages.

Moneylenders usually do not accept deposits. They lend their own money or money that they have borrowed (often from formal sources but also from other moneylenders). They lend mostly for a rather short-term period, which is sometimes as short as a workday. To the extent that moneylenders borrow money from banks, they provide an important linkage with the formal financial sectors. Moneylenders sometimes demand land as collateral but because land titling and land markets are less common in Africa than in Asia, moneylenders are more prevalent in the latter.

Many Governments and scholars have depicted the high interest rates of moneylenders as usurious. In India, for example, the Government attempted to displace the village moneylender by promoting cooperatives in the 1950s and expanding branches of banks in the 1970s. The role of the moneylender declined over the decades but did not disappear, partly because the commercialization of agriculture led to higher demand for the services of the trader-moneylender.[11]

Pawnbrokers take tangible property, such as jewellery, as collateral for a loan. If, after an agreed period, the loan and the interest are not repaid, the

11 See Clive Bell, "Interactions between institutional and informal credit agencies in rural India", *The World Bank Economic Review*, vol. 4, No. 3 (September 1990), pp. 297-327.

pawnbroker keeps the property.[12] The advantage of the pawnbroker over collateralized loans is that with the former there are no costs involved and no uncertainty in regard to seizing the collateral. The pawnbroker wants only assets that he or she can appraise quickly and easily before a loan is given. However, selling the property might involve some costs. Nonetheless, transaction costs are low; interest rates are therefore lower than those of moneylenders but usually higher than those of the other forms of informal finance.

Pawnbrokers sometimes also act as money keepers, mostly without paying interest, and sometimes they even charge a fee. Money keepers, who just keep money safe for a small fee, often also lend money to their customers, usually at no interest and in amounts smaller than the borrower's savings.

There are also indigenous banks that are considered part of the informal sector. They are similar to moneylenders but offer more services, including savings facilities and trade finance. They are able to keep transaction costs down owing to simple offices and procedures and because of their information advantages. They have been particularly prevalent in Asia. At independence, India had a sophisticated indigenous banking system which had developed over centuries. Indigenous bankers in India have often combined several activities and lent their own money. Some Governments, such as those of India and the Republic of Korea, suppressed indigenous banks but in other countries they were absorbed or developed into formal banks.

A final informal financial transaction is one where extension of credit by a miller, trader, shopkeeper, employer or landlord is tied to other economic transactions. It is common in Asia, but also exists in, for example, West Africa. In one form of the transaction, a loan for seeds and fertilizers is tied to future sales of the crop. Another possibility is one where farm workers obtain a loan from a farmer during the slack season for a promise to work during the peak season. The lender has particular advantages because of the information gained as a result of the trade or renting relation with the borrower. This relation also makes enforcement easier. Transaction costs are also low for the borrower and effective interest rates are about the same as, or lower than, those of formal loans. The terms are flexible, ranging from four months to three harvests, should the yield be poor. Such lenders normally do not accept deposits and most lending is conducted from their own resources; but they do borrow from the formal sector and sometimes accept deposits.

Advantages and disadvantages of informal finance

Informal finance is very flexible and has low transaction costs but the extent of financial intermediation is small and has limited potential. Most informal financial institutions lend only small amounts of their own resources and do not take deposits. Saving and lending are usually performed by different institutions. Moreover, the geographical area serviced by any informal institution is often restricted, for example, to the village, and very little—if any—financial intermediation takes place over large distances. Reliance on social sanctions for enforcement limits the size of the group, while the lack of collateral leads to small and short-term loans, and the lack of deposit mobilization and accumulation limits the possibilities for expansion of informal finance. Nevertheless, many moneylenders, pawnbrokers, merchants and

[12] In some countries, pawnshops are operated by the local government.

landowners borrow part of the money they lend from formal financial institutions. Informal finance can therefore be a link in a larger national chain of financial intermediation.

SURMOUNTING THE LIMITATIONS OF INFORMAL FINANCE

There are several means to overcome at least partly the limitations of informal finance. Governments have long directed formal institutions to provide financial services to the poor. More recently, other initiatives, especially ones involving microfinance, have come to the fore. Semi-formal microcredit-dispensing institutions have borrowed those features of the informal sector that allow them to keep transaction costs and the risk of default low. Most of these institutions, however, require government intervention.

Bringing traditional formal institutions to the poor

Between the 1950s and 1970s, many Governments in the developing world directly intervened in financial markets, particularly in rural areas, to ease finance constraints, address equity issues and counter the urban bias in other policies. Governments nationalized commercial banks or required private banks to make loans of a certain amount to specific sectors or target groups, guaranteed the loans and subsidized the interest rates. Governments also created development and agricultural banks and cooperatives to provide financial services and reach their development goals, following the example of some of the developed countries during the nineteenth century. Agricultural development institutions often provided credit, seeds, extension services, technology and other services as a package.

These institutions have had a mixed record. Several suffered from high loan default rates, were not able to become financially sustainable, did not reach the targeted population and were a drain on the government budget or were dependent on foreign aid. High default rates resulted from the weak pressures on borrowers to repay, which arose from weak incentives on loan officers to enforce repayment. Loans often went to wealthy and influential people who could divert the funds to unintended purposes, did not feel a need to repay, could use their influence to delay repayment or could avert the seizure of collateral.

However, this experience was not universal. For example, the Badan Kredit Kecamatan in Indonesia and the Bank for Agriculture and Agricultural Cooperatives (BAAC) in Thailand have been very successful in reaching the poor and making a profit.[13] In other countries, reforms, often modelled on microfinancing principles, have allowed development and agricultural banks and cooperatives to continue to play an important role in providing financial services to the poor. Some evidence suggests that government-sponsored schemes can be as successful as semi-formal ones, as long as techniques are adopted that take into account the information, screening and enforcement problems discussed above.

Postal savings

The experience of postal savings systems in developing countries has been mixed and in some countries the system has been abolished or privatized.

[13] See, for example, Jacob Yaron, "What makes rural financial institutions successful?", *The World Bank Research Observer*, vol. 9, No. 1 (January 1994), pp. 49-70.

However, in other cases, these institutions have been efficient collection points for savings and have offered financial services to people who might otherwise not have been serviced.

Some postal savings systems have acted merely as conduits for the flow of funds to the national Treasury; in other cases, funds may be redeposited in the commercial banking sector or in the wholesale money market. In yet other countries, such as France, Italy and Japan, postal savings funds have been used for developmental purposes. There are significantly higher rates of savings deposits and public participation in the postal savings system in such countries than in countries that pass the resources to the Treasury. In the case of Japan's 124-year-old postal savings system, the funds were dedicated to modernization and development, and the elimination of foreign borrowing. Publicity for postal savings accounts historically stressed development themes. In Japan's post-war period, postal savings resources were channelled, *inter alia*, through public institutions such as the Japan Development Bank to domestic regional development banks. In addition, the Government of Japan established public corporations to lend to small and medium-sized businesses, and for housing finance and household mortgages, and infrastructure construction. In the light of such success, this is a model that might be revisited (see box IV.1).

Credit cooperatives or unions

Governments have also often played a role in the establishment of credit cooperatives or credit unions. Credit unions are owned by their members, who are tied together by employment, village, profession or other forms of association. Credit unions provide both credit and savings services to their members. They originated in the middle of the nineteenth century in Europe and can now be found all over the world. At the end of 1997, the World Council of Credit Unions counted 34,839 credit unions in 83 countries with nearly 96 million members.

Goals, size and operational principles of credit unions vary. They can be formal, semi-formal or informal, depending on their specific characteristics. Moreover, various combinations of internal and external funds exist. Where cooperatives are informal and not regulated, they gain some flexibility, but are limited in their access to finance from the central bank or commercial banks. When they have access to formal loans, the scope for financial intermediation increases dramatically.

Many credit unions and, in particular, agricultural credit cooperatives have been created in developing countries by Governments, non-governmental organizations, or donors. These actors have functioned as catalysts and as providers of funds and technical assistance, while Governments have also subjected cooperatives to policy directives.

Sometimes a federation of credit unions is created within a country, which allows funds to be moved over larger geographical areas, thereby raising opportunities for intermediation. In Togo, for example, a federation of 93 credit unions was established in 1983. By 1995, the federation consisted of 155 unions with 50,000 members. The federation manages a central fund which transfers funds between those unions with surpluses and those with deficits. In addition, the federation has easier access than the member unions to financial institutions, through which members can increase funds for lending, place liq-

14 See, for example, Timothy Besley, "Savings, credit and insurance", in *Handbook of Development Economics*, vol. III, Jere Behrman and T.N. Srinivasan, eds. (Amsterdam, Elsevier, 1995); and Monika Huppi and Gershon Feder, "The role of groups and credit cooperatives in rural lending", *The World Bank Research Observer*, vol. 5, No. 2 (July 1990), pp. 187-204.

uid funds in low-risk financial instruments and diversify risk. However, there have also been difficulties. The growth of the federation stretched the demand for management skills beyond capacity and the larger need for management resources led to an increasing dependence on external funds. Moreover, group cohesion declined with the increase in members, leading to more bad loans. The withdrawal of one donor in 1994, however, prompted a "shake-up" and forced the federation to decentralize, implement measures to better control lending and costs, charge members for services and train managers.

As exemplified in this case, the performance of credit unions has been mixed, largely because of monitoring and collusion problems.[14] As the lenders are the owners, there is no incentive for usurious lending by a credit union. Yet, monitoring of borrowers in a cooperative is more difficult than in a ROSCA because the former is larger and less personal. Also, with the cooperative's being larger, members may feel less restrained in trying to take advantage of the institution for personal gain. For example, borrowers could try to effect a shrinkage of the spread between interest charged on loans and interest paid on deposits, which reduces financial sustainability and increases the dependence on external funds.

The success of a cooperative can be increased by proper training of members and management, by relying on savings of members rather than on outside funds and by restricting activities to those that can be carried out with the institutional and management capabilities that exist. When a credit union can draw easily on loans from Governments and donors, an impression may be created that the union will be bailed out in case of default. In such situations, repayment rates are likely to be low, as a result of moral hazard. In contrast, when their own funds are at risk, members of the credit union are given a stake in the institution and incentives for repayment are larger.

Innovations combining the formal and informal

The mixed results with development finance institutions, combined with the general movement away from direct government interventions in markets, have contributed to a rethinking about how best to deliver financial services to the poor. A number of innovations seek to combine the best characteristics of the informal and the formal financial sector.

Linkages between formal and informal institutions

Linkages between informal and formal institutions which can increase the amount of funds within the informal financial sector, may take several forms (see figure VII.1). Several linkages, as indicated above, arose autonomously, as traders, landowners, moneylenders or pawnbrokers took loans from formal financial institutions and lent proceeds to individual borrowers who did not have access themselves to formal loans. These lenders can also serve as intermediaries who screen credit applications from groups, such as ROSCAs. Moreover, there have been cases, for example, in the Republic of Korea, where banks sought deposits from informal lenders and used the deposits to lend to borrowers that had been selected by the informal lenders. In this way, the bank increases its market share, the informal lender transfers the risk of default to the bank, and the depositors are more secure and receive interest.

Figure VII.1.
CHANNELS TO PROVIDE FINANCIAL SERVICES TO THE POOR

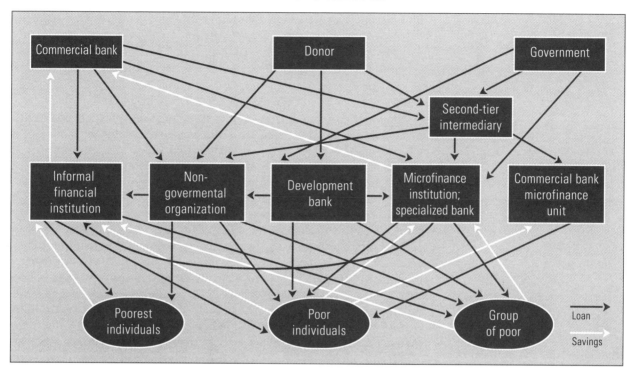

Source: UN/DESA.

The second type of linkage encompasses lending by formal institutions directly to group-based informal financial institutions, such as ROSCAs and credit unions. In Senegal, for example, a reform of the agricultural credit programme entailed forming village groups which elected a president who, functioning as an intermediary, screened, allocated and enforced credit terms. Similar arrangements exist in the Philippines.[15] Moreover, in several countries, banks allow group savings to be used as collateral or a screening device. In countries such as India and the Republic of Korea, banks have created ROSCAs themselves.

Group savings can be deposited at a bank, making savings safer, and increasing the group's income through interest earnings. However, group savings that accumulate in a bank are not necessarily being lent to group members. This raises a more general concern that, if deposits by the poor are placed in formal institutions, they may leave the community. There is an argument that bank lending portfolios should be diversified and thus that not every dollar deposited should be lent locally. However, there is a case to be made for directing some bank deposits back into the local community. In the United States of America, for example, the Community Reinvestment Act of 1977 encourages banks to lend to and service the same community that they take deposits from (the performance is evaluated by the Office of the Comptroller of the Currency).

A final linkage of formal to informal institutions can be effected through local non-governmental organizations, which act as intermediaries and borrow on their own account for onlending to individuals or self-help groups. The non-governmental organizations then do the screening, monitoring and

15 See Matthew Warning and Elisabeth Sadoulet, "The performance of village intermediaries in rural credit delivery under changing penalty regimes: evidence from Senegal", *The Journal of Development Studies*, vol. 35, No. 1 (October 1998), pp. 115-138; and Maria Sagrario Floro and Debrai Ray, "Vertical links between formal and informal financial institutions", *Review of Development Economics*, vol. 1, No. 1 (February 1997), pp. 34-56.

enforcement, based on their knowledge of the borrowers. This linkage has become a prominent part of the upscaling of microfinance institutions as discussed below.

Microcredit

Since the 1980s, a new approach has revolutionized thinking about how to provide small uncollateralized loans to the poor. This approach, often referred to by the term *microcredit*, adapted lending techniques from the informal financial sector. These techniques keep administrative costs down, reduce risk and provide incentives for repayment which could substitute for a lack of collateral (see table VII.2). Costs are reduced by employing quick and simple procedures which keep documentation to a minimum. Loan approvals are decentralized to make best use of local information. Bad debt losses are curtailed through effective incentives for repayment, such as group pressure, denying access to future loans in case of delinquency and granting access to larger loans in case of on-time repayments. In addition, sometimes there are repayment stimuli, such as savings requirements. In order to cover (the bulk of) costs, interest rates are usually higher than those commercial or development banks are allowed or would dare to charge. Many of the poor are able and willing to pay interest at these rates because they are generally lower than the rates of other sources to which they have access. Moreover, the small size of loans and high interest rates will discourage potential large borrowers who have access to commercial bank loans with lower interest rates, and thus the difficulties in public credit programmes of earlier decades may be avoided.

While originally pioneered by non-governmental organizations, albeit funded by Governments or donors, microcredit now also encompasses lending programmes by commercial or specialized banks, credit unions, parastatals and other semi-formal or formal financial institutions (see figure VII.1).

Microcredit loans may be extended to a group that allocates them among its members or to an individual member of a group. In both cases, the group is jointly responsible for repayment. Frequently, loan repayments are due at weekly or monthly group meetings to instil repayment discipline and allow peer pressure to operate. In addition, group-lending schemes apply sanctions. Some cut off access to loans to all group members after one defaults, but other schemes are less strict.

Microcredit was introduced in Asia in the 1970s and became popular in the development literature in the 1980s. The prominence of group lending is largely a result of the success of the Grameen Bank in Bangladesh, which has received considerable attention. The Grameen Bank has been able to provide credit to 2 million poor people as of 1996 and get repaid. It has been imitated in more than 45 countries, including developed countries.

Success in replicating the Grameen Bank has been mixed, although a few successful schemes have attracted attention. The scale and repayment rates of other group-based lending schemes are nearly all smaller than those of the Grameen Bank. The scale of the institutions range from a few hundred thousand members to a few hundred and repayment rates are more typically between 70 and 90 per cent, compared with the 98 per cent reported by the Grameen Bank.[16]

[16] It is not always clear how these rates are calculated and the method most commonly followed is questionable (see Richard Rosenberg, "Independent review of UNCDF microfinance activities", United Nations Capital Development Fund (UNCDF), May 1998, p. 7).

Attempts to blindly copy the Grameen Bank have not been very success-ful. Socio-economic and cultural conditions different from those in South Asia require adaptation and innovation and the most successful replicators are those that have modified the model. Even within a single country, differ-ences between borrowers (for example, with regard to loan size and risk) necessitate a variety of institutions. However, competition between different agencies has led to copying of well-publicized examples rather than innova-tion to meet local needs.[17]

One of the issues is whether borrowers need to be grouped. In some com-munities, groups readily form but in others, a catalyst is needed. This, in turn, raises several questions. Who should organize and bear the costs of group for-mation: the lender, the borrower or a third party such as the Government or a donor? What are the criteria to be used for membership in the group? To max-imize repayment rates, should the group be more homogeneous (because its social cohesion would be larger) or more heterogeneous (because it is less like-ly that all borrowers would default at the same time)? Should the group admit only women (because it would enhance the empowerment of women by creat-ing women's networks, exchanging information and training)? How is the com-mon interest created that is needed to keep the group together and make it func-tion? How large should the group be (large groups reduce the transaction costs per loan but increase the costs of peer-monitoring within the group)? Should organizers of Grameen-type banks restrict their efforts to communities in which "social capital" is high and prospective groups already exist?[18]

Once established, there are considerable costs involved in operating a group. Group lending involves frequent meetings, often weekly, where peer pressure encourages repayment and information and advice are exchanged, for example, not only on running a small business but also on social matters such as family planning, health care, education and empowerment.

In addition, project selection in groups is not straightforward. There is a danger that individual group members might select riskier projects because repayment is a joint responsibility. Group members therefore prefer to assess other members' projects, and this entails a social dynamic within the group. If this does not happen, the probability of default rises.

Furthermore, many group-lending schemes (including the Grameen Bank) remain dependent on subsidies, despite the high repayment rates. There is some evidence that the high repayment rates are related less to the fact that loans are made to a group than to the fact that default precludes future access to loans. Furthermore, men control a large share of the loans, while women account for the bulk of the borrowers and bear the liability of repayment. There is evidence that violence and aggressive behaviour have increased in households that bor-row from the Bank.[19]

The alternative to the group-lending model is microcredit for individuals, as in Indonesia. Such institutions also locate geographically close to the borrow-er and screening of loans is based on personal knowledge (referred to as char-acter-based lending). However, individual lending can be expensive and loans tend to be larger in order to reduce transaction costs per loan. Transaction costs can also be reduced over time as the lender learns more about a specific bor-rower through subsequent loans.

[17] "So in Bangladesh we found that competition was basically amongst solidarity group approaches ... that copied the Grameen approach. Similarly in Indonesia institutions compete with variations of the individual model" (see David Hulme and Paul Mosley, *Finance against Poverty*, vol. 1 (London and New York, Routledge, 1996), p. 167).

[18] See, for example, Nitin Bhatt and Shui-Yan Tang, "The problem of transaction costs in group-based microlending: an institutional perspective", *World Development*, vol. 26, No. 4 (April 1998), pp. 623-637.

[19] See, for example, Anne Marie Goetz and Rina Sen Gupta, "Who takes the credit? gender, power, and control over loan use in rural credit programs in Bangladesh", *World Development*, vol. 24, No. 1 (January 1996), pp. 45-63; Linda Mayoux, "Women's empowerment and micro-finance programmes: approaches, evidence and ways forward", mimeo (Milton Keynes, United Kingdom of Great Britain and Northern Ireland, The Open University, January 1998), pp. 37-38; and Aminur Rahman, "Micro-cred-it initiatives for equitable and sustainable develop-ment: who pays?", *World Development*, vol. 27, No. 1 (January 1999), pp. 67-82.

20 See, for example, Jacob Yaron, McDonald Benjamin and Stephanie Charitonenko, "Promoting efficient rural financial intermediation", *The World Bank Research Observer*, vol. 13, No. 2 (August 1998) pp. 147-170.

21 See Md. Rezaul Karim and Mitsue Osada, "Dropping out: an emerging factor in the success of microcredit-based poverty alleviation programs", *The Developing Economies*, vol. 36, No. 3 (September 1998), pp. 257-288. The authors show that, in one Grameen Bank branch, drop-out rates were generally higher than the increase in new members, raising questions about the viability of the programme. Moreover, they estimate that 88 per cent of the drop-outs did not move out of poverty (assuming that it takes five years to move out of poverty, as others have argued).

22 See David Hulme and Paul Mosley, *Finance against Poverty*, vol. 1 (London and New York, Routledge, 1996), pp. 95, 103 and 114; Shahidur R. Khandker, *Fighting Poverty with Microcredit: Experience in Bangladesh* (Oxford, Oxford University Press, 1998), p. 148; and Mark M. Pitt and Shahidur R. Khandker, "Household and intra-household impact of the Grameen Bank and similar targeted credit programs in Bangladesh", *World Bank Discussion Papers*, No. 320, 1996.

One of the most successful organizations providing individual microloans is the Unit Desa programme of the Bank Rakyat of Indonesia (BRI-UD), a State-owned bank that operates on a commercial basis. The Government of Indonesia prompted the establishment of the programme in 1984 when it forced BRI's loss-making public credit programme to become financially sustainable or face liquidation. The new system of village banks introduced by BRI became profitable within 18 months by promoting deposits, charging interest rates for loans that covered costs, using information from peers and village leaders to screen loans and providing incentives for clients and employees to increase loan repayment.[20] Collateral is desirable but not mandatory. At the end of 1996, BRI-UD had 3,595 offices, 2.5 million outstanding loans with a total value of $1.7 billion and an average loan size of $680. BRI-UD is so successful that profits from the Unit Desa programme are used to cover losses in BRI's lending to large clients.

Microlending schemes have served millions of poor people; however, this does not necessarily mean that poverty has been reduced. Although disentangling the multiple factors that influence poverty is difficult, many practitioners have argued that the effects of credit are positive as long as clients repay loans and reborrow. A large majority of borrowers are continuing members (85 per cent in the case of the Grameen Bank as of 1994), although drop-out rates have been increasing in some programmes and many probably dropped out before they graduated out of poverty.[21] The few studies that have investigated the impact on poverty found a generally positive impact of credit, particularly if the borrower is a woman. However, while there is evidence of gains in household consumption, nutrition, education and contraceptive use, the impact on asset accumulation, productivity and technology—and hence on achieving a sustainable output increase—is less positive, making the long-run impact on poverty less clear.[22]

Microfinance institutions: upscaling, borrowing and taking deposits

Institutions that provide microcredit and other financial services have been under increasing pressure from Governments and donors to become financially sustainable. Microfinance non-governmental organizations rely on a mix of government and donor grants, soft loans and commercial loans for their funding and the objective is to reduce the grant element. This involves becoming more like a bank, for example, accepting deposits, raising funds on capital markets, increasing interest rates to levels that cover costs and enlarging operations to benefit from economies of scale. The challenge is to maintain those aspects of microfinance that allow lending to the poor while keeping costs low.

Upscaling often involves the transformation of a non-governmental organization into a specialized financial institution or a bank which becomes subject to prudential requirements (such as maintaining a minimum level of reserves) and also incurs higher central overhead on such items as salaries and offices. Two well-known examples are the Grameen Bank, which started as a project and became a chartered bank in 1983 by a government ordinance, and Banco Solidario (known as BancoSol) in Bolivia, which transformed itself from a non-governmental organization to a commercial bank, becoming the first private commercial bank to specialize in microfinance and the largest bank by number of clients in Bolivia. BancoSol became a bank to be able to take deposits and raise funds from the capital market, and it has been successful in these activities.

A microfinance institution that can borrow on commercial terms can tap an important source of funds for lending to the poor. One well-known network of microcredit programmes (ACCION International) raised more than a quarter of its funds from commercial banks loans in 1991. Such a borrower must be able to pass on the cost of the funds to its borrowers, however, if it is to service the loan without subsidy. Non-governmental organizations can and do charge higher interest rates than banks to cover (at least part of) the higher costs of administering loans. For example, the Small Industries Development Bank of India lent to non-governmental organizations at a 9 per cent interest rate; the non-governmental organizations lent to self-help groups at a rate up to 15 per cent, and to individuals at 30 per cent. This kind of linkages can become important although very few—if any—non-governmental organizations rely solely on commercial loans.

Borrowing on commercial terms, however, is not always a solution. Many non-governmental organizations are not creditworthy, the most important constraint being their management capacity. These problems are reduced when non-governmental organizations transform themselves into more formal institutions. In other cases, these constraints have been alleviated by creating second-tier institutions or using microfinance networks as intermediaries between banks and non-governmental organizations. These institutions also provide technical assistance. Examples are the People's Credit and Finance Corporation (PCFC) in the Philippines, which is a public second-tier institution, and Palli Karma-Sahayak Foundation in Bangladesh. Second-tier institutions work best when a strong retail capacity is already present, rather than with the expectation that the institutions will create this capacity, although they can play a role in strengthening capacity. Governmental and donor involvement can be an important support to the second-tier institutions through technical assistance in improving the capacity of the institutions, through guarantees or through additional funds. There is, however, a danger that second-tier organizations can be used for purposes of political influence by Governments or donors.

One particular form of intermediary institution is an investment fund created either by the Government or by private individuals, to invest in small and medium-sized enterprises (SMEs), either directly or through another organization such as a non-governmental organization. The fund borrows from banks and invests in SMEs and makes a profit on the interest rate spread.[23]

One of the most important aspects of the upscaling of microfinance institutions entails the taking of savings deposits. Savings had been deemed the forgotten half of rural finance in the 1980s, and remained largely forgotten in the early 1990s;[24] but there has been an increasing emphasis on the importance of savings for the poor. While not all poor people want credit, most—if not all—poor people use and benefit from savings institutions; this is one reason that postal savings institutions continue to exist. The poor have always saved, for example, by accumulating cattle ("saving on the hoof") or jewellery. When savings institutions are available, poor people build deposits to accumulate for future investment, to create a stepping stone for access to credit, to protect their cash against theft or—and not least—to insure against risk and unforeseen

[23] These funds should be distinguished from wholesale or "apex" funds that channel donor resources to small and medium-sized enterprises (SMEs) through non-governmental organizations, which serve as retail institutions, although the distinction is not always clear because many funds rely on a mix of private, governmental and donor funds.

[24] See Robert C. Vogel, "Savings mobilization: the forgotten half of rural finance", in *Undermining Rural Development with Cheap Credit*, Dale W. Adams, Douglas H. Graham, and John D. von Pischke, eds. (Boulder, Colorado, Westview Press, 1984).

emergencies. Liquidity, safety, unlimited withdrawals, convenience and easy access are critical. There is usually a demand for different kinds of savings accounts by different clients, ranging from the poorest to small entrepreneurs, and research is required to establish the appropriate mix of products to be offered in any particular case.

Savings—even small deposits spread over a large number of people—are a potentially large and stable source of funds for lenders. Moreover, compulsory savings schemes to accompany borrowing enhance the financial discipline of the borrower and increase repayment rates. Compulsory savings require that the borrower save a fixed amount when the loan is received or regularly in addition to making the loan repayments. The amount saved is returned to the borrower if the loan is repaid on time. Savings schemes—compulsory or voluntary—are also associated with higher repayment rates on loans because they increase the net worth of borrowers, are an insurance against default and give the borrower a stake in the institution, thereby increasing the pressure to repay.

The transition from a credit-dispensing institution to an institution that takes voluntary deposits is a fundamental one. Accepting deposits is a different service than providing credit, and introducing deposit accounts makes an organization more complex: it requires staff training, changes in management, liquidity and risk management, and new information and security systems. Introducing savings accounts could also rapidly increase the size of the institution, as the demand for savings opportunities usually exceeds many times the demand for credit. The reason for this is partly that, as noted above, although even the poorest have the capacity and desire to save, they do not have much capacity to take on debt. For example, BRI-UD held 16.2 million savings accounts at the end of 1996, increased from 7.3 million in 1990, and amounting to $3 billion, compared with less than $26 million in 1983. The number of savings accounts was six and a half times the number of loans. This ratio appeared to have increased further during the financial crisis (see box VII.1). At Bank

Preliminary evidence suggests that microfinance institutions weathered the financial crisis in Asia relatively well, with repayment rates generally affected only slightly.[a] Institutions serving poor traders and vendors suffered less than those serving small and medium-sized enterprises (SMEs). In Indonesia in particular, the Unit Desa Programme of the Bank Rakyat of Indonesia (BRI-UD) hardly suffered a decline in repayment rates, while commercial and rural banks faced sharp increases in non-performing loans. Also, despite the severity of the crisis in 1997 and 1998, BRI-UD enjoyed a significant increase in deposits, probably as a result of a flight to safety after the Government started to guarantee deposits in January 1998 and provide liquidity to commercial banks (including BRI-UD) but not to rural banks. Preliminary evidence also suggests that microfinance institutions with links to commercial banks were generally hit harder by the financial crisis and reduced lending drastically. BRI-UD also reduced lending but this was not a result of a lack of funds, as deposits soared. In Malaysia and the Philippines, lending by microfinance institutions with linkages declined, as it was more difficult to obtain funds from commercial banks. In some countries, such as the Philippines, an increase in demand for microloans was observed, perhaps as a result of a decline in formal lending or an increase in demand for informal sector products as a fallout of the crisis.

Box VII.1.

MICROFINANCE
IN THE MIDST OF THE
ASIAN FINANCIAL CRISIS

[a] See Paul B. Mcguire and John D. Conroy, "Effects on microfinance of the 1997-1998 Asian financial crisis", paper presented at the Second Annual Seminar on New Development Finance at the Goethe University of Frankfurt, 21-25 September 1998 (Brisbane, Australia, The Foundation for Development Cooperation, November 1998).

Dagang Bali, there are 30 times more savings accounts than loans, although in other countries the ratios are lower and, in some, below 1.

Only a few institutions have the capacity and financial footing to make the transition to a deposit-taking institution and manage a large and rapidly growing loan portfolio. Expansion can mean lower average costs as a result of economies of scale, but it can also mean higher monitoring costs (as borrowers are further away geographically) and more risks (as less information is available on new and more distant borrowers). There has been at least one financial crisis in a microfinance institution (Finansol in Colombia) that resulted partly from rapid growth of lending and inadequate management and accounting systems.

Introducing savings into an institution also implies changes on the lending side. Group lending, in particular, becomes less attractive to the lender relative to loans to individuals, especially as the institution will have some information about the savings account-holder. Also, as individual savings balances grow, the institution becomes disposed towards making larger loans to its savers, at least its richer savers. Indeed, in the case of BRI-UD, for example, the average loan amounted to $680 in 1996 and the average savings account to $185.

Finally, some have also argued that upscaling and increasing financial sustainability require that the institutions reduce or eliminate non-financial services, as these are often dependent on funds from government or donors.

Commercial banks downscale

A number of commercial banks (perhaps a few dozen) have started to provide loans to the poor and small entrepreneurs. This has been the result of political pressures, encouragement and support from donors, social concerns or commercial motivation. Most of these initiatives have imitated aspects of informal institutions or microfinance to reduce risk and transaction costs. Banks often start a microlending programme after witnessing the success of microfinance institutions. While some banks that provide microcredit have experimented with group lending, nearly all focus on individual loans, largely because of the larger transaction costs involved in creating and maintaining the group.

Two kinds of banks provide microcredit. First are banks that were once non-governmental organizations providing microcredit and that have transformed themselves into regulated banks. Examples are the BancoSol and the Caja de Ahorro y Crédito Los Andes in Bolivia. Second are multi-service banks that have established an independent microlending unit, or a special microlending window, or that provide small loans as a fully integrated service.

Banks that venture into microcredit generally have more problems establishing themselves in the microfinance business than banks that were previously non-governmental organizations.[25] This can often be traced to the fact that microcredit programmes in large banks depend on one individual. Such banks usually adopt fewer microlending features and bank management is less committed. However, the more independent the unit is, the more likely it is to introduce microlending features. The outreach of this kind of bank is still limited (each bank disburses typically a few thousands loans) and the share of microcredit in the total portfolio is usually low.

25 See Mayada M. Baydas, Douglas H. Graham and Liza Valenzuela, "Commercial banks in microfinance: new actors in the microfinance world", mimeo, Microenterprise Best Practices, Development Alternatives, Inc., Bethesda, Maryland, United States of America, August 1997.

26 See A. Schoombee, "Commercial banking services for micro-enterpreneurs in South Africa", *The South African Journal of Economics*, vol. 66, No. 3 (September 1998), pp. 337-363; and Jo Ann Paulson and James McAndrews, "Financial services for the urban poor: South Africa's E Plan", *World Bank Policy Research Working Paper*, No. 2016, November 1998.

In general, the microlending units are subsidized by other operations of the bank for a few years, but subsequently they are able to break even or become profitable. Technical assistance and subsidized external funds are crucial during the first few years and donor funds and rediscount lines from Governments also often help bridge the start-up costs.

In South Africa, a case in point, the political situation after the end of apartheid compelled commercial banks to make an effort to provide financial services to the rural and urban poor and alleviate some of the socio-economic inequalities that had resulted from past discrimination.[26] Nedcor, Standard Bank and Amalgamated Banks of South Africa (ABSA) have created divisions to serve poor employed blacks, while First National Bank developed a linkage scheme with stokvels (South African ROSCAs) although this was shelved after five years owing to low demand for loans. These initiatives are quite young, but there are some early results: Standard Bank introduced a pilot project for loans between 1,000 and 6,000 rand (R) in black townships, but the project failed because of the high costs and unwillingness to charge high interest rates owing to the negative perceptions that this would create. ABSA's Nubank also provides loans this size, but it charges full-cost interest rates and was breaking even after two years in operation. These four banks also operate small business units, but do not lend below R 30,000 and therefore exclude many potential clients.

While the South African situation is unique, commercial bank initiatives elsewhere have also been prompted by financial sector liberalization reforms that led to more competition. Local banks, in particular, have looked to new market niches to cope with increased competition which often comes from new foreign entrants who pay less attention to small borrowers (see chap. V).

WHAT HAS BEEN LEARNED?

A broad array of financial institutions have emerged to service the poor over the last few decades. But are they sufficient? Do the poor now have adequate access to financial services? What has been the effect of financial liberalization on the interaction between the informal and formal markets? Is there still a role for government?

The continuing role of informal finance

It has often been argued that the informal sector is partly or entirely a result of "financial repression", a term used by economists to depict the effects on the financial sector of government controls on interest rates and other interventions. The idea is that the policy interventions distort prices and incentives in the financial sector, reduce the level of financial activity relative to a "free market" situation and drive some activity into the informal sector. The obverse is that the informal sector should be smaller if financial repression is reduced. Financial liberalization should lead to lower interest rate spreads, greater access to formal finance and increased flows between the formal and informal sectors. Yet, the evidence from a number of cases does not support this argument. For example, the informal sector expanded significantly in four African countries, along with the real economy, while the ratios of formal deposits and credit to gross domestic product (GDP) changed little or fell after financial liberalization. Moreover, interest rate spreads remained high and banks continued to be biased towards large firms.[27]

This result is not hard to understand in the light of the preceding discussion of how informal finance copes with creditors' information problems and the high cost of small transactions. Financial liberalization will not change these facts and therefore the informal financial sector will remain, although it might become smaller.

It is useful to make a distinction between the autonomous part and the reactive part of the informal financial sector. The autonomous part develops as a result of specific characteristics of the local economy, as it serves segments of the population that are excluded from the formal sector. The reactive part is a result of the policy controls imposed on the formal financial sector. The reactive part might decline as the formal sector is liberalized, but the autonomous part might not.

The interface between the formal and informal financial sectors comprises a group of borrowers who could tap either source and a group of informal lenders who could draw on resources from the formal sector. Otherwise, the credits in each sector travel in circuits that remain largely within each sector. In particular, banks will not service those segments of the population that are too risky and too costly. Moreover, if the interface between the sectors is very small, improving overall credit conditions in the formal sector may not improve conditions at all for the people who are still dependent on the informal sector. In other words, policy makers should not assume that reform of the formal financial sector by itself would meet the needs of people in the informal sector. "Trickle down" will reach only some of them.

Lending to the poor and profitability

The increasing emphasis in recent years on improving the financial sustainability of microfinance institutions is partly a result of declining aid flows and the realization that even existing aid flows will not be sufficient to attain the goals of the Microcredit Summit of February 1997 to provide microloans to 100 million poor people by the year 2005.[28] It has been argued that financial sustainability is compatible with outreach to the poor and contributes to poverty alleviation, although this is largely based on a few high-profile cases.

Making microfinance institutions sustainable is crucial, as nobody is served well by institutions that fail. Institutions are more likely to fail once they are perceived as being temporary, as repayment rates will consequently decline. Dependence on outside contributions increases uncertainty, as the continuation of these contributions is outside the direct control of the institutions. Moreover, it has been argued (based on the experience with rural credit programmes of the 1950s and 1960s) that grants and subsidies to microfinance institutions in themselves tend to induce lower repayment rates, as they are regarded as charity.

Whether or not aimed at making a profit, microfinance institutions can improve their financial performance. One of the most important challenges of lending to the poor is to reduce costs to levels that are as low as possible within the goals set by the institutions. Certain design features can help, including

[27] See William F. Steel and others, "Informal financial markets under liberalization in four African countries", *World Development*, vol. 25, No. 5 (May 1997), pp. 817-830; and Ernest Aryeetey and others, "Financial market fragmentation and reforms in Ghana, Malawi, Nigeria, and Tanzania", *The World Bank Economic Review*, vol. 11, No. 2 (May 1997), pp. 195-218.

[28] See document A/52/113-E/1997/18 of 4 April 1997, annex I, containing the Declaration and Plan of Action of the Microcredit Summit; annex II, containing the Summit Communiqué; and annex III, containing the text of the message for the Microcredit Summit from the Chairman of the Group of 77 and China.

strengthening the incentive to repay by denying future loans in case of default and by increasing the size of successive loans, increasing the frequency of repayments, giving loan officers financial or other incentives to increase repayment rates and offering savings and insurance facilities.

Most experts agree that microfinance institutions can become financially self-sustaining but may take as long as 10 years to become so. However, the vast majority of the many thousands that exist will not become self-sustaining.[29] Most significantly, in trying to become profitable, there is a risk that these institutions may lose their focus on the poor. For example, there would be strong incentives to raise interest rates or reduce average loan costs by increasing average loan size. Both courses of action are likely to discourage borrowing by the poor. Indeed, clients that are less poor are better at repaying loans.

A recent study argues that financially sustainable microfinance institutions have a greater impact on the income of borrowers than subsidized institutions because of the selection bias against the poorest. Besides offering higher interest rates, the successful institutions require more frequent loan instalments and operate savings schemes, which reduce default rates and attract borrowers with financial discipline. According to the same study, in 13 out of 21 cases borrowers with incomes below the poverty line suffered a decline in income after they had received a loan. The poorer the borrower, the smaller the percentage increase in income from the loan.

More generally, most microcredit programmes already have a bias against the poorest, even if they aim at reaching them. The poorest people generally do not seek credit because it is too risky to assume a debt burden that they cannot afford, and they do not have the skills (such as accounting, marketing and management skills) and assets (such as land and livestock) to make productive use of credit. Moreover, when people form themselves into groups for loans, the groups exclude the poorest, as they are considered the worst credit risks. For 10 out of 12 programmes, borrowers had higher income levels than a control group of non-borrowers and only the borrowers of two programmes in Bangladesh had average incomes below the poverty line.[30] Even the Grameen Bank has mostly served the group just below the poverty line.

While the poorest will make relatively little use of credit, they can use other financial services and ancillary services that microfinance institutions sometimes make available to their clients, in particular training to enhance the effect of loans. For example, the Bangladesh Rural Advancement Committee (BRAC) requires borrowers to go through three to six months of rigorous training. The Start-Up Fund in South Africa goes even further and uses training as the only selection mechanism and monitoring device. It requires prior participation in a small business training programme (a "township Master of Business Administration (MBA)"), for which a loan applicant has to pay, and does not screen applicants otherwise; nor does it monitor the business operation or enforce default.[31] On the other hand, the Grameen Bank does not regard raising the skills of borrowers as essential and only trains borrowers on how to bank with Grameen (although it does provide information on social issues during its training).

Non-financial services, such as literacy classes and training, can greatly enhance the impact of loans to the poor, but they also add costs to the operation of the organization and much of the costs cannot be recovered through revenues

29   See, for example, Jonathan Murdoch, "The microfinance schism", *Development Discussion Paper*, No. 626, Harvard Institute for International Development, February 1998; and Richard Rosenberg, "Independent review of UNCDF microfinance activities", UNCDF, May 1998.

30   See David Hulme and Paul Mosley, *Finance Against Poverty*, vol. 1 (London and New York, Routledge, 1996), pp. 88 and 109-112.

31   See Jens Reinke, "How to lend like mad and make a profit: a micro-credit paradigm versus the Start-Up Fund in South Africa", The Journal of Development Studies, vol. 34, No. 3 (February 1998), pp. 44-61. It should be noted that the method used by Reinke to calculate profits excludes the costs of capital.

from lending. As only the richer clients can be charged for non-financial services, additional funding needs to be ensured so that these services can be made available to all clients. To increase transparency and improve accountability, these funds need to be separated from lending operations.

In addition, as noted above, the financial services for the poorest are different from the financial services for the less poor. The poorest have a relatively high demand for saving facilities and for loans for special occasions and emergencies. Some microfinance institutions have group emergency funds and insurance schemes that extend loans in case of injuries and death or illness of a family member. However, non-governmental organizations are often not allowed to take deposits, and microfinance institutions that establish savings accounts for the public are often subject to regulation and upscaling, thereby becoming less attuned to the needs of the poorest. In this regard, there appears to be an institutional gap that is in danger of increasing.

The role of government and the international community

Governments, donors (including international non-governmental organizations) and multilateral institutions, including several United Nations organizations, have often been crucial in acting as a catalyst for private initiatives in microfinance. They cover set-up costs, finance training of borrowers and provide technical assistance during an initial period. Governments also provide incentives and support to encourage microlending by commercial banks. Even the most successful institutions, such as the Grameen Bank, BancoSol and BRI-UD, have received considerable external assistance from donors or the government, particularly in the early phases. Governments, non-governmental organizations and the international community will continue to play a crucial role, not least in ensuring that the poorest have access to financial services (and training).

Some have argued that *the* most important constraint on expanding microfinance is local capacity to implement programmes. The task for Governments and the international community is to identify and select those institutions that have this capacity and to then make a long-term commitment to them, as it takes as many as 10 years and the surviving of at least one shock (economic, weather-related or political) before an institution proves itself to be financially sustainable.[32]

Another area where Governments and the international community can play an important role encompasses the issue of governance and accountability. As funders, they have the leverage to require adequate data on costs, financial performance and impact. Knowing why a programme does not perform according to expectations or stated objectives is important and provides lessons about the factors that determine success. Currently, there is increasing emphasis put on financial sustainability but little on impact. This is partly related to the costs and difficulties in measuring impact, but the international community could focus more attention on assisting in developing methodologies for cost-effective impact assessment.

Most—if not all—experts agree that microfinance institutions need to be regulated or supervised only when they take voluntary deposits from the general public and these deposits are explicitly or implicitly insured by the gov-

[32] See Richard Rosenberg, "Independent review of UNCDF microfinance activities", UNCDF, May 1998.

33 For an overview of the issues and options, see Shari Berenbach and Craig Churchill, "Regulation and supervision of microfinance institutions: experience from Latin America, Asia and Africa", *Occasional Paper*, No. 1, The MicroFinance Network, 1997; and Hennie van Groening, Joselito Gallardo and Bikki Randhawa, "A framework for regulating microfinance institutions", *Policy Research Working Paper*, No. 2061, World Bank, February 1999.

ernment. Regulation needs to be specifically designed for semi-formal institutions in order that they may retain their flexibility and simple procedures and documentation. Moreover, there are a range of microfinance institutions, with different risk profiles, degrees of deposit taking and linkages to formal institutions. This requires a multi-tier regulatory framework with thresholds on, for example, deposits and commercial borrowing.[33]

CONCLUSION

The types and role of the various financial institutions that serve the poor differ substantially from country to country, with different degrees of public and private involvement. Some countries rely more on non-governmental organizations, others rely more on specialized banks, still others on commercial banks and some have an important infrastructure of public agricultural banks which serve the poor in rural areas. In Indonesia and Thailand, for example, non-governmental organizations are relatively unimportant and public programmes dominate (although the financial crisis in Indonesia seems to have triggered an interest by the Government in non-governmental organizations). In the Philippines and many African countries, on the other hand, non-governmental organizations play a larger role. There is also a difference in emphasis, often related to cultural differences, between group lending and individual lending. For example, group lending dominates in Bangladesh and individual lending in Indonesia. Informal financial institutions such as ROSCAs are relatively important in several African countries, while credit unions dominate in Ecuador. Moreover, the relative importance of different institutions can change over time. In Bangladesh, for example, informal loans accounted for 64 per cent of rural credit in 1985 but only for 21 per cent in 1991/92, while microcredit (from non-governmental organizations, the Grameen Bank and cooperatives) increased its share of rural credit from 9 to 45 per cent over that period.

Microfinance institutions are an important innovation which has already made a substantial contribution in extending credit to population groups that are not served by formal institutions. They are still evolving, however—sharpening their operational goals and procedures and learning how best to target financial services to the poor and women (see box VII.2). Microfinance institutions are increasingly endeavouring to boost their own financial sustainability and to operate under market discipline, thereby becoming more formal.

One of the most important challenges of microfinance is to reduce operating costs while maintaining the focus on the poor, *inter alia*, by keeping the loan size of a first-time borrower small. Pressures to raise the financial sustainability of microfinance institutions might challenge their commitment to serve the poorest. It is important that the poorest receive the financial services they need—most of all savings facilities and emergency loans. Providing these services, as well as training, is a public responsibility, but it is one that can be shared with the private sector. Microfinance institutions can reduce the degree of subsidy needed to achieve their conflicting objectives, but most will need to continue to receive a measure of subsidy if they are to retain their unique character and mission: only a small percentage of them will become financially self-sustaining. This should not be seen as a problem: while assuring efficient use of funds, support for the remainder can constitute an appropriate use of public moneys.

Microfinance institutions are not, however, the "magic bullet" that will solve all the problems of poverty. Credit is an important but not the only constraint on raising the incomes of the poor. Other constraints that keep the productivity of labour, hence incomes, low include a lack of human capital, material assets and access to inputs. The poorest people, in particular, have a low demand for credit because they have relatively low capacity to make profitable use of it and their capacity to service debt is virtually nil. Nevertheless, the poorest still need financial services and an important aspect of development policy should be to ensure that they receive them, not only for their own benefit but also for the benefit that their savings, properly used, can bring to the economy in general.

Box VII.2.

TARGETING FEMALE-HEADED HOUSEHOLDS IN MICROFINANCE

Many financial institutions that focus on providing small loans have a high proportion of loans that go to women, often accounting for more than 80 per cent of a portfolio. Many of these institutions have undertaken the targeting of women as an instrument to both empower women and alleviate poverty; that is to say it has been argued that channelling credit to women is more likely than lending to men to improve nutrition, health and educational attainment (which argument was confirmed recently by a study of microcredit programmes in Bangladesh[a]). Moreover, the push to financial sustainability of microfinance institutions has also led to a push for lending to women because their repayment rates have proved to be higher.

However, targeting women does not lead in itself to the empowerment of women.[b] In three programmes in Bangladesh, for example, men at least partially control 63 per cent of the loans given to women. This percentage declined significantly for women who were widowed, separated or divorced and for activities that were dominated by women such as those involving poultry, sericulture and fish.[c] These facts, combined with evidence that female-headed households are generally poorer and more vulnerable, suggest an argument for targeting female-headed households rather than women.[d] All in all, microcredit can play an important role in the empowerment of women but the success depends crucially on the incorporation of an empowerment strategy within microcredit programmes and also on wider economic, social and political policies.

[a] See Shahidur R. Khandker, *Fighting Poverty with Microcredit: Experience in Bangladesh* (Oxford, Oxford University Press, 1998).

[b] See Linda Mayoux, "Women's empowerment and micro-finance programmes: approaches, evidence and ways forward", mimeo (Milton Keynes, United Kingdom of Great Britain and Northern Ireland, The Open University, January 1998).

[c] See Anne Marie Goetz and Rina Sen Gupta, "Who takes the credit? gender, power, and control over loan use in rural credit programs in Bangladesh", *World Development*, vol. 24, No. 1 (January 1996), pp. 45-63.

[d] See Ashok Rai, Giorgio Topa and Sajeda Amin, "Does microcredit reach the poor and vulnerable? evidence from northern Bangladesh", mimeo, March 1999.

VIII VENTURE CAPITAL IN DEVELOPING AND TRANSITION ECONOMIES?[1]

In the knowledge-based global economy, a country that relied on a development model of "importing" known and well-tested technologies from foreign sources, including from foreign firms, would, in effect, be consigning itself to permanently following the leaders. It would not obtain the substantial benefits that come from introducing a new product and later, when it was on the point of replacing this with a higher-technology product, licensing its production to lower-wage producers. Its workforce might "learn by doing", but it would always be a few steps behind the leaders in the industry: by the time that the imported technology had been learned, it would be out of date. This will be the experience of the developing and transition economies, even the fast-growing ones, unless they, too, develop the capacity to participate in and contribute to the knowledge-based global economy. The question is how and where they develop this capacity. The topics to be discussed in the present chapter are currently pertinent to only some countries and with respect to only certain activities, but a vibrant and expanding venture capital industry can be expected to play a growing role in economic development in the twenty-first century.[1]

Much of the growth in employment in the major industrialized countries has come not from the expansion of well-established companies but from the creation and growth of small and medium-sized enterprises. These small companies, many of which are set up with the aid of venture capital, often have a heavy export focus and can generate much greater revenues from each dollar spent on research and development than can larger companies. Had it not been for the possibility of starting up a small company to exploit a new idea, it is possible that many ideas of potential benefit to humanity would never have been generated. The concentration of many high-technology start-up companies in the medical technology field is a dramatic case in point.

VENTURE CAPITAL AND FINANCING HIGH-RISK VENTURES

The surge of technological advance and innovative ideas gave rise to, and was itself encouraged by, the modern venture capital industry. Venture capital, the financing of entrepreneurs, has existed for a long time. Wealthy private individuals, family members and sometimes even sovereigns of States (as in the case of the Spanish monarchs backing the project of the Genovese sailor Christopher Columbus) have been prepared to put up their own money to back a risky—but potentially very profitable—venture proposed by an entrepreneur.

Often such ventures concerned the exploration and development of remote mineral deposits which, it was thought, scientific advances had made viable. For instance, through the work of the London-based Copper Ventures syndicate, the Zambian copper mining industry had been established in the 1920s, even though one of the premises on which the venture was based—that a new treatment process would render the known oxide copper deposits economic—turned out to be erroneous.[2]

Traditional forms for obtaining finance—bank loans, issuing bonds or stock market flotations—were often unavailable for the high-risk activity of developing new products from the results of research on the frontiers of knowledge. The essentially conservative nature of the banking industry, in which a depositor's money is entrusted to a financial institution which is obligated not to take undue risks with it, precluded its major involvement in such high-risk ventures. However, some banks have invested the funds of their wealthiest clients in ventures. Similarly, only a well-established company could expect to meet the requirements for listing on a stock exchange.

While entrepreneurs still obtain funds in many ad hoc ways, the venture capital industry is a formal source of the financing needed to develop an idea into an enterprise that can be listed on a stock market or merged with or acquired by an existing company with a direct interest in the product. It is a rapidly expanding industry: the total stock of venture capital funds in the only two developing and transition regions for which data are available—Asia and Central and East Europe—rose from $300 million in 1990 to over $7 billion in 1995.[3] Thus, much of the analysis in this chapter, especially concerning the developing and transition economies, will of necessity be anecdotal and descriptive, relying on reports from the financial and business press, rather than the systematic analysis that could come only with the accumulation of experiences and a large and publicly accessible database covering many countries.[4]

It is the purpose of venture capitalists not to earn a steady income from holding stocks or bonds issued by a company that they invest in, but rather to realize a capital gain by selling their interest when the company is floated or when it is acquired by merger or acquisition. The "ideal" is that the capital gain should be several times the investment in the particular venture in order to compensate the venture capitalist for the many ventures that resulted in a complete loss and never reached the flotation stage. One early survey of the earnings of companies in the portfolio of venture capital companies showed that 40 per cent had been either total or partial losses, 30 per cent had been "living dead" (making an inadequate return to justify the effort devoted to them), 20 per cent had made a return of 2 to 5 times the money invested in them, 8 per cent had made a return of 5 to 10 times the investment and 2 per cent had made a return greater than 10 times the investment.[5] However, it is difficult to say that the ideas behind the group of companies that were total losses, about 15 per cent of the total, are complete failures, as they might have been used successfully by other companies.

The modern venture capital industry emerged to finance high-technology companies in the most technologically advanced of the developed countries, the United States of America. However, the industry is also of relevance to any country that wishes to establish a thriving small and medium-sized business sector.[6] This is particularly relevant to the provision of employment opportuni-

[2] One of the ideas behind the Copper Ventures syndicate—the treatment by the Perkins process of the Bwana Mkubwa oxide ores—proved a failure. However, the participants in the syndicate were also interested in exploration in Zambia (they discovered several new deposits) and the re-examination of known deposits. When they re-evaluated by diamond drilling what had been previously written off as a smaller mine—Roan Antelope (now Luanshya)—they discovered much greater quantities of easily treatable sulphide ores. For more information on the role that Copper Ventures and in particular Sir Alfred Chester Beatty played in developing the Zambian copper industry, see Simon Cunningham, *The Copper Industry of Zambia* (New York, Praeger, 1981); and A. J. Wilson, *The Life and Times of Sir Alfred Chester Beatty* (London, Cadogan Publications, Ltd., 1989).

[3] Anthony Aylward, *Trends in Venture Capital Finance in Developing Countries,* IFC Discussion Paper, No. 36 (Washington, D.C., International Finance Corporation (IFC), 1998), p. 4 (this publication is also available on the IFC Web site at www.ifc.org).

[4] "The relatively short history of most venture capital investment in developing countries and the inherent lack of documentation of private financing arrangements means that there is little published analysis at even a basic descriptive level of the scope of venture capital operations in developing countries" (Aylward, op. cit., p. 4).

[5] Edward W. Kane, "Understanding the venture capital market", in *Investing in Venture Capital* (Washington, D.C., The Institute of Chartered Financial Analysts, December 1988), p. 14.

[6] For instance, a report prepared by the Secretariat of the United Nations Conference on Trade and Development (UNCTAD) suggested that "while few developing countries are able to create or support high-technology enterprises that are characteristic of venture capital financing in the United States, they can offer attractive market niches based on specific comparative advantages or the application of new technologies or deregulation, e.g. to agrobusinesses, horticulture, telecommunications etc." (United Nations Conference on Trade and Development, *Experiences of Country Funds and Venture Capital Funds in Developing Countries: Pilot Seminar on the Mobilization of the Private Sector in Order to Encourage Foreign Investment Flows towards the Least Developed Countries (LDCs): "Investment Opportunities in Pre-Emerging Markets"* (UNCTAD/UNIDO), Geneva, 23-25 June 1997 (UNCTAD/GDS/GFSB/1, 16 June 1997), p. 39).

ties, as much of the growth of employment in many countries has come from this sector.

The United States of America model

The modern venture capital industry arose in the United States in the late 1940s with the launching of American Research and Development, which made the initial investment into Digital Equipment Corporation.[7] The company was formed by the President of the Massachusetts Institute of Technology, a Harvard Business School professor and local business leaders to develop products from technologies developed during the Second World War.[8] From the 1960s to the 1970s, the industry was funded largely by insurance companies.

In early 1979, the United States Department of Labor clarified the "prudent man" rule in the Employment Retirement Income Security Act. It ruled that portfolio diversification was a consideration in determining the prudence of an individual investment. Thenceforth, pension funds considered that investing a small amount of their assets in the venture capital industry did not breach the "prudent man" rule, thus opening a large source of funding.[9]

The United States venture capital industry then started its rapid expansion: capital commitments to independent private funds rose from $0.2 billion in 1978 to $3.4 billion in 1983. In 1998, the amount of capital invested by venture capital funds was $16 billion, a 12 per cent increase from 1997. Of this, $5.4 billion went to computer software and service companies, $2.8 billion to communications, $2.2 billion to medical and health-related companies and $1.0 billion to biotechnology companies. The State of California received $6.5 billion and Massachusetts $1.8 billion.[10] Stanford University, the California Institute of Technology, the University of California at San Diego and the University of California at Berkeley were prominent among the academic institutions driving the venture capital industry in California.

Understanding this growth of venture capital as a mode of financing requires seeing it embedded in a process by which new ideas are brought to commercial fruition. The United States met all the requirements for a healthy venture capital industry and the industry has made a substantial contribution to United States innovative activity.[11] The first requirement was the generation of ideas that could be marketable. The universities and research institutes of the United States, backed by considerable government funding for military research during the cold war, generated an abundance of ideas that could be turned to civilian uses. However, the ethos of military research, secrecy, is incompatible with the openness to new ideas and the vigorous exchange of ideas within the research community that a vibrant high-technology civilian economy requires. On the other hand, the decline in military research and development from the peak of the 1980s released a large number of scientists who were able to turn their energies to civilian uses. The venture capital industry emerged to turn their ideas and creativity into products. In particular, two of the centres of military research, which were in California and Massachusetts, became the backbone of the civilian venture capital industry.

At the same time, restrictions on the commercial exploitation of the results of academic research were removed, breaking the "ivory tower" mentality that had imposed a strict separation between commercial and academic life. The fact that university personnel or recipients of government research funds were

[7] Kane, loc. cit., p. 11.

[8] See Paul A. Gompers and Josh Lerner, "What drives venture capital fundraising", *Brookings Papers on Economic Activity, Microeconomics 1998* (Washington, D.C., The Brookings Institution, 1998), p. 151.

[9] Australia, Canada, Ireland, the Netherlands and the United Kingdom of Great Britain and Northern Ireland have similar "prudent man" legislation. For a discussion of venture capital in the European Union, see "Risk capital: a key to job creation in the European Union", communication of the European Commission, April 1998.

[10] Figures from the National Venture Capital Association (as given in its Web site www.nvca.org).

[11] A recent study on the impact of venture capital on innovation in the United States found it did have a substantial impact and that the jump in disbursements since 1995 might trigger an additional wave of innovative activity. See Samuel Kortun and Josh Lerner, "Does venture capital spur innovation?", National Bureau of Economic Research Working Paper Series, No. 6846 (Washington, D.C., December 1998) (also available on the Internet at www.nber.org/papers/w6846).

no longer prevented from obtaining commercial benefit from the results of their research also boosted the development of the venture capital industry. In 1980, the United States Government adopted the Bayh-Dole Act, which explicitly allowed recipients of government grants to retain title to inventions made using government funds. The concentration of research in Massachusetts and California meant that there was already a network of scientists who knew each other and who could, if necessary, cooperate to turn their ideas into commercial products. California law, in particular, regarded "post-employment covenants not to compete" as unenforceable, and it is thought that this further contributed to the mobility of staff.[12]

Another factor assisting the generation of new ideas in the United States was its openness to foreign talent. It was estimated that one in four people with a science degree living in the United States in 1997 was born outside the country.[13] The United States, then, had the "critical mass" of research talent that gave a potential investor the confidence that any technical difficulties experienced in bringing the development of a research idea to the production stage could be resolved, if not by the originator of the idea, then at least by another member of the research community.

The second advantage of the United States was its pool of managerial talent, able to guide an enterprise from the idea stage to the flotation or acquisition or merger stage. Research scientists themselves would probably not have been able to negotiate all the pitfalls involved in turning an idea into a marketable proposition. In many cases, a "business angel" was essential for the commercial realization of a new discovery. These business angels were themselves often scientists, cognizant of the latest scientific advances, and thus able to grasp the significance of the new advances being made.[14]

A third advantage enjoyed by the United States was the presence of investors who not only had the funds available for investment but were prepared to risk their own money, often as members of a partnership, in the hope of realizing substantial gains from such risk-taking. Their willingness to risk their funds also required an assurance that they would be able to enjoy the benefits of their capital gains—that, for instance, tax laws would be sympathetic to sudden and large capital gains. The United States lowered the capital gains tax for long-term investments. Moreover, as noted above, it had facilitated the growth of the venture capital industry by allowing pension funds to invest a small percentage of their assets in venture funds. In addition, a portion of the endowments of universities and foundations could be invested in the venture capital industry.

A final set of financial backers of the venture capital industry were large corporations with an interest in the technology on which the venture capital companies were concentrating. Rather than seek to undertake the work in-house, using their own scientists and facilities, it was frequently more advantageous for large companies to help fund the work of other researchers who were pursuing promising ideas. They would hope to purchase outright the companies that were spun off if they developed a technology that could be incorporated in their products or contribute to their corporate strategy. Again, such corporations would seek to invest in a known business environment where they could expect to be able to enjoy many of the benefits coming from the results of the research and development effort.[15]

12 See "A survey of Silicon Valley", Supplement to *The Economist*, 29 March 1997, p. 12.

13 Ibid., p. 6.

14 A related matter is the corporate culture and favourable environment for business in the United States of America. Individuals can start an enterprise quite easily without having to surmount a wall of obstacles in the form of unnecessary or incomprehensible bureaucratic procedures.

15 These rights could be simply marketing rights or non-exclusive rights to manufacture the product—they need not imply complete control.

The fourth advantage was the presence of large, highly liquid and well-regulated stock exchanges. These exchanges provided the venture capitalists with confidence that they would be able to float their companies once they were thought to be viable. Because of stringent listing and disclosure requirements, those buying shares in the initial public offering (IPO) were assured that they were purchasing stock in what might be considered a risky, but not a fraudulent enterprise.

While the New York Stock Exchange is the most widely known stock market, the National Association of Securities Dealers Automated Quotations System (Nasdaq), which is an electronic exchange concentrating in smaller companies, was the choice of start-up companies. Over 70 per cent of the companies quoted on Nasdaq were financed with venture capital.[16] Nasdaq has also been the favoured exchange for many non-United States firms wishing to raise capital. Over 100 Israeli firms have been floated on Nasdaq. In August 1998, the first IPO by a Singapore company on Nasdaq took place.[17] In March 1999, the first Indian company, a software company, was listed on Nasdaq. The Indian National Association of Software and Service Companies (NASSCOM) expected a further 10 Indian companies to be listed on foreign exchanges in the next two years.[18]

Nasdaq is the largest electronic screen-based market in the world, with the ability to handle trading volume in excess of 1 billion shares a day. Over 5,500 companies are listed on Nasdaq. At the end of 1998, its capitalization was $2.6 trillion.

The National Association of Securities Dealers (NASD) is the self-regulatory organization responsible for Nasdaq, in accordance with the Maloney Act of June 1938 whose stated aim was "to effectuate a system of regulation...in which the members of the industry will themselves exercise as large a measure of authority as their natural genius will permit". This principle of self-regulation served the securities industry well. Market innovation helped promote the listing of small and medium-sized companies, especially in the high-technology industry, while protecting the interests of the individual investor. Technology itself helped Nasdaq expand, as it employed the industry's most sophisticated surveillance systems and regulatory specialists to protect investors and provide a fair and competitive trading environment.

A Nasdaq listing helps a company attract talented people to whom it can offer stock options as part of their own compensation package. These are agreements to sell shares in the firm to the employee at a pre-set price within a pre-set period. If the company is successful, this can be a very attractive supplement to the salary. Stock options have the further benefit of not involving the firm in direct cash payments in its formative years. Furthermore, a large exchange such as Nasdaq where many experts trade has the ability to price a new issue more fairly than a young exchange which would tend to undervalue an issue.[19]

A fifth advantage unique to the United States is the very large size of its domestic market. It is a matter not just of high incomes and large population, but also of the uniform laws and standards confronting the manufacturer of a particular product. In contrast, even in free trade areas and economic unions, such as the European Union (EU), differences between national safe-

16 *Financial Times*, Supplement on Information Technology, 5 May 1999, p. VII.

17 *Financial Times*, Supplement on Singapore, 30 March 1999, p. VI.

18 "Silicon subcontinent", *Financial Times*, 15 March 1999.

19 *World Link*, July/August 1998, p. 77.

ty and quality codes can delay the sale of a product among the different nations in the grouping.

One question arises immediately from this review, namely, Why has the United States been the main venue of the venture capital industry? Should other countries try to copy the United States model (or some other, possibly innovative model) and if they should, what steps might national Governments and the international community take to assist them? To address these questions, examples will be given from the different experiences of a variety of countries that sought to promote venture capital.

Innovation-generation: not necessarily "high tech"

As described above, the venture capital industry arose in the United States to fill an unmet need for capital to finance the transition from an idea to a functioning business enterprise. In this case, the ideas were primarily the products of research. There are other ideas that venture capital could be asked to exploit which are linked not so much to technological innovations, as to creating a new market for particular goods and services. The most recent examples would encompass the numerous enterprises that were established in the transition economies after the start of transition to supply the pent-up demand for goods and services that had been unavailable or illegal under the previous regime. Computer services, fast-food restaurants, discotheques, cellular phones, house repair and renovation, fashion magazines and speedy photographic processing are but a few of the numerous goods or services that could be supplied once central planning ended. Similarly, in developing and even developed countries, there are many needs that could conceivably be exploited profitably.[20]

These examples differ from the high-technology products that emanate from the venture capital industry in the United States in that the risk involved in their exploitation is not so much a technical risk—concerning whether the product the entrepreneur wishes to produce will function so as to make consumers wish to purchase it—as a market risk. Is there a market for the product at the particular price at which it can be supplied?

The steps that have to be taken to obtain the finance to start up these new and risky ventures are similar to those that have to be taken in the case of a new high-technology product. The research into whether the product or service can be supplied at a profit by the entrepreneur still has to be undertaken, and the question whether the potential market is large enough has to be investigated. Management is also needed to bring the idea successfully to the stage where a company can be floated.

Combating brain drain

What has to be exploited in a new venture is usually not something geographically fixed, like an oil well or a mine. Being essentially an idea, it is eminently transportable. There is thus an alternative to exploiting the idea in the country of its generation—it can be taken to the huge market of the United States. Access to the United States is especially easy, as so many in the global scientific community have been educated there and already have the contacts that can help them obtain the required finance and management assistance. Therefore, if a country with a large scientific community wants to discourage

20 For instance, the founder of TelePizza, S.A. (Ltd.), realized that with the modernization of the Spanish economy had come a change in eating habits: "Women were entering the labour force and exhausted working couples could no longer afford Spain's quaint habit of heavy dinners at 10 p.m." He saw a nascent market for fast food and that sizeable profits could be made from satisfying that demand—and saw correctly on both counts. In March 1999, a decade after being started with an initial investment of $100,000, the company was worth $2 billion, having increased 990 per cent since the IPO in November 1996 (*Forbes,* 22 March 1999, p. 96). The company recently unveiled a new venture—Vending Pizza—through which it would sell pizza through vending machines (*Financial Times,* 27-28 March 1999).

brain drain, exploit to the full its domestic scientific skills and thereby expand its domestic exports and employment, it might well strive to develop its own venture capital industry.

For instance, in Taiwan Province of China, the Hsinchu Science Park was set up in 1980 with the explicit aim of encouraging Taiwanese technologists to return from the United States. The entrepreneurs were offered various tax breaks, and promised a considerable degree of independence. By 1997, the park housed a network of small companies employing 50,000 people.[21]

Another reason for a country to seek to develop a vibrant venture capital industry is that there is a "feedback loop": it can help to enhance and modernize the country's research capability. The problems that universities have faced globally in obtaining government finance have made them more receptive to partnerships with private industry to exploit more fully the skills of their staff and their research facilities. The universities obtain funds directly to enable them to upgrade their facilities, thereby producing higher-quality research and attracting and retaining better staff. Moreover, the extra incomes that the staff obtain can persuade them not to move to higher-paying positions in other countries. Preventing this brain drain has been a major factor behind the commercial exploitation of the talents of the staff of even the most prestigious universities in the developed countries. For instance, the founder of Oxford Analytica was a North American graduate of the University of Oxford, who returned to Oxford as a lecturer and saw that providing an extra income to his colleagues for their analyses would help prevent their exodus. He saw himself as providing "brains without the drain".[22]

CONDITIONS FOR THE DEVELOPMENT OF VENTURE CAPITAL

Nurturing ideas that could be marketable

As described above, one of the essentials for a vibrant venture capital sector is the continuous generation of marketable ideas. A venture capital fund operates by choosing a few among a large number of propositions. In order to close five deals a year, a venture capital fund would need something in the order of at least 100 serious new inquiries.[23]

The generation of new technology ideas was greatly assisted in the United States by many decades of heavy government sponsorship of research and development for military purposes—and by the downsizing of the military which released the pool of scientists concerned. Another country having a substantial research base which it was able to release for its own venture capital industry is Israel. With the beginning of the Middle East peace process, it, too, reduced the scale of its military research.

Israel, moreover, also paid considerable attention to civilian research and development. In 1995, these expenditures amounted to 2.2 per cent of gross domestic product (GDP), a slightly higher percentage than that of the United States (2.1) and of the United Kingdom of Great Britain and Northern Ireland (1.9).[24] Israel traditionally devoted considerable expenditures to education and thus had a highly educated population at the beginning of the 1990s. In 1995, it was spending 6.6 per cent of its gross national product (GNP) on education, a proportion higher than the average for the developed countries (5.2 per cent)

21 See "Survey of Silicon Valley", Supplement to *The Economist*, 29 March 1997, p. 15.

22 See David R. Young, "The Oxford Analytica story: Oxford in brief", *The American Oxonian*, vol. LXXXIII, No. 1 (winter 1996).

23 United Nations Conference on Trade and Development, Experiences of Country Funds..., p. 39.

24 State of Israel, Ministry of Industry and Trade, *The Israeli Economy at a Glance 1997* (May 1998), p. 25 (also available on www.tamas.gov.il).

and for the developing countries (3.8 per cent), and had highly sophisticated scientific and engineering institutions such as the Weizmann Institute and the Technion University. It also was well acquainted with the newest technology—in 1995, it had 53.5 Internet users for every 1,000 people, compared with 38 per 1,000 in the United States, and 18 per 1,000 in the industrialized countries as a whole. In addition, in what was a fortuitous positive development, about 700,000 people primarily from the former Union of Soviet Socialist Republics (USSR) and educated in that country according to very high standards came to Israel—a country with a population of about 4.7 million in 1990—in the early 1990s. A large percentage of these Russian-speaking immigrants were particularly suited to high-technology industries.

Stimulated, in particular, by the influx of people with high technological expertise but little knowledge of modern commercial methods, the Israeli Government introduced a special programme of "technological incubators".[25] The programme, which was first implemented in 1991, provides prospective entrepreneurs with physical premises, financial resources, tools, professional guidance and administrative assistance. The criteria for proposed projects were that they be based on an innovative technological idea that aimed to develop a product with export potential. A project would stay in the incubator for approximately two years, at the end of which period the entrepreneur should have carried his or her idea to the stage of explicit product definition and proved technological and marketing feasibility. The State aimed to be reimbursed up to the sum of its grant through royalties on sales. The grant was limited to $160,000 each year, and could be a maximum of 85 per cent of the approved budget.

The project has been highly successful, with 55 per cent of the companies that left the "incubator" stage having become self-sustaining, and the rest having been discontinued. However, even where projects failed, the people involved had little trouble finding new work in their fields. Even though half the members of the project teams at the incubator had to be recent immigrants, the programme was not seen as a job-creation enterprise—it stressed entrepreneurship only. The State's involvement was not open-ended but limited in that the enterprise had to be able to stand on its own feet and attract domestic or foreign capital after the two-year period.

A similar scheme was introduced in France, with the Ministry of National Education, Research and Technology creating 12 biotechnology incubators which could offer accommodation for two years to start-up companies.[26] The French Government also took steps to promote the commercialization of research ideas by proposing legislation to allow government scientists to participate financially in start-ups without giving up their jobs. The legislation would also encourage institutes to establish technology transfer units. Similarly, the Republic of Korea abolished a rule that university researchers could not set up their own companies while remaining on the faculty.[27]

One initiative by the German Government to promote the commercialization of research was the BioRegio competition of 1995, in which the Science Ministry offered government funding to the regions that best promoted biotechnology. Three regions—Munich, Cologne-Dusseldorf and Rhine/Neckar—won, but other regions were encouraged to enter into action.

In addition, there is considerable scope for cooperation in research and development between companies of different countries. The advantages of such

25 For details of Israel's "technological incubator" programme, see State of Israel, Ministry of Industry and Trade, Office of the Chief Scientist, *Technological "Incubators" in Israel* (December 1997) (also available on the Web at http://incubators.org.il).

26 "Initiatives create a new climate", *Financial Times, Life Sciences: Biotechnology*, 15 March 1999, p. V (information on the French Government's programmes is available on the World Wide Web at http://www.education. gouv.fr/creation).

27 *Far Eastern Economic Review*, 4 March 1999, p. 53.

cooperation for both parties are the sharing of costs and reduction of risks. Partnerships can facilitate entry into new markets, access to know-how and technologies that would not be otherwise available to each of the participants, heightened awareness of the market opportunities in the partner countries and the possibility of joint commercialization in a third country where one of the partners has particular advantages.

Cooperation in research and development also can take place at the governmental level. For example, the Binational Industrial Research And Development (BIRD) Foundation was established by the United States and Israeli Governments in 1977 to promote private sector cooperation. It proved commercially successful: its initial endowment was $110 million and as of 1997 it supported 500 projects which generated over $6 billion in direct and indirect sales. Recently, Israel, Jordan and the United States formed the Trilateral Industrial Development (TRIDE) to promote trinational cooperation among their private firms. Each participant is to provide $2 million. TRIDE will support 50 per cent of the development and pre-marketing expenses for a new product and the balance will come from the participating companies. As of 1998, two projects had been approved: one for the development of Arabic scanner software and document archiving products, and the other for Technological Education for Speakers of Arabic (TESA). In December 1996, Israel and Singapore founded the Singapore-Israel Industrial Research and Development Fund. As described below, Singapore is actively supporting its venture capital industry.

Building a pool of entrepreneurial talent

The managerial services that a successful venture capital industry requires are twofold—first, the talent to manage the venture capital fund itself and to invest the funds wisely, taking into account the high risks involved; and second, the managerial talents to bring the idea to fruition as a successful business proposition. The venture capitalists themselves help to choose the management of the venture in which they are investing.

In the United States, there is a pool of financial and entrepreneurial talent, not just prepared to take risks but also able to assess the relative riskiness of different business propositions. The venture capitalists themselves often need a scientific background so as to have some understanding of the ideas being developed by research scientists. This managerial talent is itself able to tap into and obtain the talent necessary to bring a business to the flotation stage.

These talents are the products of a vibrant market economy but are also, to some extent, rooted in business ethos and practices. In some countries, the culture of taking risks is more accepted and failure to succeed in a business is not viewed with any moral disapprobation. Indeed, in the United States, failures in several endeavours are considered part of a learning process for the successful venture capitalist.[28] In a culture that frowns upon risk-taking and discourages mobility, and where failure results in social disgrace, it is difficult for a venture capital industry to flourish. Similarly, the fact that the venture capital industry also requires a firm to share its project ideas and business plans with outsiders and to cede some ownership and control can again result in a clash with local cultural norms.[29]

[28] "A person is not a good venture capitalist until we can count his or her battle scars ... Anyone who has not lost a company and not fired friends is not a venture capitalist" (Stanley Pratt, "Current opportunities and future prospects: part I", in *Investing in Venture Capital* (Washington, D.C., The Institute of Chartered Financial Analysts, December 1998), p. 73).

[29] International Finance Corporation, *Investment Funds in Emerging Markets*, Lessons of Experience Series, No. 2 (Washington, D.C., IFC, 1996), p. 27 (an executive summary of the document is available on the International Finance Corporation's Web site at www.ifc.org).

The tax and legal systems can help foster the venture capital industry and reduce if not overcome some of the traditional cultural impediments to entrepreneurship. The legal system can help by making it easier to start up again after a business failure (as in the United States with the bankruptcy provisions under Title 11 of the United States Code). A legal system in which bankruptcy incurred criminal penalties, as in some European countries in the previous century, would be a severe hindrance to entrepreneurship. The taxation system can also help by granting favourable treatment to capital gains that are realized when a company is floated and to the substantial earnings, including those from exercising stock options, that managers of start-up companies may expect.

Many developing and transition economies lack a pool of entrepreneurs and potential venture capitalists. The UNCTAD secretariat estimated that "the supply of potential venture capital managers in developing countries is virtually non-existent" and that "a good venture capitalist will learn through experience, but this takes time and the poor performance of inexperienced managers will impact on the initial results of a venture capital institution".[30]

[30] United Nations Conference on Trade and Development, *Experiences of Country Funds...*, p. 40.

Developing and transition economies are taking steps to encourage entrepreneurship, especially in high-technology industry, for example, by changes in the tax code. For example, in the March 1999 budget in India, the Employee Stock Option Scheme was put on a par with international norms, as the Government realized that stock options could attract high-quality professionals. The Government proposed to charge a concessional tax rate of 10 per cent on dividends received from stock options linked to Global Depositary Receipts (GDRs)—a mechanism for issuing equity shares internationally (see chap. VI)—of resident Indian companies, as long as the GDR was that of an information technology software and services company. This legislation was expected to further motivate companies to issue GDRs or American Depositary Receipts (ADRs)—a similar vehicle for issuing shares on the United States market—and provide dollar stock options to their employees. Moreover, dividends or long-term capital gains of a venture capital fund or a venture capital company arising from investments in equity shares in a venture capital undertaking would not be included in computing taxable income. Indian companies could also issue "sweat equity" shares—shares issued at a discount or for a consideration other than cash in exchange for providing know-how or making available rights in the nature of intellectual property.[31]

[31] Details from the 31 March 1999 press release of NASSCOM (available at http://www.nasscom.org/press.htm).

In India, NASSCOM acts as a consultative body in assisting central and State Governments in making policies friendly to the information technology industry and, as illustrated above, it has achieved considerable successes in having its recommendations enacted. In Singapore, a private sector committee is advising the government on changes in regulations to help technological entrepreneurs. It pointed out that too many rules inhibited entrepreneurs. The Government recognized that the country would have to accept failure as part of the learning curve towards success and said that it would change the laws, including bankruptcy laws, and regulations, if necessary, to foster the entrepreneurial spirit.

Government financial support for the venture capital industry

By its very nature, venture capital is concerned with high risks which should be incurred only by those who have the expertise to see a venture through to fruition. Thus the provision of funds cannot really be separated from an understanding of the risks involved and therefore an intimate knowledge of the industry involved. It is not an industry that lends itself, then, to government control and direction, but rather to indirect government backing and oversight.

There are examples of government success in investing to bolster the venture capital industry, albeit when the foundations for success were already present. In the case of Israel, for example, there was a pool of talented people who, it was felt, would develop their ideas outside the country, particularly in the United States, if they did not have access to funding domestically. Thus, the Government founded the Yozma Venture Capital Fund in June 1992 which began operations in January 1993 with $100 million in capital.[32] Its aim was to attract international investors to Israel and promote the growth of high-technology export-oriented industries. The Yozma Fund also invested directly in companies, concentrating on early stage start-ups.

Ten Yozma-initiated venture capital funds were created with experienced venture capital partners outside Israel who themselves raised another $150 million. Foreign investors were expected to bring not just capital but also the expertise needed to set up a viable domestic venture capital industry. The foreign participants included some major corporations with a global presence who could help Israel reach international markets. They would also help develop a cadre of Israeli venture capital professionals.

The Yozma Fund was privatized at a considerable profit for the Government after it had achieved its objective of establishing a thriving domestic venture capital industry. In 1993, private technology venture funds raised $49 million, and Yozma funds $149 million, while in 1997 private funds raised $573 million and Yozma funds $5 million.

Other Governments are seeking to invest in local venture capital funds. The Indian Government's State-owned funds are to make $50 million available for venture capital for the software industry. Like Israel, India has considerable scientific talent—the second largest pool of English-speaking scientific professionals in the world, and 1,715 educational institutions and polytechnics which train more than 55,000 computer software professionals on an annual basis, in addition to the graduates of the Indian Institutes of Technology.[33]

Even before a venture capital fund becomes involved in a project, there is need for capital to develop the idea up to the stage where it can attract the interest of a fund. In the example of Israel given above, the "incubator" scheme provided much of the finance and also technical guidance. In the Republic of Korea, a promising development is the emergence of "angel clubs", the first of which was founded in 1997. "Angels" are wealthy individuals who pool their own money to invest in a start-up venture in its infancy. The idea is to help the young company stand financially and to offer informal management guidance. In the Republic of Korea, angels are typically retired or seasoned business executives, with a wide network of contacts.[34]

[32] Details of the Yozma Funds are from Israel Venture Association, *1997 Yearbook* (Tel Aviv, Israel Venture Association in association with the Giza Group, 1997) and *1998 Yearbook* (Tel Aviv, Israel Venture Association in association with the Giza Group, 1998). Yozma translates as "initiative".

[33] Details from *Financial Times Survey India: Information Technology,* 2 December 1998, p. V.

[34] See *Far Eastern Economic Review,* 4 March 1999, p. 53.

Enter the venture capital fund

The venture capital fund will wish to see its investment achieve a high rate of return. This means that it will be able to add value to the original idea or prototype by the provision not only of finance but of all the other necessary components of a successful development package leading to a functioning company—research and technical expertise to turn the prototype into a marketable product, market research and marketing expertise.

Once the stage at which the venture capital fund can be approached has been reached, all parties should realize that financing will be forthcoming only on certain conditions. In exchange for providing the finance and management skills, the venture capital fund will take a large interest in the company. This interest (even before the interest resulting from the financial investment) is likely to be about 20-25 per cent of the company. As the development of the product is the result of what is essentially a partnership between the original entrepreneur and the venture capital fund, the conditions for any successful partnership apply—trust between the partners, close cooperation, openness and transparency. When the partners are from different countries, this trust is facilitated if they both "speak the same language" or at least understand each other's customs—not necessarily linguistic, but legal, scientific and accounting. In this respect, the adoption of uniform accounting standards and similar and clear legal codes concerning bankruptcy, the protection of property rights, and the legal requirements for forming a company and listing it on the stock exchange can only facilitate understanding and therefore cooperation between partners from different countries.

This partnership has to last for several years—in the developed countries, 5 to 8 years in many industries, and over 10 years in biotechnology—until the stage when the venture is ready for its IPO or for sale to or merger with another company. Periods of at least this length are probably required in developing and transition economies. Along the way, there are large, but inherently unavoidable risks—not least that the new product will simply fail, technically or in terms of demand, when taken from the prototype to the market. Also, there could be changes in the tax or regulatory regime affecting the product or service to be provided or the right of the venture capital fund to the patent over the new product could be infringed, either because of inadequate property rights legislation, or because of widespread disregard for existing laws. There are also human risks and uncertainties; for example, there could be a fundamental revision of the assumptions behind the original plan whereby the original owner would want to retain control of the enterprise rather than sell it. All such developments would reduce the capital gains to be derived from the sale of the venture capital fund's interest, and the prospects for such developments would likely deter the investment of venture capital.

Growth of stock markets for venture-based companies

As described above, many non-United States high-technology companies are listed on Nasdaq. The Nasdaq idea is spreading to other countries. For example, in December 1998, the Nasdaq-Amex group ("Amex" is the abbreviation of "American Stock Exchange") and the Stock Exchange of Hong Kong announced a partnership to provide investors with free information on a new joint Internet Web site of companies traded on each exchange. In addition, the European Association of Securities Dealers Automated Quotation (EASDAQ) was modelled on Nasdaq and those companies that choose to list on both markets enjoy nearly identical admission and reporting requirements. It was set up by venture capitalists, investment bankers, securities dealers and investment institutions to provide a highly regulated, liquid market, with trading taking place through its 14 European members. With one regulatory structure, one rule book and a single trading and settlement system, it is able to offer investors, its members and its companies "a single, transparent, European stock market". Its founders and shareholders came not just from Europe but also from the United States and Israel. The first share was traded in November 1996 and in March 1999, 40 companies were trading on EASDAQ, of which 12 were also trading on Nasdaq. It is a sign of the international character of the venture capital industry that 23 companies issued their securities in dollars, 8 of the companies were incorporated in the United States and 1 was incorporated in Israel. The market capitalization at the end of March 1999 was $17.5 billion.[35]

Individual European stock exchanges have also established their own programmes to promote small enterprises. The London Stock Exchange launched the Alternative Investment Market (AIM) in June 1995. It had a simpler entry structure than the main exchange—it placed no restriction on the size of companies that joined, the length of their operating record or the percentage of shares in public hands. However, its shares are not so much in the high-technology industries as in smaller companies and its index has not performed as well as the later European arrivals that are dedicated to high-growth companies.[36]

In Paris, Nouveau Marché started trading in March 1996, the Neuer Markt in Frankfurt in March 1997 and both the Nieuwe Markt (NMAX) in Amsterdam and the Euro.NM in Brussels in April 1997. These four markets joined to form EURO.NM which is not so much a single market like EASDAQ as a network of individual exchanges depending on marketing cooperation, regulatory harmonization and technical cooperation between its members. Milan joined later and three other new market exchanges—Copenhagen, Stockholm and Zurich—are set to join by the end of June 1999. By the end of 1999, its membership could include exchanges in Finland, Ireland, Norway, Portugal and Spain.[37] At present, the Neuer Markt dominates EURO.NM—in September 1998, it had 81 per cent of the total market, the Nouveau Marché had 13 per cent and NMAX and Euro.NM had 5 per cent and 1 per cent, respectively. EURO.NM is larger than EASDAQ or AIM and at the end of December 1998 it listed 165 companies with a capitalization of $36.9 billion.

Developing and transition economies are also taking steps to make it easier to float the companies nurtured by venture capital funds. For instance, in 1992, Taiwan Province of China eased the public listing rules for high-technology companies.[38] Malaysia launched the Mesdaq, modelled on Nasdaq, in April 1999.[39]

As venture capitalists are able to make an adequate return by investing in a company that floats for a few million dollars, one good indicator of a vibrant corporate culture in which the venture capital industry can thrive is not so much the number of firms listed on a stock market, or even their average size (which could indicate simply that the corporate sector was composed of a few behemoths and that entry was restricted) but rather the number of listed enter-

[35] The information on EASDAQ is drawn from its Web page (http://www.easdaq.be).

[36] *Financial Times,* 22 April 1999.

[37] *Financial Times,* 29 April 1999.

[38] *Far Eastern Economic Review,* 19 September 1998, p. 63.

[39] *Financial Times,* 30 April 1999.

prises per head of the population. In the case of the United States, this figure is 33 firms per million people. The average market capitalization of a listed company was $1,227.7 million in 1997. The only developing economies that equalled or exceeded this first figure were, significantly in view of their promotion of venture capital: Israel, with 109 firms per million people (average market capitalization, $70.7 million), Hong Kong Special Administrative Region (SAR), with 101 (average market capitalization, $628.2 million), Singapore, with 88 (average market capitalization, $350.9 million) and Malaysia, with 33 (average market capitalization, $132.2 million).[40] Of the developed countries, only Australia, Denmark, Canada and the United Kingdom had a larger number of listed firms per head of the population than the United States. There is, then, considerable room for a continued expansion in the number of listed firms in all countries, and with the further development of the venture capital industry such expansion can be expected.

Creating market opportunities

The Indian Government set up a National Task Force on Information Technology and Software Development in May 1998 to foster the rapidly expanding information technology industry in India. It set targets of $50 billion for Indian software exports and of $35 billion for the size of the domestic market in 2008, up from $1.5 billion and less than $1 billion, respectively, in 1997/98. The Indian industry itself has taken steps to expand its overseas markets by developing its client base. NASSCOM launched a special programme—NIESA (NASSCOM's India Europe Software Alliance) to identify joint venture and strategic alliances in the computer software sector between India and Europe. It also formed a special interest group on the euro (SIG-EURO) to bring together overseas and Indian clients looking for euro solutions with Indian software houses. NASSCOM organized its first euro seminar in Edinburgh in September 1998.

The "Y2K" problem—rewriting computer programmes to properly interpret the year 2000 in computer data and not read it as the year 1900—is providing Indian software companies with substantial market opportunities. The Government assisted with special tax breaks for Y2K exercises by domestic firms in India—all such expenditure was to be treated as current expenditure and would be accorded 100 per cent depreciation benefit.

The Indian Government is also taking steps to expand the domestic market of one of the most important avenues for venture capital—the Internet. In early 1999, there were only 172,000 Internet subscribers in India and 535,000 users. In January 1999, the Government announced the end of the public sector monopoly in Internet service provision and in March 1999 the telecoms regulator ordered large cuts in fees for leased lines. The private sector development of the telecoms infrastructure could thus provide new business opportunities.

The Indian market is large by the standards of developing countries. For developing and transition economies more generally, the international market may be essential. In this regard, multinational firms can enlarge the market by calling on local firms to supply their inputs. Multinational firms can work with other foreign firms, including venture capital firms, and local entrepreneurs, to set up the required local enterprises. Thus, easing direct investment by

[40] Calculations based on figures in International Finance Corporation, *Emerging Stock Markets Factbook 1998* (Washington, D.C., IFC, 1998).

multinational firms can be part of an open market policy to foster a local venture capital industry.

In general, the expansion of the size of the market, through trade agreements, research and development linkages, cooperation between domestic and foreign firms, liberalization of domestic regulations, and standardization and simplification of health and safety standards, serves to encourage the development of the high-growth firms that are predominantly backed by venture capital.

THE VENTURE CAPITAL INDUSTRY IN THE LIGHT OF THE FINANCIAL CRISIS

The venture capital industry is concerned with the provision of finance without standard collateral. By its nature it is a high-risk and high-return activity which can, however, be a very important part of a modern economy. There are many ways in which Governments can encourage the development of ideas and the taking of risks by creating an environment, and particularly a tax regime, favourable to venture capital. When all the ingredients are in place for a thriving high-technology sector—in particular, a large and vibrant scientific community—direct government financial assistance to the venture capital industry can prove decisive, as in the case of Israel. As more countries put these ingredients in place, the further expansion of the venture capital industry beyond the few countries in which it is currently concentrated can be expected. As the examples in this chapter have shown, this is a very dynamic and rapidly expanding industry—it can be considered one of the most successful exports of the United States—and considerable changes can be expected in the next few years.

The venture capital industry and the related private equity financing industry (which comes in at a later stage than venture capital) involve local and international private investors in doing what the venture capitalist industry has proved very successful at doing—"picking winners", that is to say, setting up companies that have thrived, adding new products and creating job opportunities. It might be added that, although the ability of Governments to "pick winners" had long been doubted, the Asian crisis served to show that some private banks, awash with cheap money, could also prove disastrously inept at choosing companies in which to invest.

The Asian crisis also lowered the share prices of Asian firms and thus tended to make the purchase of a local enterprise more attractive than the investment of risk capital in the establishment of a new enterprise. However, the crisis highlighted the importance of pushing ahead with what the countries in the region had long seen to be necessary—development of their own high-technology enterprises and upgrading of their industrial structures in order to take full advantage of the knowledge-based modern market economy. It thus provided an extra boost to the creation of local venture capital industries and a further incentive to involve foreign venture capital firms with their technical expertise and management and marketing skills.

As a case in point, between 1990 and March 1999, the Singapore Government's Economic Development Board Investments Company set up three venture capital funds, Seed Ventures, Seed Ventures II and Seed Ventures III, to cooperate with foreign venture capital funds in establishing technology-based and innovative start-up companies. The foreign firms were to co-sponsor and manage the funds. One of the companies that was established had a market capitalization in excess of $1 billion in 1996 and was listed on Nasdaq. In April 1999, the Singapore Government announced its intention to launch a $1 billion Technopreneurship Investment Fund to boost entrepreneurship in high-technology industries. The fund was part of a four-step plan involving education, production facilities, regulation and financing. The moneys were to be released within the next three months in order to set up funds that would work with private funds. It was thought that the new fund would have done well if it had committed all its resources within 18 to 24 months.

The same foreign venture capital fund that was involved with Singapore's Seed Ventures, Walden International Investment Group, was appointed in late 1998 as a manager of the official Hong Kong Applied Research Fund, together with two local private funds, Hong Kong and Shanghai Banking Corporation (HSBC) Private Equity Management and AsiaTech Ventures. The three private venture capitalist firms were expected to help develop a culture of technology investment and entrepreneurship in Hong Kong SAR. They could draw on networks in other parts of the world to tap the latest technology market trends.[41]

These networks have had several linkages in China and Taiwan Province of China. For instance, in October 1998, the W.I. Harper Group of San Francisco and Beijing Enterprises Holdings, Ltd., signed a memorandum of understanding to jointly set up the Beijing High Technology Development Fund. The fund would invest in information technologies, biotechnology and other industries. Its aim was to establish strategic links between Beijing and international high-technology companies and to transfer venture capital management expertise to Beijing. The Beijing Enterprises Holdings, Ltd., is the sole overseas listed conglomerate controlled by the Beijing Municipal Government for channelling capital, technologies and management expertise into Beijing development priorities, and was listed on the Hong Kong Stock Exchange in May 1997. W.I. Harper had been founded in 1989 to provide international banking and advisory services to the Walden Group, and in 1995 began offering its services independently. It has offices in San Francisco, Taipei, Hong Kong SAR and Beijing. Similarly, the new fund would be headquartered in Hong Kong SAR, but would have branch offices in Beijing, Taipei and San Francisco. It would not just invest in Beijing but also emphasize a collaboration model which would include Taiwan Province of China, the United States and Europe. In January 1999, the Fund signed a Strategic Alliance with Tsinghua University Enterprises Group, a subsidiary of Tsinghua University, Beijing. Besides attracting foreign interest through its universities, Beijing has developed a high-technology industrial park which has welcomed many companies from Taiwan Province of China and foreign countries.

International assistance to establish the venture capital industry

The rapid growth of the venture capital industry outside the United States suggests that this industry is one that other countries very much wish to see established. International institutions are also seeing the advantages from a development perspective of supporting the formation of venture capital and pri-

41 *Asia Computer Weekly,* 16-22 November 1998.

vate equity industries in developing and transition economies and are accordingly lending assistance.

The International Finance Corporation (IFC), in a 1996 review of its experience with investment funds in developing and transition economies, found that the financial returns on its venture capital funds had been "poor", with the unweighted nominal return on 21 venture capital funds at June 1995 having been a negative 0.6 per cent and the weighted return 1.9 per cent.[42] It found that "management was the most important determinant of fund performance ... Good venture capital managers provide more than equity to firms: they supply advice on marketing, management and industrial contacts ... But venture capital management skills are scarce in developing countries".[43]

IFC, however, continues to support the venture capital industry for three purposes: (a) to meet the needs of the transition economies and China, as over half of the IFC's venture capital fund approvals have targeted transition economies and China since 1990; (b) to meet the equity needs of small and medium-sized firms, since it found that venture capital funds remained the most effective way for IFC to invest equity in small and medium-sized firms; and (c) to build management capacity. Preliminary indications suggest that there has been continuing improvement in the funds' performance "perhaps reflecting better structuring, more experienced managers and firms' owners accepting the concept of third party equity". IFC considered that private equity funds in emerging markets were too new for evaluation of their financial performance, but that the lessons from their investment included the fact that "continued government reforms and privatization are needed to supply a pipeline of investments ... and good managers are critical, to bring both financial and industry contacts and to adapt to changes in underlying markets".[44]

The Asian financial crisis has increased the need for venture and private equity capital to put their managerial and marketing skills and financial support behind the promotion of high-growth and high-technology industries in the region, and to support companies that, before the crisis, had been fundamentally sound, but currently were in difficulty. In May 1999, IFC announced that it was investing $100 million in the Asia Opportunities Fund, Limited, a new private Asian investment fund which would invest in healthy companies with high-quality management teams needing capital to expand or reduce debt as well as in businesses being spun off by conglomerates. The fund's aim is to help fundamentally sound companies in East and South-East Asia thrive and thereby contribute to the economic development of the region. Its partner in the fund, Chase Capital Partners, the private equity investing arm of Chase Manhattan Corporation, is to contribute $250 million.[45]

The European Bank for Reconstruction and Development is supporting the venture capital industry in the transition economies. The funds that it supports make independent decisions about the projects in which they invest, but those decisions are consistent with the Bank's overall investment policy.[46] As an example of its work, in December 1998, it supported the first venture capital fund devoted to investing in Croatia. The rationale for assistance was that "if the arrival of venture capital, albeit on a tiny scale, begins to reap rewards, ... it could pave the way for a reassessment of Croatia among foreign investors".[47]

There is experience as well at the level of bilateral cooperation. For example, as of April 1999, the United States Overseas Private Investment

[42] IFC, *Investment Funds in Emerging Markets...*, p. 27.

[43] Ibid., p. 5.

[44] Ibid.

[45] IFC press release 99/143, 10 May 1999. As part of the deal, IFC plans to establish a $100 million Asian Debt Facility to enable the fund management company to offer a complete financial package to the investee companies. In addition, it will establish a $50 million Asian Co-Investment Equity Facility to leverage its Asia Opportunities Fund investments by taking direct equity stakes for its own account.

[46] See European Bank for Reconstruction and Development, *Alternative Sources of Finance* (London, October 1998), p. 3.

[47] *Financial Times,* 14 December 1998.

Corporation (OPIC) was investing in 25 direct investment funds with geographical restrictions, such as, for example, a fund investing in equity in information technology, telecommunications and consumer goods in India. The reasons given by the private companies undertaking such investments are instructive: the Draper International India fund considered that "with growth coming from deregulation, the increased demand for services and goods has created significant opportunities for companies operating in India". However, there were "few venture capitalists in India with proven and relevant investment experience who can play a supportive role in building a company," and the fund would help to add value through its access to information and resources in both India and Silicon Valley".[48]

Draper International, Warburg Pincus and Intel have recently backed India's leading Internet portal company, Rediff, in its plan to launch a sophisticated new portal site for ethnic Indians in the United States. Roughly 60 per cent of this community of 1.2 million is connected to the World Wide Web, and includes many Silicon Valley entrepreneurs. The company aims to expand later to the 20 million ethnic Indians living in Europe, Africa and Asia.

OPIC supports the funds by guaranteeing 70 per cent of the private financing raised through a zero coupon bond—the other 30 per cent has to be in pure equity form. These two pieces are sold as a unit to private investors, thereby reducing the overall risk and therefore the cost of capital. (The rate of return demanded from pure equity investment in many emerging markets would be prohibitive.)

CONCLUSION

By sponsoring the venture capital industry in developing and transition economies, donor agencies are helping establish a potentially important financial mechanism to help advance the domestic private sector. Local venture capital industries are already helping to create and develop small and medium-sized private enterprises that can be the locus of rapid employment and productivity growth. In addition, the venture capital fund is a very cost-effective and efficient mechanism for disbursing financial resources. Venture capitalists and local entrepreneurs have an interest in quick, although prudent, disbursement. Decisions are made by managers of funds who have the authority—and the financial incentive—to act quickly and decisively.

Finally, but also importantly, the success of the venture capital industry in a developing or transition economy requires the country to promote what are in any case important elements of a development agenda: a well-educated labour force, an environment friendly to investment, a tax code that encourages and rewards risk-taking, high accountancy standards and transparent business practices. These are factors that are often summed up under the rubric of "good economic governance". Moreover, once under way, the venture capital industry can produce a powerful domestic constituency in favour of furthering this agenda—namely, the local entrepreneurs, a group to which Governments are increasingly listening. In this sense, as well as directly, venture capital can be part of an effective partnership for economic development in the twenty-first century.

[48] Information on Venture Capital in India from the Web pages of Draper International, India.

IX CHALLENGES FOR DEVELOPING AND TRANSITION ECONOMIES IN THE GLOBAL FINANCIAL SYSTEM

The participation of developing and transition economies in international financial markets expanded significantly over the past decade. As a result, their domestic financial structures have been increasingly exposed to the dynamics of global finance, which have themselves been rapidly evolving.

The globalization of financial markets during the 1990s has had profound consequences for countries at all points along the development spectrum. Some developing and transition economies experienced a large increase in access to external financial resources and as a result, net financial flows to these two groups of economies as a whole almost tripled from $71 billion in 1990 to over $200 billion in 1996. Net private capital flows over the seven-year period 1990-1996 summed to $1 trillion or about 3 per cent of the gross domestic product (GDP) of these economies at that time, against $165 billion (about 1 per cent of GDP) in the nine years between 1973 and 1982.[1]

Also, the structure of capital flows became more diverse. There was a shift from long-term bank loans mainly to Governments, the major vehicle of international financing in the 1970s and 1980s, to short-term bank loans, bonds and local currency obligations, with the share of private borrowers increasing from less than 25 per cent of total external debt obligations to more than 50 per cent. In addition, equity flows, especially direct investment, rose significantly.

The explosive growth in international capital flows created valuable opportunities for the countries that could access them. Economic theory had argued that free capital movement would encourage a more efficient international allocation of savings, with capital flowing to countries whose abounding investment prospects exceeded domestic saving. Here was a chance to see if this was true. Also, unrestricted capital flows would facilitate cross-border trade in goods and services, both through more trade-related direct investment and greater financing of trade. At the same time, greater capital mobility meant a broadening international diversification of financial asset holdings which would enable investors anywhere in the world to achieve higher risk-adjusted rates of return.[2]

However, as financial crises demonstrated in Mexico in 1995, in East Asia in 1997, and in the Russian Federation and Brazil in 1998-1999, greater integration of emerging market economies into the rapidly moving world of global finance also carries large risks, as it exposes economies to sudden and dramatic reversals in capital flows, that is to say, to extreme

[1] International Monetary Fund (IMF), *International Capital Markets: Developments, Prospects, and Key Policy Issues* (Washington, D.C., September 1998), p. 59.

[2] See Barry Eichengreen and Michael Mussa, "Capital account liberalization and the IMF", *Finance and Development*, December 1998, p. 17.

financial volatility. The damage precipitated by these reversals has been substantial—much larger, in fact, relative to the underlying causes than in the past. While the old-style balance-of-payments crises were driven by unsustainable current-account imbalances, the new crises were driven by swings in components of financial flows and these inflicted major shocks to the domestic financial systems of the affected countries. The present chapter thus looks at different parts of international finance that have been seen as sources of volatility in emerging markets and asks how exposure to such volatility may best be managed.

"HIGH-TECH" INTERNATIONAL FINANCE

One source of the greater volatility in the global financial system has been its rapid evolution in recent years. Dramatic advances in computer and telecommunications technologies have radically reduced costs of financial intermediation and facilitated the introduction of new financial instruments. Also, electronic trading has, compared with older, paper-based systems, increased many-fold the speed of financial transactions. Along with the technological innovations, many of the impediments to the free flow of capital across borders have been dismantled and domestic financial markets deregulated in developed and many developing and transition economies.

Another important change in the pattern of financial intermediation has been the growing role of non-bank institutional investors, along with increasing securitization and growing marketability of assets. Commercial banks have also increased their involvement in the securities business, as part of competitive responses to the evolving financial sector, as noted in chapter IV. Most of these developments began in developed economies, especially the United States of America, but they quickly entered the domain of international finance.

The result of the developments has been the proliferation of turnover-oriented, transaction-driven finance which is displacing the traditional buy-and-hold approach to financial investment.[3] Incentives within financial institutions encourage maximization of short-term gains, possibly at the expense of the firm's overall risk exposure and long-term strategy. Also, because of increasing securitization, longer-term bilateral financial relationships are being increasingly replaced by financing through the markets, making the individual debt relationships anonymous (see chap. V). As a result, investment horizons are shrinking. Together with the technology enabling investors to initiate massive transactions with very speedy execution, as well as rapidly and constantly flowing information, this is leading to huge and sudden shifts in the supply and demand for funds.

Derivatives and emerging market economies

The market for derivative financial instruments provides a case in point of how "high-tech" changes in international finance have affected developing and transition economies.[4] Foreign currency forward and futures contracts have existed for a long time, but there has been an explosion in the volume of transactions in these and other instruments, such as currency and interest-rate swaps (where debtors or creditors exchange payment obligations to better fit their

[3] See Jurgen Stank, Deputy Governor of the Deutsche Bundesbank, "The worldwide currency situation and international monetary cooperation", speech in Kromberg, Germany, 4 December 1998, p. 9 (http://www.bundesbank.de).

[4] The present section draws heavily on William V. Rapp and Mark Scher, "Financial derivatives and emerging market economies", Department of Economic and Social Affairs discussion paper, forthcoming.

immediate needs). These instruments are used because they add liquidity and flexibility to financial markets.

Derivative contracts are now written by many types of financial institutions and on many kinds of financial instruments, domestic and international. Mostly they involve separating out some of the risks embodied in a financial instrument and shifting the risk from one party who does not want to bear it to another who does. New derivatives are constantly being designed and some have become quite complex, mimicking, for example, the effect of purchases and sales of securities without actually undertaking the transactions.

The notional value of international financial derivatives outstanding at the global level reached about $86 trillion as of mid-1998.[5] These products have become an integral part of the global financial system, as well as an important source of profits for several major financial services companies. They are considered a fundamental aspect of trading and risk management worldwide and in many cases the turnover in the derivatives markets is far larger than the actual needs of the markets to which they are related.[6] Most trading activity and the largest users of these products are located in financial centres, such as London, New York and Tokyo. It may well be, however, that the highly leveraged futures instruments that are most often traded for speculation have added an extra measure of financial instability, not only to the international financial system, but also to the flows to the developing and transition economies.

Derivative contracts have increasingly been written on underlying securities or loans of emerging markets, in some cases by financial institutions from those countries. For example, before the East Asian crisis struck, banks from the Republic of Korea participated in triangular credit swaps involving Indonesian companies and international investment banks through which the banks of the Republic of Korea channelled funds to Indonesian borrowers. The Indonesian firms received credit that they might not otherwise have accessed in the standard way and the banks of the Republic of Korea made a significantly higher return than they had been used to, albeit with the obligation to compensate the investment banks if the Indonesian firms defaulted (which they did).[7] With hindsight, the highly speculative nature of such transactions was easier to see.

Direct impact: pro-cyclical volume of derivatives

One lesson of the recent financial crises is that the liquidity added to financial markets by derivatives is "pro-cyclical": it tends to be readily available during booms and much of it disappears during crises. This reduces the utility of derivatives in managing risk since writers of derivatives will cease to provide cover when it is most needed. However, some regulations might improve the situation.

Several market participants have suggested that changes in the availability of derivatives may have aggravated the Asian financial crisis.[8] At the beginning of the crisis, a number of dollar borrowers who attempted to cover their exposure to devaluation risk in South-East Asia found that the available forward foreign exchange cover had been fully used by speculators.[9] There is, however, much in the structure of the international derivatives market that makes this result an expected one.

[5]   About $72 trillion was in derivatives provided "over the counter" and another $14 trillion was in exchange-traded derivatives, in both cases mostly in foreign exchange or interest-rate contracts (see Bank for International Settlements (BIS), *Central Bank Survey of Foreign Exchange and Derivative Market Activity, 1998* (Basel, May 1999), table A.3).

[6]   See William V. Rapp, "Foreign firms in Japan's securities industry in the 1980s and post-bubble economy", in *Post Bubble Japanese Business*, Raj Aggarwal, ed. (Dordrecht, Netherlands, Kluwer Academic Publishers, forthcoming), chap. 7.

[7]   Moreover, the banks of the Republic of Korea did not show any loans to high-risk Indonesian firms on their books, as their transactions were with international banks (for details, see Salih Neftci, "FX short positions, balance sheets and financial turbulence: an interpretation of the Asian financial crisis", Working Paper Series III, No. 11 (New York, Center for Economic Policy Analysis, New School for Social Research, October 1998).

[8]   There is also a view that derivatives markets have not added to the difficulties in the Asian crisis and that they do not add to financial volatility; see, for example, Christian Jochum and Laura Kodres, "Does the introduction of futures on emerging market currencies destabilize the underlying currencies?", *IMF Staff Papers*, vol. 45, No. 3 (September 1998), pp. 486-520.

[9]   This is not to say that speculators sought to bring down the Thai baht, the first currency to fall, but rather that some financial institutions and a few non-financial institutions saw the deteriorating situation and "merely put on positions that would become profitable should the baht decline" (Christopher Rude, "The 1997-1998 East Asian financial crisis: a New York market-informed view", in *Global Financial Turmoil and Reform: A United Nations Perspective*, Barry Herman, ed. (Tokyo, United Nations University Press, 1999), p. 374n.

This is because of the global structure of the industry. A small number of global financial institutions dominate the derivatives markets worldwide, owing to economies of scale and scope, as well as learning. They have brought their expertise and dominance in the advanced financial markets to smaller markets. They have not done this uniformly across the many markets that have mushroomed in Asia, Latin America and elsewhere over the last few years, but have selected particular markets in which to concentrate. As the smaller markets are similarly subject to economies of scale, information and learning, certain banks became specialists in these markets. In good times, these banks accumulate positions from derivatives transactions in the local market which they then sell to the international market. This removes their exposure and allows them to take on new positions. In times of crisis, however, the intermediaries will find it difficult to sell off their exposure; therefore, the local market's capacity becomes limited by the exposure limits of the local specialist banks and these limits could themselves be reduced in the light of an emerging crisis. Thus, the volume of activity in the local derivatives market expands and contracts according to how the local market is perceived internationally.

Indeed, emerging market derivative volume expanded dramatically during the boom period. The consequences of this activity for local interest rates and currency values are difficult to evaluate; but as seen in the dramatic movement of the dollar exchange rate of the Japanese yen in October 1998, the effect can be substantial.

The main mechanism by which the derivatives market affects the cash market arises from hedging or arbitrage strategies of the local banks, whereby the bank selling a derivative simultaneously buys the underlying asset. For example, when a bank sells a forward dollar contract to an importer wanting to lock in the local currency cost of his coming payment obligations, the bank then buys dollars in the spot market, which it invests until the due date. Immediately, however, this puts downward pressure on the spot exchange rate.[10] By the same token, derivative contracts on interest rates or stock-market indices can affect the prices of these underlying assets.

Derivatives can have other effects, such as shortening the maturity of government foreign borrowing. This is because the longest maturity in forward foreign exchange contracts or foreign exchange futures in most emerging markets is one year. If forward cover is readily available to market participants, there will be an incentive for many international investors to buy the short-term domestic currency treasury bills, and to cover the exchange-rate risk with a forward contract. The short-term debt market will thus become more liquid and the pricing more favourable than for longer-term bonds. Governments will then have an incentive to issue more shorter-term securities, skewing their debt profile.

A Government might even become overconfident and take on excessive short-term debt because it mistakenly believed that because the debt was denominated in domestic currency, it was relatively safe from a foreign currency run. It simply had to be rolled over every 30 or 60 or 90 days. However, to the extent that the foreign purchases of domestic currency debt were matched by forward currency contracts, a substantial net demand for foreign currency could open up. Indeed, this kind of situation seems to have played a role in Mexico and Thailand, given their quick loss of reserves once the crisis began, as well as in the Russian default, given the large losses associated with the ruble cover provided by Russian banks.

[10] If importers with obligations due in 30, 60 and 90 days all decide to hedge at once, this can create very heavy pressure on the spot market and break an exchange-rate peg.

This discussion suggests that Governments in developing and transition economies would need to be aware of how derivatives are being used and their impact on underlying financial markets. Derivatives can offer definite benefits to these economies, including hedging the returns on commodity production or financial exposures to certain projects. However, if introduced too early in the development process, they may also expose these countries' financial institutions to excessive risk. Also, they may not be the best way to promote local financial markets as places to raise capital for local businesses and economic development, since large amounts of funds might be drawn into speculative investments seeking high returns from stock or bond movements. Moreover, the cost of such financial crises as may arise from derivatives trading are easier to absorb in the developed economies than in the emerging markets.

Admittedly, calling for a policy on the introduction of derivatives is easier than specifying what that policy should be. Is there a proper sequencing? Should one begin by first developing a foreign exchange market and the use of forwards via the banking system and then introduce futures for foreign exchange, bonds and finally stocks? Furthermore, should derivatives for bonds and stocks be postponed until the cash market has reached a certain size and liquidity? The data do not exist to answer these questions; but given recent market failures, such policy question seems to be an important area for research before returning to "business as usual" in terms of freely using derivatives for any kind of transaction in the emerging markets.[11]

Indirect impact: misperceiving the source of risk

After the Russian default and currency collapse in August 1998, a sequence of events followed that by October 1998 threatened the financial system of the United States and perhaps the industrialized world. It prompted extraordinary measures to prevent the collapse of Long-term Capital Management, a prominent "hedge fund", and caused an unprecedented 10 per cent swing in the yen/dollar exchange rate on 8 October. It underlined how far the interlocking leverage in the global financial system had moved and how dangerous it had become. This degree of systemic risk and contagion caught the attention of policy makers and market participants and set in motion both the easing of monetary conditions in the United States and Europe and the commitment to speed reform of the international financial architecture. It also had a misplaced fallout for the emerging markets.

Many market participants saw the source of the instability as being in the emerging economies, rather than in a global system of markets and regulations that permitted—even encouraged—excessive leverage and speculation. Therefore, not only did creditors "unwind their positions" (reduce their risk exposure) in the developed countries, but they also pulled back on loans and financing in emerging markets. This increased the potential for liquidity problems in already fragile economies and caused new swings in foreign exchange and asset values in these countries, which in turn made their financial instruments appear even riskier. Higher risk led to the demand for higher expected returns, reducing the perceived investment values and trade opportunities, and so on in a downward spiral.

Reinforcing the tendency of developed-country financial institutions to focus their attention on difficulties in the emerging economies was the fall in

[11] One idea, for example, might be for regulators in emerging economies to impose a "real transaction rule" or "real business reason" in order to restrict use of domestic derivatives markets to those hedging a real business risk, arising, for example, from possible changes in interest rates, currency values or commodity prices. The speculators on the other side of the market would only be international players who (under improved international rules) should be better monitored and capitalized; local speculators would be limited to transactions in cash markets (see Rapp and Scher, loc. cit.).

stock prices of several major financial institutions that were considered to have had excessive exposure to emerging markets, such as Bank of Boston, Citicorp and Lehman Brothers. The Chairman of Lehman Brothers even had to make a public statement confirming the firm's strength and solvency. Goldman Sachs had to postpone its long-awaited public offering of shares.

Most executives in United States corporations are compensated on the basis mainly of their company's stock performance and thus these bankers have had few incentives to return to previous levels of exposure to the emerging markets. Not only was there an immediate withdrawal of funds, but the supply of funds remained restricted for some time for all emerging markets, as bank stock valuations discouraged lenders from returning well after the worst of the crisis had passed. As one indication, the interest-rate spreads on some emerging market debt that had jumped from 300 to 1,600 basis points (from 3 to 16 percentage points) at the height of the crisis, were still over 1,000 basis points in early March 1999.[12]

The large players in global derivatives are also the large international commercial and investment banks that finance major projects in emerging markets. They also supply much of the trade finance. Thus, crises that lead to capital losses for these banks, for example, in the derivatives side of their business, reduce their ability and willingness to increase their exposure for other types of activity, in particular project finance and other longer-term lending that is central for development. In short, in a highly uncertain and fearful environment, the smallest borrowers with the weakest reputations, whether or not justified, are going to be the ones that suffer disproportionately.

Part of the problem is that, until recently and despite little regulation, there have been relatively few major failures involving international derivatives trade, even though the number of market participants is large, the market size huge, and the transaction volume immense. Such failures as have occurred could have been, and were, considered one-time situations and not indicative of any systemic problems.[13] However, while most policy makers have been generally sanguine about the rapid development and immense scope of leveraged transactions, those losses raise some important questions. They stem from the fact that there is substantial leverage implicit in all financial derivatives and more risk than is realized.

This can be stated in terms of probabilities: derivatives are typically constructed and priced on the basis of a 95 per cent confidence interval for a probability distribution on future outcomes drawn up from historical data (whose continued relevance is assumed). The question is which transactions will fall outside this range, and when, and how large they will be. The question becomes many times more complicated when attention shifts from the individual derivative to the net exposure of the financial firm that engages in very many of these transactions on a daily basis. Indeed, very elaborate computer models have been developed to keep track of the evolving exposure of a financial firm as it shifts in and out of a wide variety of derivatives during the trading day.

The key question, in other words, is whether the possibility of rare but disastrous events is given adequate attention. The answer based on the recent experiences seems to be no. Events with 5 per cent probability of occurrence have been considered anomalies and so their potential consequences were not calculated or included in the risk-management computer models. The task

[12] See Lehman Brothers, "Global EMG Model Portfolio for March 1999", *Global Sovereign Markets Weekly*, New York, 5 March 1999.

[13] Examples of derivative-related failures that regulators have considered isolated events are the bankruptcy of Barings and the financial crisis of Orange County, California, as well as the very large derivative-related losses at County NatWest, Sumitomo Shoji, Procter and Gamble, Daiwa Bank, J.P. Morgan, Metallgesellschaft and Bankers Trust. The hedge fund related losses at Bank of America and Long-term Capital Management are in this category too.

ahead—a major preoccupation in both private and official bodies concerned with the issue—is to establish a stronger set of best practices for managing risk in financial firms and disclosing relevant information to regulators and the market (see below).

Open securities markets in emerging market countries

While the global system has been seen as a highly efficient structure, it also appears to have facilitated the transmission of financial disturbances far more effectively than ever before. The vastly accelerated pace of financial activity, its complexity, and its volume, as well as much shorter investment horizons have contributed to cycles of huge capital flow to a national market, creating a "bubble" in financial asset prices, followed by the sharp declines in asset prices and reversal of flows.

The phenomenon of "herd behaviour"

The massive withdrawal of foreign money from East Asia in 1997-1998 has been a painful reminder that financial systems are subject to periods when market judgements become heavily one-sided, that is to say, subject to "herd behaviour".[14] Simultaneous moves in several security—and hence currency—markets could hardly be explained by a synchronous shift in economic fundamentals. Rather, it is a general phenomenon that cross-country correlations of price movements in financial markets increase significantly during crisis periods.[15]

Herd behaviour is not new by any means. However, it seems that over the past decade the motives behind the collective rush in or out of a country in response to a change in sentiment have become stronger and the results of this rush more widespread and damaging. There appears to have been an increasing convergence in the behaviour of different categories of market participants, including banks. Many seemingly diverse institutions have similar risk exposures and, consequently, may become vulnerable to the same adverse event.

There is also a widespread practice of "following the leader", which is the firm or trader that is perceived to be the most successful or experienced. Not to be "left behind", investors make enormous efforts to predict the effect of new information on their peers, rather than work out what this information can tell about the underlying assets themselves.

Emerging and transition markets are more susceptible to herd mentality of investors and volatility than developed countries, as they are still marginal for international investors. One aspect of this is that they are often treated as one asset class. Consequently, during periods of financial stress, funds are often pulled out of a group of similar markets simultaneously when investors spot signs of trouble in one of them. When the withdrawal begins, it becomes rational, even for those investors who have not changed their opinions about a particular market, to follow the herd. During such periods, "momentum-based" investors find themselves in a much more favourable position than their "fundamentals-based" peers. In such circumstances, financial investors who count on herd behaviour make better profits than others who do not. Even so, this is not to say that foreign investors necessarily "cause" the volatility in the securities markets of a country (see box IX.1).

[14]   See Richard Cooper, "Should capital account convertibility be a world objective?", in Stanley Fischer and others, *Should the IMF Pursue Capital-Account Convertibility?*, Essays in International Finance, No. 207 (Princeton, New Jersey, Princeton University, May 1998), pp. 15-16.

[15]   See, for instance, Taimur Baig and Ilan Goldfajn, "Financial Market Contagion in the Asian Crisis", *IMF Working Paper*, No. 155 (Washington, D.C., November 1998).

Box IX.1

ARE EMERGING ECONOMY STOCK PRICES TOO VOLATILE?

It is in the nature of equity shares traded in stock markets that their prices change continuously and over time by possibly large amounts. Are the fluctuations in some sense too large, especially in emerging markets? The answer seems to be that panics in stock markets, large or small, are "irrational" and that short-term circuit-breakers to temporarily halt trading are a helpful pause. With this exception, however, the prices of stocks should be allowed to find their own level in a competitive market. Governments should seek to prevent private manipulation of stock markets and not themselves try to manipulate stock prices.

Dealing with panic selling

"Circuit-breakers"—such as a decision-rule to suspend trading in a security for hours or the rest of a trading day or to temporarily close the stock exchange in the midst of a price collapse—serve to prevent an inherent instability in stock markets from moving price downswings well beyond the values at which they would settle. Various factors might accelerate price declines into a panic. First, for example, if the price of a stock starts to fall and further decline is expected, holders of the share may rush to sell. The absence of hard information about the company and a surge of sell orders can start a herdlike stampede, dropping the price significantly. A second factor is the consequence of market participants' being able to buy stock "on margin" through their stock broker, that is to say, partly with funds borrowed from the broker, with the shares of stock (and cash) on deposit with the broker being pledged as collateral for the loan. If the stock price drops sharply, the value of the collateral may fall enough to force the shareholder to put up additional collateral or sell the shares and repay the loan, making for further downward pressure on the market price. Third, in fast-moving stock markets, sell orders can be triggered by pre-set instructions to brokers or computer programs. Most significantly, in the midst of a panic, with the market moving very fast, participants cannot keep track of the range of buy-and-sell offers, as needed for appropriate pricing; in such a situation, it is said that prices become "uninformative". A circuit-breaker to halt trading at this point and let information on the state of the market accumulate can be a market-enhancing measure.[a] While this is so in developed markets, it is even more the case in the thinner emerging markets. An enforced pause can also calm the psychological side of the panic.

Not dealing with falling stock prices

It is a different matter when share prices fall over a sequence of days, months or years and it is the clear intention of the market to reprice the securities. This happens regularly in all markets after securities prices have risen well out of proportion to profit expectations of the firms. The total capitalization of the Japanese market in 1998 was one third of what it had been in 1989. The New York Stock Exchange is now thought by many to be in a bubble phase of its expansion, although as is always the case in such situations, many people expect that the unusually high ratio of stock prices to corporate earnings will last indefinitely.

Stock markets in emerging economies have been subject to especially large and rapid swings upward and downward. In Mexico, for example, the stock-market index declined by about 50 per cent from its peak at the beginning of 1994 to its low in early 1995. More recently, the market index in Indonesia declined by 45 per cent in the few months between May and September of 1997.

[a] See Bruce Greenwald and Jeremy Stein, "The Task Force report: the reasoning behind the recommendations", *Journal of Economic Perspectives*, vol. 2, No. 3 (summer 1988), pp. 3-23, referring to the Task Force on Market Mechanisms of the United States President, formed after the global stock-market crash of October 1987.

Box IX.1 (continued)

The problem in this volatility is that the downswings often cause major economic disruptions. Thus, in certain economies, including Japan, the government directed official resources into the market to try to bolster demand and prevent stock prices from falling further. The major weakness that the collapse in share prices exposes is usually in the banking system. In a stock-market crash, financial institutions find themselves holding claims or collateral whose value is fast evaporating. This only underlines the importance of strong financial sector regulation, as well as sound macroeconomic policies.

Do foreigners raise volatility?

In the recent emerging markets collapse, sellers of stock were also taking their funds out of the country, putting downward pressure on pegged exchange rates. Thus, bolstering confidence in the stock market was aimed in part to bolster confidence in the currency.[b] One question is thus, Did foreign purchases of shares in the recently liberalized markets first drive up share prices to unsustainable levels and then cause the crash by exiting? Some researchers have pointed to the larger amplitude of boom-bust cycles in the 1990s in Asia which coincided with large capital flows. Large inflows relative to the level of liquidity in these markets would have a disproportionate impact on prices and result in "exuberant" valuations; a reversal in sentiment would, equally, cause large price declines.

Given the perception of higher risk in emerging markets and serious problems of information, investors could be more skittish than in established markets;[c] that is to say, investors, in seeking to diversify their portfolios, should undertake considerable research into many companies in each market before they purchase and sell the shares of a selection of them. This would be costly. Instead, sets of equities in the various emerging markets tend to be treated as an asset class to be bought and sold together, with funds reallocated among markets in quick entries and exits.[d]

In addition, international portfolio managers have incentives to act similarly, moving into and out of individual markets in a wave, as each investor tends to follow the actions of others. They tend to copy their competitors in order to achieve results that are at least not too far below the average. The aim, in other words, is to maintain a favourable performance record relative to competitors, as this is how portfolio managers are compensated.

This notwithstanding, several studies could find no statistical evidence that large inflows since the beginning of the 1990s had increased short-term volatility as compared with the 1980s.[e] Economic reform and financial liberalization had apparently led to "exuberance" on the part of domestic investors as well as foreigners.[f]

On the other hand, many of the local investors in emerging Asia were buying shares on their home market in part using funds borrowed from foreign banks, making the international link important. Indeed, the proposal made in several quarters to discourage excessive short-term capital movements across the borders of developing and transition economies seems quite germane in the context of stock-market volatility.

b   See I. Grabel, "Financial markets, the state and economic development: controversies within theory and policy", *International Papers in Political Economy*, vol. 3, No. 1 (1996); and Asian Development Bank and World Bank, "Managing global finance integration in Asia: emerging lessons and prospective challenges—overview", Asian Development Bank and World Bank Senior Policy Seminar, Manila, 10-12 March 1998.

c   See Martin Mayer, "The Asian disease: plausible diagnoses, possible remedies", Jerome Levy Economics Institute, Bard College, Working Paper, No. 232 (April 1998); G. Kaminsky and S. Schmukler, "On booms and crashes: is Asia different?", mimeograph, February 1998; M. Pomerleano, "The East Asia Crisis and Corporate Finances: The Untold Micro Story", *World Bank Policy Research Working Paper 1990* (October 1998); and I. Grabel, loc. cit.

d   See K. Sharma, "Understanding the dynamics behind excess capital inflows and excess capital outflows in East Asia", in *Global Financial Turmoil and Reform: A United Nations Perspective*, B. Herman, ed. (Tokyo, United Nations University Press, 1999), pp. 405-430.

e   See A. Richards, "Volatility and Predictability in National Stock Markets: How Do Emerging and Mature Markets Differ?", IMF Staff Papers, No. 43 (Washington, D.C., September 1996), pp. 456-501; S. Claessens, "The emergence of equity investment in developing countries: overview", *The World Bank Economic Review*, vol. 9, No. 1 (January 1995), pp. 1-17; and C. R. Harvey and A. H. Roper, "The Asian bet", paper presented at the World Bank Group-Brookings Institution Conference, "Preventing crises in emerging markets", 26 and 27 March 1999, Palisades, New York.

f   See P. Blair, "Stock market liberalization, economic reform and emerging market equity prices", Massachusetts Institute of Technology, Cambridge, Massachusetts, mimeograph, September 1997.

During periods of herdlike behaviour, investors begin viewing most pessimistically the situation in any country that bears the slightest resemblance to the situation of the first victim of the crisis. For instance, a historical high correlation between returns on money market instruments in national currencies in Thailand and the Czech Republic which had nothing to do with economic fundamentals encouraged investors to sell koruny on signs of strains in the baht.[16]

Finally, herd behaviour has been accentuated by the use of state-of-the-art risk management systems in the chief international financial institutions.[17] A jump in market volatility in one country will automatically generate an upward revision of risk associated with correlated countries, triggering sell orders, margin calls and reluctance to extend credit lines.

Portfolio adjustment effects

One phenomenon that aggravates contagion is portfolio adjustment by international fund managers. In response to a market crisis in a particular country or region, international funds tend to liquidate positions in better-performing markets in order to realize capital gains to make up for their losses elsewhere and to raise liquidity. A sudden drop in liquidity owing to the falling prices in one market or for one kind of asset may thus induce a sale of other assets, even with no change in fundamentals in the other market.

Given that the markets of most developing and transition economies are thin relative to the portfolios of international fund managers, the impact of such induced sales can be devastating. This can be seen in the fact that only 1 per cent of total equity holdings by the institutional investors of the seven major industrialized countries is equivalent to 27 per cent of the market capitalization in Asia and 66 per cent in Latin America.[18]

Such global investors, moreover, come not only from industrialized countries, but also from emerging economies themselves. For instance, in December 1997, investors from the Republic of Korea were forced to liquidate their holdings of Brazilian and Argentine dollar-denominated bonds in order to cover their dollar obligations and restore falling liquidity. The subsequent fall of prices on Latin American bonds then forced Brazilian banks, which had purchased these bonds on borrowed funds, to sell local currency-denominated assets for dollars, thereby increasing pressure on the exchange rate of the real.[19] Banks in Brazil and the Republic of Korea were also forced to liquidate their holdings of Russian treasury bills. Those holdings were about $6 billion out of approximately $20 billion held by non-residents at the end of 1997.

Banks and currency markets

The currency turmoil in one country after another has raised questions about how currency markets operate. Except where there is central bank exchange control, foreign exchange in developing and transition economies is largely traded in an interbank market that is highly opaque.[20] This makes attempts by monetary authorities to monitor market activity and take the appropriate policy response quite difficult. The same opaqueness, however, helps monetary authorities mask their intentions when they engage in open-market interventions to alter market perceptions and prices.

The foreign exchange markets of most emerging economies are relatively thin. Hence, when confidence is lost in a pegged exchange rate, "one-way" bets

[16] Bank for International Settlements (BIS), *68th Annual Report* (Basel, 8 June 1998), pp. 108-109.

[17] Peter Garber, "Buttressing capital-account liberalization with prudential regulation and foreign entry", in Fischer and others, op. cit., pp. 32-33.

[18] BIS, *68th Annual Report...*, p. 90.

[19] See Christopher Walker, "Contagion: How the Asian crisis spread", *ADB Review* (Asian Development Bank), vol. 30, No. 4 (1998), p. 12.

[20] Unlike trading on an organized exchange, where the volume and price of each trade are posted, it is often not easy for participants to determine the strength of demand and supply in the market.

on devaluation can rapidly soak up the liquidity in the market. Relatively small transactions are then able to push markets into a tailspin.

Also, potential participants in such currency markets have combined resources that are much larger than the foreign exchange reserves of the monetary authorities. Consequently, the currency market presents profit opportunities to market participants that have the ability to move markets in their favour, owing to the size of their purchases or sales.[21]

Currency speculation may be especially devastating for countries that have fixed or tightly managed exchange-rate regimes, as has been the case in many emerging and transition economies.[22] In this case, a depreciation from a fixed exchange rate may go far past the level where a currency would have been if it had not been fixed initially.

Perils of short-term foreign debt

Exceptionally high leverage (the ratio of debt to equity) in open financial markets is a sign of excessive risk-taking which leaves financial systems and economies vulnerable to loss of confidence. In this regard, it has been argued that the overall degree of leverage in the system that was viable even a decade ago may not be appropriate in today's more volatile financial environment.[23]

Moreover, it matters whether the bulk of the debt is long-term or short-term. Financial mishaps can result from almost any financial transaction. However, in virtually all recent cases, the major trigger that turned seemingly minor imbalances into a crisis was short-term debt, particularly cross-border debt.

These concerns are particularly relevant to banks. As discussed in chapter IV, their assets (loans) are typically less liquid than their liabilities (deposits) and therefore they always need to carefully manage their liquidity so as not to be caught out by maturity mismatches. If banks have lax lending or borrowing practices, they can develop severe liquidity problems and become a source of systemic risk. Short-term interbank lending, especially across borders, may turn out to be the weakest link in the global financial system.

In most cases, financial crises follow sustained periods of large increases in cross-border bank borrowing, with a high and growing proportion of these loans being short-term. By the time the Asian crisis began, short-term foreign bank debt in East Asia was measured as close to 65 per cent of the total.[24] The boom in short-term exposure continued in full swing until the very onset of each national crisis. For instance, growing financial strains did not deter foreign banks from raising their exposure to the Russian Federation until the outbreak of crisis in the third quarter of 1998.[25]

Conversely, commercial banks also account for the bulk of funds withdrawn during a crisis. For instance, more than 86 per cent of the capital that left Thailand in 1997 represented the withdrawal of credit by international commercial banks.[26]

Short-term capital inflows can accumulate over time into a large stock of foreign liabilities. Ultimately, they may exceed the liquid international assets of the country. The ratio of short-term debt to official reserves reached over 950 per cent in Mexico in 1995. At the end of 1997, it stood at 315 per cent in the Republic of Korea, 177 per cent in Indonesia, 115 per cent in Thailand and almost 310 per cent in the Russian Federation.[27] Conversely, the fact that the reserves of the Eastern European countries as a group were on average three

[21] For a discussion of different views on the nature of currency market activity, see, for instance, the International Organization of Securities Commissions (IOSCO), "Causes, effects and regulatory implications of financial and economic turbulence in emerging markets", interim report, September 1998, pp. 31-33.

[22] See IMF, "Mechanics of speculative attacks", in International Capital Markets: Developments, Prospects, and Key Policy Issues (Washington, D.C., November 1997), pp. 37-38.

[23] Alan Greenspan, "The structure of the international financial system", remarks at the Annual Meeting of the Securities Industry Association, 5 November 1998, p. 5 (http://www.frb.fed.us).

[24] The share of short-term debt was actually higher than the data indicated because of the practice, whose spread was reflected in Asian and Latin American bonds and bank loans, of including a "put option" which gave the lender the right to demand early repayment (the "put" in this case is an option to sell the security back to the issuer, usually at par). See IMF, Policy Development and Review Department, Involving the Private Sector in Forestalling and Resolving Financial Crises, advance copy (Washington, D.C., 15 April 1999), chap. I, "Foreground", pp. 26-32 (http://www.imf.org).

[25] BIS, International Banking and Financial Market Developments: BIS Quarterly Review, November 1998, p. 10.

[26] IOSCO, "Causes, effects and regulatory implications of financial and economic turbulence in emerging markets"..., p. 44.

[27] Institute of International Finance (IIF), Report of the Working Group on Financial Crisis in Emerging Markets (Washington, D.C., January 1999), p. 25.

times greater than short-term debt helped these countries withstand the 1997-1998 global financial turmoil.

It has been argued that if initial liquid foreign liabilities are large relative to short-term assets, then an exogenous shock or a sudden loss of confidence may prompt holders of the liabilities to attempt to liquidate them.[28] Levels of short-term debt in excess of liquid assets do not necessarily lead to crisis, but they make a country vulnerable to financial turmoil. The transformation of this vulnerability into crisis requires a sudden reversal of perceptions that induces short-term creditors to expect the flight of other short-term creditors. Once crisis starts, even countries that seem only slightly exposed may be overwhelmed by capital outflows.[29] It has also been stressed that sudden changes in perceptions are very hard to predict and they tend to be much greater than the magnitude of the change in underlying fundamentals warrants.[30]

The problem of moral hazard

The recent experience in Asia and the Russian Federation suggests that lenders and borrowers systematically underestimated the riskiness of their actions. In particular, the risk premiums for loans to the emerging market economies between mid-1995 and mid-1997 were at levels well below what could be justified by economic fundamentals.[31] Lenders and borrowers either misjudged the reality or assumed adverse developments would not hurt them very much. The international banks might have assumed that their lending was at least partly protected by international rescue programmes, and domestic lender-of-last-resort facilities. This relaxed their concern about excessive debt accumulation and the quality of credit and risk analysis.

The presumption of the official support would most likely have affected the short-term lenders. In this regard, it has been argued that the massive foreign official assistance, which allowed holders of short-term dollar-linked Mexican government paper to escape without any loss in 1994-1995, may have weakened investors' feeling of responsibility for their own actions thereafter.[32] It may also have shifted the pattern of capital flows towards short-term foreign currency debt, as holders of other forms of Mexican paper suffered heavy losses.

During the Asian crisis, most investors with funds in the affected countries have taken losses, but to a very different degree. Equity investors are estimated to have lost about 70 per cent for the year ending June 1998, while bank losses might have been between 5 and 10 per cent of claims.[33] In this regard, international lenders' assumptions about being bailed out were correct and for the future might reinforce debt rather than equity finance and short- rather than longer-term flows. Indeed, countering this phenomenon is one motivation for the most recent thrust of international policy to "involve the private sector" more intimately in crisis resolution (see below).

Excessive risk-taking on the back of an implicit official safety net may turn into financial turmoil if market participants suddenly realize that their belief was misguided. This was probably the reason the Russian crisis created much more turbulence in both emerging and mature markets than the Asian crisis. Unlike the Asian crisis, the Russian turmoil challenged fundamental assumptions about emerging market finance, particularly the belief that official support would be provided. This led investors to radically re-evaluate the balance of risks throughout the world.

[28] Roberto Chang and Andrés Velasco, "The Asian liquidity crisis", National Bureau of Economic Research, Working Paper, No. 6796, November 1998, p. 36.

[29] See Steven Radelet and Jeffry Sachs, "The onset of the East Asian crisis", mimeo, Harvard Institute for International Development, 30 March 1998, pp. 15-23.

[30] For a discussion of certain intrinsic imperfections of international capital flows, see Stephany Griffith-Jones and Jacques Cailloux, "Encouraging the longer-term: institutional investors and emerging markets", Discussion Paper, No. 16, Office of Development Studies, United Nations Development Programme, 1998, pp. 36-37.

[31] William Cline and Kevin Barnes, "Spreads and risks in emerging markets lending", Research Paper, No. 97-1, Institute of International Finance, November 1997.

[32] BIS, 68th Annual Report..., p. 135.

[33] IIF, Report of the Working Group..., pp. 57-59.

POLICIES TO LIMIT VOLATILITY

The overshooting of markets, high volatility and the opacity that surrounds various aspects of global financial activity have always been attributes of the international financial system. Nevertheless, the benefits of unrestricted global flows were thought to more than offset these drawbacks. However, the recent waves of financial turbulence were unleashed with such speed and severity that the conventional wisdom which had justified the manner in which the system operated has been seriously questioned.

Precautionary measures need to be strengthened. In addition, however, experience suggests that whatever precautions are taken, crises will continue to occur. Hence, the international financial community should be well prepared to deal with unfavourable events. Appropriate mechanisms for orderly and cooperative resolution of crises are extremely important, as poorly devised measures may not only exacerbate financial distress, but also risk inducing more frequent crises and volatility in the future.

Devising the scope for new policy actions poses enormous challenges. Both national authorities and international bodies continue to experiment, analyse and assess various types of intervention for coping with the volatile capital flows of the age of globalization.[34]

Issues in strengthening national financial systems

The crises in Mexico, Asia and the Russian Federation highlighted the importance of sound financial sectors in emerging economies.[35] In addition, the banking sector difficulties in Japan and the financial scare associated with Long-term Capital Management in the United States also sounded warnings in the developed countries. There is now, therefore, a firm consensus that a major and sustained effort is needed to strengthen the structure, functioning and supervision of financial systems in all countries. Good management and strong supervision of financial institutions are a key to withstanding economic shocks. Activity is thus under way under the auspices of several international bodies to develop and foster the implementation of new standards of sound financial practices.

Strengthening weak financial systems is, however, easier said than done. Even the most advanced countries have a lot of difficulties in the realm of prudential and regulatory controls. For instance, according to the Comptroller of the Currency of the United States, only 4 of the 64 largest North American banks practice state-of-the-art portfolio risk management.[36] Consequently, it may take most developing and transition economies many years to develop more adequate supervisory systems. There is little reason to believe, however, that the next major crisis will wait so long. It is thus in the best interests of the advanced countries in which capital flows originate not to hold responsible only emerging economies, and to take policy steps themselves to ensure that scale, direction and forms of capital flows meet the needs and capacities of the recipients.

Moreover, much of the new international effort has focused on developing and promoting minimum global standards. These do not fully take into consideration that there might be special needs in developing and transition economies, and that the introduction of post-industrial financial techniques

[34] Indeed, the severity of the reform challenge prompted an unprecedented collective analysis by various components of the United Nations Secretariat (see *Global Financial Turmoil and Reform...*). For some of the views of the United Nations Conference on Trade and Development, see *Trade and Development Report, 1998* (United Nations publication, Sales No. E.98.II.D.6), part one, chaps. III and IV. A joint statement recommending an overall United Nations Secretariat view was also prepared (see "Towards a new international financial architecture", report of the Task Force of the United Nations Executive Committee on Economic and Social Affairs, 21 January 1999 (www.un.org/esa/coordination/ifa.htm)).

[35] See, for instance, Malcolm Knight, "Developing countries and the globalization of financial markets", *World Development*, vol. 26, No. 7 (1998), pp. 1,185-1,200.

[36] As cited by Dani Rodrik, "Who needs capital-account convertibility?", in Fischer and others, op. cit., p. 59.

into less-developed financial systems may themselves create weaknesses (see discussion of derivatives above).

The scope and nature of increasingly integrated financial markets have gone far beyond traditional fragmented regulatory structures in national jurisdictions. The establishment through the machinery of the Bank for International Settlements of the Joint Forum on Financial Conglomerates in 1996 represented an initial response to this dichotomy. A further step was taken in February 1999 when the Finance Ministers of the Group of Seven (G-7) endorsed a proposal to establish a Financial Stability Forum. It initially comprises the ministries of finance, central banks and senior supervisory authorities of the G-7, as well as the international financial institutions and key international regulatory groupings. After its first meeting in April 1999, the Forum set up three working groups, comprising officials of developed and developing countries, international financial institutions and supervisory groupings. One group will focus on highly leveraged institutions (for example, hedge funds), another on volatility arising from short-term credit and the third on offshore financial centres. They are to report policy recommendations to the Forum in September.[37]

There is also general agreement that higher standards of accounting and reporting in business, banking and government activities—and better and more timely data for monitoring capital flows—are necessary for a well-functioning market environment. The problem is that greater transparency and disclosure cannot by themselves prevent future crises. More complete, accessible and timely information is supposed to enhance the ability of market participants to make efficient decisions. However, one lesson of the recent Mexican, Asian and Russian crises is that inadequate use was made of the great deal of information that was publicly available and that pointed to potential problems.[38] Market participants tend to ignore information during good times and turn to "if-only-we-had-known" rhetoric after almost each collapse.[39] More generally, financial markets do not use information efficiently. More information may reduce the size of the bubble and the crash, but will not eliminate the bubble and the crash themselves, as markets are imperfect—even when people realize *ex post facto* the error of their ways.

The lack of transparency also complicates attempts to develop early warning indicators of financial crises. However, the major obstacle thus far seems to have been insufficient understanding of the dynamics of the new global financial system.[40]

Capital-adequacy standards

As noted above, the major trigger of all recent crises has been short-term, especially interbank, debt. One proposal to discourage excessive short-term lending and shift funds to longer-term financing has been to increase the cost to banks of short-term finance by raising the capital required of the banks according to their short-term exposures. Capital requirements could be raised on borrowing banks by making the required level of bank capital dependent not only on the nature and size of the banks' assets, but also on the nature of their funding.

As for lending banks, under the current Basel capital-adequacy standards, banks have a clear incentive to lend short-term in emerging markets. This is because, in calculating the minimum level of capital that banks are required to

[37] BIS, press release 19/1999E (11 May 1999).

[38] Informal enquiries by BIS indicate that a shortage of information about international exposures of the Asian countries was not the basic problem affecting the banks' behaviour (see William White, "The Asian crisis and the Bank for International Settlements", a paper presented at the conference on Asia and the future of the world economic system, London, 17 and 18 March 1999, p. 4 (http://www.bis.org)).

[39] See Alice Rivlin, "Remarks before the Hyman P. Minsky conference on financial structure", The Levy Institute, Bard College, 23 April 1998, p. 2 (http://www.bog.frb.fed.us).

[40] For discussion of the problems of crisis prediction, see, for instance, "Leading indicators of currency and banking crises", in IMF, *International Capital Markets: Developments, Prospects and Key Policy Issues* (Washington, D.C., September 1995), pp. 173-175.

hold, the capital-backing of short-term claims on banks from any country is lower than that of long-term bank loans.[41] Raising the "risk weight" on short-term lending to banks would reduce the incentive to build up interbank exposures and the corresponding systemic risk. Such a revision of risk weights is currently being considered as part of the review of the capital-adequacy standards. It has also been suggested that capital-adequacy requirements need to be higher in developing and transition economies, as their banks operate in a more volatile and risky environment.[42]

Taken alone, a system of reserve requirements that penalizes short-term flows is not likely to impose sufficient discipline on the market. The regulations can be evaded through derivative transactions that could convert long-term funding into an overnight foreign exchange loan.[43] This would call for extending the scope of surveillance to include over-the-counter (OTC) derivative markets. However, certain practical difficulties, in particular the complexity of data collection, have been stressed.[44] There have been proposals to induce a shift of derivative activities towards organized exchanges, where every trade is public information. The shift could be encouraged by increasing capital requirements for OTC derivative transactions.[45]

There is also a need to improve prudential standards for certain types of non-bank financial institutions, as the risks being borne by them are increasingly similar to those facing banks. In this regard, the imposition of some form of risk-based liquidity requirement on international institutional investors, including mutual funds, has been proposed.[46] This is intended to lower their needs to liquidate investments in case of rising redemptions and, hence, to reduce the need for rapid changes in investment holdings and thus smooth international capital flows.

The Asian crisis as well as the post-Russian Federation turmoil has drawn attention to the activities of unsupervised financial service providers, notably so-called highly leveraged institutions (HLIs)[47] and, first of all, hedge funds. Their impact on the market is considered to be significant. Specific forms of regulation of these entities have not yet been agreed. There is, however, a consensus that institutions whose investment activities and market impact are essentially similar to those of their regulated counterparts should not evade regulation only because of their different form and structure. Also, much attention has focused on HLIs' relationships with banks, which are the major providers of funds for HLIs' activities.[48]

The financial safety net

Poorly designed or too generous government safety net arrangements may encourage private debtors and creditors to take excessive risk, thereby increasing the likelihood of the crisis.[49] For instance, explicit or implicit government guarantees of loans to the domestic banking systems and, in some cases, to non-financial firms in East Asia might have contributed to excessive foreign borrowing and lending.

Given the importance of financial intermediation, the burden of managing risk in the financial system should not lie with the private institutions alone. However, a complete insulation of the private sector is equally harmful. Hence, there should be some form of allocation of the burden of risk between the public and private sectors, with central banks responsible for managing

[41] The principle was that short-term lending was less risky than longer-term loans and that loans extended to other banks were less risky than loans to corporations.

[42] "Towards a new international financial architecture"…, p. 16.

[43] Garber, loc. cit., p. 30.

[44] IOSCO, "Causes, effects and regulatory implications of financial and economic turbulence in emerging markets"…, p. 81.

[45] Martin Mayer, "The Asian Disease: Plausible Diagnoses, Possible Remedies", Public Policy Brief, The Jerome Levy Economics Institute of Bard College, No. 44, 1998, pp. 31-32.

[46] IOSCO, "Causes, effects and regulatory implications of financial and economic turbulence in emerging markets"…, p. 72.

[47] These are financial institutions that are subject to little or no direct regulatory oversight and limited disclosure requirements, and that take on significant debt.

[48] See Basel Committee on Banking Supervision, "Banks' interactions with highly leveraged institutions", Basel, January 1999; and "Sound practices for banks' interactions with highly leveraged institutions", Basel, January 1999.

[49] See Group of 22, Report of the Working Group on Strengthening Financial Systems (Washington, D.C., October 1998), p. VI.

only systemic disruptions. Especially in emerging markets, there is a need for clear distinction between government support of the banking system as a whole and support available to any individual bank when the system is deemed not to be at risk. This means, for instance, that individual banks should be allowed to fail. This also means that Governments need to untangle themselves from the "too big to fail" doctrine (see chap. V), for example, by promoting more competition in the domestic financial sector and reducing the range of activities allowed to banks that are accorded lender-of-last-resort protection. Also, implicit guarantees not only of non-financial firms, which are typical, but also of the more risk-oriented non-deposit financial institutions need to be reviewed.

The provision of assistance to deposit-taking institutions during a systemic crisis may be accompanied by an increase in required capital which shifts more of the burden of a prospective bank failure onto the shareholders and gives a larger cushion to the guarantor. Also, it has been stressed that attention should be paid to appropriate "pricing" of the guarantee arrangements so as to reflect the risks being insured by the government and to deter outlandish borrowing.[50] The "price" could be in the form of an explicit premium or extra reserve requirement on a bank's interbank liabilities, with the reserves earning low or even zero interest rates.

Managing international finance during currency crises

One major challenge is to develop mechanisms that could provide during periods of financial market stress either additional resources sufficient to cover at least short-term foreign debt or greater payments flexibility.

Resources for times of crisis

The primary form of government defence against the disruption of capital flow reversals is foreign currency reserves. In an era of open capital accounts it may be prudent to hold much larger reserves than before. In this regard, it has been argued that demand for reserves will likely increase with the subsequent rise of international capital flows.[51]

A related type of defence is to supplement reserves with an open credit line from foreign lenders for drawing from in certain unfavourable circumstances. For instance, Argentina, Mexico, Indonesia and several other countries have negotiated contingent credit facilities with large foreign banks. The participating country pays a commitment fee for the availability of the facility to a consortium of international banks and receives the right to draw down on the facility at a predetermined interest rate up to pre-established limits.

Such facilities provide access to supplementary liquidity at a lower price than that of holding an equivalent quantity of additional reserves. Like reserves, contingent credit and liquidity facilities can help prevent crises by enhancing investors' confidence that liquidity will be available in the event of unexpected volatility. Thus, the banks' commitment and capacity to provide the credit must be unshakeable. The charge for drawing on such a facility, however, need not be low.[52] The attractiveness of contingent credit lines as a vehicle for liability management led the Inter-American Development Bank (IADB) to propose its own participation in such arrangements, together with the private sector.

50 Group of 22, *Report of the Working Group on International Financial Crises* (Washington, D.C., October 1998), p. 7.

51 Stanley Fischer, "On the need for an international lender of last resort", paper prepared for delivery at the joint luncheon of the American Economic Association and the American Finance Association, New York, 3 January 1999, p. 10 (http://www.imf.org).

52 At the end of September 1998, the Mexican Government drew $2.66 billion from its $3 billion contingent line of credit at an interest rate that was, at the time, considerably below market. This led to proposals to modify such agreements and to relate the terms of the drawdown to market conditions at the time of the drawdown (see IIF, *Report of the Working Group...* p. 36).

The International Monetary Fund (IMF) recently introduced an international public-sector version of such facilities, when the Executive Board established the Contingent Credit Lines on 25 April 1999. Member countries can make arrangements under this facility only before they enter into crisis, assuming the Fund approves of the Government's macroeconomic policies, as expressed through the Fund's regular consultations with all its members. The intention is to prevent the spread of the contagion to soundly managed economies in the event of an international crisis. If the funds are actually needed, the Government requests an "activation" review, which the Executive Board is authorized to conduct expeditiously. If approval is granted—this is in contrast with the private credit lines, which are automatic—the country can draw substantial sums for repayment in 1.5 years (the period can be extended one year), although it will be paying a penalty interest rate that begins at 3 percentage points above that on regular IMF drawings and rises half a percentage point each 6 months, up to 5 percentage points total.[53]

There is also scope for financial innovations so as to provide more insurance against adverse market developments than is typical in the financial arrangements currently used. For instance, there have been suggestions to consider the addition of options to new sovereign bonds and interbank credit lines that would allow a debtor Government or debtor banks to extend the maturity of a bond or credit line for a specified period of time at a predetermined spread. Such options could be exercised to ease pressure in the event of a liquidity crisis.[54] Another proposal is to design debt instruments that would automatically reduce payments in response to certain unfavourable economic developments.[55]

"Involving the private sector" in crisis resolution

The international treatment of financial crises has changed profoundly in the 1990s in comparison with the 1970s and 1980s, with the major difference being in the scope of private sector financial involvement. Private sector participation in the form of rescheduling of bank claims and provision of new loans accounted for 50 to 70 per cent of the support packages at the outset of the Latin American debt crisis in 1982-1983. In the succession of financial crises that began with Mexico in 1994-1995, however, the extent of private sector contribution has been much more limited. The private sector directly participated in only two of the six major international support packages in 1995-1998, those for the Republic of Korea and Indonesia, with the involvement in the Republic of Korea being much smaller than the average in the 1980s.[56]

There are several reasons for the changed participation of private creditors. Many procedures to resolve international financial crisis were developed and proved effective during the 1980s. They were designed, however, for an environment in which a relatively small number of international banks provided most of the capital flows to developing-country Governments. Also, claims of individual banks were relatively large and mostly medium-term and to a large degree provided through organized syndicates. Since then, the larger scale and greater diversity of capital flows to emerging markets have significantly reduced the relevance of the procedures used in the past.

The almost sole reliance on official support to respond to these recent crises stemmed, at least initially, from the aim of quickly resuming the private capital inflows. The common aim of recent packages has been to quickly restore private

[53] See *IMF Survey*, 10 May 1999, p. 133.

[54] Group of 22, *Report of the Working Group on International Financial Crises* (Washington, D.C., October 1998), pp. 11-12.

[55] See, for instance, IMF, Policy Development and Review Department, *Involving the Private Sector...*, chap. I, pp. 12-13.

[56] The other packages were for Brazil, Mexico, the Russian Federation and Thailand (see IIF, *Report of the Working Group...*, p. 48).

sector confidence. Debt rescheduling and other mechanisms that were applied in the 1980s might have been considered counter-productive.

However, the surprising severity of the financial crises and the realization that private funds would not be quick to return induced a shift in the international approach to crisis resolution. Following the ad hoc renegotiation process with bank creditors of the economy of the Republic of Korea at the start of 1998, the IMF decided to review its policy on crisis intervention.

One concern behind the review relates to the fact that bailouts in the 1990s involved handing over relatively large amounts of public sector foreign exchange to both foreign lenders and domestic investors in emerging economies, with the resulting redistribution of wealth benefiting the rich at the expense of others.[57] It has also been suggested that the bailouts might increase the fragility of the world financial system, as they would encourage behaviour that could lead to a repeat or worsening of the same problem in the future.[58] According to this line of reasoning, the prospect of emergency financing encourages private lenders to assume excessive risk exposures in emerging markets until a crisis becomes imminent (the "moral hazard" problem). Then, they overreact.

These concerns notwithstanding, there is a widespread belief that it would not be realistic to abandon public sector support arrangements in a crisis, even if the policy of bailing out debtor countries may create a moral hazard. The reason is that international capital flows can be extremely volatile and such volatility is contagious, exhibiting the classic signs of financial panics.[59] Current thinking about an overall solution is thus to mix a measure of official financial support with a shifting of more of the financial burden—and thus risk—to the private creditors. Such burden-sharing with the private creditors would be achieved by involving them in an agreed refinancing or provision of new credit in a future crisis. Raising their risk is expected to temper the moral hazard problem as well.

Sharing the burden is an easy principle to accept, but a very difficult and controversial one to put into practice, not least because of inherent conflict between ensuring systemic stability and achieving market-driven outcomes. For example, "bailing in" the private sector should not be limited to foreign investors. Stopping a massive exodus of resident capital is equally important. Otherwise, resources provided by the international community would simply finance additional private capital outflow by residents, and such outflows can be large.

A search is thus on for mechanisms to give private sector lenders incentives to act in tandem with the government authorities. The goal is to supplement official financial assistance by financial flows from other sources in the event of crisis, in a way that ensures that the private sector's exposure is maintained or increased.[60] This could contribute importantly to orderly restructuring and speed up the restoration of normal credit flows.

Private investors' behaviour in a liquidity crisis is almost always myopic. Indeed, the prospect that private creditors might have been forced to contribute to a financial rescue package for Brazil appears to have accelerated capital flight in late 1998. Economists describe such a situation as a "collective action" problem. If each creditor tries to collect on its loan, the debtor will go into cri-

[57] Michael Bordo, "International rescues versus bailouts: an historical perspective", paper prepared for the Cato Institute's 16th Annual Monetary Conference, Washington, D.C., 22 October 1998, p. 7.

[58] Charles Calomiris, "The IMF's imprudent role as lender of last resort", *The Cato Journal*, vol. 17, No. 3 (1998).

[59] See Fischer, "On the need for an international lender of last resort" ...

[60] See Michel Camdessus, "Capital flows, crises, and the private sector", remarks to the Institute of International Bankers, Washington, D.C., 1 March 1999, p. 5 (http://www.imf.org).

sis, but if the creditors agree to be patient and roll over their maturing claims, they may all recover all their loans. The international community has the power to organize the individual creditors so as to produce a more positive collective-action outcome.

Consequently, under extreme circumstances and in the absence of private sector voluntary cooperation, it might be necessary to force investors into orderly crisis resolution through international support for a temporary halt to payments to all creditors. The IMF already has a mechanism to signal its support for a country in such circumstances, called "lending into arrears". The IMF has recalled, officially, that this mechanism is available and that it could be deployed in extreme situations.[61] However, the international community has yet to reach a consensus on what constitutes an extreme situation and how to handle it. It is important that it continue to try to do so because strong leadership from the international community when the next crisis begins can make that crisis a much shorter-lived one, with lower economic costs imposed on the population of the crisis country, than the events of 1997-1999.

The role of capital controls

The Asian crisis has raised doubts about the validity of the concept of unfettered financial markets and drawn attention to various forms of government intervention. In particular, there has been renewed interest in capital control measures as a means to cope with volatile capital flows, especially in crisis situations. It has been argued that the restrictions on short-term, especially interbank, flows in order to limit excessive foreign exchange exposure of domestic institutions, or help to lengthen the maturity of foreign liabilities may be part of an appropriate strategy to prevent crises, as they partially insulate the country from the disruptive effects of sudden reversals in market sentiment.[62]

Supporters of preventive capital controls cite the experience of several Latin American countries and, first of all, Chile, which in 1991 imposed disincentives on a broad range of short-term capital inflows.[63] The effect has been to lengthen the average maturity of financial inflows. The controls have also affected the overall volume of flows.[64]

The opponents of capital controls stress that "world-class" risk management systems and effective prudential regulation could work far better than capital restrictions, which the market would in any event eventually find a method of evading. However, as noted above, for most emerging economies the development and implementation of sufficiently strong prudential regulations and supervision will take quite a long time. In this case, even opponents of capital controls agree that they may perform a role.[65] The banking systems of East Asian countries were not weaker than those in China or India, which were untouched by the crisis. Capital controls in the latter cases are thought to have discouraged the build-up of short-term liabilities and shielded these countries from the contagion.[66]

Hot money flows and attempts to control them are principally associated with pegged exchange rates. It has been suggested that, instead of imposing capital controls to preserve pegged rates, it would be better for developing countries to adopt a permanently fixed exchange rate supported by a currency board, or to allow the exchange rate to float. It is argued that as capital-market

[61] See IMF, "Report of the Managing Director to the Interim Committee on progress in strengthening the architecture of the international financial system", 26 April 1999, para. 33 (http://www.imf.org).

[62] For a review of the debate on capital controls, see Giancarlo Corsetti, Paolo Pesenti and Noureil Roubini, "What caused the Asian currency and financial crisis? Part II: The policy debate", National Bureau of Economic Research, Working Paper, No. 6834, December 1998, pp. 21-26.

[63] In September 1998, under pressure from the global financial turmoil, Chile suspended its policy with the goal of stimulating capital inflows and reducing pressure on the currency. The authorities stated that they intended to reintroduce their policy measures as conditions warranted. For a description and assessment of the policy, see Manuel Agosin and Ricardo Ffrench-Davis, "Managing capital inflows in Chile", in Global Financial Turmoil and Reform ..., pp. 161-187.

[64] Carlos Massad, "The liberalization of the capital account: Chile in the 1990s", in Fisher and others, op. cit. pp. 34-46.

[65] See Barr Johnson and Natalia Tamirisa, "Why Do Countries Use Capital Controls?", IMF Working Paper, No. 181 (Washington, D.C., December 1998), p. 15.

[66] See ADB Economic Analysis and Research Division, "Exchange controls: the path to economic recovery in Asia?", ADB Rreview (Asian Development Bank), vol. 30, No. 4 (1998), pp. 14-19.

integration increases, countries will be forced increasingly towards more pure floating or more purely fixed regimes.[67]

Currency boards may be attractive to only a limited number of countries, as the rigidity of these arrangements makes the country more vulnerable to shocks, including changes in the exchange rate of the reserve currency vis-à-vis third-country trading partners.[68] Consequently, for many countries that are not prepared to fix the nominal exchange rate of their currencies permanently, a measure of control of the most volatile kinds of capital movements may be an attractive policy choice.

Exchange-rate flexibility can discourage short-term lending and borrowing. However, it has been argued that, except in large, diversified economies, the free movement of capital and floating exchange rates are basically incompatible because the exchange rate exerts too large an influence on the national price level.[69]

A number of developing countries have shown interest in the temporary resort to capital controls as a strategy to mitigate the extent of a crisis. The most prominent case here is the introduction of capital controls by Malaysia in September 1998. The move was aimed at assisting the efforts to revive the economy by allowing interest rates to fall behind the new capital-account barrier.

The opponents of capital controls have also been stressing that even if there are some short-run benefits associated with capital controls, these benefits are more than offset by long-term costs in terms of inferior macroeconomic performance. There is, however, no clear empirical evidence of this.[70]

The imposition of ad hoc restrictions in crisis situations appears to be even more controversial than preventive capital controls. It has been argued that ad hoc controls in one country may cause widespread contagion as investors will act pre-emptively in many countries.[71] Yet, there exists an opposing view that despite certain drawbacks, the resort to temporary restrictive measures on capital transactions may be justified not only in emergency situations, but also when these measures are necessary for balance-of-payments or macroeconomic management reasons.[72]

While there is strong disagreement about costs and benefits of capital controls, especially the temporary crisis variant, there exists a policy direction that reflects a widespread consensus—the imposition or retention of selective controls that can be fitted within an overall framework of increasing liberalization of a financial system. The consensus view assigns great importance to caution, gradualism and proper management in the difficult and unpredictable process of financial liberalization.[73] As there is a plurality of well-argued views on this score, it seems most appropriate that the decisions on the degree of openness of the capital account should be left to the discretion of national Governments, without pressures for hasty external opening being imposed from outside.[74]

DOMESTIC FINANCIAL SYSTEMS, CAPITAL-ACCOUNT LIBERALIZATION AND VOLATILITY: CONCLUDING REMARKS

The preceding discussion has shown that financial liberalization and the integration of developing and transition economies into the international financial system carry significant risks. At the same time, it is unrealistic to expect this process to be reversed or even stopped. Hence, the question to be

---

[67] See Lawrence Summers, "Building international financial architecture", paper prepared for the Cato Institute's 16th Annual Monetary Conference, Washington, D.C., October 1998, p. 5.

[68] The recent crises have also ignited the discussion of the adoption of the United States dollar as the national currency of the country. The move would be aimed at reducing interest rates, inflation and volatility. The issue is being debated in several countries, including Argentina, Canada and Mexico.

[69] See Richard Cooper, loc. cit. pp. 18-19.

[70] For instance, Dani Rodrik (loc. cit., pp. 60-64) has shown that in a large number of developing economies, there is no positive correlation between liberalized capital accounts and growth, investment and low inflation.

[71] Rudiger Dornbusch, "Capital controls: an idea whose time is past", in Fisher and others, op. cit., p. 23.

[72] See, for instance, Manuel Guitian, "Economic policy implications of global financial flows", Finance and Development, March 1999, p. 28; and Donald Mathieson, Anthony Richards and Sunil Sharma, "Financial crises in emerging markets", Finance and Development, December 1998, p. 31.

[73] See Staff Team led by Barry Eichengreen and Michael Mussa, Capital Account Liberalization: Theoretical and Practical Aspects, Occasional Paper, No. 172 (Washington, D.C., IMF, 1998).

[74] This is the view, for example, in "Towards a new international financial architecture"..., pp. 17-19.

answered is under what conditions financial liberalization, especially capital-account liberalization, could be beneficial rather than harmful, that is to say, how the advantages of an open capital account could be maximized and the risks minimized.

Unfortunately, thus far there has been no clear answer to this question. The benefits, costs and risks of any chosen path and pace of financial liberalization will vary from country to country, depending on initial conditions. Governments with different economic objectives can reasonably choose different policy strategies, for instance, with respect to the degree of openness to short-term capital movements over the medium term. However, it would be positively dangerous to expose underdeveloped domestic financial structures to the ebbs and flows of global finance under the assumption that external market forces could successfully substitute for carefully designed and consistently implemented reform policies. In other words, external financial liberalization should not be considered an isolated or primary goal, achievement of which automatically raises sophistication and resilience of the domestic financial system. Rather, it should be part of a concurrent, integrated and comprehensive policy approach to macroeconomic and structural reform with individual elements of this policy package reinforcing each other.

It must be remembered, above all now that the world financial system is in a period of calm, that policy makers were taken by surprise—indeed, judging by the results of the past two years, overwhelmed—by the dynamic new world of global finance. Policy advice that was confidently propounded at mid-decade, in particular, on the benefits accruing from completely unfettered international financial flows, may reappear and gain a new hearing. It might be argued, for example, that the sequencing was wrong the first time around and that domestic financial systems in developing and transition economies should be better prepared next time. While those systems must certainly be strengthened, one must not lose sight of the consequences of the first set of errors in terms of devastating economic contractions and untenable increases in poverty in the directly affected countries, not to mention an international economic environment of slow growth of world trade, very low commodity prices, and a very substantial net transfer of financial resources out of the developing countries, as described in part one of the present *Survey*. This needs to be a time for reflection, analysis and policy experimentation, so that the advantages of the new global financial industry can be captured for development and the dangers can be held at bay.

ANNEX | STATISTICAL TABLES

ANNEX
STATISTICAL TABLES

The present annex contains the main sets of data on which the analysis provided in the *World Economic and Social Survey,* 1999 is based. The data are presented in greater detail than in the text and for longer time periods, and incorporate information available as of 30 April 1999.

The annex was prepared by the Development Policy Analysis Division of the Department of Economic and Social Affairs of the United Nations Secretariat. The annex is based on information obtained from the United Nations Statistics Division and the Population Division of the Department of Economic and Social Affairs, as well as from the United Nations regional commissions, the International Monetary Fund (IMF), the World Bank, the Organisation for Economic Cooperation and Development (OECD), the United Nations Conference on Trade and Development (UNCTAD) and national and private sources. Estimates for the most recent years were made by the Development Policy Analysis Division in consultation with the regional commissions.

Forecasts are based on the results of the May 1999 forecasting exercise of Project LINK, an international collaborative research group for econometric modelling, which is coordinated jointly by the Development Policy Analysis Division and the University of Toronto. The LINK itself is a global model that links together the trade and financial relations of 79 country and regional models which are managed by over 60 national institutions and by the Division. The models assume that the existing or officially announced macroeconomic policies as of 15 April are in effect. The primary linkages are merchandise trade and prices, as well as interest and exchange rates of major currency countries. The model generates a consistent solution by an iterative process, and thus a complete matrix of trade flows and price changes, among other variables, is determined endogenously. The one significant exception is the international price of crude oil, which is derived with the help of a satellite model of the oil sector. In this case, the average price of the basket of seven crude oils of the Organization of the Petroleum Exporting Countries (OPEC) was seen to rise by 4 per cent in 1999 and assumed to rise by 24.2 per cent in 2000.

COUNTRY CLASSIFICATION

For analytical purposes, the *World Economic and Social Survey* groups all the countries of the world into one of three mutually exclusive categories: developed economies, economies in transition and developing countries. The composition of these groupings is specified in the explanatory notes that appear at the beginning of the *Survey*. The groupings are meant to reflect basic economic conditions in each region or subregion. Several countries have characteristics that could place them in more than one grouping (in particular, economies in transition), but for purposes of analysis the groupings were made mutually exclusive. The groupings do not reflect a judgement of the stage of development of individual countries. Different groupings of countries may be deemed appropriate at different times and for different analytical purposes.

The nature of each of the three main analytical groupings remains unchanged and may be given in broad strokes. The developed economies have the highest material standards of living on average. Production is heavily and increasingly oriented towards the provision of a wide range of services; agriculture is typically a very small share of output and the share of manufacturing is generally declining. On average, workers in developed countries are the world's most productive, frequently relying on advanced production techniques and equipment. The developed economies are often global centres for research in science and technology. Internationally, the Governments of developed countries are likely to offer assistance to other countries and they do not generally seek foreign assistance.

Among the developed economies, Australia, Canada, Japan, New Zealand and the United States of America are listed separately. The European countries are grouped as follows: the "EU-15", which comprises all current members of the European Union (EU); and "other Europe", which is composed of those Western European countries that are not current EU members (Iceland, Malta, Norway and Switzerland). Data on EU cover the 15 current members of the Union for all years. Additionally, the EU countries are further organized into two groups: "EU-11" which comprises all countries that are members of the European monetary union (Austria, Belgium, Finland, France, Germany, Luxembourg, Ireland, Italy, the Netherlands, Portugal and Spain); and "other EU", which comprises the remaining EU countries (Denmark, Sweden and the United Kingdom of Great Britain and Northern Ireland). Finally, the seven largest economies measured in terms of gross domestic product (GDP), namely, Canada, France, Germany, Italy, Japan, the United Kingdom and the United States, are also referred to as the "major industrialized countries" (the Group of Seven).

The economies in transition are characterized by the great social transformation that they began at the end of the 1980s, when they fully turned away from centralized administration of resource allocation as the main organizing principle of their societies towards the establishment or re-establishment of market economies. The shock to their economies was severe, entailing a substantial decline in output and deterioration in social and economic conditions.

Some of these economies began the transformation process having many of the characteristics of developed economies and some had—and retain—several characteristics of developing economies. But while a case might be made for grouping individual economies in transition with the developed or developing countries, the fact that for purposes of analysis in the present *Survey* their most distinguishing characteristic at this time is taken to be their transitional nature, opposes such a grouping.

The group of economies in transition is divided into three sub-groups: one is Central and Eastern Europe, called Eastern Europe for short, which comprises Albania, Bulgaria, the Czech Republic, Hungary, Poland, Romania, Slovakia and the successor States of the Socialist Federal Republic of Yugoslavia (namely, Bosnia and Herzegovina, Croatia, Slovenia, the former Yugoslav Republic of Macedonia, and Yugoslavia); a second group comprises members of the Commonwealth of Independent States (CIS); and the third encompasses the Baltic States (Estonia, Latvia and Lithuania). In some cases, data are shown for the former Soviet Union until 1991 and for the aggregate of its successor States from 1992, so as to facilitate analysis of trends over time. Corresponding data for individual successor States of the Soviet Union are included as available.

The rest of the world is grouped together as the developing economies. It is a heterogeneous grouping, although one with certain common characteristics. Average material standards of living in developing countries are lower than in developed countries and many of these countries have deep and extensive poverty. In addition, developing countries are usually importers rather than developers of innovations in science and technology and their application in new products and production processes. They also tend to be relatively more vulnerable to economic shocks.

Based on the classification used by the Population Division and the United Nations Statistics Division, the *Survey* has adopted the following standard designations of geographical regions for developing countries: Africa, Latin America and the Caribbean, and Asia and the Pacific (comprising Western Asia, China and Eastern and Southern Asia, including the Pacific islands).

Other distinctions are also made for analytical purposes. The ability to export fuel or the need to import fuel has a large effect on the capacity to import—and on the growth of output, as growth in developing countries is often constrained by the availability of foreign exchange. The developing countries are therefore divided into fuel exporters and importers. Fuels, rather than energy sources more broadly, are considered because fuel prices are more directly linked to oil prices and oil prices are particularly volatile and have a considerable impact on incomes and on the purchasing power of the exports of the countries in question.

A country is defined as a fuel exporter if, simultaneously:

a Its domestic production of primary commercial fuel (oil, natural gas, coal and lignite but excluding hydro- and nuclear electricity) exceeded domestic consumption by at least 20 per cent;

b Its value of fuel exports amounted to at least 20 per cent of total exports;

c It was not classified as a least developed country.

The list of fuel-exporting countries comprises Algeria, Angola, Bahrain, Bolivia, Brunei Darussalam, Cameroon, Colombia, the Congo, Ecuador, Egypt, Gabon, Indonesia, the Islamic Republic of Iran, Iraq, Kuwait, the Libyan Arab Jamahiriya, Mexico, Nigeria, Oman, Qatar, Saudi Arabia, the Syrian Arab Republic, Trinidad and Tobago, the United Arab Emirates, Venezuela and Viet Nam. All other developing countries are classified as fuel-importing countries.

Two sub-groups of the fuel-importing developing countries are sometimes identified in the tables of the *Survey*. One is a group of four exporters of manufactures, namely, the four Asian economies considered to constitute the first generation of successful exporters of manufactures (Hong Kong Special Administrative Region (SAR), the Republic of Korea, Singapore and Taiwan Province of China).

The other sub-grouping is the least developed countries. Unlike the preceding groupings, which were created by the Secretariat for the convenience of economic and social analysis, the list of least developed countries is decided by the General Assembly, on the basis of the recommendations of the Committee for Development Policy, until 1998 known as the Committee for Development Planning. The Committee for Development Policy reviews criteria for identifying the least developed countries and considers the eligibility of individual countries. The basic criteria for inclusion require being below certain thresholds with regard to per capita GDP, an economic diversification index and an "augmented physical quality of life index".[1] There are at present 48 countries on the list.[2]

Starting with the 1997 *Survey*,[3] a new classification of "net-creditor" and "net-debtor" countries was introduced. It is based on the net foreign asset position of each country at the end of 1995, as assessed by IMF in the *World Economic Outlook*,[4] October 1996. The list of net-creditor countries comprises Brunei Darussalam, Kuwait, the Libyan Arab Jamahiriya, Oman, Qatar, Saudi Arabia, Singapore,[5] Taiwan Province of China and the United Arab Emirates.

A final sub-grouping sometimes employed is sub-Saharan Africa, which groups together all the African countries south of the Sahara desert, excluding Nigeria and South Africa. These latter two countries overwhelm the smaller economies of the region in terms of GDP, population and international trade and so aggregate measures give a distorted picture of the situation in the smaller African economies. The intent in the grouping is to overcome this shortcoming.

DATA QUALITY

Statistical information that is consistent and comparable over time and across countries is of vital importance when monitoring economic developments, discussing social issues and policy and poverty, or assessing environmental change. The multifaceted nature of these and other current issues, such as the high mobility of capital and people, and economic regionalization, calls for an integrated approach to national and international data.

The 1993 revision of the System of National Accounts (SNA)[6] and the latest edition of the IMF *Balance of Payments Manual*[7] (the IMF Manual) constitute a major step forward in efforts to develop an integrated and harmonized system of statistics that reflects the economic and social change of the past two decades. The 1993 SNA embodies concepts, definitions and classifications that are interrelated at both the macro- and microlevels. Concepts in the IMF Manual have been harmonized, as closely as possible, with those of the 1993 SNA and with the Fund's methodologies pertaining to money, banking and government finance statistics. In addition, through a system of satellite accounts, which are semi-integrated with the central framework of the SNA, it is possible to establish linkages between national accounts data and other par-

[1] See report of the Committee for Development Planning on its thirty-first session (*Official Records of the Economic and Social Council, 1997, Supplement No. 15* (E/1997/35)), chap. VI.

[2] Afghanistan, Angola, Bangladesh, Benin, Bhutan, Burkina Faso, Burundi, Cambodia, Cape Verde, Central African Republic, Chad, Comoros, Democratic Republic of the Congo, Djibouti, Equatorial Guinea, Eritrea, Ethiopia, Gambia, Guinea, Guinea-Bissau, Haiti, Kiribati, Lao People's Democratic Republic, Lesotho, Liberia, Madagascar, Malawi, Maldives, Mali, Mauritania, Mozambique, Myanmar, Nepal, Niger, Rwanda, Samoa, Sao Tome and Principe, Sierra Leone, Solomon Islands, Somalia, Sudan, Togo, Tuvalu, Uganda, United Republic of Tanzania, Vanuatu, Yemen and Zambia.

[3] United Nations publication, Sales No. E.97.II.C.1 and corrigenda.

[4] Washington, D.C., IMF, 1996.

[5] Singapore and Taiwan Province of China are classified by the International Monetary Fund (IMF) as advanced countries and thus are not included in IMF's group of "net-creditor" developing countries.

[6] Commission of the European Communities, IMF, OECD, United Nations and World Bank, *System of National Accounts, 1993* (United Nations publication, Sales No. E.94.XVII.4).

[7] IMF, *Balance of Payments Manual*, 5th ed. (Washington, D.C., IMF, 1993).

ticular fields of economic and social statistics, such as the environment, health, social protection and tourism.

Governments are increasingly reporting their data on the basis of these standards and, where available, these data are incorporated into the statistics in this annex. However, there continue to be deep-rooted weaknesses underlying some of the national and international statistics that are perforce used in this *Survey* and other international publications. Inconsistency of coverage, definitions and data-collection methods among reporting countries sometimes mar the easy interpretation of data published by international agencies.

Another perennial problem is late, incomplete or non-reported data. Although adjustments and estimations are possible, and are made in selected cases, there is a need in some areas for timely reporting not only on an annual basis, but also quarterly or even more frequently. Considerable progress has been made by some developing countries and economies in transition in publishing annual and quarterly data on a timely and regular basis, whereas major lacunae have developed in the case of other economies in transition, in conflict or at war.

On the one hand, a widespread source of inaccuracy involves the use of out-of-date benchmark surveys and censuses or obsolete models and assumptions about behaviour and conditions. On the other hand, when statistical administrations seek to improve their estimates by using new sources of data and updated surveys, there can be discontinuities in the series. National income estimates are especially affected, sometimes being subject to revisions of the order of 10-30 per cent.[8]

National accounts and related indicators mainly record market transactions conducted through monetary exchange. Barter, production by households, subsistence output and informal sector activities are not always recorded; together, the omitted items can constitute a large share of total activity and lead to an underestimation of national output by perhaps up to 40 per cent. As the degree of underestimation varies across countries, output comparisons may give faulty results. In addition, as the non-market sector is absorbed into the mainstream of production over time through increasing monetization, the extent of output growth will be overstated based on the extent of this shift (see "Data definitions and conventions" below for illustrations of such difficulties).

Weaknesses at the national level become major analytical handicaps when comparisons are made between countries or groupings of countries at a given time or over a period of time. Missing, unreliable or incompatible country data necessitate estimation and substitution on the part of international organizations if they are to retain consistent country composition of aggregated data over time. In particular, the absence of reliable GDP estimates for many developing countries and economies in transition requires the use of estimates in preparing country aggregations for many data series, as GDP weights often underlie such aggregations.

There are also problems with other types of statistics, such as unemployment, consumer price inflation and the volume of exports and imports. Cross-country comparisons of unemployment must be made with caution owing to differences in definition among countries. For this reason in particular, table A.7 employs the standardized definitions of unemployment rates which, in certain cases, differ substantially from national definitions.

[8] Wilfred Beckerman, "National income", in *The New Palgrave: The World of Economics*, John Eatwell, Murray Milgate and Peter Newman, eds. (New York, The Macmillan Press, Limited, 1991), p. 486.

Consumer price indices are among the oldest of the economic data series collected by Governments, but they are still surrounded by controversy even in countries with the most advanced statistical systems, owing in particular to the introduction of new goods, and changes in the quality of goods and consumer behaviour which are often not captured because of, *inter alia*, infrequent consumer-spending surveys and revisions to sample baskets of commodities.

There are no clear-cut solutions to many of the problems noted above. Even when there are, inadequate resources allocated to the improvement of statistical systems and reporting can perpetuate statistical shortcomings. In this light, it is advisable to approach economic and social indicators as presented in this *Survey* as approximations and estimations, especially at the aggregate level.

DATA DEFINITIONS AND CONVENTIONS

Aggregate data are either sums or weighted averages of individual country data. Unless otherwise indicated, multi-year averages of growth rates are expressed as compound annual rates of change. The convention followed is to identify the *period of change* in a multi-year growth rate and omit the base year; for example, the 10-year average growth rate of a variable in the 1980s would be identified as the average annual growth rate in 1981-1990. Year-to-year growth rates are expressed as annual percentage changes.

Historical data presented in the statistical annex may differ from those in previous editions because of updating, as well as changes in the availability of data for individual countries.

Output

National data on real GDP are aggregated to create regional output figures and national practices are followed in defining real GDP for each country. The growth of output in each group of countries is calculated from the sum of GDP of individual countries measured at 1993 prices and exchange rates. National currency data for GDP in 1993 were converted into dollars (with adjustments in selected cases)[9] and extended forward and backward in time using changes in real GDP for each country. This method is believed to supply a reasonable set of aggregate growth rates for a period of about 15 years, centred on 1993. The base year has to be moved from time to time to reflect the changed composition of production and expenditure over long periods.

Most individual countries, however, do not use 1993 as the base year for their accounts. In the case of the United States, the base year itself has a very specific meaning because GDP data are calculated in terms of a "chain-weighted" index. According to this method, the growth rate of real GDP for any year is the average of the GDP growth rate calculated in the prices of that year and the growth rate calculated in the prices of the previous year. A time series of the real GDP is then calculated by applying these growth rates to the dollar value of GDP in the base year; for the United States, this is currently 1992.[10]

Developed economies

Beginning in 1991, aggregate economic growth data for Germany included the former German Democratic Republic. Because official data for the level of

[9] When individual exchange rates seem outside the bounds of "realism", alternative exchange rates are substituted. Averages of the exchange rates in relevant years might be used, or the exchange rate of a more normal year might be adjusted according to relative inflation rates since the time the exchange rate was deemed "correct".

[10] See Charles Steindel, "Chain-weighting: the new approach to measuring GDP", *Current Issues in Economics and Finance*, Federal Reserve Bank of New York, December 1995; for details, see United States Department of Commerce, *Survey of Current Business*, January/February 1996, pp. 1-118.

GDP for the unified Germany began with 1991, the first year for which a growth rate could be calculated from official data was 1992. The growth rate in 1991, as shown in table A.2, was a weighted average of official and estimated GDP growth rates in the two parts of Germany, with the weighting based on the level of GDP in 1991, as published by the *Statistisches Bundesamt* (Federal Statistical Office) of Germany.

Economies in transition

Starting with the *World Economic Survey, 1992*,[11] there was a switch to GDP from net material product as the measure of aggregate output of economies in transition. For the purpose of arriving at an analytically useful timeseries in real and nominal terms, adjustments were made, notably in the case of the former Soviet Union, to the gross national product (GNP) data published in terms of local currency. In many instances, there were neither fully reliable national accounts data nor meaningful exchange rates for the 1980s, and this continued into the 1990s in several cases. Thus, a set of weights had to be estimated from fragmentary data (and a series of approximate growth rates of GDP in constant prices was constructed for the Soviet Union for 1981-1990).

Subsequently, new data became available that warranted updating the estimates of the weighting scheme. In addition, with the shift in base year from 1988 to 1993, it has become possible to introduce national estimates of GDP into the calculation of base-year GDP values and weights. These have been revised for this *Survey*.

The extent of economic activity not captured by national statistics and its evolution over time have become an especially acute concern in some economies in transition. In addition, the proliferation of new modes of production, transactions and entities has rendered the previous institutional and methodological framework for statistics inadequate. A comprehensive reform of national statistical systems has thus been under way in many economies in transition. As a result, important revisions to several data series have been released and further revisions of past and current performance are expected. In the meantime, the statistical information provided, especially for many of the successor States of the Soviet Union, as well as for other economies in transition, must be treated as tentative estimates subject to potentially large revision.[12]

Developing countries

Beginning with the *World Economic Survey, 1997*,[13] estimates of the growth of output in developing countries have been based on the data of 95 economies, accounting for an estimated 97 per cent of the 1993 GDP and 98 per cent of the 1993 population of all developing countries and territories. The sample countries account for more than 95 per cent of the GDP and population of each of the geographical regions into which the developing countries are divided, with the exception of sub-Saharan Africa for which the countries included in the sample make up 90 per cent of GDP and 93 per cent of the population.

The veracity of estimates of output and of other statistical data of developing countries is related to the stage of development of their statistical systems. In Africa in particular, there are wide divergences in the values of the economic aggregates provided by different national and international sources for many countries. In addition, data for countries in which there is civil strife or war

[11] United Nations publication, Sales No. E.92.II.C.1 and Corr. 1 and 2.

[12] See *World Economic and Social Survey, 1995* (United Nations publication, Sales No. E.95.II.C.1), statistical annex, sect. entitled "Data caveats and conventions".

[13] United Nations publication, Sales No. E.97.II.C.1 and corrigenda.

OUTPUT AND PER CAPITA OUTPUT IN THE BASE YEAR

	GDP (billions of dollars)		GDP per capita (dollars)	
	Exchange-rate basis 1993	PPP basis 1993	Exchange-rate basis 1993	PPP basis 1993
World	24 145	30 499	4 449	5 620
Developed economies of which:	19 002	17 006	23 242	20 801
United States	6 558	6 553	25 025	25 006
European Union	6 925	6 593	18 753	17 854
Japan	4 275	2 628	34 332	21 105
Economies in transition	502	1 842	1 223	4 487
Developing countries By region:	4 641	11 651	1 105	2 775
Latin America	1 405	2 539	3 089	5 582
Africa	429	1 001	656	1 530
Western Asia	713	1 066	3 424	5 119
Eastern and Southern Asia	1 495	4 441	876	2 603
China	599	2 603	510	2 215
By analytical grouping:				
Net-creditor countries	506	644	9 485	12 071
Net-debtor countries	4 136	11 006	998	2 655
Net fuel exporter countries	1 270	2 697	1 648	3 500
Net fuel importer countries	3 372	8 954	978	2 596
Memo items:				
Sub-Saharan Africa	130	337	339	879
Least developed countries	130	569	245	1 074

Source: UN/DESA.

often provide only rough orders of magnitude. Finally, in countries experiencing high rates of inflation and disequilibrium exchange rates, substantial distortions can invade national accounts data.

Alternative aggregation methodologies for calculating world output

The *World Economic and Social Survey* utilizes a weighting scheme derived from exchange-rate conversions of national data in order to aggregate rates of growth of output of individual countries into regional and global totals, as noted above. This is similar to the approach followed in other international reports, such as those of the World Bank. However, IMF and OECD, in *World Economic Outlook* and *Economic Outlook* respectively, use a scheme for aggregation in which the country weights are derived from national GDP in "international dollars", as converted from local currency using purchasing power parities (PPPs). The question of which approach to use is controversial.[14]

[14] See World Economic and Social Survey, 1995..., statistical annex, sect. entitled "Alternative aggregation methodologies for GDP".

The motivation for PPP weights is that, when aggregating production in two countries, a common set of prices should be used to value the same activities in both countries. This is frequently not the case when market exchange rates are used to convert local currency values of GDP. The PPP approach revalues gross production (actually, expenditure) in different countries using a single set of prices. The PPP conversion factor is in principle the number of units of national currency needed to buy the goods and services that can be bought with one unit of currency of the *numéraire* country, the United States. In principle as well as in practice, however, PPPs are difficult to calculate because goods and services are not always directly comparable across countries, making direct comparisons of their prices correspondingly difficult. This is particularly the case for such services as health care and education, for which it is hard to measure output as well as prices.

One problem in employing PPP estimates for calculating the relative sizes of countries is that the most recently completed set of PPP prices, which was for 1985, covered only 64 countries.[15] Estimates for a new benchmark year (1993) covering a larger set of countries is being prepared by the International Comparison Programme (ICP).

This notwithstanding, certain regularities had been observed, on the one hand, between GDP and its major expenditure components when measured in market prices and, on the other, between GDP and its components measured in "international" prices as derived in the ICP exercise. On that basis (and using other partial data on consumer prices), a technique was devised to approximate PPP levels of GDP and its major expenditure components for countries that had not participated in ICP, the results having come to be known as the Penn World Tables.[16]

Neither the PPP approach nor the exchange-rate approach to weighting country GDP data can be applied in a theoretically pure or fully consistent way. The data requirements for a truly global ICP are enormous, although in each round the ICP coverage grows. Similarly, since a system of weights based on exchange rates presumes that those rates are determined solely by the trade in goods and services and that domestic economies operate under competitive and liberal conditions, its application has been constrained by exchange controls and price distortions in many countries. Moreover, there are a large number of non-traded goods and services in each country to which the "law of one price" does not apply. However, the global trend towards liberalization may make possible a more consistent application over time of the exchange-rate method. Even so, the methods are conceptually different and thus yield different measures of world output growth.

These differences can be seen in table A.1 for the periods 1981-1990 and 1991-1998. The estimates employ the same data for the growth rates of GDP of individual countries, and data are employed for the same number of countries in both sets of averages. The columns differ only in the weights used to form the averages, which are shown in the table entitled "Output and per capita output in the base year".[17]

The table suggests that the world economy as a whole has grown faster when country GDPs are valued at PPP conversion factors, even though the growth rates for the main groupings of countries do not differ much when data are converted at PPP rather than at exchange rates. The reason for this is that the Asian

[15] See *World Comparisons of Real Gross Domestic Product and Purchasing Power, 1985: Phase V of the International Comparison Programme*, Series F, No. 64 (United Nations publication, Sales No. E.94.XVII.7 and Corr.1).

[16] See Robert Summers and Alan Heston, "The Penn World Table (Mark 5): an expanded set of international comparisons, 1950-1988", *Quarterly Journal of Economics*, vol. 106, No. 2 (May 1991), pp. 327-368 (current versions of these data are made available through the Internet or on diskette from the National Bureau of Economic Research, Cambridge, Massachusetts, United States of America; Internet address: http://www.nber.org/pwt56.html).

[17] The purchasing power parity (PPP) data are preliminary estimates of the Penn World Table.

developing countries, which account for a large share of the GDP of the developing countries, have grown more rapidly than the rest of the world in the 1990s and their weight under PPPs is higher than it is under the exchange-rate scheme. The influence of China is particularly important. In 1993, the total GDP of all developing countries excluding China was 2.2 times larger when valued at PPPs rather than at exchange rates, but China's GDP was 4.3 times larger. Valued at exchange rates, the GDP of the developing countries excluding China grew between 1991 and 1998 at about the same rate as GDP valued at PPPs, that is to say, 3.7 per cent versus 3.9 per cent. When China is included, however, the growth rates are 4.6 and 5.4 per cent, respectively.

International trade

The main source of data for tables A.14 is the IMF *Direction of Trade Statistics* database, while tables A.15 and A.16 are drawn from the more detailed trade data in the United Nations External Trade Statistics Database (COMTRADE).

Trade values in table A.13 are largely based on customs data for merchandise trade converted into dollars using average annual exchange rates and are mainly drawn from IMF, *International Financial Statistics*. These data are supplemented by balance-of-payments data in certain cases. Estimates of dollar values of trade include estimates by the regional commissions and the Development Policy Analysis Division.

As of 1 January 1993, customs offices at the borders between States members of the EU, which used to collect and check customs declarations on national exports and imports, were abolished as the Single European Market went into effect. A new system of data collection for intra-EU trade, called INTRASTAT, has been put in place. INTRASTAT relies on information collected directly from enterprises and is linked with the system of declarations of value-added tax (VAT) relating to intra-EU trade to allow for quality control of statistical data. There nevertheless remains a discontinuity owing to the changes in methodology.

Estimates of trade values and volumes for the economies in transition are tentative for two reasons. First, there was a switch, mainly in 1991, from intraregional trade at arbitrarily set prices in transferable roubles to trade at world market prices in convertible currency. Second, many of the data-collection systems in the region are not yet up to world standards. These shortcomings mainly affect the reliability of calculations of changes in volumes for the CIS countries. Estimates for Central and Eastern European countries are produced by the Economic Commission for Europe (ECE).

Unit values that are used to determine the volume measures of exports and imports for groupings of developing countries are estimated in part from weighted averages of export prices of commodity groupings at a combination of three- and four-digit Standard International Trade Classification (SITC) levels, based on COMTRADE (the weights reflect the share of each commodity or commodity group in the value of the region's total exports or imports). Unit value and volume changes for Latin America and the Caribbean are supplied to the Division by the Economic Commission for Latin America and the Caribbean (ECLAC). Estimates for Africa draw in part upon IMF estimates for the *World Economic Outlook*.

LIST OF TABLES

I. GLOBAL OUTPUT AND MACROECONOMIC INDICATORS

Table A.1.

WORLD POPULATION, OUTPUT AND PER CAPITA GDP, 1980-1998

| | Growth of GDP (annual percentage change) | | | | Growth rate of population (annual percentage change) | | Population (millions) | | GDP per capita Exchange-rate basis (1993 dollars) | |
| | Exchange-rate basis (1993 dollars) | | Purchasing power parity (PPP) basis | | | | | | | |
	1981-1990	1991-1998	1981-1990	1991-1998	1981-1990	1991-1998	1980	1998	1980	1998
World	2.7	2.4	3.1	3.0	1.8	1.4	4367	5813	4078	4789
Developed economies *of which:*	2.9	2.0	2.8	2.1	0.6	0.5	756	839	18184	25649
United States	2.9	2.6	2.9	2.6	1.0	0.9	230	274	20551	28313
European Union[a]	2.3	1.7	2.3	1.7	0.3	0.3	355	374	15041	20838
Japan	4.0	1.3	4.0	1.3	0.6	0.2	117	126	23483	35873
Economies in transition[b]	1.5	-3.4	1.9	-3.4	0.7	0.1	378	411	2261	1206
Developing countries *by region:*	2.4	4.6	3.8	5.4	2.1	1.7	3233	4564	993	1278
Latin America	1.0	3.4	1.3	3.2	2.0	1.7	354	493	3262	3395
Africa	1.9	1.8	2.0	2.3	2.9	2.7	455	746	786	663
Western Asia	-2.2	2.4	-0.6	2.8	3.4	2.5	137	235	6224	3502
East and South Asia	7.2	6.8	6.7	4.9	1.9	1.5	2287	3090	369	920
Region excluding China *of which:*	6.6	5.2	5.8	7.1	2.2	1.7	1306	1857	510	1015
East Asia	7.1	5.3	6.5	5.1	1.9	1.6	414	568	1150	2506
South Asia	5.3	4.8	5.2	4.8	2.3	1.8	892	1289	213	358
China	9.1	10.8	9.1	10.8	1.5	1.0	981	1233	181	777
by analytical grouping:										
Net-creditor countries	1.5	4.3	1.3	4.1	3.2	2.0	37	59	10250	10393
Net-debtor countries	2.5	4.6	4.0	5.5	2.1	1.7	3196	4505	886	1158
Net fuel exporters	-0.7	2.5	1.1	3.0	2.6	2.1	559	855	2298	1695
Net fuel importers	4.1	5.4	4.9	6.1	2.0	1.6	2674	3730	720	1175
Memo items:										
Sub-Saharan Africa	1.7	1.7	1.2	2.6	3.0	2.9	262	440	438	353
Least developed countries	2.1	2.1	2.4	3.8	2.6	2.5	379	600	282	258

Source: UN/DESA.

[a] Including the eastern *Länder* (States) of Germany from 1991.
[b] Including the former German Democratic Republic until 1990.

Table A.2.
DEVELOPED ECONOMIES: RATES OF GROWTH OF REAL GDP, 1991-1999

Annual percentage change[a]

	1991-1998	1991	1992	1993	1994	1995	1996	1997	1998[b]	1999[c]
All developed economies	2.0	0.8	1.6	0.8	2.6	2.2	3.0	2.8	2.0	1¾
United States	2.6	-0.9	2.7	2.3	3.5	2.3	3.4	3.9	3.9	3½
Canada	2.1	-1.9	0.9	2.3	4.7	2.6	1.2	3.8	3.0	3
Japan	1.3	3.8	1.0	0.3	0.6	1.5	5.1	1.4	-2.9	-1½
Australia	3.2	-1.3	2.7	4.0	5.3	4.1	3.7	2.8	4.7	3
New Zealand	2.0	-2.3	0.6	5.1	5.5	3.3	2.7	2.0	-0.3	2½
EU-15	1.7	0.8	1.0	-0.6	2.8	2.4	1.6	2.5	2.7	2
EU-11	1.6	1.2	1.4	-1.0	2.5	2.3	1.4	2.4	2.8	2¼
Austria	2.1	3.4	1.3	0.5	2.4	1.7	2.0	2.5	3.3	2¼
Belgium	1.7	1.6	1.5	-1.5	2.6	2.3	1.3	3.0	2.9	1½
Finland	1.4	-7.1	-3.6	-1.2	4.6	5.1	3.6	6.0	4.7	3¼
France	1.6	0.8	1.2	-1.3	2.8	2.1	1.6	2.3	3.2	2¼
Germany	1.4	1.2	2.2	-1.1	2.3	1.7	0.8	1.8	2.3	2
Ireland	6.8	2.0	4.2	3.1	7.3	11.1	7.4	9.8	9.5	6¾
Italy	1.1	1.1	0.6	-1.2	2.2	2.9	0.7	1.5	1.4	1½
Luxembourg	4.2	3.1	1.8	8.7	4.2	3.8	3.0	4.8	4.7	3½
Netherlands	2.5	2.3	2.1	0.3	2.6	2.3	3.1	3.6	3.8	2
Portugal	2.4	2.3	1.9	-1.4	2.4	3.0	3.2	3.7	4.1	3
Spain	2.1	2.3	0.7	-1.2	2.3	2.7	2.4	3.5	3.8	3¼
Other EU	1.7	-1.1	-0.5	1.2	3.9	2.9	2.3	3.0	2.3	1
Denmark	2.5	1.4	1.3	1.6	3.6	3.1	3.5	3.5	2.3	1½
Greece	1.9	3.5	0.4	-0.9	1.5	2.0	1.8	3.2	3.5	3¾
Sweden	1.0	-1.1	-2.0	-2.2	3.3	3.9	1.3	1.8	2.9	2¼
United Kingdom	1.8	-2.0	-0.5	2.1	4.3	2.7	2.4	3.2	2.1	½
Other Europe										
Iceland	2.4	1.1	-3.4	1.0	3.7	1.0	5.5	5.0	5.6	4¼
Malta	4.5	6.3	4.7	4.5	4.0	9.0	4.2	1.6	2.0	1¾
Norway	3.7	3.1	3.3	2.7	5.5	3.9	5.5	3.4	2.0	1
Switzerland	0.4	-0.8	-0.1	-0.5	0.5	0.6	0.0	1.7	2.1	1
Memo item: Major industrialized countries	1.9	0.7	1.7	0.9	2.6	2.1	3.1	2.7	1.7	1¾

Source: UN/DESA, based on IMF, *International Financial Statistics.*

[a] Data for country groups are weighted averages, where weights for each year are the previous year's GDP valued at 1993 prices and exchange rates.
[b] Partly estimated.
[c] Forecast, partly based on Project LINK.

Table A.3.
ECONOMIES IN TRANSITION: RATES OF GROWTH OF REAL GDP, 1993-1999

Annual percentage change[a]	1993	1994	1995	1996	1997	1998[b]	1999[c]
Economies in transition	-6.1	-5.1	0.6	0.7	2.4	0.2	-½
Central and Eastern Europe and Baltic States	-2.3	3.9	5.6	4.0	3.7	2.6	1½
Central and Eastern Europe	-2.0	4.1	5.7	4.0	3.6	2.5	1½
Albania	9.7	8.3	13.3	9.0	-6.9	7.9	3
Bulgaria	-1.4	1.8	2.8	-10.2	-7.0	3.0	0
Croatia	-8.0	5.9	6.8	6.1	6.4	2.7	-1
Czech Republic	0.5	3.3	6.4	3.9	1.0	-2.7	-1
Hungary	-0.6	3.1	1.4	1.4	4.5	5.1	3½
Poland	3.8	5.1	7.1	6.0	6.9	4.8	3½
Romania	1.6	3.9	7.1	4.0	-6.9	-6.6	-4
Slovakia	-3.6	4.8	7.0	6.5	6.6	4.4	-2
Slovenia	2.9	5.3	4.2	3.5	4.5	4.0	3
The former Yugoslav Republic of Macedonia	-9.0	-1.9	-1.2	0.7	1.5	3.0	1½
Federal Republic of Yugoslavia	-30.8	2.7	6.0	5.9	7.5	2.6	..
Baltic States	-14.0	-4.2	2.1	4.0	7.7	4.1	1¼
Estonia	-9.0	-2.0	4.3	4.0	11.4	4.0	1
Latvia	-14.9	0.6	-0.8	3.3	6.5	3.8	1
Lithuania	-16.2	-9.8	3.3	4.7	6.1	4.4	1½
Commonwealth of Independent States	-9.5	-14.1	-5.4	-3.7	0.5	-3.4	-3¼
Armenia	14.8	5.4	6.9	5.8	3.1	5.5	4
Azerbaijan	-23.1	-19.7	-11.8	1.3	5.8	10.0	6
Belarus	-7.6	-12.6	-10.4	2.8	11.4	8.3	-1
Georgia	-25.4	-11.4	2.4	10.5	11.0	4.0	2
Kazakhstan	-9.2	-12.6	-8.2	0.5	1.7	-2.5	-3
Kyrgyzstan	-16.0	-20.0	-5.4	-7.1	9.9	4.6	3
Republic of Moldova	-1.2	-31.2	-3.0	-8.0	1.7	-5.0	-3
Russian Federation	-8.7	-12.7	-4.1	-3.5	0.8	-4.8	-4
Tajikistan	-11.0	-18.9	-12.5	-4.4	1.3	5.3	3
Turkmenistan	-10.0	-18.8	-8.2	-8.0	-26.0	4.5	5
Ukraine	-14.2	-23.0	-12.2	-10.0	-3.0	-1.7	-3
Uzbekistan	-2.3	-4.2	-0.9	1.6	2.4	2.8	1

Sources: UN/DESA and ECE.

a Country group aggregates are averages weighted by GDP in 1993 dollars (for methodology, see *World Economic Survey, 1992* (United Nations publication, Sales No. E.92.II.C.1 and corrigenda), annex, introductory text).
b Partly estimated.
c Forecast, based in part on Project LINK.

Table A.4.
DEVELOPING COUNTRIES: RATES OF GROWTH OF REAL GDP, 1991-1999

Annual percentage change										
	1991-1998	1991	1992	1993	1994	1995	1996	1997	1998[a]	1999[b]
Developing countries[c] *of which:*	4.6	3.2	5.0	5.2	5.7	4.8	5.7	5.5	1.7	2½
Latin America and the Caribbean	3.4	3.3	2.9	3.5	5.8	0.4	3.8	5.4	2.4	0
Net fuel exporter	3.1	4.6	4.0	2.1	3.8	-3.5	4.2	6.2	3.6	2
Net fuel importer	3.6	2.6	2.3	4.4	6.8	2.5	3.6	5.0	1.8	-1¼
Africa	1.8	0.8	-0.4	-0.6	2.0	2.8	4.5	2.7	2.5	3
Net fuel exporter	1.9	1.7	1.0	-1.8	0.5	3.7	3.7	3.2	3.0	3
Net fuel importer	1.7	0.2	-1.4	0.2	3.1	2.2	5.0	2.4	2.2	2¾
Western Asia	2.4	-5.0	5.5	4.3	-0.9	4.1	4.8	5.2	1.3	½
Net fuel exporter	1.4	-8.7	5.7	3.2	-0.2	2.0	4.0	5.2	0.4	-1
Net fuel importer	4.1	1.9	5.3	6.3	-2.0	7.6	5.9	5.2	2.6	3
East and South Asia	6.8	6.9	7.8	7.9	8.6	8.2	7.4	6.2	1.2	4¾
Region excluding China *of which:*	5.2	6.2	5.6	5.9	7.0	7.3	6.5	5.0	-1.9	3¼
East Asia	5.3	7.2	6.0	6.5	7.6	7.6	6.6	5.2	-4.1	2½
South Asia	4.8	2.9	4.2	3.9	5.2	6.2	6.0	4.6	5.5	5½
Memo items: Sub-Saharan Africa (excluding Nigeria and South Africa)	1.7	-0.3	-1.2	-3.0	1.8	4.2	5.0	4.0	3.1	3¾
Least developed countries	2.1	-0.5	0.5	-1.2	1.8	4.1	4.7	4.4	2.8	3
Major developing economies										
Argentina	5.7	8.9	8.7	6.0	8.3	-3.1	4.4	8.4	4.2	-1½
Brazil	2.4	0.1	-1.1	4.1	6.2	4.2	2.9	3.0	0.2	-2½
Chile	7.0	7.1	10.5	6.0	5.4	9.9	7.0	7.1	3.5	2
China	10.8	9.2	14.2	13.5	12.6	10.5	9.6	8.8	7.8	7½
Colombia	3.5	1.6	4.0	5.1	6.3	5.4	2.1	3.0	0.6	-¾
Egypt	3.5	2.3	2.5	2.0	2.3	3.2	4.0	5.9	5.7	4¾
Hong Kong SAR	4.0	5.1	6.3	6.1	5.3	4.7	4.8	5.2	-5.0	-½
India	4.9	2.0	4.0	3.9	5.4	6.7	6.4	5.1	5.6	6
Indonesia	4.2	7.0	6.5	6.5	7.5	8.1	8.0	4.7	-13.1	-2½
Iran (Islamic Republic of)	3.2	6.0	6.0	2.6	1.8	4.2	5.0	2.5	-2.5	-2½
Israel	4.8	6.2	6.6	3.4	6.6	7.1	4.5	2.1	1.9	2½
Korea, Republic of	5.4	9.1	5.1	5.8	8.6	8.9	7.1	5.5	-5.8	4½
Malaysia	6.4	8.6	7.8	8.3	9.2	9.5	8.2	7.8	-6.8	1½
Mexico	3.1	4.3	3.7	1.9	4.6	-6.2	5.5	7.0	4.8	3
Nigeria	2.8	4.8	3.0	2.3	1.3	2.2	3.3	3.1	2.8	3½
Pakistan	4.4	6.7	5.1	3.1	4.2	4.9	5.2	1.3	4.9	4½
Peru	5.2	2.6	-0.9	5.8	14.7	10.0	2.3	7.4	0.8	2½
Philippines	2.7	0.0	0.0	2.1	4.4	4.8	5.5	5.2	-0.5	2½
Saudi Arabia	1.5	6.0	3.0	1.6	-2.7	-0.2	4.0	3.0	-2.0	-2¼
Singapore	7.2	6.7	6.0	9.9	10.1	8.9	7.0	7.8	1.5	1
South Africa	1.1	-1.0	-2.2	1.3	2.7	3.4	3.2	1.7	0.0	1¼
Taiwan Province of China	6.3	7.6	6.8	6.3	6.5	6.1	5.6	6.8	4.8	4¾
Thailand	4.9	8.5	7.8	8.3	8.7	8.6	6.7	-0.4	-8.0	1¼
Turkey	4.0	0.8	5.0	8.1	-6.1	8.0	7.0	6.8	3.1	3½
Venezuela	2.4	9.7	6.1	0.7	-3.0	3.1	-1.3	5.1	-0.7	-¾

Source: United Nations.

[a]   Preliminary estimates.
[b]   Forecast, based in part on Project LINK.
[c]   Covering countries that account for 98 per cent of the population of all developing countries.

Table A.5.
DEVELOPED ECONOMIES: INVESTMENT, SAVING AND NET TRANSFERS, 1980-1997

Percentage of GDP		Gross domestic investment	Gross domestic saving	Net financial transfer
Total[a]	1980	23.5	23.7	-0.3
	1985	21.4	21.8	-0.4
	1990	22.1	22.1	-0.1
	1995	20.9	21.5	-0.6
	1996	20.6	21.4	-0.7
	1997	20.6	21.4	-0.8
Major industrialized countries[a]	1980	23.2	22.7	0.5
	1985	21.4	20.9	0.5
	1990	21.8	21.8	0.0
	1995	21.0	21.5	-0.5
	1996	20.8	21.1	-0.3
	1997	20.6	21.0	-0.4
European Union (15)	1980	22.9	22.0	0.9
	1985	19.5	20.9	-1.4
	1990	21.8	22.1	-0.4
	1995	19.3	21.1	-1.9
	1996	18.9	21.2	-2.2
	1997	18.9	21.2	-2.2
Germany[b]	1980	23.4	22.9	0.5
	1985	19.6	23.1	-3.5
	1990	21.4	27.3	-5.9
	1995	21.9	22.7	-0.8
	1996	20.7	21.9	-1.2
	1997	21.3	22.8	-1.5
Japan	1980	32.2	31.3	0.9
	1985	28.2	31.5	-3.4
	1990	32.3	33.0	-0.7
	1995	28.6	30.1	-1.5
	1996	29.9	30.5	-0.5
	1997	28.5	29.7	-1.2
United States of America	1980	20.0	19.4	0.6
	1985	20.1	17.2	3.0
	1990	16.9	15.5	1.4
	1995	17.2	15.7	1.4
	1996	17.5	16.0	1.5
	1997	18.1	16.7	1.5

Sources: OECD, *National Accounts;* and national information supplied to the United Nations Statistics Division.

[a]   National data converted to dollars for aggregation at annual average exchange rates.
[b]   Prior to 1991, data referring to Western Germany only.

Table A.6.
DEVELOPING ECONOMIES: INVESTMENT, SAVING AND NET TRANSFERS, 1980-1997

Percentage of GDP												
	Gross domestic investment				Gross domestic saving				Net transfer of resources			
	1980	1985	1990	1997	1980	1985	1990	1997	1980	1985	1990	1997
All developing countries by region:	25.8	23.6	25.2	26.9	28.7	24.1	25.7	26.5	-2.9	-0.5	-0.5	0.3
Africa	24.9	22.4	22.8	22.1	29.3	21.7	19.5	17.8	-4.4	0.7	3.2	4.3
Latin America	24.8	19.1	19.6	22.1	23.6	23.8	21.7	20.5	1.2	-4.8	-2.1	1.6
East and South Asia (excluding China)	26.1	24.3	29.2	29.6	24.1	24.5	28.9	28.8	2.0	-0.2	0.4	0.9
East Asia	29.6	25.1	31.8	31.9	29.7	28.6	33.0	32.1	-0.1	-3.5	-1.2	-0.2
South Asia	21.0	23.1	23.6	22.7	15.7	18.3	19.9	18.2	5.3	4.7	3.7	4.4
Western Asia	23.6	20.7	23.5	21.7	40.5	19.0	24.1	23.3	-16.9	1.7	-0.6	-1.6
by analytical grouping:												
Net-creditor countries	24.2	23.2	24.7	25.6	56.9	27.4	29.4	30.3	-32.7	-4.1	-4.7	-4.7
Net-debtor countries	26.0	23.6	25.3	27.0	24.4	23.7	25.3	26.1	1.7	-0.1	0.0	0.9
Net fuel exporters	25.2	22.1	24.0	24.3	37.4	23.9	25.8	25.9	-12.2	-1.8	-1.8	-1.6
Net fuel importers	24.6	21.2	24.3	25.2	20.6	21.8	23.8	23.0	4.0	-0.7	0.4	2.2
Four exporters of manufacturers	34.1	26.2	31.2	31.2	29.6	32.3	34.2	32.4	4.5	-6.0	-3.0	-1.2
Memo items:												
Sub-Saharan Africa	17.6	14.3	16.1	18.5	10.4	11.0	10.2	12.6	7.2	3.3	5.9	5.9
Least developed countries	19.4	15.5	16.4	19.1	7.0	5.4	7.2	10.0	12.4	10.1	9.2	9.1
Selected developing countries												
Argentina	25.3	17.6	14.0	20.1	23.8	23.1	19.7	18.4	1.4	-5.5	-5.7	1.7
Brazil	23.3	19.2	20.2	21.3	21.1	24.4	21.4	18.6	2.2	-5.2	-1.2	2.6
China	35.2	37.8	34.7	38.2	34.9	33.7	37.5	42.7	0.3	4.1	-2.8	-4.5
Egypt	27.5	26.7	28.8	17.7	15.2	14.5	16.1	13.0	12.4	12.1	12.7	4.7
India	21.0	24.2	25.2	24.0	17.4	21.1	22.4	20.0	3.5	3.1	2.8	4.0
Indonesia	24.1	26.1	30.8	30.9	38.0	28.6	33.2	30.6	-14.0	-2.5	-2.4	0.3
Korea, Republic of	31.6	29.6	36.9	35.0	24.2	30.9	36.4	34.2	7.4	-1.3	0.5	0.7
Mexico	27.2	20.8	23.1	26.4	24.9	25.9	22.0	26.4	2.3	-5.1	1.1	0.0
Nigeria	21.3	9.0	14.7	15.3	31.4	12.6	29.4	21.9	-10.2	-3.7	-14.6	-6.5
Peru	29.0	18.4	21.1	24.6	32.0	24.9	21.6	20.8	-3.0	-6.5	-0.4	3.8
South Africa	28.3	19.9	17.1	15.9	36.5	29.0	23.1	17.0	-8.2	-9.1	-6.0	-1.1
Thailand	29.1	28.2	41.4	35.0	22.9	25.5	33.8	35.7	6.3	2.7	7.5	-0.7
Turkey	18.2	16.5	24.3	25.1	11.4	13.4	20.1	19.3	6.8	3.1	4.3	5.8

Source: United Nations, based on World Bank, *1999 World Development Indicators* (CD-ROM), and United Nations Secretariat estimates.

Table A.7.
DEVELOPED ECONOMIES,[a] CENTRAL AND EASTERN EUROPE
AND BALTIC STATES: UNEMPLOYMENT RATES, 1991-1999

Percentage of total labour force									
	1991	1992	1993	1994	1995	1996	1997	1998[b]	1999[c]
All developed economies	6.6	7.6	8.0	8.0	7.6	7.7	7.4	7.0	6¾
United States	6.8	7.4	6.8	6.0	5.5	5.4	4.9	4.5	4¼
Canada	10.4	11.3	11.2	10.4	9.5	9.7	9.2	8.3	7¾
Japan	2.1	2.1	2.5	2.9	3.1	3.3	3.4	4.1	5
Australia	9.5	10.8	11.0	9.8	8.6	8.6	8.6	8.0	8
New Zealand	10.3	10.3	9.5	8.1	6.3	6.1	6.6	7.6	7¾
EU-15	7.9	9.6	10.9	11.5	11.0	11.3	11.0	10.3	9½
EU-11	7.9	9.6	11.0	12.1	11.8	12.3	12.3	11.4	10½
Austria	3.4	3.5	4.0	3.8	3.9	4.3	4.4	4.4	4¼
Belgium	6.6	7.3	8.9	10.0	9.9	9.7	9.2	8.8	8½
Finland	7.2	12.4	17.3	17.4	16.2	14.6	12.7	11.4	10½
France	9.4	10.4	11.7	12.3	11.6	12.3	12.5	11.8	11½
Germany[d]	4.2	7.7	8.1	9.6	9.3	10.8	11.7	10.7	9
Ireland	14.8	15.4	15.6	14.3	12.3	11.6	9.9	7.8	7
Italy	8.8	9.0	10.3	11.4	11.9	12.0	12.1	12.3	12
Luxembourg	1.7	2.1	2.7	3.2	2.9	3.0	2.8	2.8	2¾
Netherlands	5.8	5.6	6.6	7.1	6.9	6.3	5.2	4.0	3½
Portugal	4.0	4.2	5.7	7.0	7.3	7.3	6.8	4.9	4¾
Spain	16.4	18.5	22.7	24.1	22.9	22.2	20.8	18.8	17¼
Other EU	8.0	9.4	10.2	9.5	8.5	8.1	7.2	6.8	7
Denmark	8.5	9.2	10.1	8.2	7.2	6.8	5.6	5.1	4½
Greece[e]	7.7	8.7	9.7	9.6	10.0	10.3	10.4	10.3	9¾
Sweden	3.3	5.9	9.1	9.4	8.8	9.6	9.9	8.2	7½
United Kingdom	8.8	10.1	10.5	9.6	8.4	7.7	6.5	6.3	6½
Other Europe	3.2	4.1	4.7	4.4	4.1	4.3	4.2	3.6	3¼
Iceland	1.5	3.1	4.4	4.8	5.0	4.3	3.9	3.1	2¾
Malta[e]	3.6	4.0	4.5	4.0	3.6	3.7	4.4	4.5	0
Norway	5.6	6.0	6.1	5.5	5.0	4.9	4.1	3.3	4
Switzerland	2.0	3.1	4.0	3.8	3.5	3.9	4.2	3.7	3
Memo item:									
Major industrialized countries	6.2	7.1	7.2	7.2	6.8	7.0	6.8	6.5	6½

Table A.7 (continued)	1991	1992	1993	1994	1995	1996	1997	1998[b]	1999[c]
Central and Eastern Europe[f]									
Albania			22.0	18.0	12.9	12.3	14.9	17.6	15
Bulgaria			16.4	12.8	11.1	12.5	13.7	12.2	14
Croatia			16.6	17.3	17.6	15.9	17.6	18.6	15
Czech Republic			3.5	3.2	2.9	3.5	5.2	7.5	8½
Hungary			12.1	10.9	10.4	10.5	10.4	9.1	10½
Poland			16.4	16.0	14.9	13.2	10.3	10.4	12
Romania			10.4	10.9	9.5	6.6	8.8	10.3	12
Slovakia			14.4	14.8	13.1	12.8	12.5	15.6	16½
Slovenia			15.5	14.2	14.5	14.4	14.8	14.6	15
The former Yugoslav Republic of Macedonia			30.3	33.2	37.2	39.8	42.5	31.0	38
Yugoslavia			24.0	23.9	24.7	26.1	25.6	27.2	..
Baltic States[f]									
Estonia			5.0	5.1	5.0	5.6	4.6	5.1	5
Latvia			5.8	6.5	6.6	7.2	6.7	9.2	9
Lithuania			3.4	4.5	7.3	6.2	6.7	6.9	8

Sources: UN/DESA, based on data of OECD; national statistics and direct communications from national statistical offices to ECE secretariat.

[a]   Unemployment data are standardized by OECD for comparability among countries and over time, in conformity with the definitions of the International Labour Office (see OECD, *Standardized Unemployment Rates: Sources and Methods* (Paris, 1985)); national definitions and estimates are used for other countries.

[b]   Partly estimated.

[c]   Forecast.

[d]   Prior to January 1993, data do not include new *Länder* (States).

[e]   Not standardized.

[f]   Because of the comparability problem, figures are not given for the Commonwealth of Independent States.

Table A.8.
DEVELOPED ECONOMIES: CONSUMER PRICE INFLATION, 1991-1999[a]

Annual percentage change									
	1991	1992	1993	1994	1995	1996	1997	1998	1999[b]
All developed economies	4.3	3.2	2.8	2.2	2.3	2.1	2.1	1.4	1
United States	4.2	3.1	3.0	2.5	2.8	2.9	2.4	1.6	1¾
Canada	5.6	1.5	1.9	0.2	2.2	1.5	1.7	1.0	1
Japan	3.3	1.7	1.2	0.7	-0.1	0.2	1.7	0.6	-½
Australia	3.2	1.0	1.8	1.9	4.7	2.6	0.3	1.6	2
New Zealand	2.6	1.0	1.4	1.7	3.8	2.6	0.9	1.3	1¼
EU-15	4.9	4.4	3.6	3.0	3.0	2.5	2.1	1.7	1¼
EU-11	4.3	4.3	3.7	3.0	2.8	2.4	1.8	1.3	1¼
Austria	3.3	4.1	3.6	3.0	2.3	1.8	1.3	0.9	1
Belgium	3.2	2.4	2.7	2.4	1.4	2.1	1.6	1.0	1¼
Finland	4.1	2.6	2.2	1.1	0.9	0.6	1.3	1.4	1½
France	3.2	2.4	2.1	1.7	1.7	2.1	1.1	0.7	¾
Germany	3.6	5.1	4.4	2.7	1.9	1.5	1.8	0.9	1
Ireland	3.2	3.1	1.4	2.3	2.5	1.7	1.5	2.4	2¾
Italy	6.3	5.1	4.5	4.0	5.3	3.9	2.0	2.0	1½
Luxembourg	3.1	3.2	3.6	2.2	2.0	1.4	1.4	0.9	1
Netherlands	3.1	3.2	2.6	2.8	2.0	2.1	2.1	1.9	1½
Portugal	11.4	8.9	6.8	4.9	4.1	3.2	2.1	2.8	2¾
Spain	5.9	6.0	4.6	4.8	4.6	3.6	2.0	1.8	1¾
Other EU	7.1	4.6	3.1	3.3	3.8	2.7	2.9	3.1	1½
Denmark	2.4	2.1	1.3	2.0	2.0	2.2	2.1	1.8	2¼
Greece	19.5	15.8	14.5	10.9	8.9	8.2	5.5	4.8	3
Sweden	9.0	2.8	4.5	2.6	2.5	0.0	0.8	-0.1	0
United Kingdom	5.9	3.7	1.6	2.5	3.4	2.5	3.1	3.4	1½
Other Europe									
Iceland	6.8	3.9	4.1	1.6	1.6	2.3	1.8	1.7	1¾
Malta	2.5	1.7	4.1	4.2	4.0	2.6	3.1	3.9	3¼
Norway	3.4	2.3	2.3	1.5	2.5	1.2	2.6	2.2	2½
Switzerland	5.8	4.1	3.4	0.8	1.8	0.9	0.4	0.1	¼
Memo item:									
Major industrialized countries	4.1	3.0	2.6	2.1	2.2	2.1	2.2	1.4	1

Source: UN/DESA, based on data of IMF, *International Financial Statistics.*

[a]   Data for country groups are weighted averages, where weights for each year are consumption expenditure for the year valued at 1993 prices and exchange rates.
[b]   Forecasts.

Table A.9.
ECONOMIES IN TRANSITION: CONSUMER PRICE INFLATION, 1993-1999

Annual percentage change							
	1993	1994	1995	1996	1997	1998[a]	1999[b]
Central and Eastern Europe							
Albania	85.0	21.5	8.0	12.7	33.1	21.0	18
Bulgaria	72.9	96.2	62.1	123.1	1082.6	22.3	5¼
Croatia[c]	1516.6	97.5	2.0	3.6	3.7	6.0	6
Czech Republic	20.8	10.0	9.1	8.9	8.4	10.7	4½
Hungary	22.6	19.1	28.5	23.6	18.4	14.2	9
Poland	36.9	33.2	28.1	19.8	15.1	11.7	7½
Romania	256.2	137.1	32.2	38.8	154.9	59.3	46
Slovakia	23.1	13.4	10.0	6.0	6.2	6.7	12½
Slovenia[c]	31.7	21.0	13.5	9.9	8.4	8.0	6¼
The former Yugoslav Republic of Macedonia[c]	353.1	121.0	16.9	4.1	3.6	1.0	10
Yugoslavia	..[d]	..[d]	71.8	90.5	23.2	30.4	..
Baltics States							
Estonia	89.6	47.9	28.9	23.1	11.1	10.6	4
Latvia	109.1	35.7	25.0	17.7	8.5	4.7	3
Lithuania	410.1	72.0	39.5	24.7	8.8	5.1	2
Commonwealth of Independent States							
Armenia	3731.8	4964.0	175.5	18.7	13.8	8.7	10
Azerbaijan	1129.7	1129.7	1663.9	411.5	19.8	-0.8	4
Belarus	1190.9	2219.6	709.3	52.7	63.9	73.2	213
Georgia	4084.9	22470.6	177.6	39.4	6.9	3.6	20
Kazakhstan	1662.7	1879.5	175.9	39.1	17.4	7.3	6
Kyrgyzstan	1208.7	278.1	42.9	30.3	25.5	12.1	10
Republic of Moldova	1751.0	486.4	29.9	23.5	11.8	7.7	15
Russian Federation	875.0	309.0	197.4	47.8	14.7	27.8	100
Tajikistan	2884.8	350.3	682.1	422.4	85.4	43.1	12
Turkmenistan	3128.4	2562.1	1105.3	714.0	83.7	16.8	20
Ukraine	4734.9	891.2	376.7	80.2	15.9	11.0	45
Uzbekistan	1231.8	1550.0	315.5	56.3	73.2	29.0	29

Sources: ECE and UN/DESA.

[a] Partly estimated.
[b] Forecasts.
[c] Retail prices.
[d] Annual rates of hyperinflation of over 1 trillion percentage points.

Table A.10.
DEVELOPING COUNTRIES: CONSUMER PRICE INFLATION, 1991-1999[a]

Annual percentage change	1991	1992	1993	1994	1995	1996	1997	1998[b]	1999[c]
Developing countries by region:	81.6	132.9	253.9	134.6	20.9	16.8	11.0	10.8	11½
Africa	96.0	172.3	111.9	244.7	40.4	36.6	13.3	9.3	9¼
East and South Asia	7.7	7.0	8.3	12.0	9.9	6.7	4.5	7.9	4¾
Region excluding China *of which:*	9.5	7.2	5.7	7.1	6.9	6.1	5.2	11.4	6
East Asia	8.4	6.1	5.4	6.1	5.9	5.2	4.4	12.2	4¾
South Asia	13.0	10.9	6.6	10.0	10.2	8.9	7.8	9.1	9¾
Western Asia	27.9	29.0	27.0	41.6	40.7	33.0	30.7	26.5	35¼
Latin America and the Caribbean	210.6	354.1	757.8	326.4	23.5	19.5	11.7	9.0	11¾
Memo items:									
Sub-Saharan Africa (excluding Nigeria and South Africa)	283.3	532.6	336.2	780.3	86.9	94.9	30.3	17.0	16½
Least developed countries	366.0	687.1	430.4	997.7	103.5	119.0	35.7	19.6	19½
Major developing economies									
Argentina	171.7	24.9	10.6	4.2	3.4	0.2	0.5	0.9	0
Brazil	440.8	990.2	2186.3	930.0	25.0	11.1	6.0	3.5	10
China	3.3	6.4	14.7	24.1	17.1	8.3	2.8	-0.8	2
Hong Kong SAR	11.6	9.3	8.5	8.2	9.1	6.0	5.2	1.0	1¾
India	13.9	11.8	6.4	10.2	10.3	8.9	7.2	9.5	10½
Indonesia	9.4	7.5	9.7	8.5	9.5	8.0	6.7	57.6	20½
Israel	19.0	11.9	11.0	12.3	10.1	11.3	9.0	8.6	6
Korea, Republic of	9.3	6.2	4.8	6.2	4.5	4.9	4.4	8.6	2
Malaysia	4.4	4.7	3.6	3.7	5.3	3.5	3.3	5.4	4
Mexico	22.7	15.5	9.7	6.9	35.0	34.4	20.6	15.9	19½
Saudi Arabia	4.9	-0.1	1.0	0.6	4.9	1.2	0.1	0.1	4
South Africa	15.3	13.9	9.7	9.0	8.6	7.3	8.5	7.2	7¼
Taiwan Province of China	5.4	4.5	3.0	4.1	3.7	3.1	1.6	1.1	1¼
Thailand	5.7	4.1	3.4	5.1	5.8	5.9	5.6	8.0	2
Turkey	66.0	70.1	66.1	106.3	88.1	80.3	85.7	70.0	89

Source: UN/DESA, based on data of IMF, *International Financial Statistics.*

[a] Weights used are GDP in 1993 dollars.
[b] Preliminary estimates based on data for part of the year.
[c] Forecasts.

Table A.11.
MAJOR DEVELOPED ECONOMIES: FINANCIAL INDICATORS, 1991-1998

	1991	1992	1993	1994	1995	1996	1997	1998
Short-term interest rates[a] *(percentage)*								
Canada	7.4	6.8	3.8	5.5	5.7	3.0	4.3	5.1
France	9.5	10.4	8.8	5.7	6.4	3.7	3.2	3.4
Germany	8.8	9.4	7.5	5.4	4.5	3.3	3.2	3.4
Italy	12.2	14.0	10.2	8.5	10.5	8.8	6.9	5.0
Japan	7.5	4.6	3.1	2.2	1.2	0.5	0.4	0.4
United Kingdom	11.8	9.4	5.5	4.8	6.0	5.9	6.6	7.1
United States	5.7	3.5	3.0	4.2	5.8	5.3	5.5	5.4
Long-term interest rates[b] *(percentage)*								
Canada	9.8	8.8	7.9	8.6	8.3	7.5	6.4	5.7
France	9.1	8.6	6.9	7.4	7.6	6.4	5.6	4.7
Germany	8.6	8.0	6.3	6.7	6.5	5.6	5.1	4.4
Italy	13.2	13.3	11.3	10.6	12.2	9.4	6.9	4.9
Japan	6.5	4.9	3.7	3.7	2.5	2.2	1.7	1.1
United Kingdom	9.9	9.1	7.9	8.1	8.3	8.1	7.1	5.5
United States	7.9	7.0	5.8	7.1	6.6	6.4	6.4	5.3
General government financial balances[c] *(percentage)*								
Canada	-7.2	-8.0	-7.5	-5.5	-4.3	-2.0	0.9	2.0
France[d]	-2.0	-3.9	-5.7	-5.7	-4.9	-4.1	-3.0	-2.9
Germany[d,e]	-3.3	-2.6	-3.2	-2.4	-3.3	-3.4	-2.6	-2.1
Italy	-10.1	-9.6	-9.5	-9.2	-7.7	-6.6	-2.7	-2.7
Japan	2.9	1.5	-1.6	-2.3	-3.6	-4.3	-3.3	-6.1
United Kingdom	-2.8	-6.5	-8.0	-6.8	-5.8	-4.4	-2.0	0.6
United States	-3.3	-4.4	-3.6	-2.3	-1.9	-0.9	0.4	1.6

Sources: United Nations, based on IMF, *International Financial Statistics*; and OECD, *Economic Outlook*.

[a]   Money market rates.
[b]   Yield on long-term government bonds.
[c]   Surplus (+) or deficit (-) as a percentage of nominal GNP or GDP; some for 1998 are OECD estimates.
[d]   As of 1992, deficits are calculated using "Maastricht" definition.
[e]   Including balances of the German Railways Fund from 1994 onwards and the Inherited Debt Fund from 1995 onwards.

Table A.12.
SELECTED COUNTRIES: REAL EFFECTIVE EXCHANGE RATES, BROAD MEASUREMENT, 1991-1998[a]

1990 = 100	1991	1992	1993	1994	1995	1996	1997	1998
Major developed economies								
Australia	98.6	91.2	85.7	90.0	87.6	96.4	97.9	89.8
Austria	99.6	103.5	107.7	109.4	112.0	110.6	107.5	107.9
Belgium	100.6	104.3	106.4	110.1	113.0	111.7	107.5	108.5
Canada	97.6	91.4	89.0	88.7	92.3	91.5	92.6	90.4
Denmark	98.7	102.2	104.4	104.7	107.7	108.1	106.0	108.6
Finland	94.9	83.2	74.1	79.4	85.2	84.1	81.8	80.4
France	97.9	101.7	103.1	102.6	103.2	103.2	98.6	99.3
Germany	97.9	100.7	101.0	99.8	104.9	100.5	95.0	96.3
Greece	101.7	105.9	107.3	105.8	107.1	112.2	114.3	111.1
Ireland	98.3	101.5	96.2	97.6	97.7	100.1	100.8	98.2
Italy	101.0	98.4	85.0	83.3	81.1	91.5	91.3	93.5
Japan	104.8	106.7	121.7	126.5	127.5	108.8	103.4	100.2
Netherlands	97.8	100.9	103.8	103.8	105.3	103.3	99.0	100.7
New Zealand	97.2	89.9	93.5	100.0	107.5	117.8	121.3	106.0
Norway	99.8	101.8	99.8	98.7	101.0	100.6	102.5	97.8
Portugal	103.8	111.5	107.7	104.1	103.8	105.2	104.4	104.0
Spain	98.3	95.4	83.3	79.5	82.6	82.7	79.3	79.3
Sweden	98.6	97.2	81.5	83.7	90.7	95.4	91.4	91.8
Switzerland	100.8	101.0	104.7	111.1	117.7	115.9	108.7	110.9
United Kingdom	102.8	99.8	91.5	92.4	89.3	92.0	105.9	109.7
United States	101.2	101.1	103.3	100.6	95.7	100.2	106.4	113.8
Developing economies								
Argentina	115.4	113.4	115.0	111.4	108.9	112.8	120.4	122.6
Brazil	80.4	73.1	82.2	94.2	100.2	98.6	104.8	103.4
Chile	106.1	113.9	113.9	113.9	120.3	126.6	135.1	128.5
Colombia	103.3	108.7	110.2	118.3	117.1	121.5	132.8	126.1
Ecuador	107.3	111.7	128.8	137.4	134.7	136.8	148.1	152.0
Hong Kong SAR	103.5	106.3	111.7	114.5	113.0	121.2	131.5	137.3
India	85.5	78.9	75.3	77.8	75.3	74.7	82.3	79.7
Indonesia	101.0	99.6	101.6	100.3	98.8	103.5	96.7	47.7
Korea, Republic of	96.9	88.4	85.8	84.1	85.6	88.5	83.8	66.1
Kuwait	115.5	130.4	133.6	134.1	125.6	130.3	139.7	147.6
Malaysia	98.8	106.5	109.6	106.4	106.1	111.3	108.7	83.0
Mexico	106.2	107.8	116.6	112.2	78.9	89.8	102.8	102.3
Morocco	100.8	100.4	103.7	104.5	107.4	111.1	110.7	115.5
Nigeria	90.7	74.0	93.6	141.1	223.5	294.0	340.8	380.2
Pakistan	100.1	98.0	98.7	104.8	105.0	105.7	110.4	110.7
Peru	93.3	98.4	91.0	97.6	97.9	102.1	106.1	105.7
Philippines	97.0	105.7	97.4	104.3	103.5	114.7	109.1	91.7
Saudi Arabia	102.2	98.5	102.9	99.9	96.3	103.3	114.7	125.6
Singapore	102.5	105.3	106.2	109.2	110.3	115.0	117.0	113.0
South Africa	103.2	103.1	102.2	98.0	96.3	90.1	96.7	85.2
Taiwan Province of China	97.1	94.7	91.6	90.5	91.3	88.7	90.3	87.2
Thailand	102.4	98.7	100.2	99.5	97.7	105.6	97.6	88.5
Turkey	97.1	89.1	92.6	72.8	75.6	74.3	78.4	77.8
Venezuela	99.8	100.7	104.0	109.3	139.1	119.1	139.3	157.1

Source: Morgan Guaranty Trust Company, *World Financial Markets*.

[a]   Indices based on a "broad" measure currency basket of 22 OECD currencies and 23 developing-economy currencies (mostly Asian and Latin American). The real effective exchange rate, which adjusts the nominal index for relative price changes, gauges the effect on international price competitiveness of the country's manufactures due to currency changes and inflation differentials. A rise in the index implies a fall in competitiveness and vice versa. The relative price changes are based on indices most closely measuring the prices of domestically produced finished manufactured goods, excluding food and energy, at the first stage of manufacturing. The weights for currency indices are derived from 1990 bilateral trade patterns of the corresponding countries.

II. INTERNATIONAL TRADE

Table A.13.

WORLD TRADE: CHANGES IN VALUE AND VOLUME OF EXPORTS AND IMPORTS, BY MAJOR COUNTRY GROUP, 1991-1999

Annual percentage change									
	1991	1992	1993	1994	1995	1996	1997	1998[a]	1999[b]
Dollar value of exports									
World	2.5	7.1	0.1	13.5	19.4	4.3	3.5	-2.3	3
Developed economies	2.0	5.9	-2.6	12.5	18.9	2.6	2.3	0.3	3
of which:									
North America	5.3	6.1	4.7	11.2	14.6	6.4	9.3	-0.7	5¾
Western Europe	-0.5	5.4	-6.9	13.7	22.5	3.0	-1.5	1.8	2½
Japan	9.5	8.0	6.6	9.6	11.6	-7.3	2.5	-7.9	¼
Economies in transition	-14.1	8.9	5.6	17.5	29.1	8.0	2.2	-2.1	8
Central and Eastern Europe[c]	-7.5	7.5	◆8.8	16.3	30.1	5.7	6.5	13.5	9
Former Soviet Union/CIS[d]	-21.0	10.5	1.9	19.0	27.9	10.9	-1.8	-17.0	7
Developing countries	5.9	10.2	6.3	15.5	19.5	7.6	6.4	-6.5	2¼
Latin America and the Caribbean	0.6	6.7	9.4	16.4	20.9	10.2	10.4	-2.4	5¼
Africa	-2.8	1.1	-9.6	2.7	12.5	19.7	2.5	-15.0	-1
Western Asia	-9.0	7.4	-1.0	6.6	12.3	13.6	-5.7	-24.1	3½
East and South Asia	14.0	12.8	10.7	16.8	21.3	5.0	4.0	-6.9	1¾
China	15.8	18.1	7.1	33.1	22.9	1.6	20.8	0.5	0
Memo items:									
Fuel exporters	-5.4	5.2	-3.4	5.9	15.9	19.5	0.5	-9.9	3½
Non-fuel exporters	10.8	12.0	9.0	18.5	21.3	4.4	6.7	-4.7	1½
Dollar value of imports									
World	3.0	6.9	-1.2	13.3	19.4	4.8	2.8	-2.3	3¼
Developed economies	0.7	4.4	-5.8	13.4	18.0	3.6	2.6	1.9	4¼
of which:									
North America	-1.1	7.9	8.7	13.7	11.3	6.2	10.3	4.6	4½
Western Europe	1.5	3.9	-13.1	13.0	20.7	2.3	0.0	3.8	5¼
Japan	0.7	-1.6	3.6	13.9	22.0	4.0	-3.0	-17.2	-1½
Economies in transition	-16.7	5.2	0.8	13.0	33.4	13.9	9.0	0.5	1
Central and Eastern Europe[c]	-3.0	14.0	◆14.1	14.1	37.0	16.5	6.7	13.0	8¾
Former Soviet Union/CIS[d]	-30.1	-6.7	-21.3	10.2	24.4	6.7	15.9	-19.0	-16
Developing countries	12.4	14.0	9.7	13.0	21.0	6.3	4.3	-10.2	3½
Latin America and the Caribbean	17.8	22.2	11.6	18.6	11.6	9.7	16.2	5.2	-1
Africa	-1.3	9.6	-4.9	5.8	21.2	2.0	6.0	-1.0	3
Western Asia	9.5	11.1	6.3	-7.9	23.1	9.3	0.6	-6.4	3½
East and South Asia	14.0	11.9	10.0	18.4	24.8	5.3	2.0	-20.0	4¼
China	19.6	26.3	27.9	12.2	11.6	7.6	2.5	-1.5	7¾
Memo items:									
Fuel exporters	14.4	16.1	-1.6	3.9	9.5	7.8	7.1	-5.7	6¼
Non-fuel exporters	12.0	13.9	12.6	15.4	23.8	5.8	3.7	-12.0	2

Table A.13 (continued)

	1991	1992	1993	1994	1995	1996	1997	1998[a]	1999[b]
Volume of exports									
World	4.1	5.4	4.3	10.5	9.4	4.8	8.8	3.6	3
Developed economies	3.3	3.9	2.5	9.5	7.3	4.2	9.2	4.0	3¼
of which:									
North America	5.0	6.8	5.3	9.0	9.1	6.2	10.9	3.7	4¼
Western Europe	2.4	3.5	2.8	11.4	7.6	3.8	7.7	5.4	3
Japan	2.5	1.5	-2.4	1.7	3.3	0.6	9.6	-3.7	1½
Economies in transition	-18.0	11.0	5.7	2.7	13.7	6.0	-0.9	6.9	6¾
Central and Eastern Europe[c]	-8.1	8.5	◆8.9	0.2	16.7	4.5	0.8	15.0	8
Former Soviet Union/CIS[d]	-27.7	14.2	1.9	5.8	10.0	7.9	-2.9	0.2	6½
Developing countries	10.8	9.0	8.7	14.1	13.7	6.5	9.9	1.9	2
Latin America and the Caribbean	4.7	6.3	10.3	9.2	9.9	9.3	12.8	7.8	6
Africa	2.8	0.8	-0.9	11.7	7.3	8.2	5.2	-0.9	5
Western Asia	2.9	8.0	7.3	8.1	6.0	9.0	-0.7	-1.5	-¼
East and South Asia	15.8	10.5	10.6	14.5	16.6	5.8	9.3	0.1	1
China	18.2	15.7	6.8	31.0	18.9	2.4	26.3	4.1	-1¼
Memo items:									
Fuel exporters	6.1	6.9	2.6	5.7	9.0	15.1	4.9	1.2	2
Non-fuel exporters	12.7	10.0	9.1	15.0	16.5	5.9	11.3	2.9	1¾
Volume of imports									
World	4.4	5.9	4.9	10.5	7.8	6.1	9.0	3.0	4
Developed economies	2.5	4.4	1.1	11.1	7.0	4.9	8.7	5.9	5¼
of which:									
North America	-0.9	7.9	9.6	12.0	7.2	5.6	13.3	10.3	7
Western Europe	4.2	3.4	-2.8	10.0	5.9	4.4	7.6	6.1	5½
Japan	4.0	-0.4	2.9	13.6	12.5	3.5	2.7	-10.0	¼
Economies in transition	-22.5	0.8	0.8	9.6	9.9	13.8	9.0	2.0	¾
Central and Eastern Europe[c]	-2.5	12.0	◆14.3	13.0	11.4	17.9	7.6	10.0	7¾
Former Soviet Union/CIS[d]	-38.5	-13.4	-21.5	1.3	6.0	2.4	13.6	-15.0	-15
Developing countries	14.7	11.3	15.3	9.5	9.7	8.5	10.2	-4.7	2½
Latin America and the Caribbean	20.8	22.5	10.8	14.4	4.2	8.4	23.1	7.2	-2¼
Africa	-0.7	-0.3	-2.1	2.0	10.8	3.8	6.3	2.0	4
Western Asia	12.3	9.0	12.7	-11.1	11.3	11.8	6.4	-2.6	3
East and South Asia	16.8	9.7	17.4	14.8	12.5	8.2	8.4	-12.7	3
China	21.4	23.1	36.4	9.1	0.1	11.4	9.4	6.0	7¼
Memo items:									
Fuel exporters	16.7	13.6	4.1	-0.2	-1.0	11.2	13.8	-0.2	5½
Non-fuel exporters	14.9	11.6	20.2	11.9	11.6	8.7	10.1	-6.7	1

Source: United Nations, based on data of United Nations Statistics Division, ECE, ECLAC and IMF.

◆ Indicates break in the series.
a Preliminary estimates.
b Forecast.
c As of 1993, transactions between the Czech Republic and Slovakia are recorded as foreign trade.
d CIS countries since 1992.

Table A.14
DIRECTION OF TRADE: EXPORTS (F.O.B.), 1985-1998

		Destination[a]													
		World[b]	Devd.	EU	US	Japan	EIT	EE	CIS	RF	Devg.	LAC	Africa	SSA	WA	ESA
		Bn. $	Percentage													
World[b]	1985	1874.5	68.1	34.0	17.5	5.9	..	..	..	..	23.9	4.5	3.7	1.0	5.0	8.7
	1990	3378.4	72.2	40.0	14.5	6.1	..	..	..	..	22.9	3.9	2.8	0.8	3.5	11.3
	1995	5068.5	65.4	34.6	14.8	5.9	4.1	2.2	1.7	1.0	29.2	4.9	2.3	0.6	3.2	15.7
	1996	5281.0	64.8	33.8	15.1	6.0	4.5	2.4	1.8	1.1	29.4	5.2	2.3	0.6	3.4	15.5
	1997	5612.0	64.6	34.6	15.5	5.4	4.6	2.4	1.9	1.1	29.5	5.6	2.2	0.6	3.4	15.2
	1998[c]	5608.6	66.0	36.0	16.1	4.6	5.0	2.7	1.9	1.1	27.6	6.0	2.3	0.7	3.5	12.9
Developed	1985	1276.5	72.7	38.6	16.8	3.5	..	..	..	..	23.0	4.6	4.1	1.0	5.1	7.4
economies	1990	2438.1	76.4	45.8	12.4	4.2	..	..	..	..	20.0	3.9	2.8	0.7	3.3	9.1
(Devd.)	1995	3315.3	70.6	41.6	12.4	3.9	3.4	2.3	1.0	0.8	25.0	5.1	2.4	0.5	3.1	12.6
	1996	3420.1	70.1	40.9	12.5	3.9	3.9	2.5	1.1	0.8	25.1	5.4	2.3	0.5	3.4	12.3
	1997	3625.9	70.1	41.8	12.7	3.6	4.1	2.6	1.2	0.9	24.9	5.9	2.1	0.5	3.5	11.8
	1998[c]	3703.7	71.8	43.3	13.4	3.1	4.4	2.9	1.2	0.9	22.8	6.3	2.2	0.5	3.5	9.1
of which:																
European Union	1985	637.3	79.3	50.2	13.8	1.5	..	..	..	..	18.0	2.1	4.6	1.2	6.1	5.6
(EU)	1990	1350.8	82.0	54.9	10.9	2.5	..	..	..	..	15.3	1.7	3.1	0.9	4.5	7.5
	1995	1752.7	76.8	50.4	10.0	2.7	3.6	2.2	1.0	0.8	17.2	1.9	2.6	0.7	4.2	10.0
	1996	1785.1	75.9	50.4	10.3	2.8	3.9	2.3	1.1	0.8	17.7	1.9	2.5	0.7	4.7	10.0
	1997	1942.5	74.4	49.1	10.6	2.6	4.2	2.4	1.3	1.0	18.4	2.2	2.5	0.7	5.4	10.0
	1998[c]	2021.5	75.2	50.1	11.3	2.0	4.5	2.6	1.3	0.9	17.3	2.5	2.5	0.6	5.1	8.7
United States	1985	327.5	61.4	22.0	..	10.6	..	..	..	..	36.6	14.5	3.5	0.8	5.2	11.5
(US)	1990	491.5	63.9	23.7	..	12.4	..	..	..	..	34.6	13.7	2.0	0.4	3.4	14.2
	1995	752.2	57.3	19.0	..	11.0	1.1	0.4	0.6	0.5	41.5	16.5	1.7	0.3	3.5	17.8
	1996	795.9	56.5	18.4	..	10.8	1.2	0.4	0.8	0.5	42.2	17.5	1.7	0.3	3.7	17.3
	1997	867.3	55.5	20.6	..	9.6	1.2	0.4	0.7	0.5	43.3	19.4	1.7	0.3	3.6	16.7
	1998[c]	904.5	56.7	22.2	..	8.6	1.2	0.4	0.7	0.6	42.0	21.1	1.5	0.3	4.1	13.1
Japan	1985	110.2	58.0	12.2	37.6	..	..	..	..	..	39.4	4.4	2.2	0.5	6.5	19.4
	1990	207.6	58.6	19.1	31.7	..	..	..	..	..	40.1	3.4	1.9	0.4	3.5	29.2
	1995	298.7	47.7	14.8	27.5	..	0.5	0.2	0.3	0.3	51.7	4.2	1.7	0.3	2.2	38.6
	1996	314.5	47.1	14.3	27.5	..	0.5	0.2	0.3	0.2	52.3	4.1	1.4	0.3	2.7	38.7
	1997	305.0	48.3	15.6	28.1	..	0.6	0.3	0.3	0.2	51.1	4.7	1.3	0.3	2.9	36.9
	1998[c]	257.7	53.9	18.4	30.4	..	0.7	0.3	0.3	0.3	45.4	5.2	1.4	0.3	3.6	29.8
Economies in	1995	210.0	50.7	40.0	3.9	1.8	34.9	12.9	19.8	8.6	13.6	1.0	1.3	0.1	3.9	4.0
transition	1996	237.0	50.1	39.3	4.4	1.6	35.1	13.0	19.3	8.4	13.6	1.2	1.4	0.1	4.0	3.4
(EIT)	1997	260.4	51.6	43.2	3.8	1.5	34.6	12.4	19.1	8.0	13.3	1.1	1.2	0.1	4.2	3.1
	1998[c]	279.5	51.4	43.3	4.2	1.2	34.6	12.4	19.1	7.9	13.5	1.1	1.4	0.2	4.4	2.6
of which:																
Eastern Europe	1995	113.3	63.1	56.4	2.5	0.3	26.6	17.9	7.9	4.8	9.0	1.0	1.8	0.2	3.2	2.5
(EE)	1996	126.5	63.2	56.6	2.5	0.3	27.2	17.6	8.0	4.8	9.1	1.0	2.0	0.2	3.0	2.5
	1997	137.2	66.0	60.6	2.8	0.4	26.5	16.3	8.6	5.1	7.3	0.7	1.4	0.2	2.7	2.0
	1998[c]	149.9	67.0	60.6	3.4	0.5	26.1	16.5	7.8	4.1	6.7	0.8	1.3	0.1	2.4	1.6

Table A.14 (continued)		World[b]	Devd.	EU	US	Japan	EIT	EE	CIS	RF	Devg.	LAC	Africa	SSA	WA	ESA
		Bn. $	Destination[a] — Percentage													

		World[b] Bn. $	Devd.	EU	US	Japan	EIT	EE	CIS	RF	Devg.	LAC	Africa	SSA	WA	ESA
Commonwealth of Independent States (CIS)	1995	85.8	40.7	26.5	5.2	3.1	41.0	9.5	28.7	11.0	18.0	1.1	0.9	..	4.7	6.4
	1996	95.2	39.6	25.2	6.1	2.7	40.7	10.0	27.5	10.7	17.9	1.3	0.9	..	4.9	4.8
	1997	104.5	38.6	27.3	4.7	2.6	41.6	9.9	27.8	10.2	19.0	1.4	1.1	0.1	5.7	5.0
	1998c	108.6	35.7	26.0	5.1	2.0	42.9	9.3	29.6	11.2	20.7	1.5	1.5	0.2	6.6	4.2
of which: Russian Federation (RF)	1995	52.8	49.6	31.6	6.6	4.1	31.8	10.5	18.5	..	18.2	1.2	0.9	..	4.1	6.3
	1996	58.0	48.9	30.7	7.6	3.5	33.4	11.4	18.4	..	16.5	1.4	0.8	..	4.3	4.7
	1997	63.6	47.1	32.9	5.8	3.4	36.0	11.6	19.5	..	16.4	1.5	0.9	0.1	4.7	4.3
	1998c	63.2	45.1	32.2	6.4	2.8	37.2	11.2	20.9	..	17.4	1.6	1.2	0.2	5.1	3.3
Developing countries (Devg.)	1985	447.4	64.0	26.0	23.0	13.4	..	..	..	..	30.6	4.9	2.9	1.0	5.4	13.9
	1990	774.4	61.6	23.8	22.4	12.6	..	..	..	..	34.1	4.2	2.6	1.0	4.1	19.1
	1995	1479.0	55.1	17.1	22.3	11.2	1.4	0.6	0.8	0.6	41.4	5.1	2.4	0.9	3.2	24.7
	1996	1553.0	54.8	16.9	22.5	11.1	1.5	0.6	0.9	0.6	41.5	5.3	2.3	1.0	3.2	24.6
	1997	1657.9	54.3	17.3	23.3	10.2	1.6	0.7	0.9	0.7	42.1	5.7	2.5	1.0	3.1	24.6
	1998c	1550.3	55.2	18.6	24.1	8.5	1.8	0.7	1.0	0.6	40.6	6.0	2.7	1.1	3.2	22.0
of which: Latin America and the Caribbean (LAC)	1985	83.8	71.7	22.0	40.0	5.2	..	..	..	..	22.4	13.4	2.8	0.6	2.6	2.9
	1990	131.5	71.9	22.4	38.8	5.6	..	..	..	..	24.7	17.1	1.6	0.3	2.1	4.6
	1995	249.5	68.6	15.1	44.6	4.0	0.9	0.4	0.5	0.5	28.7	20.2	1.3	0.2	1.3	4.7
	1996	272.6	68.5	13.4	47.3	3.5	1.1	0.5	0.6	0.5	28.6	20.4	1.3	0.2	1.3	4.3
	1997	315.0	68.5	13.3	48.5	3.3	1.1	0.4	0.6	0.5	28.2	20.7	1.4	0.2	1.2	3.7
	1998c	335.7	66.8	13.6	45.8	2.8	1.4	0.5	0.9	0.7	29.3	22.1	1.4	0.2	1.3	3.1
Africa	1985	69.6	72.8	50.3	14.7	2.9	..	..	..	..	13.3	3.2	4.2	2.1	2.5	1.8
	1990	92.9	71.0	46.5	14.8	3.0	..	..	..	..	14.3	1.1	7.0	3.6	2.3	2.8
	1995	118.1	66.5	43.6	13.3	2.9	1.4	1.0	0.4	0.2	23.5	1.9	10.6	7.4	3.1	6.8
	1996	119.0	66.6	42.2	14.1	2.9	1.4	0.9	0.4	0.2	25.1	2.5	10.6	7.5	3.5	7.6
	1997	123.7	64.8	43.7	15.0	2.7	1.6	0.9	0.6	0.3	26.2	2.8	10.8	7.9	3.5	7.6
	1998c	130.4	62.4	44.4	12.6	2.8	1.7	0.9	0.7	0.3	27.8	2.8	12.0	8.8	3.6	7.6
of which: Sub-Saharan Africa (SSA)	1985	18.2	75.2	47.3	17.8	2.6	..	..	..	..	19.2	2.9	9.5	6.4	1.1	3.9
	1990	25.7	74.0	44.0	18.7	3.2	..	..	..	..	22.0	1.9	12.9	8.9	1.0	5.0
	1995	31.6	69.3	39.9	19.0	3.4	1.5	0.9	0.5	0.3	27.2	1.3	14.3	9.0	1.8	6.3
	1996	33.9	67.8	37.3	19.5	2.6	1.7	1.0	0.6	0.4	29.1	2.3	14.7	9.6	1.7	7.1
	1997	35.4	64.6	38.9	21.3	2.5	2.7	1.4	1.2	0.9	31.0	1.7	15.2	10.5	1.8	6.8
	1998c	37.9	62.7	41.5	16.8	2.5	2.8	1.6	0.9	0.5	32.7	1.4	17.6	12.3	2.0	7.8
Western Asia (WA)	1985	94.6	57.7	27.8	6.3	20.5	..	..	..	..	32.5	4.2	2.6	1.1	11.7	13.7
	1990	117.3	59.7	24.0	13.7	17.7	..	..	..	..	31.3	3.0	2.9	0.7	10.5	14.1
	1995	162.5	54.9	22.6	11.4	17.1	3.5	1.3	2.1	1.2	38.4	1.8	3.4	0.8	9.4	22.4
	1996	177.9	53.1	22.3	10.2	17.5	3.4	1.1	2.3	1.1	38.8	1.3	2.7	0.8	8.1	25.1
	1997	191.4	51.1	21.0	10.7	16.8	3.7	1.1	2.5	1.3	38.9	1.3	3.7	0.9	7.0	25.0
	1998c	195.9	49.6	22.9	11.3	13.1	3.9	1.0	2.8	1.1	37.3	1.2	3.9	1.0	7.7	22.2

Table A.14 (continued)		Destination[a]														
		World[b]	Devd.	EU	US	Japan	EIT	EE	CIS	RF	Devg.	LAC	Africa	SSA	WA	ESA
		Bn. $	Percentage													
East and	1985	145.2	62.5	12.0	30.2	16.2	..	..	..	..	33.9	1.5	2.0	0.7	4.3	26.1
South Asia	1990	332.7	60.7	16.8	24.7	14.4	..	..	..	..	36.2	1.4	1.6	0.6	2.4	30.9
(including	1995	697.5	50.5	14.2	20.2	11.5	1.2	0.4	0.6	0.5	47.1	2.3	1.6	0.5	2.8	41.6
China)	1996	726.6	49.5	14.0	19.5	11.5	1.3	0.4	0.7	0.6	47.9	2.5	1.6	0.5	2.8	42.2
(ESA)	1997	748.7	49.7	15.1	20.1	10.3	1.5	0.5	0.7	0.5	48.5	2.8	1.7	0.6	2.8	42.5
	1998[c]	609.3	51.9	16.7	21.9	8.6	1.6	0.6	0.7	0.5	46.0	3.0	2.1	0.8	2.9	39.6

Source: UN/DESA, based on IMF, *Direction of Trade Statistics*.

[a]   Owing to incomplete specification of destinations in underlying data, shares of trade to destinations do not add up to 100 per cent.
[b]   Including data for EITs; before 1994, data for EITs are highly incomplete.
[c]   Estimates.

Table A.15.
COMPOSITION OF WORLD MERCHANDISE TRADE: EXPORTS, 1985-1997

Billions of dollars and percentage

							Primary commodities										
									of which:								
	Total exports (billions of dollars)			Total			Food			Agricultural raw materials			Fuels		
Exporting country group	1985	1990	1997	1985	1990	1997	1985	1990	1997	1985	1990	1997	1985	1990	1997
World (billions of dollars)	1606.3	2848.5	5490.4	596.1	797.5	1127.9	160.2	268.8	425.6	77.7	119.2	173.7	332.1	372.7	458.8
World (percentage share)				100.0	100.0	100.0	100.0	100.0	100.0	100.0	100.0	100.0	100.0	100.0	100.0
Developed economies	1021.1	1865.1	3600.6	40.0	45.1	49.4	59.4	63.0	63.9	60.5	62.2	61.8	24.6	23.0	30.2
Economies in transition[a]	89.4	124.6	230.0	7.2	6.1	7.2	3.4	3.5	3.6	5.1	5.3	6.5	9.7	8.2	11.0
Developing countries	495.7	858.9	1659.8	52.7	48.8	43.4	37.2	33.5	32.4	34.4	32.5	31.7	65.7	68.8	58.8
Africa	78.1	92.5	122.4	11.5	8.5	7.1	6.1	4.1	3.7	4.6	5.1	3.9	16.0	13.7	11.4
Latin America	107.6	154.3	299.9	12.7	11.0	11.7	16.1	14.5	14.3	8.0	7.3	8.9	11.9	9.3	9.8
East and South Asia	210.8	459.1	1051.7	13.7	13.4	13.2	12.9	13.1	12.5	20.3	19.0	17.8	12.7	12.3	12.2
of which:															
East Asia	159.0	333.7	774.8	9.4	9.0	9.2	7.8	8.0	7.4	15.3	13.9	14.0	9.0	8.3	9.2
South Asia	24.5	63.3	94.3	1.8	2.2	1.6	2.5	2.3	2.0	1.8	2.3	1.3	1.4	2.4	1.4
China	27.3	62.1	182.6	2.4	2.2	2.4	2.6	2.8	3.2	3.2	2.7	2.5	2.2	1.6	1.6
Western Asia	99.2	153.0	185.8	14.8	16.0	11.4	2.2	1.9	1.9	1.4	1.1	1.2	25.1	33.6	25.4
Memo items:															
Sub-Saharan Africa	22.5	29.7	34.6	3.1	2.6	2.3	4.6	2.6	2.4	3.0	3.1	2.6	2.3	2.3	2.2
Least developed countries	24.3	58.4	61.5	2.5	2.9	1.9	2.4	2.0	1.2	2.4	3.0	2.1	2.4	3.9	2.5

Table A.15 (continued)

Exporting country group	Total (billions of dollars)			Manufactures											
				of which:											
				Textiles			Chemicals			Machinery and transport			Metals		
	1985	1990	1997	1985	1990	1997	1985	1990	1997	1985	1990	1997	1985	1990	1997
World (billions of dollars)	983.4	1992.0	4183.4	86.8	178.2	342	120.5	236.4	512.7	472.4	953.1	2134	88.3	152.7	258.8
World (percentage share)	100.0	100.0	100.0	100.0	100.0	100.0	100.0	100.0	100.0	100.0	100.0	100.0	100.0	100.0	100.0
Developed economies	77.1	73.3	70.1	46.2	42.1	39.2	82.7	81.0	80.8	83.8	79.7	74.7	70.3	65.2	63.1
Economies in transition[a]	4.6	3.7	3.2	3.3	2.1	4.3	4.9	3.6	3.5	4.8	3.7	1.8	7.2	8.5	13.2
Developing countries	18.3	23.0	26.6	50.5	55.7	56.5	12.4	15.4	15.6	11.4	16.5	23.6	22.3	26.3	23.7
Africa	1.3	1.1	0.8	2.0	2.5	2.5	1.8	1.4	0.9	0.3	0.3	0.2	5.5	6.2	3.2
Latin America	3.4	3.3	3.9	3.2	3.4	5.7	3.7	2.9	2.8	2.6	2.6	3.6	8.5	9.4	7.9
East and South Asia	12.5	17.3	20.6	42.3	47.3	44.7	5.0	8.2	10.0	8.0	13.2	19.1	6.9	8.7	10.8
of which:															
East Asia	10.1	12.9	15.6	28.5	30.4	26.3	3.2	4.7	6.9	7.2	10.3	17.1	6.0	6.1	7.0
South Asia	1.1	2.2	1.3	5.3	5.7	6.4	0.7	2.0	1.1	0.6	1.5	0.5	0.5	1.2	0.9
China	1.2	2.2	3.7	8.5	11.2	12.0	1.2	1.6	2.0	0.2	1.4	1.5	0.5	1.4	2.9
Western Asia	1.2	1.3	1.3	3.0	2.5	3.6	1.9	2.9	1.9	0.5	0.4	0.6	1.4	2.0	1.9
Memo items:															
Sub-Saharan Africa	0.4	0.5	0.2	0.5	0.5	0.5	0.4	0.3	0.1	0.1	0.2	0.1	2.4	2.2	0.6
Least developed countries	0.7	1.6	0.5	1.6	1.6	1.0	0.6	1.6	0.3	0.6	1.6	0.4	2.3	2.6	0.6

Source: UN/DESA.

[a] Data for 1997 including trade flows between the States of the former USSR. Prior to 1992, these flows were considered internal.

Table A.16.
COMPOSITION OF WORLD MERCHANDISE TRADE: IMPORTS, 1985-1997

Billions of dollars and percentage

Importing country group	Total imports (billions of dollars)			Primary commodities Total			Food			Agricultural raw materials			Fuels		
	1985	1990	1997	1985	1990	1997	1985	1997	1996	1985	1990	1997	1985	1990	1997
World (billions of dollars)	1606.3	2848.5	5490.4	596.1	797.5	1127.9	160.2	268.8	425.6	77.7	119.2	173.7	332.1	372.7	458.8
World (percentage share)				100.0	100.0	100.0	100.0	100.0	100.0	100.0	100.0	100.0	100.0	100.0	100.0
Developed economies	1090.0	1941.6	3593.0	71.9	68.6	66.7	65.1	66.2	68.3	64.5	66.0	63.0	76.2	69.0	66.3
Economies in transition[a]	92.3	128.9	257.3	5.8	5.5	5.9	7.6	8.2	6.5	6.7	3.9	3.6	4.5	4.2	6.2
Developing countries	424.0	778.0	1640.1	22.3	25.9	27.4	27.3	25.6	25.2	28.8	30.1	33.4	19.2	26.8	27.4
Africa	60.3	98.8	103.8	3.1	3.0	2.3	6.1	4.9	3.5	4.1	3.7	2.9	1.5	1.4	1.1
Latin America	75.1	110.7	321.5	4.3	4.4	5.3	4.4	4.7	5.5	4.2	3.9	6.0	4.4	4.5	5.1
East and South Asia	204.3	467.3	1034.9	11.0	15.2	16.8	9.2	10.9	12.2	17.2	19.8	21.1	10.7	18.3	19.3
of which: East Asia	142.0	379.1	834.1	7.9	12.0	12.5	6.9	8.6	10.3	11.2	13.7	13.3	7.4	13.4	14.3
South Asia	24.8	37.5	59.1	2.3	1.9	1.9	1.3	0.9	0.8	3.0	2.8	2.2	3.2	4.5	2.9
China	37.5	50.7	141.7	0.8	1.2	2.5	1.0	1.3	1.1	3.1	3.4	5.6	0.1	0.3	2.1
Western Asia	84.3	101.2	179.9	4.0	3.3	3.0	7.6	5.2	4.0	3.2	2.8	3.3	2.7	2.7	1.9
Memo items: Sub-Saharan Africa	20.6	29.6	33.3	1.1	1.0	0.7	2.2	1.5	1.1	0.9	0.8	0.7	0.8	0.7	0.4
Least developed countries	18.6	27.4	25.9	1.4	1.0	0.6	2.1	1.6	0.9	1.3	1.7	0.7	1.8	2.7	0.5

Table A.16 (continued)															
	Manufactures														
	Total (billions of dollars)			*of which:*											
				Textiles			Chemicals			Machinery and transport			Metals		
Importing country group	1985	1990	1997	1985	1990	1997	1985	1990	1997	1985	1990	1997	1985	1990	1997
World (billions of dollars)	983.4	1992.0	4183.4	86.8	178.2	342.0	120.5	236.4	512.7	472.4	953.1	2133.9	88.3	152.7	258.8
World (percentage share)	100.0	100.0	100.0	100.0	100.0	100.0	100.0	100.0	100.0	100.0	100.0	100.0	100.0	100.0	100.0
Developed economies	65.6	68.0	65.5	69.9	69.5	67.3	60.1	61.6	63.5	65.2	66.8	64.8	58.3	63.9	61.7
Economies in transition[a]	5.7	4.2	4.0	5.3	2.6	3.9	6.6	4.4	5.0	5.9	5.1	3.6	8.4	4.4	4.3
Developing countries	28.6	27.9	30.6	24.7	27.9	28.8	33.3	34.0	31.5	28.9	28.1	31.7	33.2	31.7	34.0
Africa	4.0	3.6	1.8	2.6	2.5	1.7	4.7	4.5	2.2	4.3	4.0	1.8	3.2	3.2	2.0
Latin America	4.9	3.8	6.1	2.3	2.1	4.5	7.3	5.9	7.5	5.6	4.0	6.3	3.4	3.4	4.9
East and South Asia	13.7	16.9	19.3	13.5	19.8	19.3	16.2	19.4	18.4	13.5	16.9	20.2	19.5	20.0	23.2
of which:															
East Asia	9.4	13.8	15.8	10.9	15.8	14.9	10.5	14.7	13.2	9.4	14.1	17.2	8.9	14.9	17.9
South Asia	1.3	1.0	0.8	0.7	0.9	0.4	2.7	2.0	1.5	1.1	0.7	0.6	2.2	3.1	1.5
China	3.0	2.0	2.7	1.8	3.1	4.0	3.1	2.7	3.7	3.0	2.1	2.5	8.4	2.1	3.8
Western Asia	6.0	3.6	3.4	6.2	3.5	3.4	5.1	4.1	3.3	5.6	3.2	3.3	7.1	5.0	3.9
Memo items:															
Sub-Saharan Africa	1.4	1.1	0.6	1.2	0.8	0.6	1.6	1.1	0.7	1.6	1.3	0.6	0.8	0.7	0.5
Least developed countries	1.2	1.0	0.4	1.3	1.2	0.5	1.3	0.9	0.4	1.4	1.1	0.5	0.9	2.2	0.5

Source: UN/DESA.

[a] Data for 1997 including trade flows between the States of the former USSR. Prior to 1992, these flows were considered internal.

Table A.17.
INDICES OF PRICES OF PRIMARY COMMODITIES, 1980-1998

Annual percentage change[a]

			Non-fuel commodities[b]					Manufac-tured export prices[c]	Real prices of non-fuel commodities[d]	*Memo item:* crude petroleum[e]
	Food	Tropical beverages	Vegetable oilseeds and oils	Agricultural raw materials	Minerals and metals	Combined index Dollar	SDR			
1980	65.5	-6.3	-13.3	10.6	11.6	27.6	27.6	11.1	14.9	21.5
1981	-20.0	-17.8	-4.3	-12.5	-16.0	-17.0	-9.0	-6.0	-11.7	-3.5
1982	-31.8	-5.2	-19.6	-13.4	-13.2	-21.8	-16.4	-2.1	-20.1	-7.2
1983	5.3	4.3	18.9	6.8	7.6	6.3	9.8	-3.3	9.9	-10.3
1984	-15.9	14.6	34.6	0.9	-7.1	-3.4	0.0	-3.4	0.0	-2.9
1985	-13.8	-9.1	-30.6	-9.9	-4.8	-12.3	-10.7	0.0	-12.3	-4.2
1986	10.0	24.0	-38.0	2.0	-5.0	4.0	-10.0	19.8	-13.2	-49.9
1987	6.4	-34.7	17.7	16.7	18.9	2.9	-6.7	12.6	-8.7	31.0
1988	29.9	1.2	31.5	8.4	45.1	26.2	21.4	8.2	16.6	-19.7
1989	5.9	-14.6	-11.5	0.0	0.0	0.0	4.9	-1.1	1.1	21.6
1990	-6.2	-11.4	-12.9	4.7	-9.8	-5.9	-11.2	9.9	-14.4	28.6
1991	-6.6	-8.1	8.1	-0.7	-9.5	-6.3	-7.4	0.0	-6.3	-16.4
1992	-2.1	-14.0	7.5	-3.7	-3.7	-3.4	-5.7	3.0	-6.2	-1.0
1993	0.7	6.1	0.0	-6.2	-14.7	-3.5	-2.4	-5.8	2.5	-11.4
1994	10.1	75.0	24.4	15.7	12.7	18.0	13.6	2.1	15.6	-4.9
1995	5.9	1.1	10.3	15.0	20.2	9.9	4.3	11.1	-1.1	8.6
1996	6.8	-15.2	-4.2	-9.9	-12.1	-4.2	1.0	-3.6	-0.6	20.3
1997	-3.5	33.3	-0.9	-10.3	0.0	0.0	5.2	-6.6	7.1	-7.9
1998	-12.6	-17.3	7.1	-10.8	-16.0	-12.3	-11.8	-2.7	-9.9	-34.3
1997 I	-3.9	19.9	4.2	-9.3	-3.1	-2.3	0.0	-6.5	4.5	12.8
II	-5.6	47.3	-3.7	-8.7	0.5	0.2	5.0	-5.7	6.2	-7.5
III	-5.4	36.6	-6.8	-10.9	8.2	0.2	6.3	-8.5	9.5	-10.9
IV	1.4	32.3	1.5	-13.0	-2.4	0.5	6.1	-7.6	8.8	-20.6
1998 I	-8.9	9.9	2.6	-14.6	-15.8	-8.5	-5.2	-4.0	-4.8	-35.7
II	-9.8	-27.9	9.8	-11.6	-18.0	-13.6	-10.5	-4.0	-9.9	-30.0
III	-14.3	-24.5	13.3	-8.5	-17.7	-14.0	-12.3	-1.0	-13.1	-31.6
IV	-18.0	-23.4	6.8	-7.0	-14.0	-14.5	-16.6	-1.0	-13.6	-40.0

Sources: UNCTAD, *Monthly Commodity Price Bulletin*; United Nations, *Monthly Bulletin of Statistics* and *OPEC Bulletin*.

[a] For quarterly data, the comparison is with the same quarter of previous year.
[b] All non-fuel commodity indices are based on 1985.
[c] Index of prices of manufactures exported by developed countries (1985 base year until 1987 and 1990 base year thereafter).
[d] Combined index of non-fuel commodity prices in dollars deflated by manufactured export price index.
[e] Composite price of the OPEC basket of seven crudes.

Table A.18.
WORLD OIL SUPPLY AND DEMAND, 1990-1999

Millions of barrels per day										
	1990	1991	1992	1993	1994	1995	1996	1997	1998	1999[a]
World oil supply[b]										
Developed economies	15.9	16.3	16.6	16.8	17.6	18.0	18.4	18.6	18.4	18.3
Economies in transition	11.8	10.7	9.2	8.2	7.5	7.3	7.3	7.5	7.5	7.5
Developing countries	38.0	38.5	40.0	41.1	41.9	43.4	44.8	46.6	47.7	45.5
OPEC[c]	25.1	25.3	26.5	27.0	27.3	27.7	28.5	30.0	30.7	28.3
Non-OPEC developing countries[c]	12.9	13.2	13.5	14.1	14.6	15.7	16.3	16.7	17.1	17.2
Processing gains[d]	1.3	1.3	1.3	1.4	1.4	1.5	1.5	1.6	1.6	1.7
World total supply[e]	67.0	66.8	67.1	67.4	68.4	70.0	72.0	74.3	75.3	72.9
World oil demand[f]										
World total demand	66.4	66.9	67.5	67.6	68.9	69.9	71.7	73.4	73.8	74.9

Source: United Nations, based on International Energy Agency, *Monthly Oil Market Report*, various issues.

a   Forecast.
b   Including crude oil, condensates, natural gas liquids (NGLs), oil from non-conventional sources and other sources of supply.
c   Ecuador is included in OPEC through 1992 and in non-OPEC developing countries starting in 1993. Gabon is not included in OPEC starting in 1995.
d   Net volume gains and losses in refining process (excluding net gain/loss in the economies in transition and China) and marine transportation losses.
e   Totals may not add up because of rounding.
f   Including deliveries from refineries/primary stocks and marine bunkers, and refinery fuel and non-conventional oils.

III. INTERNATIONAL FINANCE AND FINANCIAL MARKETS

Table A.19.

NET IMF LENDING TO DEVELOPING COUNTRIES, BY FACILITY, 1988-1998

Billions of dollars

	1988	1989	1990	1991	1992	1993	1994	1995	1996	1997	1998
Regular facilities	-3.5	-2.4	-1.4	-1.1	0.0	-0.2	-0.8	12.5	-2.6	13.0	14.7
Repayment terms:											
3-5 years (Credit tranche)[a]	-0.4	-0.1	-1.6	0.3	1.5	-0.2	0.1	12.4	-1.4	13.6	11.6
3.5-7 years (SFF/EAP)[b]	-2.3	-2.4	-0.5	-0.7	-1.5	-1.5	-1.4	-1.6	-1.3	-0.7	-0.1
4-10 years (Extended Fund Facility)	-0.9	0.1	0.7	-0.7	-0.0	1.5	0.5	1.8	0.1	0.2	3.2
Concessional facilities	-0.3	0.9	0.2	1.1	0.8	0.2	0.9	1.5	0.2	-0.1	0.2
in order created:											
Trust Fund[c]	-0.7	-0.5	-0.4	-0.1	0.0	-0.1	-0.0	-0.0	0.0	0.0	0.0
SAF[d]	0.3	0.7	0.1	0.2	0.0	-0.1	-0.2	-0.1	-0.4	-0.3	-0.2
ESAF[d]	-	0.8	0.5	0.9	0.7	0.4	1.1	1.6	0.5	0.2	0.5
Additional facilities[e]	-0.4	0.2	-0.8	1.2	-0.9	-0.2	-0.9	-1.6	-0.7	-0.9	-0.7
in order created:											
Compensatory financing[f]	-0.4	0.2	-0.8	1.2	-0.9	-0.2	-0.9	-1.6	-0.7	-0.9	-0.7
Buffer stock[g]	-0.0	0.0	0.0	0.0	0.0	0.0	0.0	0.0	0.0	0.0	0.0
STF[h]						0.0	0.0	0.0	0.0	0.0	0.0
Total	-4.3	-1.3	-2.0	1.2	-0.1	-0.2	-0.7	12.5	-3.1	12.0	14.2
Memo items:											
Selected characteristics of higher conditionality lending agreements											
Number initiated during year	27	23	12	24	17	13	26	18	20	14	15
Average length (months)	25	25	19	22	26	24	25	23	29	33	29
Total amount committed	5.0	13.8	1.3	6.4	7.1	3.0	6.6	23.2	5.2	38.4	29.5

Source: Data of IMF, *International Financial Statistics* and *IMF Survey*.

[a] Including Supplemental Reserve Facility (SRF) (created December 1997) for use when a sudden and disruptive loss of market confidence causes pressure on the capital account and on reserves, creating a large short-term financing need (higher-cost and shorter-term than regular drawings); adding to commitments under standby or extended arrangements for up to one year, with drawings in two or more tranches.

[b] Supplementary Financing Facility (SFF) (1979-1981) and Enhanced Access Policy (EAP) (1981-present) have provided resources from funds borrowed by IMF from member States, on which the Fund pays a higher interest rate than the remuneration paid to countries that have a net creditor position with the Fund. Thus, users of SFF and EAP resources have paid a higher interest rate than on drawings from ordinary resources, which are partly subsidized (for example, in fiscal 1981/82: 6.3 per cent versus 14.8 per cent for SFF and 13.2 per cent for EAP; by 1985/86, the spread was much reduced: 7 per cent versus 9.4 per cent and 9.2 per cent). However, up to a 3 percentage point subsidy was made available for International Development Association (IDA)-eligible countries and up to half that for countries above IDA limits but under the maximum for Trust Fund eligibility in order to reduce interest on SFF drawings towards the rate on ordinary drawings. There has been no subsidy on EAP drawings.

[c] Mainly using resources from IMF gold sales, the Trust Fund lent during 1977-1981 under one-year adjustment programmes; eligibility was based on maximum per capita income criteria; loans had 10-year maturities, with repayments beginning in the sixth year; the interest rate was 0.5 per cent per year.

[d] Structural Adjustment Facility and Enhanced Structural Adjustment Facility (the first financed mainly from Trust Fund reflows and the second from loans and grants) have made loans to IDA-eligible countries with protracted balance-of-payments problems; funds are disbursed over 3 years (under Policy Framework Paper arrangements), with repayments beginning in 5.5 years and ending in 10 years; the interest rate is 0.5 per cent.

[e] All having final maturity of 7 years and repayments beginning in 3.5 years.

[f] Compensatory Financing Facility from 1963 to 1988; Compensatory and Contingency Financing Facility from August 1988.

[g] Helping to finance buffer stock purchases under approved international buffer stock arrangements; established June 1969.

[h] See description in table 20 below.

Table A.20.
NET IMF LENDING TO TRANSITION ECONOMIES, BY FACILITY, 1988-1998

Billions of dollars											
	1988	1989	1990	1991	1992	1993	1994	1995	1996	1997	1998
Regular facilities	-0.9	-0.9	0.1	2.0	1.8	0.1	0.2	4.4	3.7	2.1	3.1
Repayment terms:											
3-5 years (Credit tranche)	-0.0	-0.2	0.4	1.0	1.8	0.1	0.5	4.9	1.2	-0.0	-0.9
3.5-7 years (SFF/EAP)	-0.9	-0.7	-0.3	0.2	-0.0	0.0	-0.3	-0.0	-0.0	-0.0	-0.0
4-10 years (Extended Fund Facility)				0.8	0.1	0.0	0.0	-0.5	2.6	2.2	4.0
Concessional facilities (ESAF)						0.0	0.0	0.1	0.2	0.2	0.2
Additional facilities											
Compensatory financing	0.0	0.0	0.0	1.5	-0.1	0.0	-0.7	-0.6	-0.2	0.1	3.0
STF						2.0	2.8	0.9	0.0	-0.0	-0.5
Total	-0.9	-0.9	0.1	3.5	1.7	2.1	2.3	4.8	3.7	2.4	5.8
Memo items:											
Selected characteristics of higher conditionality lending agreements											
Number initiated during year	2	0	3	5	6	9	8	12	12	7	6
Average length (months)	12	0	12	12	12	18	18	13	28	21	32
Total amount committed	0.8	0.0	1.6	4.9	1.5	1.6	2.1	9.2	13.2	2.1	3.4

Source: Data of IMF, *International Financial Statistics* and *IMF Survey.*

Note: The Systemic Transformation Facility (STF), created in 1993 on a temporary basis, assisted economies in transition with severe balance-of-payments problems arising from discontinuance of trade arrangements under planning. For Members that had not yet had a stand-by arrangement, drawings could be made in two tranches in support of a written statement of policy reform intentions, the second 6-18 months after the first, assuming satisfactory progress towards an upper credit tranche arrangement (repayment terms are the same as for the Extended Fund Facility). See table 19 above for description of other facilities.

Table A.21.
NET ODA FROM MAJOR SOURCES, BY TYPE, 1978-1997

Donor group or country	Growth rate of ODA[a] (1995 prices and exchange rates)		ODA as percentage of GNP	Total ODA (millions of dollars)	Percentage distribution of ODA by type, 1997					
					Bilateral			Multilateral		
	1978-1987	1988-1997	1997	1997	Grants[b]	Technical cooperation	Loans	United Nations	IDA	Other
Total DAC countries	4.33	-0.71	0.22	48324	64.6	26.6	2.4	8.1	8.4	16.6
Total EU	4.78	0.28	0.33	26612	63.4	25.8	1.4	6.5	5.4	23.2
Austria	3.10	5.39	0.26	527	48.0	13.9	10.1	5.5	12.5	23.9
Belgium	1.37	-1.71	0.31	764	60.1	33.8	-2.7	5.2	7.6	29.8
Denmark	6.97	3.47	0.97	1637	61.8	7.0	-0.1	17.9	0.2	20.2
Finland	15.09	-2.17	0.33	379	53.8	15.3	-1.1	21.1	3.7	22.4
France[c]	6.07	0.02	0.45	6307	77.8	34.4	-2.1	1.8	4.5	18.0
Germany	3.70	0.18	0.28	5857	58.2	33.6	4.0	4.4	5.9	27.6
Ireland	11.75	8.94	0.31	187	64.2	39.0	0.0	9.1	3.7	23.0
Italy	17.64	-6.81	0.11	1266	28.5	4.6	7.3	13.0	0.4	50.8
Luxembourg	..	16.29	0.55	95	69.5	2.1	0.0	9.5	5.3	14.7
Netherlands	3.94	1.03	0.81	2947	78.1	31.1	-5.7	8.9	6.3	12.4
Portugal	..	14.69	0.25	250	46.0	19.2	19.2	2.4	3.2	29.2
Spain	..	13.35	0.23	1234	43.8	10.4	18.3	2.9	3.3	31.8
Sweden	1.60	0.46	0.79	1731	69.8	2.7	0.0	12.8	7.3	10.1
United Kingdom	-1.45	1.40	0.26	3433	56.1	26.0	1.5	6.1	8.4	27.8
Australia	3.03	-0.35	0.28	1061	74.5	37.4	-1.3	7.2	9.0	10.7
Canada	2.92	-1.64	0.34	2045	63.8	20.0	-4.4	7.0	14.5	19.0
Japan	7.73	-0.23	0.22	9358	53.3	20.9	16.8	6.6	14.0	9.4
New Zealand	-2.40	-0.14	0.26	154	73.4	40.3	0.0	6.5	9.1	11.0
Norway	7.91	0.94	0.86	1306	69.4	13.1	0.7	18.2	5.4	6.2
Switzerland	7.14	2.46	0.34	911	64.3	31.4	-1.2	11.5	15.3	10.0
United States	1.51	-4.36	0.09	6878	81.9	39.9	-10.1	14.4	10.2	3.6
Arab countries[d] of which:										
Saudi Arabia	..	..	..	235	33.6			66.4		
Kuwait	..	..	..	373	95.2			4.8		
Other developing countries:[d]										
Korea, Republic of	..	..	..	186	59.7			40.3		
Taiwan Province of China			..	65	100.0			0.0		

Source: United Nations, based on OECD, *Development Co-operation*, 1998 report.

[a] Average annual rates of growth, calculated from average levels in 1976-1977, 1986-1987 and 1996-1997.
[b] Including technical cooperation.
[c] Excluding flows from France to the Overseas Departments, namely Guadeloupe, French Guiana, Martinique and Réunion.
[d] Bilateral ODA including all grants and loans; multilateral ODA including United Nations, IDA and "other", including technical cooperation.

Table A.22.
REGIONAL DISTRIBUTION OF ODA FROM MAJOR SOURCES, 1986-1997

Millions of dollars, two-year averages

| Donor group or country | All developing countries | | of which: | | | | | | | |
| | | | Latin America | | Africa | | Western Asia | | South and East Asia[a] | |
	1986-1987	1996-1997	1986-1987	1996-1997	1986-1987	1996-1997	1986-1987	1996-1997	1986-1987	1996-1997
Total ODA[b] (net)	39695.6	54447.0	3941.4	7228.0	14764.1	19712.2	4080.0	3151.4	12179.4	15277.1
DAC countries, bilateral	27043.4	35716.3	3141.3	4839.2	10007.6	12103.1	2541.4	2140.7	7392.6	9472.5
Australia	524.0	813.8	1.4	0.4	39.7	58.5	1.0	1.0	452.4	676.6
Austria	149.2	359.2	5.6	25.2	102.7	102.8	14.4	17.4	0.2	81.7
Belgium	393.4	483.8	23.2	79.3	284.3	233.9	3.9	-2.4	33.0	40.0
Canada	1156.9	1285.2	140.3	142.3	360.1	347.9	4.5	12.2	320.1	226.7
Denmark	410.6	1033.8	9.0	72.4	247.1	454.3	4.1	0.0	113.5	228.6
Finland	225.2	207.4	11.8	12.0	131.4	77.9	1.2	5.9	41.9	57.6
France[c]	3575.1	5265.0	189.6	207.6	2071.6	3065.8	82.1	131.4	769.9	1105.1
Germany	2866.3	4086.8	437.2	663.3	1061.6	1522.0	377.0	283.0	461.9	932.7
Ireland	26.3	117.1	0.2	3.1	15.2	84.5	..	0.7	0.5	8.7
Italy	1682.3	632.4	143.8	69.9	1183.3	345.7	35.2	39.3	173.8	17.7
Japan	4490.5	7379.7	367.3	850.4	649.0	1148.6	251.1	282.6	2899.2	3828.3
Luxembourg	0.0	61.4	..	11.2	..	34.8	..	0.6	..	10.3
Netherlands	1299.6	2204.2	225.1	473.5	516.1	699.2	31.2	93.4	367.2	303.3
New Zealand	63.4	107.4	0.3	1.7	0.6	4.7	0.0	0.2	53.1	94.1
Norway	503.3	930.2	26.7	69.7	292.2	420.1	0.3	12.4	124.5	218.9
Portugal	11.2	160.1	..	0.8	..	155.0	..	0.4	..	-0.2
Spain	86.3	825.1	15.8	326.1	8.7	261.5	..	5.6	..	134.1
Sweden	836.3	1302.0	50.9	128.0	413.9	463.2	0.8	55.9	198.3	261.3
Switzerland	355.9	648.8	50.1	82.5	169.1	208.7	3.9	7.2	68.7	136.5
United Kingdom	1009.5	1884.3	64.1	199.3	363.5	648.4	12.6	30.4	330.3	506.5
United States	7378.0	5928.5	1379.0	1420.5	2097.5	1765.5	1718.0	1163.5	984.0	604.0
DAC countries, multilateral	9300.9	18227.8	794.2	2353.3	4133.2	7486.1	306.4	661.8	3315.1	5953.2
Total DAC	36344.3	53944.0	3935.5	7192.4	14140.8	19589.2	2847.7	2802.5	10707.7	15425.7
Arab countries bilateral[d]	3351.4	503.0	5.9	35.5	623.3	123.1	1232.2	348.9	1471.8	-148.5
multilateral	101.6	..	-3.0	..	68.2	..	32.0	..	1.1	..

Source: United Nations calculations, based on OECD, *Geographical Distribution of Financial Flows to Aid Recipients.*

[a] Including Central Asian transition economies.
[b] Excluding assistance provided by centrally planned and transition economies, owing to measurement difficulties. Donor total includes amounts to certain European countries and unallocated amounts and hence is larger than the sum of the amounts per region.
[c] Excluding flows from France to the Overseas Departments, namely Guadeloupe, French Guiana, Martinique and Réunion.
[d] Approximately 35-40 per cent of Arab bilateral aid being geographically unallocated, depending on the year.

Table A.23.
RESOURCE COMMITMENTS OF MULTILATERAL DEVELOPMENT INSTITUTIONS, 1988-1998[a]

Millions of dollars

	1988	1989	1990	1991	1992	1993	1994	1995	1996	1997	1998
Financial institutions	27609	32337	34804	39820	39757	39709	40656	43516	44701	45760	57928
African Development Bank	2177	2842	3281	3454	2996	2519	1655	802	823	1880	1742
Asian Development Bank	3194	3686	4043	4843	5095	5426	3864	5759	5878	9648	6208
Caribbean Development Bank	74	73	109	111	71	71	56	110	99	54	122
European Bank for Reconstruction and Development				89	1188	2103	2232	2616	2774	2625	2658
Inter-American Development Bank	1738	2694	4005	5661	6232	6191	5298	7454	6951	6224	10403
of which:											
Inter-American Investment Corporation		15	67	102	158	124	43	36	72	67	223
International Fund for Agricultural Development	244	277	323	281	331	383	364	414	447	430	443
World Bank Group	20182	22765	23043	25381	23844	23016	27187	26361	27729	24899	36352
International Bank for Reconstruction and Development	14411	16251	15176	17021	15551	15098	16427	15950	15325	15098	24687
International Development Association	4350	4924	6300	7160	6310	5345	7282	5973	6490	5345	7325
International Finance Corporation	1421	1590	1567	1200	1983	2573	3478	4438	5914	4456	4340
Operational agencies of the United Nations system	2493	2542	2754	3628	3683	3363	3537	3931	3726	3453	4290
United Nations Development Programme[b]	833	897	1042	1134	1027	1031	1036	1014	1231	1529	1764
United Nations Population Fund	169	194	211	212	164	206	278	340	285	322	326
United Nations Children's Fund	454	498	545	947	917	623	810	1481	1133	521	962
World Food Programme	1037	953	956	1335	1575	1503	1413	1096	1077	1081	1238
Total commitments	30102	34879	37558	43448	43440	43072	44193	47447	48427	49213	62218
Memo item:											
Commitments in units of 1990 purchasing power[c]	32720	38329	37558	43448	42175	44404	44639	43134	45686	49710	64143

Source: Annual reports and information supplied by individual institutions.

a   Loans, grants, technical assistance and equity participation, as appropriate; all data are on a calendar-year basis.
b   Including United Nations Development Programme (UNDP)-administered funds.
c   Total commitments deflated by the United Nations index of manufactured export prices in dollars of developed economies: 1990=100.

Table A.24.
EXTERNAL DEBT AND DEBT INDICATORS FOR ECONOMIES IN TRANSITION, 1988-1997

	1988	1989	1990	1991	1992	1993	1994	1995	1996	1997
	External debt (billions of dollars)									
Russian Federation/former Soviet Union[a]										
Total external debt	42.2	53.9	59.8	67.8	78.4	111.7	121.5	120.4	125.2	125.6
Long-term debt	31.0	35.7	48.0	55.2	65.2	103.4	111.6	110.1	113.0	119.5
Concessional	0.0	0.0	0.0	0.7	1.0	33.7	33.0	22.1	24.8	25.9
Bilateral	0.0	0.0	0.0	0.7	1.0	33.7	33.0	22.1	24.8	25.9
Multilateral	0.0	0.0	0.0	0.0	0.0	0.0	0.0	0.0	0.0	0.0
Official, non-concessional	1.5	2.1	5.9	8.8	10.8	23.0	34.2	44.9	50.8	49.9
Bilateral	1.3	1.9	5.5	8.4	9.3	19.3	28.5	33.3	35.5	31.3
Multilateral	0.2	0.2	0.4	0.4	0.5	1.3	1.5	2.0	2.8	5.3
IMF credit	0.0	0.0	0.0	0.0	1.0	2.5	4.2	9.6	12.5	13.2
Private creditors	29.5	33.7	42.1	45.6	53.4	46.7	44.4	43.0	37.5	43.7
Bonds	0.3	1.4	1.9	1.9	1.7	1.6	1.8	1.1	1.1	4.6
Commercial banks[b]	15.0	17.3	17.9	16.8	18.5	15.9	16.4	16.7	15.7	29.4
Short-term debt	11.2	18.2	11.8	12.6	13.1	8.3	9.9	10.4	12.1	6.1
Central and Eastern Europe										
Total external debt	144.4	156.0	169.0	185.4	191.4	226.3	240.0	254.5	263.5	265.9
Long-term debt	115.5	119.7	139.0	157.1	165.2	205.5	218.6	227.2	232.1	234.6
Concessional	5.7	4.8	5.2	5.5	15.3	47.3	45.0	35.3	37.2	36.1
Bilateral	5.6	4.7	5.1	5.4	15.2	47.1	44.9	35.1	36.9	35.7
Multilateral	0.1	0.1	0.1	0.2	0.1	0.2	0.2	0.2	0.3	0.4
Official, non-concessional	31.5	33.4	42.5	56.4	49.4	61.8	75.3	86.3	90.5	87.4
Bilateral	22.7	26.4	34.1	43.2	33.6	43.9	53.3	59.9	61.3	54.8
Multilateral	6.7	5.9	7.0	8.3	9.5	10.1	12.1	13.7	14.5	16.8
IMF credit	2.1	1.1	1.3	5.0	6.4	7.8	9.9	12.7	14.7	15.7
Private creditors	78.3	81.5	91.3	95.2	100.5	96.4	98.3	105.5	104.3	111.2
Bonds	2.9	5.0	6.9	8.5	9.2	13.4	29.9	32.1	30.2	30.3
Commercial banks[b]	48.8	51.6	52.6	50.5	49.3	44.3	30.0	32.4	35.0	50.4
Short-term debt	28.9	36.3	30.0	28.3	26.2	20.9	21.3	27.4	31.5	31.3
Hungary										
Total external debt	19.6	20.4	21.3	22.6	22.0	24.3	28.2	31.5	27.1	24.4
Long-term debt	16.2	17.1	18.3	20.5	19.7	22.3	25.8	28.3	23.7	21.0
Concessional	0.0	0.0	0.0	0.0	0.1	0.1	0.2	0.4	0.4	0.4
Bilateral	0.0	0.0	0.0	0.0	0.1	0.1	0.2	0.4	0.4	0.4
Multilateral	0.0	0.0	0.0	0.0	0.0	0.0	0.0	0.0	0.0	0.0
Official, non-concessional	2.4	2.4	3.0	5.1	5.0	5.1	5.3	4.4	3.2	2.8
Bilateral	0.1	0.1	0.1	0.5	0.6	0.6	0.6	0.5	0.3	0.2
Multilateral	1.7	1.8	2.5	3.3	3.3	3.3	3.6	3.5	2.8	2.5
IMF credit	0.6	0.5	0.3	1.3	1.2	1.2	1.1	0.4	0.2	0.2
Private creditors	13.9	14.6	15.3	15.3	14.7	17.1	20.2	23.5	20.1	17.8
Bonds	2.5	3.4	4.7	6.0	6.8	10.1	13.5	15.8	13.1	10.6
Commercial banks[b]	9.9	10.2	9.6	8.1	6.4	5.1	3.9	3.3	1.8	1.2
Short-term debt	3.4	3.3	2.9	2.2	2.3	2.0	2.4	3.2	3.4	3.4
Poland										
Total external debt	42.1	43.1	49.4	53.4	48.5	45.2	42.6	44.3	43.5	39.9
Long-term debt	33.6	34.5	39.8	45.9	44.0	42.5	41.7	42.1	40.8	36.1
Concessional	4.4	3.5	3.8	3.7	13.0	12.6	10.8	11.1	10.1	7.7
Bilateral	4.4	3.5	3.8	3.7	13.0	12.6	10.8	11.1	10.1	7.7
Multilateral	0.0	0.0	0.0	0.0	0.0	0.0	0.0	0.0	0.0	0.0

Table A.24 (continued)	1988	1989	1990	1991	1992	1993	1994	1995	1996	1997
Official, non-concessional	17.4	20.1	24.6	31.0	20.7	20.6	21.6	21.1	20.4	18.9
Bilateral	16.7	19.6	23.6	29.3	18.7	18.4	18.3	19.1	18.2	16.8
Multilateral	0.7	0.5	0.5	0.9	1.2	1.5	2.0	2.1	2.2	2.1
IMF credit	0.0	0.0	0.5	0.9	0.8	0.7	1.3	0.0	0.0	..
Private creditors	11.7	10.9	11.3	11.1	10.3	9.4	9.3	9.9	10.3	9.5
Bonds	0.0	0.0	0.0	0.0	0.0	0.0	7.9	8.1	8.3	6.6
Commercial banks	9.2	9.0	9.8	9.7	9.1	8.6	0.4	0.6	0.3	0.5
Short-term debt	8.5	8.6	9.6	7.6	4.5	2.7	0.8	2.2	2.7	3.8
					Debt indicators (percentage)					
Ratio of external debt to GNP										
Russian Federation/former Soviet Union	7.6	9.0	10.3	12.5	18.6	29.1	37.9	35.3	29.7	26.2
Central and Eastern Europe	17.5	17.4	19.7	25.7	31.1	37.6	42.6	39.8	35.6	33.4
of which:										
Bulgaria	39.6	48.0	57.1	119.6	116.2	114.6	102.3	81.2	106.5	101.3
Former Czechoslovakia	13.9	15.7	17.9	30.4	26.0					
Czech Republic						29.5	26.8	31.8	35.6	41.8
Slovakia						28.0	34.0	32.6	41.2	51.6
Hungary	71.3	73.5	67.3	70.5	61.2	65.0	70.3	73.4	62.0	55.0
Poland	64.0	54.5	88.8	72.6	58.6	53.3	46.6	37.5	32.4	29.5
Romania	7.3	2.6	3.0	7.4	13.0	15.6	19.6	20.9	28.0	32.9
Ratio of external debt to exports										
Russian Federation/former Soviet Union[c]	57.8	72.6	73.8	124.8	143.0	169.8	156.7	129.6	119.5	121.0
Central and Eastern Europe	101.6	110.0	119.1	170.0	155.7	160.9	143.5	117.8	112.3	109.8
of which:										
Bulgaria	84.8	105.4	154.0	280.5	230.1	244.4	185.7	148.7	156.2	152.6
Former Czechoslovakia	40.4	46.6	56.1	75.2	42.4					
Czech Republic						47.1	48.7	55.0	64.0	68.6
Slovakia						44.2	50.6	50.5	69.3	88.5
Hungary	173.9	169.8	172.8	180.5	158.1	212.9	246.2	175.4	132.8	94.1
Poland	253.8	261.5	251.4	286.4	249.6	246.0	162.7	118.0	109.7	95.0
Romania	23.8	9.4	17.4	42.2	63.8	73.7	75.6	70.3	94.3	103.8
Ratio of debt service to exports										
Russian Federation/former Soviet Union[c]	11.3	12.3	14.6	24.8	2.5	3.3	4.4	6.3	6.7	6.5
Central and Eastern Europe	17.9	17.1	17.3	22.2	10.5	8.0	10.0	10.6	10.6	11.0
of which:										
Bulgaria	22.2	26.8	19.4	6.6	8.7	6.5	13.0	16.5	19.3	14.4
Former Czechoslovakia	9.1	10.1	9.0	10.4	9.3					
Czech Republic						7.2	11.4	8.2	8.4	14.1
Slovakia						8.5	9.1	11.3	11.9	12.2
Hungary	31.2	29.7	34.3	31.9	35.6	38.7	49.3	39.1	41.0	29.7
Poland	10.6	9.4	4.9	5.2	7.6	9.2	11.9	11.1	6.8	6.1
Romania	33.3	16.9	0.3	2.4	9.1	6.1	8.5	10.2	12.6	15.7

Source: United Nations, based on IMF and World Bank.

[a] In 1992, the Russian Federation assumed the debt of the former Soviet Union.

[b] Government or government-guaranteed debt only.

[c] Merchandise exports only.

Table A.25.

EXTERNAL DEBT OF NET-DEBTOR DEVELOPING COUNTRIES, 1988-1998

Billions of dollars

	1988	1989	1990	1991	1992	1993	1994	1995	1996	1997	1998[a]
All countries[b]											
Total external debt	1142.2	1197.1	1289.2	1359.1	1426.1	1533.4	1699.4	1826.4	1920.3	1914.8	2465.1
Long-term debt	989.3	1023.3	1073.4	1118.8	1151.1	1223.9	1372.5	1442.3	1514.4	1519.6	2052.9
Concessional	239.7	279.0	308.7	329.1	340.8	360.1	392.9	404.3	393.6	329.3	417.9
Bilateral	181.6	215.1	236.3	248.7	255.0	267.3	287.3	290.1	275.7	217.8	294.1
Multilateral[c]	58.1	63.9	72.4	80.5	85.8	92.8	105.6	114.2	118.0	111.5	123.8
Official, non-concessional	245.4	251.5	277.0	293.5	300.7	313.0	344.3	349.2	346.0	340.5	515.1
Bilateral	105.3	110.1	115.2	124.2	133.0	137.3	157.0	145.8	156.6	135.7	225.9
Multilateral	109.1	113.5	132.0	140.8	141.2	149.8	161.4	166.8	156.8	154.7	193.8
IMF credit	30.9	27.9	29.8	28.5	26.5	26.0	26.0	36.6	32.5	50.1	95.5
Private creditors	504.2	492.8	487.7	496.2	509.6	550.7	635.3	688.8	774.8	849.7	1119.9
of which:											
Bonds	43.7	45.9	102.2	108.8	119.9	153.5	212.0	228.3	257.7	265.7	335.0
Commercial banks[d]	290.4	282.4	203.9	199.9	188.3	169.7	137.7	149.8	152.5	160.3	355.4
Short-term debt	152.9	173.8	215.8	240.3	275.0	309.5	326.9	384.2	405.9	395.3	412.2
Memo items:											
Principal arrears on long-term debt	38.1	43.3	53.3	56.6	61.5	65.2	72.3	77.4	70.9	69.0	87.9
Interest arrears on long-term debt	18.0	29.4	39.7	41.9	38.0	39.0	36.0	35.4	29.2	26.7	33.1
Latin America											
Total external debt	456.2	452.9	475.4	492.4	509.5	554.1	592.6	620.0	668.8	667.1	735.8
Long-term debt	407.1	393.4	398.0	405.6	414.9	443.3	474.7	500.5	554.3	545.1	608.7
Concessional	44.2	45.6	48.5	51.7	53.5	55.9	58.3	60.0	57.6	31.5	57.7
Bilateral	38.8	40.0	42.4	45.3	46.7	48.6	50.6	51.7	48.7	21.7	47.8
Multilateral[c]	5.4	5.6	6.1	6.4	6.8	7.2	7.7	8.4	9.0	9.7	9.9
Official, non-concessional	97.4	100.0	115.9	123.6	126.4	128.5	132.7	130.6	137.8	115.1	128.8
Bilateral	35.6	37.7	43.6	50.3	56.3	56.2	57.8	39.5	52.2	36.2	38.9
Multilateral	45.5	46.5	54.1	56.2	55.3	58.4	61.4	64.8	62.2	60.9	67.4
IMF credit	16.3	15.7	18.1	17.1	14.9	13.9	13.5	26.3	23.4	18.0	22.6
Private creditors	265.5	247.8	233.6	230.2	234.9	258.9	283.7	309.8	358.9	398.5	422.2
of which:											
Bonds[d]	18.1	19.1	76.0	79.1	81.8	108.9	158.0	172.1	199.6	198.8	212.3
Commercial banks[d]	190.4	178.7	102.7	97.4	94.6	75.3	37.5	35.2	29.4	30.0	37.4
Short-term debt	49.1	59.6	77.4	86.9	94.5	110.8	117.9	119.5	114.5	122.0	127.1
Memo items:											
Principal arrears on long-term debt	15.0	18.2	24.6	24.3	24.1	20.7	20.4	16.5	8.1	12.5	12.5
Interest arrears on long-term debt	8.6	16.5	25.6	27.0	20.9	18.0	12.7	9.5	3.2	4.3	4.3
Africa											
Total external debt	270.7	278.6	286.7	292.1	288.4	291.1	314.4	334.1	328.0	311.2	..
Long-term debt	239.4	244.6	252.4	258.6	252.4	251.1	274.3	289.0	280.6	265.3	..
Concessional	73.3	77.2	85.3	92.2	96.2	101.2	111.0	119.8	125.5	117.8	..
Bilateral	50.8	51.9	56.9	60.4	62.4	64.4	68.9	72.3	76.1	72.9	..
Multilateral[c]	22.6	25.3	28.4	31.8	33.8	36.8	42.1	47.5	49.4	44.9	..

Table A.25 (continued)

	1988	1989	1990	1991	1992	1993	1994	1995	1996	1997	1998[a]
Official, non-concessional	76.8	80.2	81.8	84.5	83.0	81.5	91.6	97.1	90.0	87.6	..
Bilateral	49.0	52.0	50.8	51.9	50.7	47.9	55.1	60.3	55.2	51.7	..
Multilateral	20.4	21.7	24.9	26.9	27.3	28.6	30.7	31.6	29.5	26.3	..
IMF credit	7.4	6.6	6.1	5.7	5.0	5.0	5.8	5.2	5.4	9.6	..
Private creditors	89.3	87.1	85.3	81.8	73.2	68.4	71.8	72.1	65.0	59.9	..
of which:											
Bonds[d]	4.7	4.5	3.6	3.1	5.1	2.9	4.5	5.3	5.9	9.3	..
Commercial banks[d]	33.0	31.8	28.0	29.3	22.9	21.3	21.9	23.3	24.9	21.3	..
Short-term debt	31.3	34.0	34.2	33.6	35.9	40.0	40.1	45.1	47.4	45.9	..
Memo items:											
Principal arrears on long-term debt	19.7	19.8	21.8	22.0	25.9	32.0	35.7	41.6	40.5	38.4	..
Interest arrears on long-term debt	8.5	10.6	11.0	11.0	13.2	17.0	18.7	20.8	20.4	18.5	..
Sub-Saharan Africa											
Total external debt	117.7	123.9	140.3	146.3	149.7	154.0	160.6	170.2	168.1	161.7	165.0
Long-term debt	105.1	108.5	121.6	126.0	127.3	129.5	138.0	145.3	142.4	137.9	142.0
Concessional	47.0	50.0	58.6	63.3	66.5	70.0	76.5	82.9	84.5	79.7	86.6
Bilateral	28.7	29.0	33.3	34.7	36.0	36.8	38.4	40.0	40.6	40.1	42.1
Multilateral[c]	18.3	21.0	25.3	28.6	30.5	33.2	38.1	42.9	43.9	39.6	44.6
Official, non-concessional	33.7	33.8	37.5	37.4	36.8	35.4	38.4	38.6	36.7	37.6	37.5
Bilateral	18.8	20.1	22.9	23.0	22.9	21.8	24.4	25.5	24.3	22.2	22.6
Multilateral	9.1	9.3	10.5	10.9	10.9	10.9	11.1	11.1	10.0	8.8	7.5
IMF credit	5.8	4.4	4.1	3.5	3.0	2.7	2.8	2.0	2.3	6.7	7.1
Private creditors	24.4	24.7	25.5	25.3	24.1	24.1	23.2	23.9	21.2	20.6	18.4
of which:											
Bonds[d]	0.4	0.4	0.3	0.3	0.2	0.2	0.2	0.3	0.2	2.7	4.9
Commercial banks[d]	7.8	8.1	8.6	8.4	8.1	8.1	8.4	9.6	12.0	8.9	4.9
Short-term debt	12.6	15.4	18.7	20.3	22.4	24.5	22.6	24.9	25.7	23.8	23.0
Memo items:											
Principal arrears on long-term debt	10.1	12.8	15.5	19.8	22.9	26.9	28.6	32.0	29.7	26.7	37.9
Interest arrears on long-term debt	4.8	6.6	7.9	9.9	11.5	14.0	14.2	15.4	14.7	12.8	18.3
Asia											
Total external debt	415.3	465.6	527.1	574.5	628.2	688.2	792.4	872.4	923.5	936.5	..
Long-term debt	342.8	385.4	423.0	454.7	483.7	529.4	623.5	652.8	679.5	709.1	..
Concessional	122.2	156.1	174.8	185.1	191.0	203.0	223.5	224.4	210.5	180.6	..
Bilateral	92.0	123.3	137.0	143.0	145.8	154.2	167.8	166.1	150.9	123.2	..
Multilateral[c]	30.2	32.8	37.8	42.2	45.2	48.8	55.7	58.3	59.6	57.4	..
Official, non-concessional	71.1	71.4	79.4	85.3	91.4	103.0	120.1	121.5	118.2	137.3	..
Bilateral	20.7	20.4	20.8	22.0	26.0	33.1	44.1	46.0	49.2	47.7	..
Multilateral	43.3	45.3	53.1	57.7	58.6	62.9	69.2	70.4	65.2	67.5	..
IMF credit	7.2	5.7	5.6	5.7	6.8	7.0	6.7	5.1	3.8	22.0	..

Table A.25 (continued)	1988	1989	1990	1991	1992	1993	1994	1995	1996	1997	1998ᵃ
Private creditors	149.5	157.9	168.8	184.2	201.4	223.4	279.9	306.9	350.8	391.3	..
of which:											
Bondsᵈ	20.9	22.3	22.7	26.6	33.0	41.7	49.5	50.8	52.2	57.5	..
Commercial banksᵈ	67.0	71.9	73.2	73.1	70.8	73.2	78.2	91.3	98.2	109.0	..
Short-term debt	72.5	80.2	104.1	119.9	144.5	158.7	168.9	219.6	244.0	227.4	..
Memo items:											
Principal arrears on long-term debt	3.4	5.3	6.9	10.3	11.6	12.5	16.3	19.3	22.3	18.1	..
Interest arrears on long-term debt	0.9	2.2	3.2	3.9	3.8	4.0	4.7	5.1	5.6	4.0	..
Least developed countries											
Total external debt	102.6	108.8	121.6	126.6	130.4	134.0	142.8	147.0	144.7	139.1	..
Long-term debt	93.3	97.8	108.6	112.1	114.2	117.5	125.0	128.9	127.5	122.2	..
Concessional	56.4	60.9	69.3	73.7	76.9	81.2	87.8	90.3	92.6	87.1	..
Bilateral	34.0	35.8	39.0	39.7	40.6	41.6	42.9	41.9	41.8	40.3	..
Multilateralᶜ	22.4	25.1	30.4	34.0	36.3	39.6	44.9	48.3	50.8	46.7	..
Official, non-concessional	22.9	22.8	24.2	23.6	22.8	21.7	22.4	23.5	21.4	23.3	..
Bilateral	14.9	15.4	16.9	16.7	16.4	15.6	16.2	16.9	16.2	14.4	..
Multilateral	3.4	3.5	3.8	3.7	3.6	3.5	3.6	3.6	3.4	3.0	..
IMF credit	4.6	3.9	3.6	3.1	2.8	2.5	2.6	3.1	1.8	5.8	..
Private creditors	14.0	14.2	15.1	14.8	14.5	14.6	14.8	15.1	13.6	11.9	..
of which:											
Bondsᵈ	0.0	0.0	0.0	0.0	0.0	0.0	0.0	0.0	0.0	0.0	..
Commercial banksᵈ	3.3	3.2	3.5	3.3	3.2	3.1	3.6	4.5	7.1	7.3	..
Short-term debt	9.4	11.0	13.0	14.5	16.2	16.4	17.8	18.1	17.2	16.9	..
Memo items:											
Principal arrears on long-term debt	9.8	12.1	15.2	18.8	21.9	25.5	29.7	33.0	31.1	28.7	..
Interest arrears on long-term debt	4.3	5.9	7.3	8.9	10.3	12.0	14.0	14.9	14.1	13.2	..

Source: United Nations, based on IMF, OECD and World Bank.

ᵃ Estimate.

ᵇ Debt of 122 economies, drawn primarily from the Debtor Reporting System of the World Bank (107 countries). For non-reporting countries, data are drawn from the Creditor Reporting System of OECD (15 economies), excluding, however, non-guaranteed bank debt of offshore financial centres, much of which is not the debt of the local economies.

ᶜ Including concessional facilities of IMF.

ᵈ Government or government-guaranteed debt only.

Table A.26.
DEBT INDICATORS AND DEBT-SERVICE PAYMENTS FOR NET-DEBTOR DEVELOPING COUNTRIES, 1988-1998

	1988	1989	1990	1991	1992	1993	1994	1995	1996	1997	1998[a]
	Debt indicators (percentage)										
Ratio of external debt to GNP											
All countries *of which:*	45.5	42.7	41.7	41.8	41.2	41.1	41.4	38.9	36.9	36.9	37.3
Latin America	55.6	47.7	44.7	44.1	41.1	40.5	38.2	38.0	37.6	34.0	36.9
Africa	73.5	74.7	68.9	73.7	71.0	72.8	79.0	76.5	68.9	63.2	..
Asia	31.4	31.5	32.8	33.0	34.6	35.0	36.7	33.3	31.4	34.2	..
Memo items:											
Sub-Saharan Africa	86.5	90.5	98.4	103.1	118.5	130.0	147.9	137.3	122.4	115.8	96.4
Least developed countries	91.1	93.4	98.0	102.7	117.5	117.9	135.5	123.7	110.4	101.0	..
Ratio of external debt to exports											
All countries *of which:*	220.2	207.1	193.0	192.6	184.7	185.2	176.3	155.0	147.8	137.5	146.2
Latin America	309.3	275.0	256.5	261.9	252.9	254.1	233.4	204.1	200.4	182.5	202.5
Africa	278.1	265.9	228.7	234.6	221.6	232.6	249.9	222.8	199.4	193.4	..
Asia	151.6	150.9	147.5	146.1	142.6	142.0	135.6	120.4	115.3	108.1	..
Memo items:											
Sub-Saharan Africa	343.4	337.7	345.1	373.6	380.5	408.7	414.5	363.1	326.7	344.5	280.2
Least developed countries	522.0	525.9	479.3	541.2	534.2	553.6	539.8	451.4	413.7	376.7	..
Ratio of debt service to exports											
All countries *of which:*	27.1	23.7	21.1	19.6	19.7	20.0	18.3	18.1	19.1	19.2	17.6
Latin America	37.1	30.4	24.6	24.3	26.4	28.4	25.8	26.9	32.1	35.6	33.8
Africa	27.2	25.4	24.6	23.8	23.7	22.7	19.7	18.1	16.2	15.4	..
Asia	21.6	19.6	18.0	16.0	15.5	15.6	14.7	14.4	14.2	13.0	..
Memo items:											
Sub-Saharan Africa	22.8	19.8	18.5	18.4	15.9	15.2	17.8	20.2	16.1	16.5	22.1
Least developed countries	20.9	20.4	15.7	16.4	12.1	12.3	12.1	19.3	12.0	10.7	..

Table A.26 (continued)

	1988	1989	1990	1991	1992	1993	1994	1995	1996	1997	1998[a]
	Debt-service payments (billions of dollars)										
All countries											
Total debt service	139.8	136.5	140.1	137.7	151.8	165.4	175.5	212.5	247.0	267.5	296.1
Interest payments	67.4	63.6	61.9	63.5	62.7	63.1	70.3	89.3	93.3	92.3	125.3
of which:											
non-concessional	64.1	59.7	57.1	58.8	57.2	57.1	64.1	82.7	87.0	86.4	118.4
Latin America											
Total debt service	54.7	50.0	45.6	45.6	53.2	61.8	65.5	81.7	106.9	130.0	123.0
Interest payments	33.3	25.9	22.8	24.1	23.0	24.3	28.8	37.5	39.4	40.0	45.4
of which:											
non-concessional	32.8	25.5	21.9	23.3	22.1	23.5	27.8	36.6	38.6	39.3	44.5
Africa											
Total debt service	26.0	26.0	30.3	29.1	30.2	27.9	24.3	26.6	26.2	24.8	..
Interest payments	11.4	11.8	12.4	11.7	12.5	9.8	9.5	10.5	11.0	9.6	..
of which:											
non-concessional	10.7	11.0	11.3	10.9	11.1	8.4	8.2	9.0	9.3	8.0	..
Asia											
Total debt service	59.2	60.5	64.2	63.0	68.4	75.8	85.7	104.2	113.8	112.7	..
Interest payments	22.7	25.9	26.7	27.7	27.1	29.0	32.0	41.4	43.0	42.7	..
of which:											
non-concessional	20.6	23.2	23.9	24.6	23.9	25.3	28.1	37.2	39.2	39.1	..
Memo items:											
Sub-Saharan Africa											
Total debt service	7.8	7.3	7.5	7.2	6.3	5.7	6.9	9.5	8.3	7.7	13.0
Interest payments	3.2	3.0	3.1	3.2	2.7	2.4	2.7	3.1	3.2	3.0	6.1
of which:											
non-concessional	2.8	2.6	2.7	2.7	2.3	1.9	2.1	2.5	2.4	2.3	5.2
Least developed countries											
Total debt service	4.1	4.2	4.0	3.9	2.9	3.0	3.2	6.3	4.2	4.0	..
Interest payments	1.7	1.6	1.5	1.6	1.1	1.3	1.3	1.7	1.4	1.4	..
of which:											
non-concessional	1.2	1.1	1.0	1.1	0.7	0.7	0.6	1.1	0.7	0.8	..

Source: United Nations, based on data of IMF, OECD and World Bank.

[a] Preliminary estimate.

Table A.27.
DEBT-RESTRUCTURING AGREEMENTS WITH OFFICIAL CREDITORS, 1988-1998

	1988	1989	1990	1991	1992	1993	1994	1995	1996	1997	1998
Number of agreements											
Developing countries, total	15	24	17	14	16	10	14	17	15	7	9
Middle-income countries	3	6	1	2	4	1	2	1	0	0	0
Lower-middle-income countries	4	6	7	9	4	3	6	7	1	1	2
Low-income countries	8	12	9	3	8	6	6	9	14	6	7
Memo item:											
Sub-Saharan Africa	9	16	9	6	9	4	10	9	10	5	6
Amounts rescheduled[a] (millions of dollars)											
Developing countries, total	9362	18600	6075	44308	12522	3394	14020	14163	11312	6276	7030
Middle-income countries	6721	6016	200	1825	7287	57	293	1030	0	0	0
Lower-middle-income countries	1342	9312	3320	34150	2628	2615	11360	11130	6724	400	4761
Low-income countries	973	2518	2445	390	2607	722	1007	2003	4588	5876	2269
Memo item:											
Sub-Saharan Africa	1299	10330	3374	1810	3687	633	5289	3117	3570	4432	2055
Average consolidation period (years)											
Developing countries, total	1.3	1.4[b]	1.5	..[c]	1.9	2.3	1.4	2.1[d]	2.3[e]	2.8	6.4
Middle-income countries	1.4	1.6	1.4	0.8	1.5	..	0.5	3.0	..	..	..
Lower-middle-income countries	1.4	1.4	1.4	..[c]	1.5	3.1	1.8	1.9	2.8	1.8	2.0
Low-income countries	1.2	1.3[b]	1.7	1.2	2.1	2.1	1.2	2.1	2.2	2.9	2.9
Memo item:											
Sub-Saharan Africa	1.2	1.3[b]	1.6	1.2	2.0	2.3	1.4	2.1	2.7	2.9	2.9

Source: UNCTAD, based on Paris Club Agreed Minutes.

Note: In 1995, Paris Club creditors introduced new concessional debt-relief measures for poor, severely indebted countries, known as the Naples terms. For the major features of current Paris Club rescheduling terms, see the report of the Secretary-General entitled "The developing country debt situation as of mid-1995" (A/50/379 and Corr. 1) of 31 August 1995, paras. 12-16, and table 2.

[a]   Including previously rescheduled debt.
[b]   Excluding Equatorial Guinea.
[c]   Owing to the menu options for Egypt, it is not possible to calculate consolidation periods.
[d]   Excluding Bolivia and Uganda, both of which obtained a 67 per cent Naples terms stock reduction agreement.
[e]   Excluding Benin, Burkina Faso, Guyana and Mali, all of which obtained a 67 per cent Naples terms stock reduction agreement; and Ghana, which consolidated arrears only as of July 1995.

UNITED NATIONS PUBLICATIONS
United Nations, Room DC2-853, New York, New York 10017, U.S.A.

UNITED NATIONS PUBLICATIONS
Palais des Nations, 1211 Geneva 10, Switzerland

Printed in the United Nations, New York • 13551—August 1999—5,615
ISBN 92-1-109135-7 • Sales Number E.99.II.C.1
E/1999/50/Rev.1 • ST/ESA/268